CHINA 2049

CHINA 2049

ECONOMIC CHALLENGES
OF A
RISING
GLOBAL POWER

Edited by

**DAVID DOLLAR
YIPING HUANG
YANG YAO**

BROOKINGS INSTITUTION PRESS
Washington, D.C.

The Brookings Institution is a private nonprofit organization devoted to research, education, and publication on important issues of domestic and foreign policy. Its principal purpose is to bring the highest quality independent research and analysis to bear on current and emerging policy problems. Interpretations or conclusions in Brookings publications should be understood to be solely those of the authors.

Library of Congress Cataloging-in-Publication Data
Names: Dollar, David, editor. | Huang, Yiping, 1964– editor. | Yao, Yang, 1964– editor.
Title: China 2049 : economic challenges of a rising global power / edited by David Dollar, Yiping Huang, Yang Yao.
Description: Washington, D.C. : Brookings Institution Press, [2020] | Includes bibliographical references and index.
Identifiers: LCCN 2019048113 (print) | LCCN 2019048114 (ebook) | ISBN 9780815738053 (paperback) | ISBN 9780815738060 (epub)
Subjects: LCSH: Economic forecasting—China. | China–Economic conditions—2000– | China—Economic policy–2000–
Classification: LCC HC427.95 .C4352 2020 (print) | LCC HC427.95 (ebook) | DDC 330.951—dc23
LC record available at https://lccn.loc.gov/2019048113
LC ebook record available at https://lccn.loc.gov/2019048114

9 8 7 6 5 4 3

Typeset in Minion Pro

Composition by Elliott Beard

Contents

Preface

NATIONAL SCHOOL OF DEVELOPMENT,
PEKING UNIVERSITY

THE BROOKINGS INSTITUTION

In 2012, the Chinese government announced Two Centennial Goals. The first is to double the 2010 GDP and per capita income for both urban and rural residents by 2021, the year when the Chinese Communist Party (CCP) celebrates its centenary. And the second is to build China into a fully de-veloped country that is prosperous, powerful, democratic, culturally ad-vanced, and harmonious by 2049, the year when the People's Republic of China (PRC) celebrates its centenary. It looks that China is well on track to achieve the first Centennial Goal, as its GDP grew by 7.4 percent per annum between 2010 and 2018 and it plans to eliminate poverty completely by 2020.

There are greater uncertainties, however, surrounding the path to the second Centennial Goal. China ascended successfully from one of the world's poorest economies in 1978 (GDP per capita at less than US$200) to a high middle-income economy in 2018 (GDP per capita close to US$10,000). And according to projections by this volume, under reasonably favorable conditions, China's GDP per capita, using purchasing power parity (PPP) measures, relative to that of the United States may rise from about one-quarter in 2018 to around two-thirds in 2049. However, the growth trajectory in reaching the middle-income level and achieving the high-income status could differ significantly, when viewed from key growth drivers and internal and external constraints for growth.

The purpose of this volume is to take stock of the new economic challenges for China when it sets out to achieve the second Centennial Goal over the coming three decades. While the various chapters examine transformation of different sectors and aspects of the economy, they focus on the central theme of China becoming a new global economic power. Specifically, these analyses seek to address three common questions: What contributed to China's past economic success? What are the most important new challenges for China and the world as China continues to ascend in the coming decades? What policies should China adopt to both facilitate rapid growth of their economy and accommodate it in the global system?

KEY DRIVERS OF PAST ECONOMIC GROWTH

After establishment of the PRC in 1949, the Chinese government adopted various policy schemes in an attempt to modernize the economy, including the socialist transformation program and the urban industrialization strategy, starting from the mid-1950s. While paces of economic development were, at times, decent and even remarkable, the central planning system was largely unsuccessful in boosting income levels during that time. This eventually led to the start of economic reform from the end of 1978, which dramatically improved economic performance. Real GDP grew by an average of more than 9.8 percent during the period 1978–2008, which was often referred to as the "China miracle."

So what contributed to this economic success during earlier decades of economic reform? The foremost driver was the reform policy, or transition from the central planned system to a free market economy. This transformation significantly increased both allocative efficiency, through better allocation of resources, and technical efficiency, through better use of resources in the same production activities. Adoption of a household farming system in the countryside in the early 1980s, for instance, led to immediate jumps of grain output, as the new scheme helped establish a direct link between efforts and rewards. Again, migration of rural surplus labor to the urban area both raised average labor productivity and supported expansion of industrial production. According to analysis in this volume, improvement in total factor productivity (TFP) roughly accounted for about four-tenths of China's GDP growth in the period 1996–2015.

A related factor was the open-door policy, or rapid integration of the Chinese economy into the world. The start of China's economic reform coincided with the wave of globalization. The combination of the two processes enabled China to participate deeply in the international division of labor. Relying on its low-cost advantage, China quickly rose to be one of the world's major exporters, especially in markets for labor-intensive manufacturing products. The ratio of exports to GDP increased from well below 10 percent in 1978 to 37 percent in 2007. And for almost two decades starting from 1993, China was among the world's largest recipient countries of foreign direct investment (FDI). Its accession to the World Trade Organization (WTO) at the end of 2001 not only further reduced China's trade and investment barriers, but also accelerated domestic structural reforms. In short, China was one of the main beneficiaries of globalization, especially during the first three decades of economic reform. And the world economy contributed export markets, investment funds, and production technologies to China.

Several other factors also played critical roles in supporting China's successful economic development, including favorable demographics, high saving and investment rates, macroeconomic and financial stability and economic foundations built during the pre-reform period. During the reform period, China experienced two waves of improvement in demographic structure, which generated the so-called "demographic dividend." The first wave (1976–1990) coincided with the start of economic reform, and the second wave (2000–2010) coincided with China's WTO accession. Both helped to accelerate economic growth. The high saving rate during the reform period was probably attributable to a number of causes, such as the life-cycle hypothesis (i.e., the saving rate being proportional to GDP growth rate), favorable demographics (lower dependency ratio), a common East Asian culture (or at least behavior), and even lack of well-developed social welfare systems (precautionary saving). A high saving rate led to a high investment rate, which, in turn, facilitated both capital accumulation and technological progress.

With exceptions of several years in the mid-1980s and early 1990s, China largely maintained macroeconomic stability, as evidenced by low levels of volatilities of growth rates, inflation rates, and external account imbalances. And during the past four decades, China was the only major emerging market economy that did not suffer from a serious financial crisis. Stable macroeconomic and financial conditions increased investor confidence and improved economic efficiency. And, finally, while the growth record of the pre-reform period was quite poor, physical infrastructure, a comprehensive industrial base (especially the heavy industries), relatively high levels of human capital, and gender equality during that time all laid good foundations for economic development after 1978.

UNDERSTANDING THE REFORM POLICY

Alongside the remarkable economic performance, it appears puzzling that, after four decades of economic transition, China's economic policy still looks quite different from the free market system. For instance, while the share of state-owned enterprises (SOEs) in total industrial output dropped from 80 percent at the start of the reform to 20 percent in recent years, SOEs still dominate in many important economic areas, particularly in some service sectors and upstream industries. Again, the government still intervenes heavily in almost all aspects of the financial system, including interest rates, exchange rate, fund allocation, and cross-border capital flows. Among 130 economies with available data in 2015, China's financial repression index, or degree of government intervention in the financial sector, ranked fourteenth. Compared with free market economies, the Chinese government still plays much more direct and proactive roles. Some of these policy distortions are often criticized by scholars for causing significant inefficiency and increasing risks. And some government interventions are also at the center of the current China-U.S. trade disputes.

So why didn't the Chinese government eliminate such policy distortions and move toward the free market economy more rapidly? To understand the rationale of such policy interventions, one needs to go back to the reform strategy adopted at the beginning of economic reform. The former Soviet Union and the Eastern European transitional economies followed the so-called "shock therapy" approach; that is, the governments dismantled the central planning system and privatized SOEs at the very start of reform. Unfortunately, such reform strategy often caused initial collapse of output and even social instability, because an economy cannot jump to the market system over night. Market mechanisms take years to develop. In contrast, China implemented the so-called "dual-track" gradual reform strategy; that is, the government continued to support the SOEs while creating more favorable conditions, on the margin, for non-SOEs to expand. This approach could suffer from potential efficiency losses, because SOEs are generally less efficient, but it ensured economic and social stability during the transition period.

This dual-track reform strategy led to the unique phenomenon of "asymmetric liberalization" between product and factor markets in China: the government almost completely liberalized the product markets, where prices are freely determined by demand and supply. Government interventions remain widespread and heavy in markets for production factors such as capital, land, and energy. Such interventions are actually effective ways of supporting the relatively less efficient SOEs, at least in the initial period. For instance, the state-dominated commercial banks continuously allocated large volumes of cheap bank loans to the SOEs. Therefore, many of the policy interventions were actually parts of the arrangements to support the dual-track strategy.

Such seemingly inefficient policy distortions, however, did not prevent China from achieving both rapid economic growth and basic financial stability during the reform period. On the one hand, the degree of government interventions was actually on the decline, albeit at a slower pace than in other transitional economies. For instance, in 1980, the financial repression index dropped from 1.0 (almost completely centrally planned) to 0.6 in 2015 (roughly halfway through financial liberalization). On the other hand, some policy interventions even played positive economic roles. Again, the SOEs often supported the government's efforts to stabilize the economy, alongside the fiscal and monetary policies. And, according to analyses in this volume, repressive financial policies actually raised GDP in China by 0.8 percentage points in the 1980s through effective conversion of savings into investment and support to investor confidence. If the market system is not well developed, then perhaps a certain degree of government intervention could be favorable.

The key lesson from China's reform experience is that we should not view policy distortions through ideological lenses. On the one hand, all government interventions have both positive effects and negative effects, and decisions on policy reform should be determined by cost-and-benefit analyses.

A lot of the earlier policy distortions were results of the dual-track reform strategy, the main purpose of which was to ensure smooth transition of the economy. But under certain circumstances, government interventions can make positive contributions to economic performance. It is easy to imagine that such situations could occur not only in transitional economies, where the market mechanism is generally under developed, but also in developed economies, where "market failure" problems are also common. Were China to liberalize its financial system completely in 1978, it would, most likely, have already suffered from a number of financial crises over the past decades.

On the other hand, it is still important to remember that the most fundamental contributor to China's economic success during the reform period was the "liberalization policy," not the "control policy." During the past forty years, the Chinese economic system converged steadily to the free market regime, although the paces of such convergence varied in time, sometimes fast, sometimes slow. Because the cost-and-benefit dynamism of policy distortion changes over time, the government has to formulate timely and flexible policy responses. The latest development suggests that policy distortions in favor of the SOEs are now imposing very high costs on the economy. For instance, according to the analysis in this volume, the net effects of repressive financial policies on China's GDP growth already turned from positive in the 1980s and 1990s to negative in the 2000s. These imply that further SOE reform and financial liberalization should be both urgent and desirable.

NEW ECONOMIC CHALLENGES

In retrospect, the onset of the global financial crisis marked an important turning point in China's macroeconomic performance. Before 2008, the Chinese economy sustained rapid economic growth, maintained basic financial stability but suffered from serious structural imbalances. And after 2008, the economy was hit by persistent growth slowdown and witnessed rising systemic financial risks but also experienced important structural rebalancing. One might describe the post-crisis economic features as important parts of the new normal, although this transition is still ongoing and may take decades to complete. The new normal is a complex phenomenon but the key takeaway is quite straightforward: future growth trajectory will be very different from the past experience. And this change was likely underpinned by a number of new trends.

The first important challenge is transition of the growth model from input-driven to innovation-driven. For several decades during the reform period, China enjoyed low-cost advantages. As long as large numbers of farmers continued to flow from the countryside to the cities, labor cost could stay low and manufacturing could continue to expand rapidly. However, now rural surplus labor is almost exhausted and per capita GDP is already close to the high-income level, and China has to rely on industrial upgrading to continue economic growth. This is the so-called "middle-income challenge." As China already lost its low-cost advantage, both the proportion of exports to GDP and the share of industry in GDP are already on the decline. The growth model has to switch from input-driven to innovation-driven. And the key question is, can China innovate?

Building innovative capability is the result of coordinated efforts in several areas. First is accumulation of human capital. While the Chinese universities produce millions of students majoring in sciences and engineering every year, the average education level of the 300 million migrant workers is junior high school. The latter could be particularly troublesome as there could be a significant mismatch between future labor demand by increasingly more sophisticated industries and supply of labor volumes of unskilled workers. Second is financial services that are suitable for supporting innovation, as the current bank-dominated financial system appears more capable of supporting extensive manufacturing expansion. Third is protection of intellectual property rights, which is also at the center of China's ongoing trade disputes with several trading partners. And fourth is the big question about appropriate industrial policy. The commonly applied government subsidies and picking-the-winner approach are often not effective and are sometimes even counter-productive.

The second important challenge is population aging. At around 2010, the second wave of "demographic dividend" gave way to population aging, as the dependency ratio started to rise from a trough of around 36 percent. This was probably also one of the drivers behind persistent growth slowdown after 2010. But the process of aging is only starting. According to projections in this volume, the dependency ratio, which measures the proportion of nonworking-age population to total population, could rise to 66 percent in 2049, while the working-age population could shrink by about

170 million in absolute number between 2019 and 2049. Population aging, especially "getting old before getting rich," could have serious consequences for the Chinese economy in the coming decades, including declining labor supply, weakening consumption demand, rising need for elderly care, and widening funding gaps of social security systems.

Fortunately, analyses in this volume also point to some potential ways of responding to some of the challenges posed by population aging. Adoption of artificial intelligence (AI), for instance, could potentially substitute for 280 million workers during the coming three decades, which is more than enough to offset the potential decline of working-age population as a result of aging. Interestingly, AI has larger substitution impacts on female, old, low-skilled workers. Similarly, continuous urbanization may also help mitigate weakening consumption demand as a result of aging. Currently, per capita consumption in urban areas is, on average, more than double the per capita consumption in rural areas. If China's urbanization rate could rise from 56 percent in 2015 to 80 percent in 2049, which was predicted by the United Nations, aggregate consumption demand could continue to expand at robust paces in the coming decades. Perhaps the greatest difficulty caused by aging is the rapidly widening funding gap of social security services. Given that the dependency ratio will rise dramatically in the coming decades, but that the social security system is not well funded, the macro tax burden of the Chinese economy will likely rise in the future.

The third important challenge is de-globalization. While China was one of the greatest beneficiaries of globalization during the past decades, it is almost impossible to continue the dependence of Chinese growth on external markets for several reasons. On the one hand, China already rose from a small-country economy to a large-country economy. Today, whatever China buys, the commodity becomes more expensive; and whatever China sells, the commodity becomes cheaper. In other words, the "spillover effects" from China's economic policies and activities are already significant enough to induce significant reactions from other countries. On the other hand, the trend of globalization has already reversed since the global financial crisis. This was because, while improving overall efficiency, globalization also caused pain by the shifts of economic activities. Certain social groups were hard hit in the form of job losses. And this backfired on globalization, as illustrated by the election of Donald Trump in the United

States and Brexit in the United Kingdom. At least in the foreseeable future, the global market is likely to stay less open than before.

There is also a new dimension of economic tension between China and the United States, or between an emerging and an existing power. China's international economic policies have gone in two important directions. One is opening of the Chinese economy to the outside world, especially the service sector. While China probably fulfilled most of the commitments it made upon WTO accession, the standards of openness look low relative to China's new level of development and its size in the world economy. The trade friction does raise a new question of whether China's economic policy would continue to be outward-oriented or would turn inward-looking. And the other is participation in international economic governance, including through the WTO and the International Monetary Fund (IMF). China is also pushing its own international economic agendas, such as internationalization of renminbi (RMB), the Asian Infrastructure Investment Bank (AIIB), and the Belt and Road Initiative (BRI). An important question is whether China and the United States can reach an accommodation to work together to reform global governance, or whether the two are destined for economic and strategic conflict. It is too early to tell how the external economic environment will look and what the exact consequences on the Chinese economy will be.

In addition to the above three challenges, there are several other important changes that China will have to face in the coming decades. One of them is environmental and climate challenges. During a large part of the reform period, China maintained relatively lax environmental standards, which probably also boosted the pace of economic growth, to a certain extent. It also helped to create the so-called "pollution haven" phenomenon after China opened up to the outside world. This was largely evident as exports, pollution, and carbon emission all grew at extraordinary paces in the years following China's WTO accession at the end of 2001. In return, China's environmental degradation was also very severe and already imposed heavy welfare losses on the country. Economic studies suggest that the costs of environmental degradation and resource depletion in China approached 10 percent of GDP, of which air pollution accounted for 6.5 percent, water pollution 2.1 percent, and soil degradation 1.1 percent. Water and air pollutions are also important causes of illness. Therefore, without seeking a low carbon and green path, China's growth model is no longer sustainable.

Other things being equal, higher environmental standards could also lead to slower GDP growth as it is conventionally measured. All of these challenges likely will exert significant influences on the Chinese economy in the coming decades, including the pace, composition, and quality of economic growth. A higher level of dependence on innovation, a rapidly ageing population, a less open international economic environment, and a more green and low-carbon development path all point to a slower pace of economic growth and an entirely different growth model. A lot of economic skills that China accumulated during the past four decades might not be as effective as before or even useful going forward. For instance, out of the three components of economic growth on the demand side—consumption, investment, and net exports—China relied almost exclusively on the latter two in the past. But this growth model is no longer sustainable.

POLICY RECOMMENDATIONS

According to forecasts in this volume, China's economic growth rate will probably slow to 2.7 to 4.2 percent in 2049, with its GDP per capita rising to about two-thirds that of the United States in the same year. If these projections turn out to be moderately accurate, then China would achieve several important goals between 2019 and 2049:

- overcoming the "middle-income trap" by successfully reaching high-income status

- becoming the largest global economic power by surpassing the size of the United States economy

- achieving the government's second Centennial Goal of becoming a fully developed economy

An immediate takeaway from this projection is that the growth slowdown will likely persist for a very long time. It is not a pure cyclic fluctuation as some believe. Before the global financial crisis, the Chinese government frequently relied on macroeconomic policies, such as fiscal and monetary measures, to stabilize economic growth. And that counter-cyclical policy was often quite effective. But it is now different; growth slowdown, from above 10 percent in 2010 to below 7 percent in 2018, was driven mainly by structural, not cyclical, factors. China's years of continuous 10 percent or even 8 percent economic growth are over permanently. Government officials and private entrepreneurs should be prepared, both psychologically and economically, for this long-term decline of growth rates.

But even these slower growth rates may not be automatically guaranteed. Many developing countries were stuck in the middle-income trap for decades, and Japan suffered from a period of economic stagnation. Several studies reveal that China's TFP and capital efficiency declined dramatically after 2008. The projections in this volume are based on the roles of economic openness and demographic structure in explaining China's economic convergence with the United States. The underlying assumption is that China has to continue productivity improvement in order to retain even the projected lower rates of economic growth. This is why the government is shifting its policy focus from demand-side counter-cyclical measures to supply-side structural reforms.

This volume sets forth the following set of policy recommendations for China to continue a robust pace of economic growth over the next three decades:

End the dual-track reform approach and realize competitive neutrality for SOEs and private enterprises. It is time to call an end to the dual-track reform strategy, which was a transitional arrangement initially, and to complete the transition to a market economy. Enforcement of competitive neutrality, particularly through the SOE reform, could be a central step in achieving this objective. First, the government should clearly specify the narrowed role and scope of SOEs. With the exceptions of a small number of "strategic industries" wherever the private sector can do well, there should be no reason to maintain a significant presence of SOEs. Second, the government should try to create a level playing field concerning entry, competition, and exit. It should resist frequently calling for SOEs to fulfill policy responsibilities. Whenever needed, the government should buy such services from the SOEs on market terms. And, third, as owners, government agencies should optimize capital management and supervision of SOEs. They should focus more on investment returns to state-owned assets, instead of interfering into the daily operations of the enterprises.

Abandon birth restrictions and build good baby—and elderly—care fa-cilities to cope with the negative consequences of aging. Rapid aging looks inevitable now, regardless of new policies. The government, however, can carefully devise some policy schemes to mitigate the pains. First, it should introduce measures to encourage fertility, including economic sup-port, childcare services, medical security, and promotion of female employ-ment, in addition to a complete removal of birth restrictions. Second, it should take steps to strengthen human capital accumulation by expanding education and training resources and increasing inputs in health. Third, it should make efforts to improve the pension system and establish a more flexible retirement mechanism. A multilevel pension insurance system as well as postponement of the legal retirement age should be helpful. And, finally, government policy should also focus on developing long-term care services. For instance, home- and community-based services, rather than simply institutional care, might be favored by the Chinese elderly.

Improve innovative capability through human capital accumulation, intellectual property protection, and sensible industrial policies. To a large extent, the issue of growth sustainability boils down to the question of innovative capability. First, accumulation of human capital becomes even more critical. This includes not only educating scientists and technicians, but also training unskilled workers. Second, the government may try to establish a more effective research and development (R&D) system through greater public and private spending in this area, better schemes linking innova-tion and mass production through better protection of intellectual property rights, and greater rewards to scientists. And, finally, China also needs to revamp its industrial policy to make it more fair, more efficient, and more transparent. The purpose of industrial policy is to encourage innovation by overcoming market failures. Therefore, industrial policy should avoid "pick-ing the winner." Instead, it should avoid restricting competition and set a clear timeline for exit.

Shift the focuses of public finance from underpinning stability to sup-porting economic efficiency and distributive equity. The fiscal system needs to be transformed in several ways. First, the priority of government expenditure should shift from economic construction to social welfare. The mix of tax revenues should evolve as the revenue share of individual income tax increases but that of corporate income tax declines. New taxes, such as property taxes, are urgently needed for distributive and local infrastructure purposes. Second, the government can try to ease current social security funding pressure by injecting state assets, extending retirement ages, and reducing excessive social security payments to retired government officials. The social security scheme should also provide more equal coverage for retired farmers. Third, the central government is trying to resolve the excessive debt burdens of some local governments. In addition to restrictions on extra-budgetary revenues, the central government may also directly assist local governments in balancing their budgets and reducing debt burdens. And, finally, the central-local fiscal relationship should evolve from a highly centralized to a more decentralized system, with the local government reducing spending responsibilities but increasing direct revenues.

Support quality development through further financial reform, cautious financial innovation, and prudent financial regulation. The financial system needs to adapt quickly in order to effectively support innovation. First, China needs more financial institutions and funding channels. Diversification of financial services could also better serve the small- and medium-sized enterprises (SMEs) through increased competition and financial innovation, such as using machine learning and big data analyses. Second, market mechanisms should play greater roles in the allocating and pricing of financial resources. Competitive neutrality should be helpful for improving funding conditions for the SMEs, many of which are innovation start-ups. Market-based risk pricing, through interest rate liberalization, can also change financial institutions' ability and willingness to serve the new economy. And, finally, financial liberalization and innovation should be accompanied by the restructuring of financial regulation, which has been largely ineffective in containing financial risks. Financial regulatory reforms should focus on policy effectiveness through the ways that regulations are enforced.

Accelerate urbanization to unlock new economic impetuses by eliminating household registration and reforming land tenure. China can generate additional economic dynamism by raising the urbanization rate from 56 to 80 percent in the coming three decades, to offset a slowing economic momentum dictated by the aging population. So far, most of the migrant workers leave their families in the villages, which has not only caused serious social problems, but also weakened overall consumption demand. One, it is time for the government to completely stamp out the feudal household registration system, which could have the equivalent system-wide effects of a resumption of the university entrance examination and adoption of the household farming. Allowing rural families into the cities could help narrow the unfair rural-urban divide, increase consumption demand, and improve infrastructure efficiency. This time the focus of the new urbanization program should be on large cities instead of small towns. Also, urbanization should be accompanied by integration of the social security system across the country. Further land system reform, even reform of the land property rights, should be considered to provide farmers with the "first bucket of gold" when they move to cities.

Apply market-based policies, such as taxes, to build a green and low-carbon development path. The government has already launched a series of initiatives and programs in these areas, though with mixed results. If the ongoing efforts continue on the current track, it is possible for China to outperform its environmental and climate change targets. It is already the world's largest producer and supplier of renewable technologies, advancing ahead of schedule. It launched the environmental tax in 2018 and switched recently from feed-in tariff to auction scheme in renewable energies, which already shows great promises. The main policy recommendation of this volume is to transition from an administrative-oriented to a market-based approach in policy design and implementation. Here the 2018 policy to clean up the environment provides a useful example. The campaign-style implementation led to the collapse of economic activities in some regions, followed by the dramatic reversal of the policy. Such policies are too volatile and often unsustainable. Market-based approaches generally make the costs of environmental cleanup more transparent and sustainable.

Further open unilaterally by giving up the status of "developing country" and constructively contributing to the international system. China's current international economic policymaking is heavily distracted by external disputes, but it should take a unilateral approach in establishing a high-quality opening regime. First, China should consider unilaterally giving up the "developing country" status, which should enable China to reaffirm its reform commitment in the WTO framework and also to reduce tensions with economic partners. After all, this is in China's own interest and China is only several years away from the high-income level. Second, it is important to balance between liberalization and stability. For instance, financial liberalization is now highly desirable, but volatile cross-border hot money flows could be damaging. Therefore, some restrictions or prudential regulations could accompany financial liberalization. Again, the best strategy for tech development is through an open innovation system. But the security of the supply chain could be at risk at times, and some measures to ensure the security of the supply chain would be desirable. And, finally, China should try to actively participate in international economic governance, including the WTO and the IMF, through constructive, not disruptive, engagement. It is also reasonable for China to add some new innovations, such as BRI and AIIB, to the international system.

PART I

SETTING THE SCENE

1

China's Economic Growth in Retrospect

YAO YANG

One of the world's defining events of the past several decades has been China's economic ascent. Seventy years ago, when the People's Republic of China (PRC) was founded, the average Chinese adult lived on an income barely above one-fifth the world average; today, the same person is able to enjoy the standard of living of the average world citizen. China is now the world's second-largest economy and largest exporter. This status was not achieved simply through an increase in population. Rather, tremendous structural transformation has taken place, as a result of which the country has one of the most complete production networks in the world. This chapter reviews China's growth experience and explains the main economic and political drivers behind the country's economic success.

In economic terms, there is probably little miracle in China's miraculous growth; the country has followed closely the tenets of neoclassical economics, aiming for high savings, high investment, accumulation of human capital, technological progress, industrialization, and so on. It also enjoyed favorable demographics and international environments during the period of high growth. What is unconventional about China is how the country has adopted those economic precepts. A lengthy period of economic planning before 1978, despite the many mistakes, laid a solid foundation of heavy industry that helped the take-off in the reform era. The country has benefited tremendously from economic opening, yet it has opened at its own pace and has kept a strong bias toward mercantilism characterized by a managed exchange rate, asymmetric policies toward export and import, and a policy of market-for-technology imposed on foreign direct investment (FDI) in some strategic sectors. Despite a wave of reform in the period 1995–2005, state-owned enterprises (SOEs) still play a significant role in the economy and enjoy privileged access to credit and market.

Over the next thirty years, China is likely to face two strong headwinds. The first is deteriorating demographics and the second is a more haphazard international environment. Deteriorating demographics will render capital accumulation a less attractive driver of sustainable growth; instead, innovation will have to move to center-stage, and domestic policy will have to change accordingly. On the international front, the increasing size of China's economy will require that the country formulate a new approach to international economic relations. Changes will have to come soon. The main purpose of this chapter is to provide some insight into where and how those changes might best occur.

The chapter starts by reviewing China's economic achievements from a historical perspective. It then discusses the four drivers of China's fast growth in the reform era, namely, the preparation undertaken during the planning period, favorable demographics, high saving and capital accumulation, and greater efficiency. This is followed by a concise look at the structural change in the Chinese economy and its consequences. The chapter closes with a brief discussion of the two strong headwinds, aging and a changing international environment, that China will have to deal with in its quest to meet its second centennial goals, to be achieved by the 2049 anniversary of the founding of the PRC.

GREAT ACHIEVEMENTS

The Chinese civilization reached its peak during the Tang and Song dynasties (AD 666–1266). During the subsequent Ming and Qing dynasties (AD 1346–1911), the Chinese economy was locked in stagnation. Although there was some growth in the agricultural sector, per capita income remained suppressed by a growing population. By the mid-nineteenth century, China had entered an extended period of secular decline that halted only with the founding of the PRC. Table 1-1, adapted from Angus Maddison (2001), provides a vivid account of China's decline and rejuvenation relative to the world over the past three centuries. Before around 1820, both China's population and its GDP kept pace with the rest of the world. After that date, the share of China's population in the world total began to decline, but its share of GDP declined faster. By 1950, per capita GDP in China was merely 21 percent of the world average. The Chinese Communist Party (CCP) inherited a dirt-poor country. Although in 2001, Angus Maddison was too optimistic about China's projected 2015 per capita GDP, China's overall achievement since 1950 was still remarkable.

From a historical perspective, China's economic resurgence started not in 1978 but in 1949. Figure 1-1 presents the growth rates in the period 1954–2018. Between 1954 and 1977, the PRC managed to grow by 6.14 percent per annum. According to the numbers shown in table 1-1, China grew 2.1 percent faster than the rest of the world in each year during the period 1950–2001. However, the growth in the first thirty years was rather haphazard and might be exaggerated by artificially inflated prices of goods produced by heavy industry, a sector deliberately promoted by economic planning. Sustainable growth has occurred only since 1978. In the forty years between

TABLE 1-1. **China in Comparison with the World, 1700–2015**

	1700	1820	1900	1950	2001	2015
Population (millions)						
China	138	381	400	5,47	1,275	1,387
World	603	1,042	1,564	2,521	6,149	7,154
China in world (%)	23	37	26	22	21	19
GDP (billions of 1990 international dollars)						
China	83	229	218	240	4,570	11,463
World	371	696	1,973	5326	37,148	57,947
China in world (%)	22	33	11	5	12	20
Per capita GDP (1990 international dollars)						
China	600	600	545	439	3,583	8,265
World	615	668	1,262	2,110	6,041	7,154
China in world	0.98	0.90	0.43	0.21	0.59	1.16

Source: Adapted from Maddison (2001).

Note: Numbers for 2015 are Maddison's 2001 projections.

1978 and 2018, China's economy managed to grow at an annual rate of 9.44 percent. As a result, in real terms the Chinese economy in 2018 was thirty-seven times as large as it was in 1978.

Apparently, China has been growing much faster than the rest of the world, particularly after 1978. As a result, China's share of the world economy, measured in nominal terms, has increased sharply, from less than 2 percent in 1978 to 16 percent in 2018 (figure 1-2). China's share of world trade was negligible in 1978 but reached 11 percent by 2018. Based on certain projections provided in chapter 2, China's GDP is set to regain its 1820 share of the world total by 2049 and China's per capita income is forecasted to be double the world average.

The living standard of the average Chinese person increased by twenty-six times in real terms in the period 1978–2018. Only a few economies in human history have managed to achieve this rapid advance in standard of living. Although income disparities remain large, the rising tide of income has lifted most people's living standard. In particular, poverty has been drastically reduced. In 1978, 30 percent of the Chinese population, or 250 million people, lived below the official poverty line, which was about US$20 per year. By the end of the 1980s, the poverty rate had been reduced by two-thirds. Today, fewer than 4 percent of the rural population live below the

FIGURE 1-1.   **Growth Rates of China's GDP: 1954–2018 (%)**

Source: National Bureau of Statistics of China (www.stats.gov.cn).

FIGURE 1-2. **China's Shares of World GDP and Exports: 1960–2018 (%)**

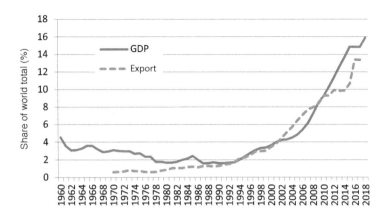

Source: Penn World Table 9.0 (Feenstra, Inklaar, and Timmer 2015).

Note: GDP and export are measured in then current dollars.

poverty line (now about US$340 per year), and the government's goal is to eradicate absolute poverty by 2020.

GROWTH DRIVERS

The classical theory of growth, promulgated in the 1950s, holds that labor, capital formation, and technological progress are the key drivers of economic growth. China has done a superb job in hewing to these tenets. From an economic perspective, then, there is no miracle to China's miraculous growth. It is worth emphasizing, however, that China began applying the precepts of classical economics even during the planning period. With focused effort, China was able to accumulate a significant stock of capital and build a solid industrial base that was conducive to its economic take-off in the reform era.

Preparation During the Planning Period

The PRC's first thirty years were marked by many failures, some of which were devastating. With painstaking effort, however, the country was able to establish a relatively solid industrial foundation, particularly in the heavy manufacturing sectors. In 1952, industry was the smallest sector in the economy, and its value added accounted for less than 20 percent of the national GDP; by 1975, industry had overtaken agriculture and the service sector to become the largest sector, and its value added was already 46 percent of the national GDP.[1] The policy China adopted, import substitution, was the state-of-the-art policy prescription for developing countries at the time. What separated China from other countries was China's high saving rate and its more rigorous planning. Despite being one of the poorest countries in the world, China managed to maintain a national saving rate of 25–30 percent most of the time. In addition, the government was able to channel the savings to targeted sectors. Despite its low efficiency, China was able to establish a relatively complete industrial base by 1978, and the country was transformed from an agrarian society into an industrializing one.

There has been a debate about whether the heavy-industry development in the planning period was worthwhile. Yao and Zheng (2008) provided an assessment by calibrating a dynamic general equilibrium model to China's real data. They found that there should be an optimal rate (31 percent) and an optimal length (twelve years) of subsidy provided to heavy industry because heavy industry possesses distinctive technical externalities coming out of roundabout production (in roundabout production, capital goods are produced first, followed by consumer goods). Compared with the optimums, the rate of subsidy implemented by the planning period was 6.6 percentage points higher than the optimal rate and the period of subsidy was thirteen years longer than the optimal length.

In addition to industrial development, China managed to improve the level of education and health of ordinary citizens. Table 1-2, adopted from Yao (2014), presents a comparison of China and India in terms of human and industrial development in 1978. At that time, the average Chinese person was one-fourth poorer than the average Indian, but China achieved higher levels of human and industrial development than India. Specifically, it is clear that China adopted a quite different approach from India's to improving human capital. While India put more emphasis on higher education, China aimed at raising the educational level of ordinary citizens. As a result, China was able to achieve a much higher adult literacy rate than India, even though India produced more university graduates than China until 2002. China's approach paid off in its early stage of economic growth, when a large number of unskilled workers were needed. China began to expand its higher education after 1998, and this corresponded to China's entry into the middle-income stage (China became a middle-income country in 2002), when more skilled workers were needed. To be sure, China's initial approach to human capital improvement was not designed to push for economic growth but to improve equality for the population. Nevertheless, this approach contributed significantly to the country's economic take-off.

Labor and Demographics

In retrospect, two decisions made by the CCP leadership at the end of the 1970s very much determined China's growth trajectory over the next several decades. One was reform and opening, and the other was family planning. These two decisions were not made out of a well-coordinated process but rather were coincidence. While reform and opening was a conscious decision, family planning was more an unthought-out reaction to the fear of a coming "population bomb" in China—the country's population was estimated to approach one billion at the time, news that astonished the Chinese leadership. Yet the two decisions enhanced each other in the next three decades. Family planning created a favorable demographic structure that helped unleash the potential of reform and opening. A large number of young people moved from the countryside to the city and made tremendous contributions to China's export-led growth and industrialization.

TABLE 1-2. **Comparisons of China and India in 1978**

	China	India
Per capita GDP (constant 2000 dollars)	155	206
Adult literacy rate (%)	65.5	40.8
Tertiary school enrollment (% gross)	0.7	4.9
Life expectancy	66	54
Infant mortality rate (%)	54.2	106.4
Share of manufacturing in GDP (%)	40.0	17.0
Share of manufacturing in employment (%)	17.3	13.0

Source: Yao (2014).

Note: China's literacy rate is for 1982 and India's literary rate is for 1981.

Figure 1-3 presents China's working-age ratios between 1960 and 2018. Before 1976, the ratio hovered at around 55 percent. It then increased to 65 percent by the end of the 1980s, mostly because family planning slowed the birth rate. The 1980s witnessed the restoration of family farming and the beginning of rural industrialization; rising working-age ratios allowed farmers to accumulate more savings from farming, which in turn helped fuel rural industrial development. As the country entered the 1990s, the trend toward rising working-age ratios was mitigated by the demographic echo caused by the baby boomers born between 1962 and 1976. Then, in the first decade of the twenty-first century, another sharp rise in working-age ratios occurred, peaking in 2009 at 74.2 percent. This by far was the most favorable demographic structure that a country has experienced (Bloom et al. 2007). The first decade of the twenty-first century registered the most dramatic growth in recent Chinese history. Much of this growth was driven by labor-intensive export, which benefited tremendously from a favorable demographic structure. Since 2009, the working-age ratio has declined almost as quickly as it rose before that year. Also, China had begun to exit from export-led growth by that time, and favorable demographics were not as badly needed as before. In a sense, China was extremely lucky because its pace of growth in the first thirty years of the reform era almost perfectly matched its demographic transition. The remaining question is whether China can complete the transformation required by a deteriorating demographic structure.

A significant consequence of rising demographic dividends in the first thirty years was a large proportion of migrant labor, mostly young people moving from the countryside to the city. They first worked in labor-intensive exporting factories, then, more recently, shifted to service sectors. Figure 1-4 shows the number of migrant workers (left axis, bars) and their share in the urban population (right axis, solid line) in the period 1993–2017. According to China's National Bureau of Statistics (NBS) definition, a migrant worker is a person who works outside his or her own county and an urban resident is a person who stays in a city for more than 180 days in a year. Figure 1-4 shows that except for a setback caused by the 1997 Asian financial crisis, the number of migrant workers increased until 2014, then stabilized at around 170 million, or about one quarter of China's total labor force. On the other hand, the share of the urban population increased steadily from less than 30 percent in 1993 to almost 60 percent in 2017.

FIGURE 1-3. **Working-Age Ratios (Share of Persons Aged 15–64 Years in the Population), 1960–2018 (%)**

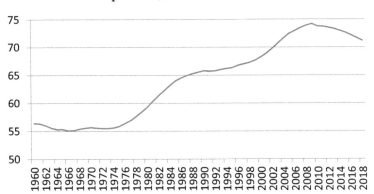

Source: NBS at www.stats.gov.cn.

A favorable demographic structure helped China's growth in the first thirty years in several ways. A direct contribution was a large supply of labor, which enabled China to conduct large-scale labor-intensive export. In the first decade of the twenty-first century, China's exports grew by a factor of 6.33 to reach US$1.5 trillion. This period coincided with the period of significant growth in the demographic dividends, as shown in figure 1-3. According to the estimates of Tian and coworkers (2013), rising working-age ratios contributed 14.6 percent of China's export growth in the period 2000–2006. The second contribution of a favorable demographic structure was low wages. There was clearly a large amount of surplus labor in the countryside before China joined the World Trade Organization (WTO); the real wage of migrant workers increased slowly, if at all. As a result, industry could enjoy Lewisian growth; that is, it could expand without much increase in labor costs. After great growth in the first decade of the twenty-first century, however, the surplus labor supply was very much depleted.[2] That depletion coincided with a decline in China's demographic dividends beginning in 2009. This has certainly contributed to China's slowdown in recent years, but the working-age ratio has remained above its 2000 level, and its level effects may remain for a while. One such effect has been a high demand for consumer goods—the third contribution of a favorable demographic structure. Young people consume more than old people when adjusted for income. This factor has been particularly helpful after China began to rely more on domestic consumption than on exports to generate growth.

Overall, rising demographic dividends were responsible for a quarter of China's economic growth (Cai and Wang 2005). In international comparisons, China's demographic structure is expected to remain favorable until the late 2020s. Once China's baby boomers, born between 1962 and 1976, retire from the workforce, however, the situation is expected to deteriorate. This is a consequence of the strict family planning policy implemented between 1979 and 2015, which has constrained workforce replacement. One of the premises of this discussion is that aging is inevitable, and over the next thirty years it will be incumbent on China to find some ways to adjust to its aging demographic structure. The discussions in subsequent chapters are all based on this premise. In the long run, demography trumps other factors in its effect on a country's growth potential. Whether China is able to meet its second centennial goals depends critically on how successfully it mitigates the negative consequences on economic growth of an aging population.

FIGURE 1-4.   **Migrant Workers as Share of the Urban Population, 1993–2017**

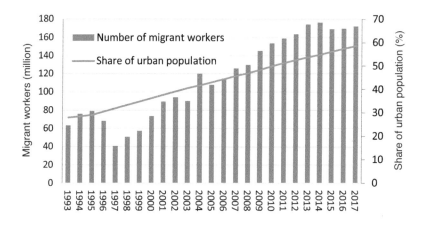

Source: Ministry of Labor and Social Security of China (various years).

Saving and Investment

Capital formation has been central to China's economic growth, both before and after 1978. The national saving rate was between 22 percent and 33 percent in the several five-year plan periods before 1978. In the context of China's very low income level at the time, this was an extraordinarily high rate. After 1978, five periods can be identified (figure 1-5). During the first period, 1978–1982, the national saving rate declined. This was caused by the reversal of the heavy-industry development strategy. During the second period, 1983–1994, the saving rate increased significantly. The third period, 1995–2000, was marked by another decline in the saving rate caused by the restructuring of SOEs, which lowered both urban household income and corporate savings. In the fourth period, 2001–2010, national savings increased dramatically. By 2010, national savings accounted for 52.6 percent of GDP, a rate only a few countries have reached. It is this period that has attracted so much academic research seeking to explain why China's saving rates, both national and household, increased so dramatically. Precautionary saving—saving in expectation of a future income shortfall— and high housing prices are the two most prominent explana-

FIGURE 1-5.   **Share of National Savings and Capital Formation in GDP, 1978–2017 (%)**

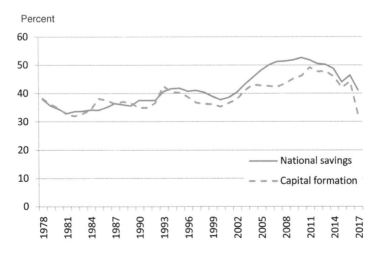

Source: National Bureau of Statistics of China (www.stats.gov.cn).

tions offered (for example, Chamon and Prasad 2010; Chen and Qiu 2011). However, precautionary saving motives cannot explain why the saving rates, including the household saving rate, declined in the third period when the old enterprise-based social security system was basically broken because of SOE restructuring. And housing prices cannot explain why the saving rates, again including the household saving rate, declined in the fifth period, from 2011 onward.

A plausible theory that provides a unified explanation for all five periods is Franco Modigliani's life-cycle hypothesis. One of the most important propositions to emerge from the life-cycle hypothesis is that a country's national saving rate is proportional to its GDP growth rate. In his last published paper (Modigliani and Cao 2004), Modigliani and his coauthor applied this proposition to explain the changes in China's national saving rate since 1950. They found that China's rising GDP growth rate could provide a good explanation for the rising saving rate after 1978. In the same vein, they attributed the rising saving rate during the fourth period (2001–2010) to accelerated growth, and its subsequent decline after 2010 they considered to be a result of decelerated growth.

Related to China's high savings is an international debate over China's contribution to global trade imbalances. In 2005, Ben Bernanke considered that a "saving glut," mainly brought about by excessive saving in Asia, was a cause of the American trade deficit (Bernanke 2005). Since then, China's high saving rates have caught international attention. For China's savings to cause global trade imbalances, China has to run a large current account surplus. Figure 1-5 also shows China's share of capital formation in GDP. By definition, the difference between savings and capital formation is a country's current account surplus. Before 1994, China's savings and capital formation were more or less balanced, but since 1994, savings have been consistently larger than capital formation, and the discrepancy was particularly large between 2004 and 2010. It was also during this period that China accumulated a large amount of official foreign reserves. However, China's current account surplus as a share of GDP began to decline, and by 2015–2016 it was barely above 2 percent.[3]

China's fixed exchange rate regime (FERR) was often picked up by American politicians and some international organizations as the main reason for China's large current account surplus in the period 2004–2010. While the FERR might have helped China export more, it is questionable whether it was the main cause of China's large current account surplus because a country's current account is a result of both international balances (exports minus imports) and domestic balances (savings minus investment), and the latter is determined by many factors, among which the exchange rate may be a less important one.[4]

At any rate, rebalancing has happened since 2010. Together with its declining share in the current account surplus, the national saving rate dropped faster than it had increased before 2010. In the seven years between 2010 and 2017, the rate declined by an average of 1.63 percentage points each year, reaching 41.2 percent in 2017. It was still high by international standards, but the rebalancing brought about by the drop was significant. Structural adjustments in both international and domestic markets have contributed to this change. In the international market, adjustments in the United States and other advanced economies have slowed the growth of consumption, very much as a belated response to the global financial crisis. Export is no longer a driver of China's growth. In the domestic market, the Chinese economy has gone through several important structural changes, among which deindustrialization has been the most significant. One of the consequences of deindustrialization is a slowdown in saving. A more detailed discussion of this topic is provided later in the chapter.

Total Factor Productivity

According to received wisdom, China's economic growth has been driven solely by capital accumulation ever since Paul Krugman questioned the so-called East Asian miracle (Krugman 1994). Econometric exercises that calculate the Solow residual seem to confirm this view.[5] For example, a meta-analysis published in 2012 and based on 5,308 observations from 150 primary studies found that the growth of China's total factor productivity (TFP) was only 2 percent per annum and had contributed 20 percent to China's overall GDP growth since 1978 (Tian and Yu 2012). By contrast, in advanced economies the contribution is in the range of 40–50 percent (Kim and Lau 1996). However, there are many problems with using the Solow residual. One of the most significant is that it fails to account for technological progress embedded in capital accumulation. It is undeniable that a factory improves its technological efficiency when it installs new, more advanced equipment, yet this improvement is highly likely to be attributed to the growth of capital stock when the Solow residual is calculated because the growth of capital stock is the first-order event.

An alternative to using the Solow residual is to calculate TFP growth by the growth in wages and the rate of return on capital (ROC). For that purpose, we may consider the standard Solow model with constant-return-to-scale technology:

$$Y = AK^{\alpha}L^{1-\alpha}, \tag{1}$$

where Y is national GDP, K is the stock of capital, L is the stock of labor, A is the index of technological progress, and $0 < \alpha < 1$ is capital's output elasticity. Then, using the identity $Y = rK + wL$, where r is the rate of return on capital and w is the wage rate, we get:

$$\hat{Y}_t = \alpha\hat{K}_t + (1 - \alpha)\hat{L}_t + [\alpha\hat{r}_t + (1 - \alpha)\hat{w}_t]. \tag{2}$$

Therefore, TFP growth is

$$\hat{A} = \alpha\hat{r}_t + (1 - \alpha)\hat{w}_t. \tag{3}$$

It is the weighted average of the growth rate of wages and the growth rate of ROC using the output elasticities of labor and capital as the weights. Wages and ROC may be subject to confounding cyclical factors, but in the long run they reflect economic fundamentals.

There are no consistent data for wages, so labor income reported by the NBS's *Flow of Funds Table* is used to substitute for wages (NBS, various years). Accordingly, the labor share of national income is taken as labor's output elasticity $(1 - a)$. ROCs are calculated from macrodata by Lu (2018). Table 1-3 presents the results for the period 1996–2015 for which data are available. On average, labor income grew by 9.2 percent per annum in this period, slightly lower than the GDP growth rate. The change in ROC was highly volatile. Consistent with China's growth cycles, ROC declined before 2000 and after 2008, but increased drastically in between. On average, though, ROC declined by 0.4 percent per annum.[6] The average contribution of labor income growth to GDP growth was 4.3 percent, whereas growth of ROC contributed −0.2 percent. TFP growth calculated by equation (1.3) is presented in the second-to-last column. On average, it was 4.1 percent per annum. Its share of contribution to GDP growth varied from year to year (exceeding 100 percent in 2001 and 2004), but on average it was 41.9 percent, right in the range of the advanced economies' results but much higher than the results arrived at by other studies.

There has been concern in recent years that capital efficiency has been declining rapidly. The evidence often cited is the increasing incremental capital-output ratio (ICOR). Before 2008, China's ICOR was around 4, close to the numbers put up by other East Asian economies. Since then, it has increased to 6.[7] However, about half of China's capital investment since 2008 has been spent to improve people's welfare (Zhang 2019). This includes spending on high-speed railways, subways, public utilities, and recreational facilities, all of which usually require government subsidies to operate. China's ICOR would decline drastically if investment in those areas were excluded.

Notwithstanding the increasing share of investment in welfare-improving infrastructure, the declining ROC since 2005 should sound an alarm. This decline has taken a toll on TFP growth. The average rate of TFP growth was 6.1 percent in 1996–2004 but dropped to 2.5 percent between 2005 and 2015. A glance at table 1-3 shows that the decline could be attributed solely to the decline of the ROC. At the time of writing, China's ROC in the manufacturing sector was around 15 percent, about the same as that of the United States but higher than Japan's (Lu 2018). However, the declining trend shows no sign of stopping. To stabilize the ROC, China needs to greatly improve how it allocates capital, particularly to reduce wasteful financial resources received by the SOE sector.

STRUCTURAL CHANGE

The Chinese economy has gone through significant structural changes since the global financial crisis. Two of them are a pivot away from export-led growth and deindustrialization. Together with those two changes, rebalancing has happened. In addition to the drop in the saving and investment rates, the share of labor income has stopped declining and the share of services has increased. On the other hand, overall growth has slowed and begun to rely more on domestic consumption.

TABLE 1-3. **TFP Growth Estimated from Growth of ROC and Labor Income, 1996–2015 (%)**

Year	GDP growth rate	Share of labor income	Growth of labor income	Labor share of GDP growth	Share of capital gains	Growth of ROC	ROC share of GDP growth	TFP growth	TFP share of GDP growth
1996	10.0	53.4	14.7	7.9	46.6	-0.5	-0.2	7.6	76.1
1997	9.3	52.8	8.1	4.3	47.2	-3.5	-1.7	2.6	27.9
1998	7.8	53.1	8.5	4.5	46.9	-7.1	-3.3	1.2	15.5
1999	7.6	52.4	6.1	3.2	47.6	-2.4	-1.1	2.0	26.8
2000	8.4	51.4	6.3	3.2	48.6	-2.7	-1.3	1.9	22.8
2001	8.3	51.5	8.5	4.3	48.5	18.3	8.9	13.2	159.4
2002	9.1	50.9	8.0	4.1	49.1	3.9	1.9	6.0	65.7
2003	10.0	49.6	7.2	3.6	50.4	5.0	2.5	6.1	61.1
2004	10.1	45.5	1.0	0.4	54.5	25.0	13.6	14.1	139.1
2005	11.3	41.4	1.2	0.5	58.6	-2.8	-1.6	-1.1	-9.9
2006	12.7	40.6	10.5	4.3	59.4	3.9	2.3	6.6	51.9
2007	14.2	39.7	11.8	4.7	60.3	4.0	2.4	7.1	50.0
2008	9.6	43.2	19.1	8.2	56.8	-15.9	-9.1	-0.8	-8.5
2009	9.2	46.6	17.9	8.3	53.4	-7.2	-3.8	4.5	49.2
2010	10.4	45.0	6.6	3.0	55.0	7.1	3.9	6.9	66.0
2011	9.3	44.9	9.1	4.1	55.1	-3.0	-1.6	2.5	26.4
2012	7.8	45.6	9.4	4.3	54.4	-4.7	-2.6	1.7	21.7
2013	7.7	46.0	9.6	4.5	54.0	-1.5	-0.8	3.6	47.3
2014	7.4	46.5	9.9	4.6	53.5	-5.4	-2.9	1.7	23.5
2015	6.9	47.9	10.1	4.8	52.1	-19.0	-9.9	-5.1	-73.4
Average	9.4	47.4	9.2	4.3	52.6	-0.4	-0.2	4.1	41.9

Sources: National Bureau of Statistics of China, "Flow of Funds" (table) (www.stats.gov.cn), and Lu (2018).

Note: TFP, total factor production; ROC, return on capital.

Changes in the Growth Pattern

Chapter 10 provides a detailed account of China's export-led growth and its transition; this section discusses it only from a macro perspective. Before 1978, China had a closed economy and its export was minimal. After 1978, three periods can be identified (figure 1-6). The first period is 1979–2001. There were large fluctuations during this period, but the average growth rate of exports was respectable, reaching 16.0 percent. One of the reasons for this respectable growth was the low starting point of China's exports. By 2001, when China joined the WTO, China's exports had managed to reach only US$266.2 billion. During the second period, 2002–2008, China's exports grew by an average of 27.3 percent per annum, thanks to the country's accession to the WTO. In a mere seven years, its volume of exports had increased by 5.37 times, to reach US$1.43 trillion. As a result, China became the largest exporter in the world. The third period is from 2009 on. During this period, the growth of exports dropped to 6.8 percent per annum. In 2009, 2015, and 2016, negative growth was registered. However, China's exports still grew faster than world trade did. At US$2.49 trillion, China's exports in 2018 made it just below the size of the seventh-largest

FIGURE 1-6.   **Exports and Their Growth, 1979–2018**

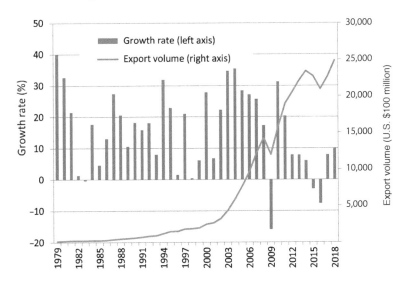

Source: National Bureau of Statistics of China (www.stats.gov.cn).

economy in the world (India) for that year. Large economies usually do not have high export/GDP ratios; it is around 10 percent in the United States and 17 percent in Japan. China reached 36 percent in 2007, with the ratio falling since then. Because China's GDP growth rate has been decelerating, it will not be surprising if exports grow more slowly in the future.

Exports contributed greatly to China's overall economic growth in the period 2002–2008. According to Lau and coworkers (2007), exports contributed 11–15 percent of China's GDP through net exports and forward and backward linkages. This means that export growth contributed three to four percentage points, or 30–40 percent of China's GDP growth in this period. In contrast, export's contribution on average has been lowered to around one percentage point since 2008. In some years it was even negative. This is a clear sign that exports are no longer a strong driver of growth, although they remain an important component of the Chinese economy.

Domestically, the Chinese economy has experienced the most significant structural change in decades. After six decades of painstaking industrialization, China entered the stage of deindustrialization right around the time of the global financial crisis. Figures 1-7 and 1-8 present the sectoral shares of employment and value added, respectively. China has followed the common patterns of structural change experienced by successful economies: the share of the primary sector in the national economy declines, the share of the tertiary sector increases, and the share of the secondary sector first increases and then declines. The last pattern is an indicator of industrialization and subsequent deindustrialization. The secondary sector's share of value added reached its peak in 2006 (48.0 percent), and its share of employment did so in 2012 (30.3 percent).[8] Because the share of employment is usually stickier than the share of value added (which is evident from figures 1-7 and 1-8), it can be concluded that China finished the period of high industrialization and entered a deindustrialization phase in 2012.

However, China's deindustrialization might have come earlier. Liu, Mao, and Yao (2018) calibrated a dynamic and multisectoral model and found that China's industrialization would have continued to around 2017 had the global financial crisis not occurred. For comparison, it was around 2017 that China reached South Korea's 1990 per capita GDP, when the latter's industrial share of employment reached its peak. China's in-

FIGURE 1-7.   **Sectoral Shares of Employment, 1954–2018**

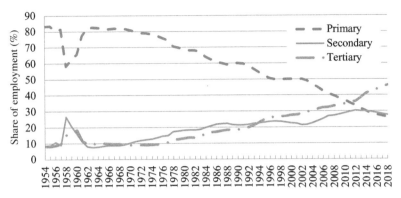

Source: National Bureau of Statistics of China (www.stats.gov.cn).

FIGURE 1-8.   **Sectoral Shares of Value Added, 1954–2018**

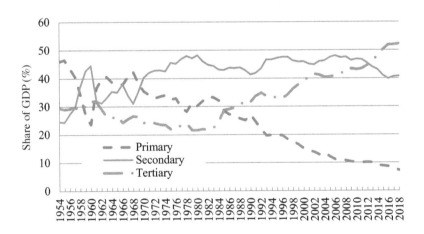

Source: National Bureau of Statistics of China (www.stats.gov.cn).

dustrialization was greatly accelerated by its export-led growth model. In the first decade of the twenty-first century, the secondary sector gained 10 percent in its share of employment, equivalent to its gains in the preceding forty years. Exit from that growth model has taken a toll on China.[9]

Consequences of Structural Change

The first consequence of structural change is a slowing of growth. When exports were able to drive growth, industrial expansion was almost unlimited because demand was not related to domestic consumption. After the economy exited from export-led growth and deindustrialization began, services became the strongest driver of growth, and their demand must be generated endogenously, within the country. During the period 2001–2010, industrial growth contributed on average 47.5 percent to China's overall growth, whereas the corresponding figure for services was 45.8 percent. Between 2011 and 2017, industry's contribution declined to 32.6 percent and the contribution of services increased to 62.2 percent.[10] These figures are indicative of a sea change in China's growth model. For one thing, they meant that many of China's policies aiming at promoting industrial development and export would have to be moderated. Unfortunately, this has not happened yet.

Industrial development is still important, of course. Studies have shown that continuous industrial upgrading is critical for a middle-income country to become a high-income one (Su and Yao 2017). However, industrial upgrading now is not automatically fulfilled by capital accumulation; rather, it must be led by innovation. One overarching theme of this book is how China is meeting the challenge of innovation.

Yet innovation is unlikely to be able to generate very fast growth. A case of comparison is Japan in the 1970s and 1980s. Japan adopted the export-led growth model in the 1950s and 1960s, and its economy was able to grow more than 9 percent per annum. The first oil crisis forced the country to abandon the export model, very much as the global financial crisis would later force China to do the same. Japan successfully transformed its economy into one based on innovation. In fact, Japan dominated the world stage of innovation in the 1970s and 1980s. Yet the country managed to grow only by an average of 3.5 percent between 1973 and 1993. After 1993, the Japanese economy virtually stopped growing. China may be able to do better than Japan did because of internal income disparities and subsequent convergence. But that requires the inland provinces to catch up with the efficiency of coastal provinces, which will not be easy (Yao and Wang 2017). Therefore, China may have to lower its expectations for the growth rate.

Deindustrialization brought more than bad news, though. The rebalancing discussed earlier was one of the good results of deindustrialization. Of course, declining saving rates also contributed to the slowdown in growth. But in general, increased consumption has brought the Chinese economy back to a more balanced growth trajectory. The most significant good news is that the share of labor income has increased, and consequently, income distribution has become better (figures 1-9 and 1-10).

FIGURE 1-9.   **Composition of National Income, 1995–2017**

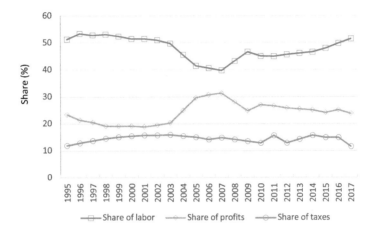

Source: National Bureau of Statistics of China, *Flow of Funds Table.*

FIGURE 1-10.   **Income Gini Coefficients, 2003–2017**

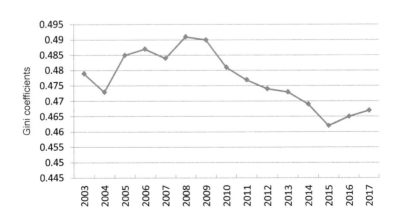

Source: National Bureau of Statistics of China (www.stats.gov.cn).

Between 1995 and 2007, the labor share declined by more than ten percentage points. Most of the gains were taken by corporate profit. This had two consequences. One was that income distribution worsened: income and wealth were concentrated among a relatively small number of capital owners. The other was that the saving rate increased because high-income capital owners have a higher propensity to save than lower-income people. Beginning in 2007, though, the labor share began to increase, and by 2017 it had regained 11.7 percentage points.

Several factors contributed to the changes in labor shares. Among them, two were the most significant. One was demographic transition. The declining period of labor shares was the period of rising working-age ratios. Labor was becoming more abundant and wages were suppressed. By around 2007, China had finally reached the Lewis turning point, and rural-to-urban migration began slowing. And finally, by 2010 demography had started to work against fast growth. The other significant factor was structural change (Liu, Mao, and Yao 2018). During the period of industrialization, labor moved from agriculture to industry (and services), and the share of industrial employment increased. But industry is the most capital-intensive sector and pays a higher ratio to capital than agriculture and services. The resulting composition effect lowered the share of labor income in the overall economy. During the period of deindustrialization, labor began to move from both agriculture and industry to services. As a result, the labor share began to increase.

It is widely acknowledged that income inequality is large in China. According to data released by the NBS, the Gini coefficient reached a peak of 0.49 in 2008 (figure 1-10).[11] This makes China one of the seriously unequal societies in the world. However, income inequality began to drop after 2008, though it went up a bit in 2016 and 2017. While the geographic relocation of growth—inland provinces have been growing faster than coastal provinces since 2008—was a factor, the most important driver of the decline probably was the increase of labor shares in the national income. Even as it is a desirable objective in itself, improved income distribution is also good for domestic consumption. After tremendous expansion in the period 2003–2012, China's economy has accumulated a significant amount of excessive capacity; the lack of effective demand has constrained faster growth. When ordinary people enjoy a larger share of national income, domestic consumption increases.

CONCLUSION

China has accomplished one of its two centennial goals. Over the next thirty years, China will face strong headwinds trying to fulfill its second centennial goal of becoming a high-income country on par with the current rich countries. Export-led and extensive expansion is no longer an option. Fortunately, the Chinese economy has successfully started its rebalancing, and innovation has become a strong driver of economic growth. The challenges China faces in the future are now primarily structural.

The first structural challenge is the declining rate of TFP growth. Though innovation will help, it alone cannot be relied on to sustain a very high TFP growth rate. In many areas, China is approaching the world technological frontiers, so it is natural to see the country's technological progress slow. On the other hand, the declining ROC will put more pressure on TFP growth. While much of the ROC's decline can be explained by deteriorating demographics and a slowing of external demand, misallocation in the financial markets cannot be ignored. SOEs take a disproportionate share of financial resources yet are much less efficient than private firms. Reforming the SOEs and the financial sector will be key to sustaining China's growth.

The second challenge is aging. Aging is a gray rhino in China; not much can be done to avoid it. China needs to learn how to continue reasonable growth in the context of an aging society. This requires a paradigm change in the country's policy framework. Several chapters of this book are devoted to discussing this change.

The third challenge is the changing international environment. Because of the sheer size of its population, China changes the world when its income level increases. When 30–40 percent of global growth comes from China, it is inevitable that every country will feel the impacts. The recent Sino-American trade disputes are probably the beginning of a long period of global adjustment to China's rise. Despite China's declining reliance on global demand, its complete production networks and a burgeoning domestic market have prevented the medium-range industries from moving out of the country. There is a possibility that the "flying geese" pattern espoused by economic theory will collapse and the train of global growth will stop at "Station China" for a long time.[12] This would not just be a problem for the rest of the world; it would above all be a problem for China. Instead of exporting goods to other countries, China must start thinking about how to bring prosperity to all in the world.

NOTES

1. Figures in this section come from *New China Statistics 30 Years* (Beijing: National Bureau of Statistics of China, 1980) if not specified.

2. See Garnaut (2010) and the papers in the same issue of *China Economic Journal*.

3. In 2017, the share went back to 9.1 percent owing to the fast growth of exports. But it became negative in 2018.

4. Economic fundamentals and macroeconomic policy are arguably the more important factors. See Yao (2014) for more discussion.

5. The Solow residual is proposed by Robert Solow in the 1950s to measure an economy's total factor productivity. It is so called because it is the residual growth rate after the contribution of labor and capital is accounted for.

6. In the first half of the 1990s, ROC was about 10 percent. Its decline in the second half of that decade took it to 8.0 percent in 2000. It then began to increase, reaching a peak of 13.7 percent in 2007. After the global financial crisis, it again declined, and by 2015 it had dropped to below 10.0 percent. Decline in this period was faster than in the latter part of the 1990s, reaching 6.2 percent per annum. See Lu (2018) for more details.

7. Calculated from data released by the NBS at www.stats.gov.cn.

8. There is debate whether the NBS's statistics of labor shares were correct. It is possible that the NBS overreported the amount of labor in agriculture because many farmers farm only on a part-time basis. The peak of the industrial labor share often reached 35 percent in other successful economies (such as South Korea). Judging by China's painstaking effort to develop industry, there is a high probability that China did the same.

9. An alternative interpretation is that industrialization in that decade was dramatic and every indicator had already reached its peak by 2012. In other words, China's industrialization was compressed into a very short period of time, and by 2012, deindustrialization was happening naturally.

10. Calculation based on NBS data.

11. Several independent surveys found higher Gini coefficients. For example, the China Family Panel Studies found that the highest Gini coefficient was 0.52, reached in 2010 (Institute of Social Science Survey 2012).

12. The "flying geese" pattern of economic development, proposed in the 1930s to describe technological development in Southeast Asia, holds that wages and other factor prices tend to increase with economic development. Japan was positioned as the lead "goose" in the V formation of Asian developing nations.

REFERENCES

Bernanke, Ben. 2005. "The Global Saving Glut and the U.S. Current Account Deficit." Sandridge Lecture. Virginia Association of Economists, Richmond, VA, March 10, 2005.

Bloom, David, David Canning, Rick Mansfield, and Michael Moore. 2007. "Demographic Change, Social Security Systems, and Savings." *Journal of Monetary Economics* 54 (1): 92–114.

Cai, Fang, and Dewen Wang. 2005. "Demographic Transition: Implications for Growth." Working paper, Institute of Population and Labor, Chinese Academy of Social Sciences, Beijing.

Chamon, Marcos, and Eswar Prasad. 2010. "Why Are Saving Rates of Urban Households in China Rising?" *American Economic Journal: Macroeconomics* 2 (1): 93–130.

Chen, Yanbin, and Zheshen Qiu. 2011. "How Do High Housing Prices Affect Household Saving Rates and Inequality of Wealth?" [In Chinese.] *Economic Research Journal* 10:25–38.

Feenstra, Robert C., Robert Inklaar, and Marcel P. Timmer. 2015. "The Next Generation of the Penn World Table." *American Economic Review* 105 (10): 3150–82.

Garnaut, Ross. 2010. "Macro-economic Implications of the Turning Point." *China Economic Journal* 3 (2): 181–90.

Institute of Social Science Survey. 2012. *The China Report 2010.* [In Chinese.] Beijing: PKU Press.

Kim, Jong-Il, and Lawrence Lau. 1996. "The Sources of Asian Pacific Economic Growth." *Canadian Journal of Economics* 29:S448–54.

Krugman, Paul. 1994. "The Myth of Asia's Miracle." *Foreign Affairs* 73 (6): 62–78.

Lau, Lawrence, Leonard K. Cheng, Xikang Chen, et al. 2007. "Non-Competitive Input-Output Model and Its Application: An Examination of the China-U.S. Trade Surplus." [In Chinese.] *Social Sciences in China* 5:91–103.

Liu, Yalin, Rui Mao, and Yang Yao. 2018. "Structural Change, the Global Financial Crisis, and the Change of China's Share of Labor Income." [In Chinese.] *China Economic Quarterly* 17 (2): 609–32.

Lu, Feng. 2018. "The Rate of Return to Capital." Manuscript, National School of Development, Peking University.

Maddison, Angus. 2001. *The World Economy: A Millennial Perspective.* Brussels: OECD, June.

Ministry of Labor and Social Security of China. Various years. *China Labor and Social Security Yearbook.* Beijing: Statistics Press.

Modigliani, Franco, and Shi Cao. 2004. "The Chinese Saving Puzzle and the Life-Cycle Hypothesis." *Journal of Economic Literature* 42 (1): 145–70.

NBS (National Bureau of Statistics). Various years. *"Flow of Funds Table"* in *China Statistical Yearbook.* Beijing: Statistics Press.

Su, Dan, and Yang Yao. 2017. "Manufacturing as the Key Engine of Economic

Growth for Middle-Income Economies." *Journal of Asian Pacific Economy* 22 (1): 47–70.

Tian, Wei, Yang Yao, Miaojie Yu, and Yi Zhou. 2013. "Demographic Structure and International Trade." [In Chinese.] *Economic Research Journal* 11:87–99.

Tian, Xu, and Xiaohua Yu. 2012. "The Enigmas of TFP in China: A Meta-Analysis." *Courant Research Centre: Poverty, Equity and Growth—Discussion Papers* 23 (2): 396–414.

Yao, Yang. 2014. "The Chinese Growth Miracle." In *Handbook of Economic Growth*, edited by Philip Agnion and Steve Durlauf, vol. 2B, chap. 7, 943–1032. Amsterdam: North Holland.

Yao, Yang, and Mengqi Wang. 2017. "Internal Convergence and China's Growth Potential." In *Technological Progress and China's Long-Run Growth*, edited by Ligang Song, Cai Fang, and Laura Johnston, chap. 5. Canberra: Australian National University Press.

Yao, Yang, and Dongya Zheng. 2008. "Heavy Industry and Economic Development: The Chinese Planning Economy Revisited." [In Chinese.] *Economic Research Journal* 43 (4): 26–40.

Zhang, Bin. 2019. "Increasing Fiscal Expenditure to Overcome the Deficiency of Effective Demand." Paper presented at a conference, "How the Financial Sector Can Support the Real Economy: Economic and Financial Policy Recommendations for 2019." The 132nd NSD Policy Talk, National School of Development, Peking University, January 18, 2019.

2

Convergence and Prospects

XUN WANG

A vigorous debate is in progress over the impact of domestic economic fundamentals on China's growth prospects. A declining growth potential and certain policies with respect to technological development loom large in these discussions, even as the ongoing China-U.S. trade dispute adds uncertainty about globalization and the world economy. One major benefit of the reform era and the opening up of China has been the skill and knowledge spillover from leading economies. Further openness is necessary for China to successfully use this knowledge to catch up economically as the aging of the population increasingly works against the country's potential GDP growth.

Even though China's growth prospects have been closely scrutinized in recent years, our understanding of the size of China's economic convergence with the leading developed economies and the time-sensitive effects on potential GDP growth is limited. This chapter focuses on the growth convergence that is primarily associated with relative per capita GDP and the fundamentals that determine the country's ability to absorb knowledge produced elsewhere and leverage technology spillover and transfer. In so doing, the chapter makes three major contributions to the literature. First, it provides a supply-side method of predicting China's growth potential over the long term, based on cross-country productivity convergence and China's demographic evolution. Second, it documents the dynamic effects of the size of the convergence and spillover, that is, how much greater openness, human capital accumulation, urbanization, and population aging affect the country's ability to absorb knowledge and utilize technology transfer. Third, it offers a new estimation framework that incorporates these elements into a nonlinear panel data model based on a catch-up growth model to investigate China's growth prospects and the convergence of China's relative per capita GDP with that of other leading economies.

For the purposes of discussion, I have identified five open economies with a relative per capita GDP comparable to China's out of 113 economies, based on their classification as open or closed (Sachs and Warner 1995). I used historical data from the comparable open economies to estimate the time-varying size of the convergence of China's per capita GDP with that of the five selected countries, the fitted value of which I used as the basis for projecting the growth of China's per capita GDP. The dependent variable (per capita GDP growth of the comparable open economies and China) is regressed on relative per capita GDP and on control variables, including human capital, urbanization, the old-age dependency ratio, and the youth dependency ratio, in a nonlinear framework.

Growth theories and empirical evidence show that real per capita income in open economies follows the law of relative convergence; that is, open economies in the same stages of development tend to exhibit similar patterns of per capita income convergence (Lucas 2009). More specifically, the lower the initial relative per capita income of an open economy, the higher the average growth rate of per capita income in the following decades. However, demographic factors do not follow such a law. Therefore, in projecting economic growth rates, we will consider both the experience of conditional convergence and country-specific demographic factors that may modify this experience.

The main findings of the chapter are as follows: (1) Growth performance diverges significantly between open economies and closed economies since openness provides developing countries the opportunity to access technology and knowledge spillover from the leading economies through economic cooperation and exchange. (2) Urbanization and the accumulation of human capital are important processes that enhance following and developing countries' ability to catch up. This finding has significant implications, especially for China and other open and transitional economies. (3) An aging population is increasingly constraining the sustainability of

China's economic growth, implying that some modification of China's birth control policy is necessary. (4) China's projected GDP growth falls from 6.66 percent (2016–2020) to 2.66 percent (2046–2050) on low growth estimates, from 6.96 percent (2016–2020) to 3.39 percent (2046–2050) on medium estimates, and from 7.20 percent (2016–2020) to 4.16 percent (2046–2050) on high growth estimates.

The chapter is organized as follows. After analyzing the importance of openness for developing countries to be able to catch up economically and which factors contribute most to growth convergence, I briefly consider the theoretical treatment of growth convergence and related empirical work on growth projections for China. The empirical framework used for growth projections for China in the next three decades is introduced and discussed, followed by projected results for real GDP growth during 2015–2020 under different scenarios. The implications for China's growth conclude the chapter.

OPENNESS AND GROWTH CONVERGENCE

The Significance of Openness

Openness is a prerequisite for developing countries to narrow the gap between themselves and more advanced economies. Increasing trade volume, one manifestation of openness, has significant effects on domestic employment (Autor, Dorn, and Hanson 2013), wage level (Melitz 2003), the efficiency of resource reallocation (Melitz and Redding 2013), and technical change (Bloom, Draca, and Van Reenan 2016). Opening gives developing countries the opportunity to access technology and knowledge spillover from the leading economies through economic cooperation and exchange; that access is vital for poorer countries to take off. In the process of opening up, it is also important for developing countries to strengthen intellectual property protection, which will help create the sort of institutional environment conducive to innovation and technology transfer.

To examine the effect of open policies on economic performance, I applied the Sachs-Warner classification (Sachs and Warner 1995) based on trade and other related policies and divided 113 economies into open and closed policies during the period 1980–2010. (Appendix table 2A-1 presents the country list and open period.) I view China as an open economy based on China's trade and other reform policies. Since the start of the reform and opening up beginning in the late 1970s, and especially after China entered the World Trade Organization (WTO) in 2001, the country has grown to be an increasingly important trading partner and among the largest recipients of foreign direct investment (FDI) in the world.

Figure 2-1 plots the average annual growth of per capita GDP during the period 1980–2010 against the 1980 per capita GDP levels, measured in 2011 U.S. dollars, for the two types of economy. As figure 2-1 shows, in most cases open economies grew faster than economies with an equivalent level of per capital GDP in the beginning but which then followed closed policies over the next thirty years. China's economic performance is remarkable in that per capita GDP kept growing at an annual rate of 6.2 percent from a starting value in 1980 of US$1,539 per capita, according to the Maddison Project (2018).

To provide a formal test of the significance of openness, I present some additional econometric evidence on the relation between openness and economic growth. The empirical strategy is similar to the one employed in a number of empirical studies on growth (such as Barro 1991). The objec-

FIGURE 2-1.   **Per Capita GDP and Growth Rates, 113 Economies**

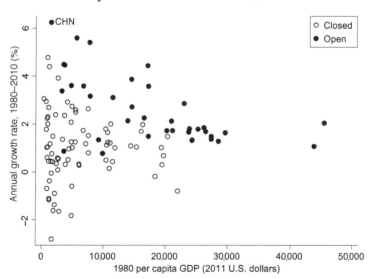

Sources: Author's calculations, based on data from Maddison Project (2018).

tive is to test whether, after controlling for the usual determinants (such as initial income, human capital accumulation, government size, and political stability), open economies grow significantly faster than closed economies.

I regressed the average growth of per capita GDP of 113 economies in the 1980–2010 period (GR8010 in table 2-1) on the following regressors: the initial value of GDP per capita; the openness status in 1980, proxied by a dummy variable, where 1 denotes open and 0 denotes closed; the initial amount of human capital, obtained from the Barro-Lee Educational Attainment Dataset (Barro and Lee 2013); the amount of government spending, proxied by the average ratio of real government spending to real GDP (government size); distortions in the prices of investment goods, proxied by the deviation of the 1980 purchasing power parity (PPP) price of investment goods from the sample mean; and the degree of political stability, proxied by the government stability index of the International Country Risk Guide (2015) data set.

The results of the regression, presented in table 2-1, are familiar from the related literature: the initial level of per capita GDP is negatively correlated with economic growth, consistent with the hypothesis of conditional convergence (Barro and Sala-i-Martín 1992). The measures of human capital accumulation and political stability positively affect growth. Government size and distortions in the prices of investment goods (denoted in the table by the producer price index, PPI) are factors negatively associated with growth, but the price distortions are insignificant.

More important, all the coefficients for openness in table 2-1 are positive and highly significant, indicating that a decision to open domestic markets to international trade helps a country's economic growth in the next three decades. The coefficients are around 1.91 to 2.17, which means that the average growth rate of open economies was around 2 percent higher than that of closed economies during the 1980–2010 period. Since we regress the status of openness in year 1980 on the average growth rate during the 1980–2010 period, reverse causality is not a big problem.

Growth Convergence of Open Economies

Historical data from high-income countries show evidence of growth convergence; that is, the poorer an open economy is during the initial period of measurement, the faster it grows in the following decades. To make it

TABLE 2-1. **Growth Regressions**

Dependent variable	GR8010		
	(1)	(2)	(3)
Initial GDP per capita, 1980	−0.052[‡]	−0.109[‡]	−0.091[†]
	(0.000)	(0.000)	(0.000)
Openness, 1980	2.169[‡]	1.906[‡]	1.918[‡]
	(0.336)	(0.318)	(0.325)
Human capital, 1980		1.219[‡]	0.881[†]
		(0.365)	(0.438)
Government size			−0.115[‡]
			(0.031)
PPI, deviation			−0.211
			(0.275)
Political stability			0.525[†]
			(0.201)
Number of observations	113	91	70
R^2	0.281	0.322	0.484

Notes: Robust standard errors are in parentheses. GR8010 denotes the average growth of per capita GDP during 1980–2010. Initial GDP per capita for 1980 is measured in thousands of 2011 U.S. dollars. PPI = producer price index.

[‡]$P < 0.01$, [†]$P < 0.05$.

clear, we chose five open economies in Asia (Japan, Singapore, South Korea, Taiwan Province of China, and Hong Kong SAR) and fourteen Western European economies (Ireland, Austria, Belgium, Denmark, Finland, France, Germany, Italy, the Netherlands, Norway, Sweden, Switzerland, the United Kingdom, and Spain) and plotted the average annual growth rate of per capita GDP in the period 1960–2010 against the 1960 per capita GDP, measured in 2011 dollars (figure 2-2).

Figure 2-2 shows that the lower the per capita GDP in 1960, the higher the economy's average annual per capita GDP growth rate between 1960 and 2010. The downward-sloping curve implies that the forces equalizing the per capita income and growth rate were operating within these nineteen open market economies. It proves empirically that the per capita GDP of low-income economies under open policies will gradually converge to the per capita GDP of high-income economies.

FIGURE 2-2. **Income and Growth Rates, Nineteen Economies**

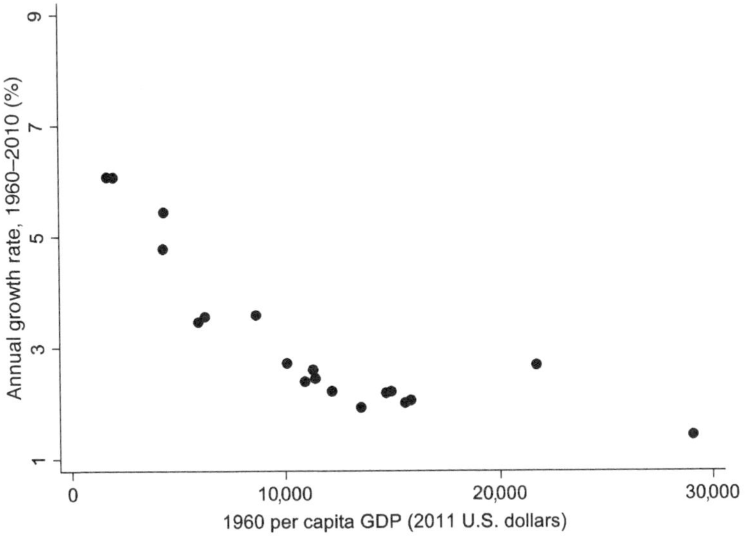

Source: Author's calculations, based on data from Maddison Project (2018).

China did not reform and open its economy until 1978. During the 1950s to 1970s, China adopted central planning and almost closed its economy to trade with the advanced economies. Market mechanisms did not play a role in the economy. Economic growth performance before and after 1978 differed significantly. Before 1978, the average annual GDP growth rate was a modest 3 percent, not much different from the growth rate of the United States. However, since the reform and opening up in 1978, China's per capita GDP growth rate has accelerated to more than 8 percent a year. Figure 2-3 shows how China's per capita GDP (in log terms) has begun to reduce the gap with the United States' GDP as a result of the opening-up policies.

Factors Associated with Growth Convergence

Certain factors have been associated with the economic growth convergence of less well-off countries with that of better-off countries, among which investment in human capital and the process of urbanization are most often pointed out. Although some have argued that these factors are correlated,

FIGURE 2-3.   **Log per capita GDP of China and United States, 1950–2014**

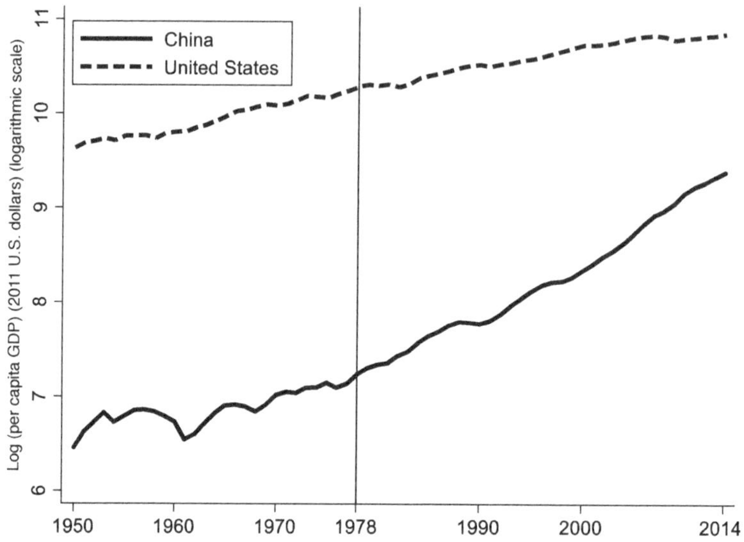

Source: Author's calculations, based on data from Maddison Project (2018).

they have different meanings. Human capital as a productive factor measures the quality of the population. Urbanization reflects the effects of the increasing concentration of information and knowledge as people move from rural to urban areas.

Human capital, usually measured by comparative levels of schooling (Wang and Yao 2003), is vital to the ability of an economy that is in the process of catching up to participate in the communication that technology transfer requires and to absorb appropriate technological transfer and knowledge. Cities are the centers of information and knowledge exchange and the recipients of technological inflows. Besides other barriers to and costs of domestic migration, including the constraints of the household registration system (*hukou* system) in China, moving from a rural area to a city requires the migrant or migrant household to have accumulated human capital.[1]

Therefore, the concentration of the population in the cities and the quality of the workers are crucial for an opening, poor economy to catch up. In poor economies, a high fraction of the population and of employment is usually in rural areas, which inhibits the accumulation of human capital since agriculture tends to be a low-skilled sector. For example, at the start of China's opening up, 82 percent of the population were concentrated in rural areas, and at that time, the human capital of China was less than half (49.3 percent) that of the United States and just 55 percent that of Japan. As a poor economy adopts opening-up policies, cities will become nodes for attracting foreign investment and technology. Improvements to the educational system, more readily available in cities, contribute to the growth of human capital, which in turn promotes the process of urbanization.

Figures 2-4 and 2-5 respectively plot the share of the urban population in the total population and human capital against an economy's per capita GDP (in logs) for 117 economies. The data on human capital are from the *Penn World Table* 9.0, a database (PWT 9.0; Feenstra, Inklaar, and Klimmer 2015). For urbanization, I used the 2018 World Development Indicators (WDI). For real income, I used the Maddison Project's 2018 data set. Figures 2-4 and 2-5 show that the wealthy economies all have relatively high levels of human capital and shares of urban population, while poorer economies have lower levels of human capital and higher shares of rural population. China's urbanization and human capital levels in 2014 (labeled "CHN") were among the medium levels in the world and suggest considerable opportunity for catching up economically with further opening in the coming decades. Appendix figures 2A-1 and 2A-2 graph urbanization and human capital against relative per capita GDP and show a similar pattern.

THEORETICAL BACKGROUND AND EMPIRICAL LITERATURE

Theories Regarding Convergence

In neoclassical growth theory, per capita GDP growth tends to be inversely related to the starting level of output or income per person (Cass 1965; Koopmans 1965; Solow 1956). In particular, if economies are similar with respect to preferences and technology, then poorer economies will grow faster than richer ones. Thus there are underlying forces that promote convergence in per capita product and income. This convergence seems to apply to growth across states and regions within an economy as well. Barro and Sala-i-Martín (1992) provided evidence of convergence across the

FIGURE 2-4.   Urbanization and Log (per capita GDP), 2014

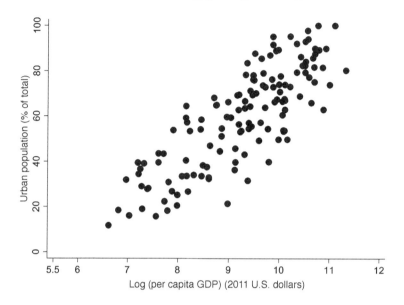

Source: Author's calculations, based on data from Maddison Project (2018).

FIGURE 2-5.   Human Capital and Log (per capita GDP), 2014

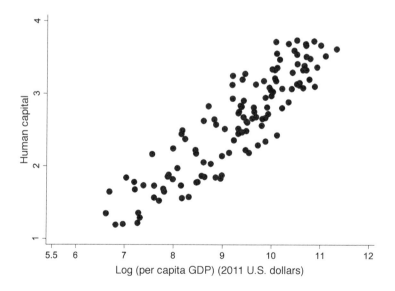

Source: Author's calculations, based on *Penn World Table* 9.0 (2019 data) (Feenstra, Inklar, and Timmer 2015).

forty-eight contiguous U.S. states and found that the U.S. states, in terms of personal income and gross state products, exhibited apparent evidence of convergence.

It is technological progress that promotes the growth of per capita output in the long run. Because of diminishing return on capital, an economy grows faster when it starts farther below its steady-state path. The evidence provided by Becker, Murphy, and Tamura (1990) shows that the convergence is local and conditional. Tamura (1991), using an endogenous growth model, predicted convergence in both the growth rates of income and the level of per capita income. And he introduced an external human capital effect in the investment sector that eliminates human capital heterogeneity, such that income convergence arises from human capital convergence. Barro and Sala-i-Martín (1997) showed that catching up between followers and leaders would generate a pattern of conditional convergence owing to the rising cost to followers of copying the leaders. Rodriguez (2006) found that it would be much easier for countries with high initial human capital stock to successfully start developing. Lucas (2009) assumed that the per capita GDP of an economy would be proportional to its human capital stock in an "AK" economy (where A is total factor productivity and K is capital) and provided evidence that the evolutional path of per capita income convergence applied to all open economies.

Empirical Literature on China's Growth Projections

A large body of literature has attempted to predict China's potential growth over a long horizon. Although the results diverge, most studies agree that China's economic growth will likely slow in the coming decades. Holz's (2008) predictions were that China's annual economic growth rates would be in the range of 5.50–10.90 percent for the period 2015–2020 and 3.98–13.51 percent for the period 2020–2025. A report by Zhang, Vandenberg, and Huang for the Asian Development Bank (2012) noted that China was expected to fulfill its growth targets of 8 percent and 6 percent for the periods 2010–2020 and 2020–2030, respectively. Eichengreen, Park, and Shin (2012) projected that China would grow at an annual rate of around 6.1–7.0 percent during 2011–2020, with the rate declining to 5.0–6.2 percent during 2020–2030. Johansson, Guillemette, and Murtin (2012) predicted that China's average annual growth rate during the periods 2011–2030 and

2030–2060 would be 6.6 percent and 2.3 percent, respectively. Cai and Lu (2013) showed that China's potential GDP growth would reach 6.08 percent during 2016–2020. Pritchett and Summers (2014) thought that China's previous rapid growth would finally return to normal growth and the annual average growth rate would fall to 5.01 percent in 2013–2023 and to 3.28 percent in 2023–2033.

Using the growth accounting method, Lu and Cai (2016) projected that China's potential growth would be 6.6 percent, 5.6 percent, 5.03 percent, 4.5 percent, 3.9 percent, 3.2 percent, and 2.5 percent during 2016–2020, 2021–2025, 2026–2030, 2031–2035, 2036–2040, 2041–2045, and 2046–2050, respectively. Li and coworkers (2017) examined the relationship between human capital and per capita income, and estimation showed China would grow at an annual rate of 3 percent during 2015–2035. Based on Lucas's framework and the assumption of constant size of convergence, Bai and Zhang (2017) found that China's potential growth would be around 6.28 percent, 5.57 percent, 4.82 percent, 3.94 percent, 3.40 percent, 3.46 percent, and 2.98 percent during 2016–2020, 2021–2025, 2026–2030, 2031–2035, 2036–2040, 2041–2045, and 2046–2050, respectively. The *World Economic Outlook 2017*, published by the International Monetary Fund (IMF, 2017), projected that China would grow 6.58 percent, 6.17 percent, 6.00 percent, 5.90 percent, 5.80 percent, and 5.70 percent seriatim during each year of 2017–2022.

Methods Used to Project Growth

The methods used in the empirical studies cited above differ. Standard economic theories show that in the long run, equilibrium output is determined by potential output or the long-run supply curve owing to flexible prices and adjustable wages. Therefore, projections of growth over a long time horizon that focus only on the demand side tend to ignore production capacity. Studies that focus on the supply side can be roughly divided into two types: simple analogies based on growth convergence theory and predictions employing growth accounting methods.

Simple analogies based on growth convergence theory hold that different economies enjoy roughly the same potential growth rate in the same development stages (Lin 2014; Zhang 2015). But such methods are problematic in that they tend to ignore differences in demographic structure and institutional environment across economies. Predictions employing growth accounting methods are based on projecting the growth of economic efficiency (total factor productivity) and productive factors. The results are highly dependent on the specification of the production function or the elasticity of capital and labor with respect to output. On the other hand, capital accumulation results from the annual growth of output, and the change per se may be the result of changes in total factor productivity.

Some other investigators have adopted methods that take into account both demand and supply, such as the computable general equilibrium model (for example, World Bank Group 2013) or the dynamic stochastic general equilibrium model (for example, IMF 2017). These approaches are relatively effective for analyzing the effects of exogenous shocks in the short term. However, different parameter selection and model specification make the results volatile and difficult to compare.

In this chapter, we employ a supply-side method to predict China's growth potential over a long horizon, based on cross-country productivity convergence and China's demographic evolution. A catch-up and spillover model between leading country and following economies is used to estimate the average growth rate of per capita GDP of the leading economy and the time-varying size of convergence or spillover, based on which the per capita GDP growth of China during 2015–2050 is projected. At the same time, this method allows us to avoid specifying production functions, classifying productive factors, and the like.

Differing from Lucas (2009) and Bai and Zhang (2017), and among others, we allow the size of the convergence to change over time, which makes it possible to examine the determinants of the size of the spillover convergence for developing countries under open economic policies. The next step involves adding the projected per capita GDP growth and the population growth to yield China's annual economic growth rates between 2015 and 2050.

DATA AND ANALYTICAL FRAMEWORK

The data used for estimation and projection are mainly from the following sources. Real GDP per capita (in 2011 U.S. dollars) is from the Maddison Project (Bolt and van Zanden 2014; Bolt et al., 2018). The human capital index and urbanization are from *Penn World Table* 9.0 (PWT 9.0, Feenstra, Inklaar, and Klimmer 2015) and the World Development Indicators (WDI), respectively. Different variants of the projected population data during 2015–2050 are from the 2017 revision of the United Nations' *World Population Prospects* (WPP 2017). To check the robustness of the estimates, we also employ real GDP at constant 2011 national prices (in millions of 2011 U.S. dollars) and the population during 1950–2014 to get the real per capita GDP and its growth rate from PWT 9.0.

Our objective is to forecast the potential GDP growth rate of China in the next three decades. As we know, real GDP can be presented as

$$Y = \frac{Y}{N} \cdot N, \tag{1}$$

where Y and N denote real GDP and the total population, respectively. Therefore, potential GDP growth can be divided into the sum of per capita GDP growth and population growth. Since we can access the historical and predicted data for population from WPP 2017, our main focus is on the projection of potential GDP per capita and its growth rate.

Our projection of China's per capita GDP is based on the framework developed by Lucas (2009), in which the income of open economies converges to a common growth level following a simple law that can be described by a few parameters. Suppose there are two groups of economies, leading economies and developing open economies. Specifically, Lucas (2009) developed a catch-up growth model based on technology spillovers. An economy's per capita production (real GDP) is proportional to its stock of knowledge. The evolution of stock of knowledge in a leading economy can be given as

$$\dot{K}(t) = \mu K(t), \tag{2}$$

where $\dot{K}(t)$ is the change in the stock of knowledge over time. The stock of knowledge of the developing open economies, $\dot{k}(t)$, can be given as

$$\dot{k}(t) = \mu k(t)^{1-\theta} K(t)^{\theta}, \tag{3}$$

where θ is the size of the convergence, indicating the follower's ability to absorb knowledge, technology transfer, and autonomous innovation. In terms of per capita income, the leader grows at a constant rate, and the growth rate of the developing follower is given as

$$\mu \left(\frac{K}{k} \right)^{\theta}. \tag{4}$$

Since $K > k$, the developing economy grows faster than the leader, at a rate that depends on relative per capita GDP and the size of convergence θ.

Therefore, the dynamic of per capita GDP growth for the follower i is given by

$$g_{y_{i,t}} = \mu \left(\frac{y_{us,t-1}}{y_{i,t-1}} \right)^{\theta_{i,t}}, \tag{5}$$

where $y_{i,t}$ denotes per capita GDP of country i at year t in 2011 U.S. dollars and g_y is the growth of per capita GDP. We chose the United States as the leading economy, and relative GDP per capita of country i at year t means the GDP per capita of country i at year t as a share of GDP per capita of the United States at year t. Differing from Lucas (2009), we further allow that the size of convergence parameter θ changes over time. We specify the determination of the size of spillover as

$$\theta_{it} = \beta_1 urban_{it-1} + \beta_2 hcapital_{it-1} + \beta_2 depyoung_{it-1} + \beta_2 depold_{it-1} + \varepsilon_{it}, \tag{6}$$

where θ_{it} is the convergence rate of country i at year t and $urban_{it}$, $hcapital_{it}$, $depyoung_{it}$, and $depold_{it}$ denote urbanization, human capital, young dependency ratio, and old dependency ratio, respectively. Then we employed the nonlinear least squares method to estimate equation (6) to produce the fitted value of the time-varying convergence rate.

Equation (5) is the baseline model for our estimation and projection. To predict the per capita GDP growth of China, we used the historical data of similar open economies in terms of relative per capita GDP to estimate the size of convergence over time and the constant, μ. Therefore, we first identified open economies similar or comparable to current China according to relative per capita GDP. For example, according to the Maddison Project (2018), GDP per capita of China relative to that of the United States in 2014 was 23.1 percent, which is basically equivalent to Japan's relative GDP per capita in 1953 (23.0 percent). Second, we estimated parameters μ and $\theta_{i,t}$ from historical data on the open economies comparable to China. Third, based on the estimated growth rate of per capita GDP of the United States, $\hat{\mu}$, we derived the future value of real GDP per capita of the United States. Based on $\hat{\mu}$, the average size of convergence, $\Sigma_i \widehat{\theta_{it}}$, the future value of real GDP per capita of the United States, and the initial relative per capita GDP of China, we obtained the future value of the growth rate and level of real GDP per capita of China.

GROWTH PROJECTIONS FOR CHINA DURING 2015–2050

Since the latest version of the Maddison Project data and the PWT have updated the data set to years 2014 and 2016, respectively, for consistency, we set 2014 as the initial year and 2015–2050 as the projection period. According to the definition of openness by Lucas (2009) and Sachs and Warner (1995), and using the relative real per capita GDP of China in 2014, we identified five open economies for purposes of comparison: Japan (from 1953), Singapore (from 1960), Hong Kong SAR (from 1960), Taiwan Province of China (from 1978), and the Republic of Korea (South Korea, from 1984). Table 2-2 shows the details from both the Maddison Project (2018) and PWT 9.0.

Predicting China's Potential per capita GDP Growth

We used historical data of five open economies in Asia—Japan (1953–2014); Singapore (1960–2014); Hong Kong SAR (1960–2014); Taiwan Province of China (1978–2014) and South Korea (1984–2014)—to estimate the parameter μ and the time-varying θ. Due to the model specification as shown in equation (5), a nonlinear least squares estimation was employed. Table 2-2

TABLE 2-2. **Real per capita GDP: China Compared with Open Economies, Historical Data**

Economy		Relative real per capita GDP	
	Year	Maddison Project	PWT 9.0
China (mainland)	2014	0.231	0.243
Japan	1953	0.230	0.249
Singapore	1960	0.241	0.251
Hong Kong SAR	1960	0.239	0.249
Taiwan Province of China	1978	0.238	0.241
South Korea	1984/1986	0.231	0.250

Sources: Data from Maddison Project (2018) and Penn World Table 9.0 (2019 data) (Feenstra, Inklaar, and Timmer 2015).

Notes: China refers only to mainland China. The growth projections for China do not include data for Hong Kong SAR, Macao SAR, or Taiwan Province of China.

shows the estimation results. To alleviate the problem of heterogeneity, robust errors clustered by economy are provided.

The estimated results, shown in columns 1 and 4 of table 2-3, indicate that the per capita GDP growth of the United States is around 2.62–2.75 percent, estimated from the historical data of the five open Asian economies used for comparison. According to historical data for the United States (Maddison Project 2018), per capita GDP growth bookended by two economic crises, the Great Depression and the Great Recession (the subprime crisis beginning in 2007), or the period 1935–2006, averaged 2.68 percent. It is interesting that 2.68 percent is within the interval of 2.62–2.75 percent. Therefore, our estimated μ is consistent with the realized growth rate of the per capita GDP of the United States during the period of 1935 to 2006.

TABLE 2-3. **Estimation Results Using Maddison Project (2018) and PWT 9.0 Data**

Dependent variable:	Per capita GDP growth					
	Maddison Project			PWT 9.0		
Constant μ	0.0262‡	0.023	0.02	0.0275‡	0.023	0.02
	(0.005)	—	—	(0.005)	—	—
Human capital	0.332‡	0.309‡	0.289‡	0.354‡	0.322‡	0.299‡
	(0.093)	(0.084)	(0.083)	(0.092)	(0.082)	(0.081)
Urbanization	1.581‡	1.789‡	1.983‡	1.628‡	1.889‡	2.091‡
	(0.433)	(0.340)	(0.343)	(0.419)	(0.003)	(0.352)
Dependence (Young)	−1.247‡	−1.418‡	−1.577‡	−1.253‡	−1.464‡	−1.625‡
	(0.454)	(0.388)	(0.391)	(0.447)	(0.398)	(0.401)
Dependence (Old)	−7.451†	−6.051†	−4.805‡	-8.975‡	−7.103‡	−5.733†
	(3.363)	(2.513)	(2.511)	(3.475)	(2.627)	(2.623)
Number of observations	240	240	240	238	238	238
R^2	0.693	0.692	0.691	0.693	0.692	0.690
Adjusted R^2	0.686	0.687	0.685	0.687	0.687	0.685

Sources: Author's calculations, based on data from Maddison Project (2018) and Penn World Table 9.0 (2019 data) (Feenstra, Inklaar, and Timmer 2015).

Notes: Robust errors cluster by economy are in parentheses. In column 2 and 5, we set $\mu = 0.023$ and estimated the other parameters. In columns 3 and 6, we set $\mu = 0.020$ and estimated the other parameters.

*P < 0.1, †P < 0.05, ‡P < 0.01.

Furthermore, the coefficients for human capital and urbanization are both significant at the 1 percent level, which indicates that both variables are significantly associated with the ability to absorb knowledge, accept technology transfer from advanced economies, and promote autonomous innovation. Coefficients for the youth dependency ratio and the old dependency ratio are significantly negative, indicating that the greater the youth dependency ratio and old dependency are, the less capacity developing countries have to absorb knowledge and technology transfer from leading economies. In keeping with historical data for the United States, we set the per capita growth rate at 2.28 percent (the average growth rate during 1961–2006) in column 2 and at 5 percent and 2 percent (the average growth rate during 1961–2006 and 1961–2016) in columns 3 and 6, respectively. The estimation results show that the coefficients do not change much.

These findings are consistent with the theoretical hypothesis and empirical evidence presented above. Since the five Asian economies selected for comparison were in the same development stage as China is currently during the initial estimation period, we computed the simple average of the estimated θ_{it} across economies, $\Sigma_i \widehat{\theta_{it}}$, to get a time-varying series of θ_t as the predicted convergence rate for China during 2015–2050. Figure 2-6 plots the time-varying size of convergence estimated from the historical data of the five open Asian economies under $\mu = 0.026$, using the Maddison Project (2018) data and PWT 9.0, respectively. The estimated trajectory first goes up and then turns down, which supports a picture of limited and conditional convergence owing to the rising costs of learning, absorbing, and innovating.

Based on the estimated parameter for the specified μ and the time-varying θ_t, and the initial value of GDP per capita of China and the United States, we calculated the predicted values for the growth rate of China's per capita GDP. Figure 2-7 shows China's potential per capita GDP growth rate during 2015–2050 according to Maddison Project (2018) data. Table 2-4 provides the average growth rate by five-year intervals for the period 2016–2050 using the Maddison Project (2018) data and PWT 9.0. The projection shows that China's per capita GDP growth rate will decline gradually, from 6.39–6.51 percent during 2016–2020 to 3.48–3.55 percent during 2046–2050, under $\mu = 0.020$, and from 6.49–6.64 percent (6.61–6.66 percent) during 2016–2020 to 3.78–3.86 percent (4.17–4.19 percent) during 2046–2050 under $\mu = 0.023$ ($\mu = 0.026/0.0275$).

FIGURE 2-6.   **Time-Varying Size of Spillover Effect for China, 2015–2050**

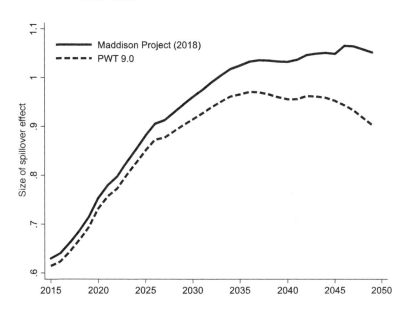

Source: Author's calculations, based on data from Maddison Project (2018) and PWT 9.0 (2019 data) (Feenstra, Inklaar, and Timmer 2015).

Note: The results are based on $\mu = 0.026$ and a medium fertility rate scenario.

Predicting China's Potential Real GDP Growth

Potential GDP growth can be calculated as the sum of the rate of per capita GDP growth and the rate of population growth. Here we borrow the IMF's predicted data on total population from the 2017 *World Population Prospects.* Population growth is projected under several scenarios: low, medium, and high fertility rate; constant fertility; and instant replacement variants. The other variants differ from the medium fertility rate variant only in the projected level of total fertility. In the high fertility rate variant, total fertility is projected to reach a fertility level that is 0.5 births above the total fertility expected with the medium fertility rate variant. In the low variant, total fertility is projected to remain 0.5 births below the total fertility rate of the medium variant.

Figure 2-8 plots the projected total population assuming a medium fertility rate during 2015–2050 for China and the United States. As shown in

FIGURE 2-7.   Potential per capita GDP Growth of China, 2015–2050

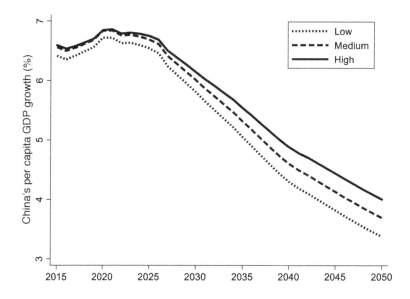

Source: Author's calculations, based on data from Maddison Project (2018).

Note: "Low," "Medium," and "High" refer to the calculation of China's per capita GDP under $\mu = 0.020$ and a low fertility rate scenario, $\mu = 0.023$ and a medium fertility rate scenario, and $\mu = 0.026$ and a high fertility rate scenario, respectively.

TABLE 2-4. **China's per capita GDP Growth Projections, 2016–2050 (%)**

Period	$\mu = 0.020$ Maddison Project	PWT 9.0	$\mu = 0.023$ Maddison Project	PWT 9.0	$\mu = 0.0262/0.0275$ Maddison Project	PWT 9.0
2016–2020	6.51	6.39	6.64	6.49	6.66	6.61
2021–2025	6.62	6.48	6.76	6.60	6.80	6.73
2026–2030	6.11	5.96	6.29	6.13	6.40	6.32
2031–2035	5.35	5.22	5.60	5.45	5.79	5.74
2036–2040	4.59	4.48	4.88	4.76	5.14	5.12
2041–2045	4.01	3.92	4.32	4.22	4.61	4.62
2046–2050	3.55	3.48	3.86	3.78	4.17	4.19

Sources: Author's calculations, based on data from Maddison Project (2018) and Penn World Table 9.0 (2019 data) (Feenstra, Inklaar, and Timmer 2015).

Notes: Projections of China's per capita GDP growth of China according to Maddison Project or PWT 9.0 under $\mu = 0.020$, $\mu = 0.023$, and $\mu = 0.0262/0.0275$ are shown in columns 1 and 2, columns 3 and 4, and columns 5 and 6, respectively.

the graph, China's population will reach a peak (14.42 billion) by 2029 and then move to a falling curve, declining to 13.71 billion by 2050. During the same period, the U.S. population is expected to experience steady growth at an average annual rate of 0.57 percent. Figure 2-9 further plots China's projected population under low, medium, and high fertility rate scenarios. It shows that China's total population will start to decline beginning in 2022, 2030, or 2045 in low, medium, and high fertility rate scenarios, respectively. The demographic decline is clearly becoming a challenge to the Chinese economy's sustainable growth.

Adding the potential per capita growth with the population growth at different variants, we obtain the potential GDP growth of China over the next three decades. To save space, we examine only three scenarios here, the low variant ($\mu = 0.020$ and a low fertility rate), medium variant ($\mu = 0.023$ and a medium fertility rate), and high variant ($\mu = 0.026$ and a high fertility rate). Figure 2-10 plots the projected GDP growth of China during 2015–2050 under these three scenarios. During this period, potential GDP growth will drop gradually from 6.70 percent in 2015 to 2.46 percent in 2050 under

FIGURE 2-8. **Total Population of China and United States, 2015–2050**

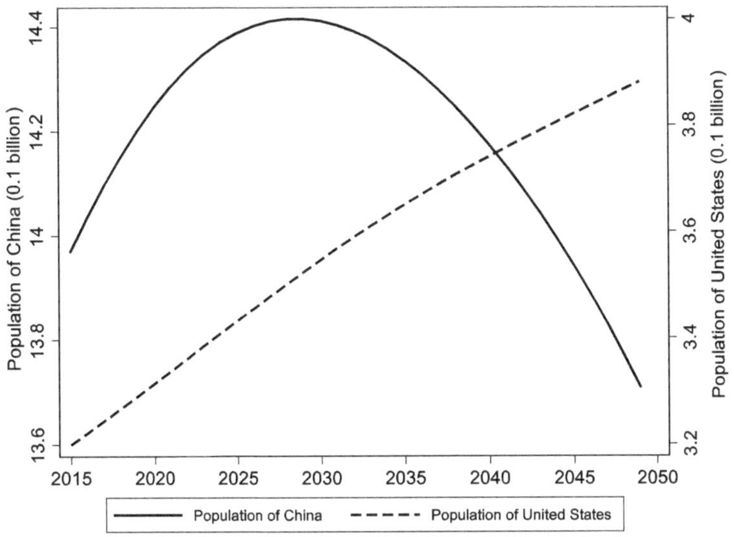

Sources: Author's calculations, based on WPP 2017 (United Nations 2017).

Note: Population data are calculated for a medium fertility rate scenario.

FIGURE 2-9.   Population Growth of China, 2015–2050

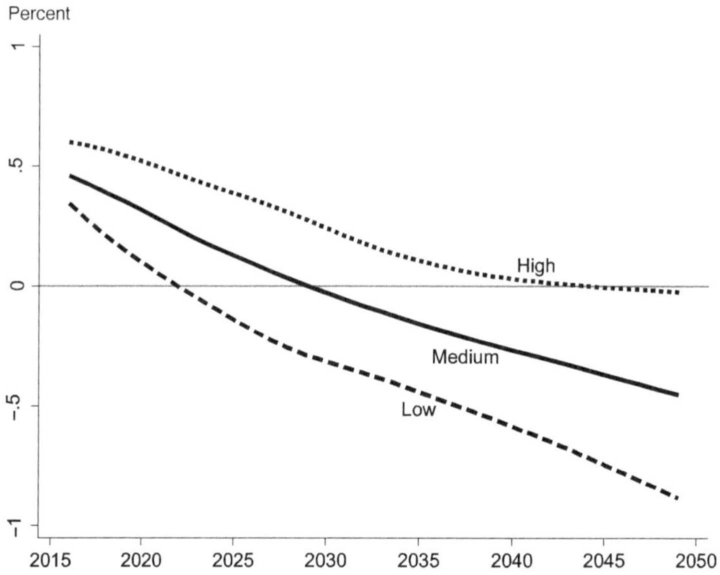

Source: Author's calculations, based on data from WPP (2017) of United Nations.

the low fertility rate variant scenario and from 7.06 percent (7.09 percent) in 2015 to 3.22 percent (3.98 percent) in 2050 under the medium variant (high variant) scenario. Appendix table 2A-2 shows the projected annual growth rate under the three scenarios during 2015–2050 using Maddison Project (2018) and PWT 9.0 data, respectively.

Table 2-5 shows China's projected GDP growth rate under the three scenarios by five-year intervals using Maddison Project (2018) and PWT 9.0 data. For the periods 2016–2020, 2021–2025, 2026–2030, 2031–2035, 2036–2040, 2041–2045, and 2046–2050, the projected GDP growth is around 6.66 percent, 6.51 percent, 5.78 percent, 4.90 percent, 4.01 percent, 3.28 percent, and 2.66 percent, respectively, under the low variant scenario, and around 6.96 percent (7.20 percent), 6.88 percent (7.20 percent), 6.24 percent (6.66 percent), 5.42 percent (5.91 percent), 4.59 percent (5.18 percent), 3.94 percent (4.62 percent), and 3.39 percent (4.16 percent) under the medium variant (high variant). Over the whole period of 2016–2050, China's potential GDP will grow at an annual rate of around 4.83 percent under the low variant scenario, around 5.35 percent under the medium variant scenario, and 5.85 percent under the high variant scenario.

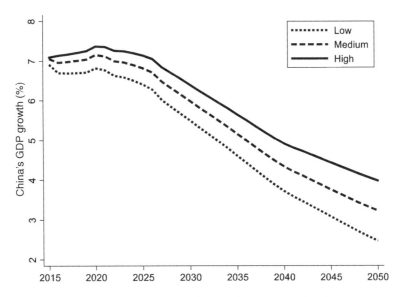

FIGURE 2-10. Projected GDP Growth of China, 2015–2050

Source: Author's calculations, based on data from Maddison Project (2018).

Note: "Low," "Medium," and "High" refer to the calculation of China's per capita GDP under $\mu = 0.020$ and a low fertility rate scenario, $\mu = 0.023$ and a medium fertility rate scenario, and $\mu = 0.026$ and a high fertility rate scenario, respectively.

TABLE 2-5. **China's Growth Projections under Different Fertility Rate Scenarios, 2016–2050 (%)**

Period	Low variant		Medium variant		High variant	
	Maddison Project	PWT 9.0	Maddison Project	PWT 9.0	Maddison Project	PWT 9.0
2016–2020	6.72	6.60	7.03	6.88	7.22	7.18
2021–2025	6.58	6.43	6.96	6.80	7.24	7.17
2026–2030	5.86	5.70	6.32	6.16	6.70	6.63
2031–2035	4.97	4.83	5.49	5.35	5.94	5.89
2036–2040	4.06	3.95	4.65	4.53	5.20	5.17
2041–2045	3.33	3.24	3.99	3.89	4.62	4.62
2046–2050	2.70	2.63	3.43	3.35	4.15	4.17
Average	4.89	4.77	5.41	5.28	5.87	5.83

Sources: Author's calculations, based on data from Maddison Project (2018) and *Penn World Table* 9.0 (2019 data) (Feenstra, Inklaar, and Timmer 2015).

Notes: "Low variant," "Medium variant," and "High variant" denote scenarios of $\mu = 0.020$ and a low fertility rate, $\mu = 0.023$ and a medium fertility rate, and $\mu = 0.026$ and a high fertility rate, respectively.

CATCHING UP AND CONVERGENCE OF CHINESE ECONOMY

In an open economy, the catching up of a developing country is expected to lead to convergence of that economy's per capita GDP growth and income with that of the leading economies'. The growth prospects depend further on the GDP growth of the leading economy and the rate at which the follower converges.

GDP per capita is often used to compare countries to assess their relative stages of development. Based on data from the Maddison Project (2018), our projection shows that China's real GDP per capita will increase from US$11,944 (2011 dollars) in 2015 to US$87,099 (2011 dollars) in 2050 under the high fertility rate scenario. Figure 2-11 graphs China's projected real GDP relative to that of the United States. It shows that China's real GDP is as much as 24 percent of that of U.S. in 2015, while after almost thirty-five years of catching up, China's real GDP will grow to be 66.4 percent of that of

FIGURE 2-11. **Relative per capita GDP of China, 2015–2050**

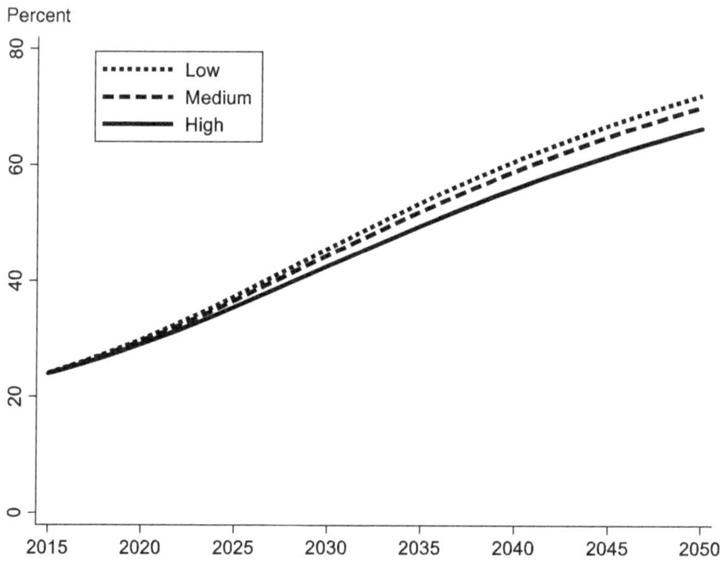

Source: Author's calculations, based on Maddison Project (2018).

Note: "Low," "Medium," and "High" refer to the calculation of China's relative per capita GDP under $\mu = 0.020$ and a low fertility rate scenario, $\mu = 0.023$ and a medium fertility rate scenario, and $\mu = 0.026$ and a high fertility rate scenario, respectively.

the United States under the high fertility rate scenario and 70.1 percent (72.1 percent) of the U.S figure under the medium and low fertility rate scenarios. The relative GDP of China in 2050 under the low scenario is roughly at the level of Spain's in 2007 (66.4 percent), Italy's in 2013 (65.1 percent), and New Zealand's (64.5 percent) and Korea's (66.7 percent) in 2014.

In this framework, when will China become the largest economy? According to our projection, China will surpass the United States in terms of GDP beginning in 2030 under the low and medium fertility rate scenarios and from 2032 under the high fertility rate scenario (figure 2-12). If the world economy continues to grow at an average rate of 3.55 percent, its average annual growth rate in 1960–2016, over the next three decades, our projection period, then China can be expected to account for 24 percent of the world economy in 2049 (figure 2-13).

To examine how much of the growth over the projection period (2015–2050) can be explained by increases in the GDP of a leading open economy

FIGURE 2-12. **Projected Real GDP of China and United States, 2017–2050**

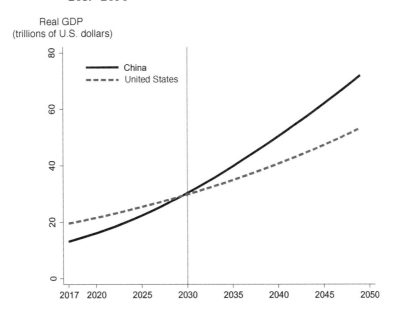

Source: Author's calculations, based on Maddison Project (2018).

Note: In the low fertility rate scenario, China will surpass the United States in terms of GDP beginning in 2030.

FIGURE 2-13. China's Share in the World Economy, 2015–2050

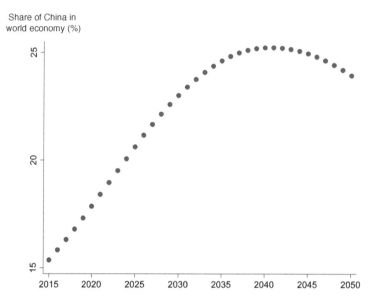

Share of China in
world economy (%)

Source: Author's calculations, based on data from Maddison Project (2018).

and how much stems from population growth and the size of the convergence, we use growth accounting. Equations (1) and (5) imply

$$\frac{\dot{Y}(t)}{Y(t)} = g_{y,us}(t) + \ln\frac{g_{y,CN}(t)}{\mu} \cdot \left(\frac{1}{\theta(t)}\right) \cdot g_\theta(t) + g_N(t) + \eta(t), \tag{7}$$

where $\eta(t) = -\frac{1}{\theta(t)}g_{g_{CN}}(t)$ serves as a residual denoting the parts of the change of the GDP growth rate of China.

We focus on the first three terms of equation (7). Figure 2-14 plots part of GDP growth attributed to the growth of per capita GDP of the United States, the growth of the size of spillover and convergence, and population growth under the scenario of $\mu = 0.026$ and a high fertility rate. The contribution of convergence declines gradually as the gap between China and United States narrows, probably due to the rising costs of learning, absorbing, and innovating by the follower, China. The part attributable to population growth declines steadily with the decreasing population of China. The role of the leading economy increases as China catches up. On average, the parts of China's projected GDP growth during 2015–2050 that result from growth of the leading economy, the size of the convergence, and population decline are

FIGURE 2-14. **Decomposition of GDP Growth of China, 2015–2050**

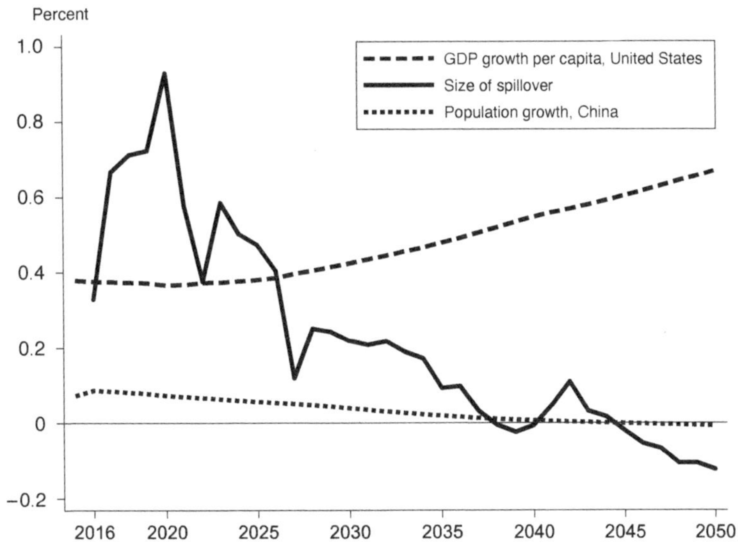

Percent

Source: Author's calculations, based on Maddison Project (2018).

Note: The results are calculated for $\mu = 0.026$ and a high fertility rate scenario.

47.8 percent, 22.3 percent, and 3.3 percent, respectively, under the scenario of $\mu = 0.020$ and a low fertility rate. And growth of the leading economy, the size of the convergence, and population growth account for 46.9 percent, 32.4 percent, and 10.6 percent of China's projected GDP growth under the scenario of $\mu = 0.023$ and a medium fertility rate, respectively.

It should be noted that further opening up is a precondition for China to catch up with, and see its economy successfully converge to, a high-income economy in the coming decades. In the context of China-U.S. trade tensions, one extreme possibility is that China totally closes its economy to the outside. In such an extreme case, the framework used above will not apply. The average growth during the pre-reform period, between 1950 and 1977, could serve as a reference growth rate of GDP under a closed economy.

According to the Maddison Project (2018), China's per capita GDP grew at an average rate of 2.86 percent during the pre-reform period. An economy that totally closes itself to the international market tends to suffer a hard landing, which means that the grow rate is likely to experience sudden decline. Suppose in this scenario that China grows at an average annual rate of 2.86 percent and United States grows at an average annual rate of 2 percent in the coming decades. Figure 2-15 shows how China's real GDP per capita would fare in this scenario. The ratio of per capita GDP in China to that of the United States would rise slowly from 23.31 percent to 31.02 percent. China would likely not escape middle-income trap and successfully find itself among the ranks of high-income economies.

In reality, China probably does not yet face deglobalization, and fully closing its door to international markets is impossible. Therefore, China's possible growth prospects might lie between the extreme of a closed-economy scenario and the various open economy scenarios we analyzed within the framework of a growth model of catch-up based on knowledge spillover.

FIGURE 2-15. **Catch Up Growth of China in a Closed-Economy Scenario, 2015–2050**

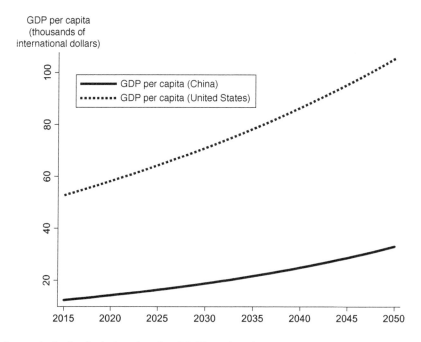

Source: Author's calculations, based on Maddison (2018).

Note: China and the United States are assumed to grow at an annual rate of 2.86 percent and 2 percent, respectively, in this figure.

CONCLUSION AND POLICY IMPLICATIONS

This chapter employed a supply-side method to predict China's growth potential over a long horizon, based on cross-country productivity convergence and China's demographic evolution. A catch-up and spillover model comparing following economies and leading country was used to estimate the average growth rate of per capita GDP of the leader and the time-varying size of convergence of the followers, based on which China's per capita GDP growth for 2015–2050 was projected. At the same time, using this method makes it possible to avoid specifying production functions, the classification of productive factors, and the like. The next step involves adding the projected per capita GDP growth and the population growth to obtain China's projected annual economic growth rates between 2016 and 2050.

For the periods 2016–2020, 2021–2025, 2026–2030, 2031–2035, 2036–2040, 2041–2045, and 2046–2050, China's projected GDP growth rate is around 6.66 percent, 6.51 percent, 5.78 percent, 4.90 percent, 4.01 percent, 3.28 percent, and 2.66 percent, respectively, in the low variant, and around 6.96 percent (7.20 percent), 6.88 percent (7.20 percent), 6.24 percent (6.66 percent), 5.42 percent (5.91 percent), 4.59 percent (5.18 percent), 3.94 percent (4.62 percent), and 3.39 percent (4.16 percent) in the medium (high) variant. Over the entire period 2016–2050, China's potential GDP will grow at an annual rate of around 4.83 percent in the low variant, around 5.35 percent in the medium variant, and around 5.85 percent in the high variant.

The time-varying size of knowledge spillover permits not only examining the trajectory of convergence but also analyzing the determinants of a country's ability to absorb knowledge and accept technology transfer from the leading economies. Empirical evidence shows that urbanization and the accumulation of human capital enhance a following country's ability to catch up economically with leading countries. The analyses and results reported in this chapter have significant implications, especially for China and other open and transitional economies.

Openness is a prerequisite for developing countries to narrow the gap between themselves and advanced economies. Opening gives developing countries the opportunity to access technology and knowledge that flows from the leading economies through economic cooperation and exchange; that access is vital for poorer economies to take off. In the process of opening up, it is also important for developing countries to strengthen intellectual property protection, which will help create the institutional environment conducive to innovation and technology transfer.

It is crucial for China to further open its markets to avoid the middle-income trap and join the ranks of high-income countries in the coming decades. Reforms in state-owned enterprises and financial markets are among the areas of most concern for private capital and foreign investors. Since significant differences in market structure and institutional mechanisms still exist between China and the advanced economies, it is quite important for China to follow the international market rules and practices as it further opens up its domestic market and expands into markets abroad.

An aging population is increasingly becoming a constraint on China's sustainable economic growth. According to UN projections, the absolute total population number for China will decrease beginning in 2030 in the medium fertility rate scenario since the aging of the population was already well under way several years ago. An aging population increases the burden on the pension and social security system while at the same time impeding the accumulation of human capital. Because of China's low total fertility rate and no noticeably strong desire to have children, it is time for China to completely eliminate its current birth control policy and consider implementing a subsidy for the second and later child.

Greater urbanization and the accumulation of human capital cannot be accomplished separately. Population quality and population agglomeration are both essential to developing countries in that they contribute to learning by doing and innovation. Urbanization is the process of migration of rural people to cities and is endogenously determined by the economic transition and development. Therefore, although there are barriers to and costs associated with migration, migration boosts human capital accumulation and provides the seedbed for the agglomeration effects of information and knowledge to take shape during the process of urbanization.

In the process of catching up, China should coordinate the relationship between the process of urbanization and human capital accumulation. In the short run, measures should be taken to improve the system for educating migrant workers' children in the city. In the medium and long term, the government should strive to reduce the income gap between urban and rural areas, which in turn will promote the movement and reallocation of educational resources across provinces and between cities and rural areas.

APPENDIX

FIGURE 2A-1. Urbanization and Relative per capita GDP, 2014

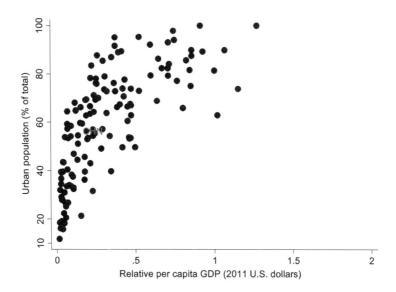

Source: Author's calculations, based on Maddison Project (2018).

FIGURE 2A-2. Human Capital and Relative per capita GDP

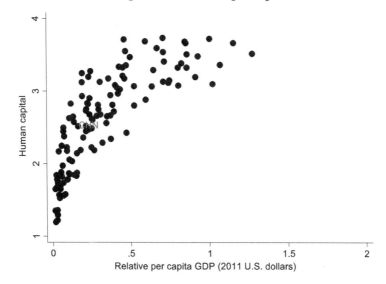

Source: Author's calculations, based on Maddison Project (2018).

TABLE 2A-1. **Open Economy Classifications**

Economy code	Economy	Open time	Open
AGO	Angola	Never open	0
ALB	Albania	1992	0
ARG	Argentina	1991	0
AUS	Australia	1964	1
AUT	Austria	1960	1
BDI	Burundi	Never open	0
BEL	Belgium	1960	1
BEN	Benin	1990	0
BFA	Burkina Faso	Never open	0
BGD	Bangladesh	Never open	0
BGR	Bulgaria	1991	0
BOL	Bolivia	1985	0
BRA	Brazil	1991	0
BRB	Barbados	1966	1
BWA	Botswana	1979	1
CAF	Central African Republic	Never open	0
CAN	Canada	1952	1
CHE	Switzerland	Always open	1
CHL	Chile	1976	1
CHN	China	1979	1
CIV	Côte d'Ivoire	Never open	0
CMR	Cameroon	1993	0
COD	Democratic Rep. of Congo	Never open	0
COG	Congo	Never open	0
COL	Colombia	1991	0
CRI	Costa Rica	1986	0
CYP	Cyprus	1960	1
CZE	Czech Republic	1991	0
DEU	Germany	1959	1
DNK	Denmark	1960	1
DOM	Dominican Republic	Never open	0
DZA	Algeria	Never open	0
ECU	Ecuador	1991	0
EGY	Egypt	Never open	0
ESP	Spain	1959	1
ETH	Ethiopia	Never open	0
FIN	Finland	1960	1
FRA	France	1959	1
GAB	Gabon	Never open	0
GBR	United Kingdom	Always open	1

Economy code	Economy	Open time	Open
GHA	Ghana	1985	0
GIN	Guinea	1986	0
GMB	Gambia	1985	0
GNB	Guinea-Bissau	1987	0
GRC	Greece	1959	1
GTM	Guatemala	1988	0
HKG	China, Hong Kong SAR	Always open	1
HND	Honduras	1991	0
HRV	Croatia	1993	0
HTI	Haiti	Never open	0
HUN	Hungary	1990	0
IDN	Indonesia	1970	1
IND	India	1994	0
IRL	Ireland	1966	1
IRN	Iran	Never open	0
ISR	Israel	1985	0
ITA	Italy	1959	1
JAM	Jamaica	1989	0
JOR	Jordan	1965	1
JPN	Japan	1962	1
KEN	Kenya	1993	0
KOR	Republic of Korea	1968	1
LKA	Sri Lanka	1991	0
LUX	Luxembourg	1959	1
MAR	Morocco	1984	0
MDG	Madagascar	Never open	0
MEX	Mexico	1986	0
MKD	TFYR of Macedonia	1994	0
MLI	Mali	1988	0
MMR	Myanmar	Never open	0
MOZ	Mozambique	Never open	0
MRT	Mauritania	1992	0
MUS	Mauritius	1968	1
MWI	Malawi	Never open	0
MYS	Malaysia	1963	1
NER	Niger	Never open	0
NGA	Nigeria	Never open	0
NIC	Nicaragua	1991	0
NLD	Netherlands	1959	1
NOR	Norway	Always open	1

TABLE 2A-1 CONTINUED

Economy code	Economy	Open time	Open
NPL	Nepal	1991	0
NZL	New Zealand	1986	0
PAK	Pakistan	Never open	0
PER	Peru	1991	0
PHL	Philippines	1988	0
POL	Poland	1990	0
PRT	Portugal	Always open	1
PRY	Paraguay	1989	0
ROU	Romania	1992	0
RUS	Russian Federation	Never open	0
RWA	Rwanda	Never open	0
SEN	Senegal	Never open	0
SGP	Singapore	1965	1
SLE	Sierra Leone	Never open	0
SVN	Slovenia	1991	0
SWE	Sweden	1960	1
SYR	Syrian Arab Republic	Closed since 1965	0
TCD	Chad	Never open	0
TGO	Togo	Never open	0
THA	Thailand	Always open	1
TTO	Trinidad and Tobago	Never open	0
TUN	Tunisia	1989	0
TUR	Turkey	1989	0
TWN	Taiwan	1963	1
TZA	Tanzania	Never open	0
UGA	Uganda	1988	0
URY	Uruguay	1990	0
USA	United States	Always open	1
VEN	Venezuela	Closed since 1993	0
YEM	Yemen	Always open	1
ZAF	South Africa	1991	0
ZMB	Zambia	1993	0
ZWE	Zimbabwe	Never open	0

Source: Sachs and Warner (1995).

Note: The rule of openness is judged by whether the economy is open not later than 1980. If it is open before or during 1980, the openness index is 1; otherwise it is 0.

APPENDIX TABLE 2A-2.   PROJECTED GDP GROWTH OF CHINA, 2015–2050 (%)

Year	Low estimate		Medium Estimate		High estimate	
	Maddison Project	PWT	Maddison Project	PWT	Maddison Project	PWT
2015	6.91	6.81	7.06	6.92	7.09	7.06
2016	6.70	6.59	6.96	6.82	7.13	7.10
2017	6.69	6.58	6.98	6.84	7.16	7.12
2018	6.70	6.58	7.01	6.86	7.21	7.16
2019	6.71	6.58	7.04	6.89	7.25	7.20
2020	6.82	6.68	7.15	7.00	7.37	7.31
2021	6.77	6.63	7.12	6.96	7.35	7.29
2022	6.63	6.48	6.99	6.83	7.26	7.19
2023	6.59	6.44	6.96	6.80	7.24	7.18
2024	6.50	6.35	6.90	6.73	7.20	7.13
2025	6.40	6.25	6.82	6.65	7.14	7.07
2026	6.27	6.12	6.71	6.54	7.05	6.98
2027	6.01	5.86	6.47	6.31	6.84	6.77
2028	5.84	5.68	6.31	6.14	6.69	6.62
2029	5.67	5.51	6.15	5.98	6.54	6.47
2030	5.49	5.34	5.98	5.82	6.39	6.31
2031	5.31	5.16	5.81	5.66	6.23	6.17
2032	5.14	5.00	5.65	5.50	6.09	6.03
2033	4.97	4.83	5.49	5.35	5.94	5.89
2034	4.80	4.67	5.33	5.19	5.80	5.76
2035	4.61	4.48	5.16	5.02	5.64	5.61
2036	4.42	4.30	4.99	4.86	5.50	5.47
2037	4.24	4.12	4.81	4.69	5.34	5.32
2038	4.05	3.94	4.64	4.53	5.19	5.17
2039	3.88	3.77	4.48	4.37	5.04	5.02
2040	3.72	3.61	4.33	4.22	4.91	4.90
2041	3.58	3.48	4.21	4.11	4.81	4.80
2042	3.46	3.37	4.11	4.01	4.72	4.72
2043	3.33	3.24	3.99	3.89	4.62	4.63
2044	3.20	3.12	3.88	3.78	4.53	4.53
2045	3.07	2.99	3.76	3.67	4.43	4.44
2046	2.94	2.86	3.64	3.56	4.34	4.35
2047	2.82	2.74	3.53	3.45	4.24	4.26
2048	2.69	2.62	3.42	3.35	4.15	4.17
2049	2.58	2.51	3.32	3.24	4.06	4.08
2050	2.47	2.40	3.22	3.15	3.98	4.00

Sources: Maddison Project (2018); *Penn World Table* (PWT, 2019 data) (Feenstra, Inklaar, and Timmer 2015).

Note: "Low estimate," "Medium estimate," and "High estimate" denote scenarios of $\mu = 0.020$ and a low estimated fertility rate, $\mu = 0.023$ and a medium estimated fertility rate, and $\mu = 0.026$ and a high estimated fertility rate, respectively.

NOTE

1. China's *hukou* system, a government-imposed household registration system started in the late 1950s, regulates rural-to-urban migration, in part for determining welfare benefits. Under it, farmers do not have the same rights as urban dwellers.

REFERENCES

Autor, D., D. Dorn, and G. Hanson. 2013. "The China Syndrome: Local Labor Effects of Import Competition in the United States." *American Economic Review* 103:12–68.

Bai, C., and Q. Zhang. 2017. "China's Growth Potential to 2050: A Supply-side Forecast Based on Cross Country Productivity Convergence and Its Featured Labor Force." [In Chinese.] *China Journal of Economics* 4 (4):1–27.

Barro, R. J. 1991. "Economic Growth in a Cross Section of Countries," *Quarterly Journal of Economics* 106:407–41.

Barro, R., and J.-W. Lee. 2013. "A New Data Set of Educational Attainment in the World, 1950–2010," *Journal of Development Economics,* vol. 104(C): 184–98.

Barro, R. J., and X. Sala-i-Martín. 1992. "Convergence." *Journal of political Economy* 100 (2): 223–51.

Barro, R. J., and X. Sala-i-Martín. 1997. "Technological Diffusion, Convergence, and Growth." *Journal of Economic Growth* 2 (1): 1–26.

Becker, G. S., K. M. Murphy, and R. Tamura. 1990. "Human Capital, Fertility, and Economic Growth." *Journal of Political Economy* 98 (5, pt. 2): S12–37.

Bloom, N., M. Draca, and J. Van Reenen. 2016. "Trade-Induced Technical Change? The Impact of Chinese Imports on Innovation, IT and Productivity." *Review of Economic Studies* 83 (1): 87–117.

Bolt, J., and J. L. van Zanden. 2014. "The Maddison Project: Collaborative Research on Historical National Accounts." *Economic History Review* 67 (3): 627–51.

Cai, F., and Y. Lu. 2013. "Population Change and Resulting Slowdown in Potential GDP Growth in China." *China & World Economy* 21 (2): 1–14.

Cass, D. 1965. "Optimum Growth in an Aggregative Model of Capital Accumulation." *Review of Economic Studies* 32 (3): 233–40.

Eichengreen, B., D. Park, and K. Shin. 2012. "When Fast-Growing Economies Slow Down: International Evidence and Implications for China." *Asian Economic Papers* 11 (1): 42–87.

Feenstra, Robert C., Robert Inklaar, and Marcel P. Timmer. 2015. "The Next Generation of the Penn World Table." *American Economic Review* 105 (10): 3150–82.

Holz, C. A. 2008. "China's Economic Growth 1978–2025: What We Know Today about China's Economic Growth Tomorrow." *World Development* 36 (10): 1665–91.

IMF. 2017. *World Economic Outlook 2017.* Washington, DC: International Monetary Fund.

Johansson, Å., Y. Guillemette, and F. Murtin. 2012. *Looking to 2060: Long-Term*

Global Growth Prospects: A Going for Growth Report. Brussels: OECD Publishing.

Koopmans, T. C. 1965. "On the Concept of Optimal Economic Growth." In *The Econometric Approach to Development Planning*. Amsterdam: North-Holland.

Li, H., P. Loyalka, S. Rozelle, and B. Wu. 2017. "Human Capital and China's Future Growth." *Journal of Economic Perspectives* 31 (1): 25–48.

Lin, Justin Y. 2014. "The Backward Advantage of Chinese Economy." *Financial Times*, March 6.

Lu, Y., and F. Cai. 2016. "From Demographic Dividends to Reform Dividends: A Simulation Based on China's Potential Growth Rate." [In Chinese.] *Journal of World Economy* (1): 3–23.

Lucas, R. E. 2009. "Trade and the Diffusion of the Industrial Revolution." *American Economic Journal: Macroeconomics* 1 (1): 1–25.

Bolt, J., R. Inklaar, H. de Jong, and J. L. van Zanden. (2018). Maddison Project Database, version 2018. "Rebasing 'Maddison': New Income Comparisons and the Shape of Long-Run Economic Development," Maddison Project Working paper no. 10.

Melitz, Mark J. 2003. "The Impact of Trade on Intra-Industry Reallocations and Aggregate Productivity Growth," *Econometrica* 71 (6):1695–725.

Melitz, Mark J., and Stephen J. Redding. 2013. "Firm Heterogeneity and Aggregate Welfare." CEP Discussion Paper 1200. London: Centre for Economic Performance.

Pritchett, L., and L. H. Summers. 2014. "Asiaphoria Meets Regression to the Mean." NBER Working Paper No. 2 0573. Cambridge, MA: National Bureau of Economic Research.

The PRS Group. 2015. *International Country Risk Guide*. https://epub.prsgroup .com/products/international-country-risk-guide-icrg.

Rodriguez, A. (2006). "Learning Externalities, Human Capital and Growth," doctoral dissertation, University of Chicago.

Sachs, Jeffrey D., and Andrew M. Warner. 1995. "Economic Reform and the Process of Global Integration." Brookings Papers on Economic Activity (1): 1-95.

Solow, R. M. 1956. "A Contribution to the Theory of Economic Growth." *Quarterly Journal of Economics* 70 (1): 65–94.

Tamura, R. 1991. "Income Convergence in an Endogenous Growth Model." *Journal of Political Economy* 99 (3): 522–40.

United Nations, Department of Economic and Social Affairs, Population Division. 2017. *World Population Prospects: The 2017 Revision*. New York: United Nations.

Wang, Y., and Y. D. Yao. 2003. "Sources of China's Economic Growth 1952–1999: Incorporating Human Capital Accumulation," *China Economic Review* 14:32–52.

World Bank Group. 2013. *China 2030: Building a Modern, Harmonious, and Creative Society*. Washington, DC: World Bank Group.

Zhang, J. Z., P. Vandenberg, and Y. P. Huang. 2012. *Growing beyond the Low-Cost Advantage: How the People's Republic of China Can Avoid the Middle Income Trap?* Manila: Asian Development Bank. 2012.

Zhang, Jun. 2015. "The Non-normality of Chinese Economy." *Financial Times*, March 18.

PART II

TRANSFORMATION OF THE DOMESTIC ECONOMY

3

Aging and Social Policy in an Era of Demographic Transition

CHEN BAI and XIAOYAN LEI

The demographic transition is an essential factor in explaining the unforeseeable development of China's social economy over the past forty years. After the founding of the People's Republic of China in 1949, China's demographics entered a new stage, with a significantly declining mortality rate. The birth rate remained high because of improvements in healthcare and living standards. As a result, the natural population growth rate was excessively high. The total fertility rate (TFR) was as high as six until the mid-1960s. However, the situation began to change as the TFR peaked at the end of the 1960s, which triggered China's demographic transition from the pattern of high births, low mortality, and high population growth to one of low births, low mortality, and low population growth.

Especially in the 1970s and 1980s, the implementation of strict family planning policies accelerated the demographic transition. According to estimates by the World Bank (figure 3-1), as the birth rate decreased, the TFR dropped sharply, from 5.8 to 2.3, and the proportion of children under age fourteen years fell from 40 percent to 28.7 percent. At the same time, the working-age population increased dramatically, from about 460 million to 730 million, accounting for nearly 65.3 percent of the total population. In addition, the average proportion of the population over age sixty-five years remained low, at less than 5 percent. Consequently, China's total population dependency ratio, that is, the ratio of the dependent population (ages zero to fourteen years and sixty-five years and older) to the working-age population (ages fifteen to sixty-four), decreased from 79.0 to 53.0, resulting in a rather light social burden.

The mushrooming working-age population and the continuing decline in the total population dependency ratio shaped a "production-oriented" demographic structure (one in which the working-age population is larger than the consumer population) (Gribble and Bemner 2012). Such an economically favorable demographic structure was in line with the launch of China's reform and opening-up policy and successfully translated into a demographic dividend that spurred unprecedented economic growth (Cai and Du 2009). According to Cai and Wang's (2005) estimate, the decline in the dependency ratio contributed 26.8 percent to growth in per capita GDP from 1982 to 2000.

The impact of the demographic dividend on economic growth has been demonstrated in various ways. On the one hand, rapid growth of the working-age population guaranteed an adequate supply of labor. In particular, rural-to-urban migration of the working-age population at the beginning of the 1990s released a large amount of rural surplus labor,

FIGURE 3-1.   **Demographic Changes in China, 1960–2017**

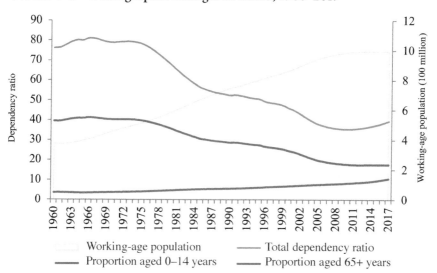

Working-age population   Total dependency ratio
Proportion aged 0–14 years   Proportion aged 65+ years

Source: Data from *Population Estimates and Projections* (database), World Bank Group, 2019.

which had accumulated in the planned economy. Workers moved from the low-productivity agricultural sector to the high-productivity industrial sector. Such migration greatly improved the efficiency of resource allocation, serving as the main source of total factor productivity (Cai and Wang 1999). Moreover, a sufficient labor supply accompanied by improvement in the quality of labor allowed China to maintain a low-cost labor advantage in the long term. Not only did the income distribution tilt toward enterprises by enhancing the savings of the business sector, but Chinese enterprises were able to achieve a late-mover advantage in participating in economic competition globally. On the other hand, the continuous decline in the dependency ratio boosted a rapid increase in the saving rate, which in turn gave rise to productivity improvement through increased capital per worker (capital deepening). It was estimated that China's household savings accounted for only 6–7 percent of GDP in the 1970s but more than 22 percent in the 2000s (Kraay 2000). In addition, the average gross domestic savings-to-GDP ratio increased from 30.5 percent in the 1970s to 45.9 percent in the 2000s (Yang, Zhang, and Zhou 2011). A high saving rate is one of the fundamental conditions for capital formation as it allows heavy investment to be a main source of GDP growth (Cai and Zhao 2012).

However, China's window of opportunity with the demographic dividend will not be open permanently. Mainly as a result of population aging, attributed to the declining TFR and increasing life expectancy, the massive growth of the working–age population and the decline in the dependency ratio will reach a turning point.

Eventually, China's demographic dividend will fade or disappear, along with an irreversible change in the structure of the population. Indeed, the demographic transition had already started at the beginning of the twenty-first century, much earlier than anyone had expected (figure 3-2). According to the Fifth National Population Census, which took place in 2000, China's TFR dropped to the rather low level of 1.22 in 2000, much lower than the replacement level of 2.1. At the same time, the proportion of people older than sixty-five exceeded the 7 percent global average first suggested by the United Nations, indicating that China has formally become an aging society. Since 2000, China's demographic structure has undergone more in-depth change. The total population growth has slowed gradually and is estimated to peak in 2029 at about 1.4 billion, after which it is expected to decline to

FIGURE 3-2.   Dependency Ratio and Population, 1961–2049

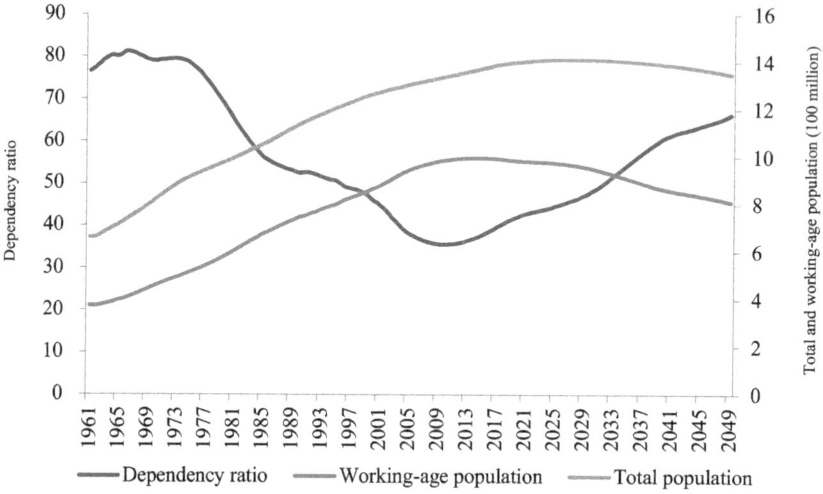

Source: Data from *Population Estimates and Projections* (database), World Bank Group, 2019.

1.35 billion in 2049. As the trend took shape, labor shortages were widely reported around 2004, first along the coastal regions, where migrant workers were in short supply, but soon spreading nationwide. China's working-age population peaked and started to decline in 2012. At nearly the same time, the dependency ratio rebounded, which ended the downward trend of more than forty years. The proportion of people over age sixty-five now exceeds 10 percent, reaching 140 million. Consequently, China is going through a new kind of demographic transition, with its demographic dividend dramatically changing into a heavy dependency burden. With this transition, China has not only the largest elderly population in the world but also one of the most rapidly aging societies.

CHARACTERISTICS AND TENDENCIES OF POPULATION AGING

Based on the most recent population projection data set released by the Population Division of the United Nations, Department of Economic and Social Affairs (*World Population Prospects: The 2019 Revision*, WPP 2019) and China's Population and Development Research Center (*China Popula-*

tion Prospects 2018, CPP 2018), population aging in China is expected to exhibit the following five main characteristics in the coming years:

Deepening of Population Aging

With the population born in the first (1949–1957) and second (1962–1970) baby booms successively moving into old age, the number of Chinese over age sixty-five is expected to tick up significantly in the next thirty years. As a result, according to the CPP 2018 estimates, there will be two growth peaks, during 2019–2022 and 2027–2038, with average annual increases in the elderly population of around 8.6 million to 11.2 million (figure 3-3). The second growth peak will be not only long-lasting but also fast-growing, with average growth of the elderly population reaching 11.2 million per year. By 2049 the Chinese population over age sixty-five will be close to 400 million (399 million), accounting for more than a quarter of the total population (28.9 percent). By that time the proportion of the elderly in China's population will be not only higher than the average for the Organization for Economic Cooperation and Development (OECD) countries but also twice that of less-developed countries.

FIGURE 3-3.   **Projected Population over Age 65 Years, 2019–2049**

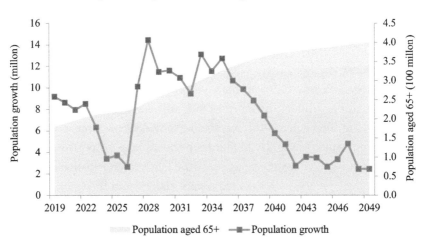

Source: Data from Population and Development Research Center, *China Population Prospects 2018.*

Shifting Composition of the Elderly, from the Young-Old to the Oldest Old

In the next thirty years, most of the growth in the elderly population will gradually shift from the young-old to the oldest old (figure 3-4). Specifically, during the period 2019–2038, the growth of the aged population will still be dominated by the younger elderly, accounting for more than two-thirds of the total elderly population. Nevertheless, this situation will change around 2041, with the proportion of the younger elderly decreasing year by year. From then on, the advanced aging process will become more and more intensified, with the growth rate of the oldest old segment increasing sharply. By 2049 the total number of Chinese oldest old will reach 137 million. This number will not only be more than the total Russian population (134 million) but will also exceed the sum of the oldest old in Europe (72 million) and North America (38 million). Moreover, the proportion of Chinese oldest old in the aged population will have risen from 19.1 percent to 34.3 percent, with a total increase of nearly 50 million in the next thirty years. By then the proportion of China's advanced-age population will be equivalent to the average proportion in Europe (36.4 percent).

Shrinking and Aging of the Working-Age Population

The working-age population, which peaked around 2012, is expected to remain at the relatively high level of more than 980 million until 2026 (figure 3-5). Nevertheless, with the arrival of the second growth peak of the elderly in 2027, there will be a rapid decrease in the working-age population, at a rate of 7.8 million per year. By 2049, China's working-age population will have dropped to 800 million (with a total decrease of nearly 200 million since 2018), accounting for nearly 60 percent of the total population, which is slightly higher than the average proportion in developed countries. Moreover, the aging of the labor force will also deepen in the next thirty years, with the median age rising from thirty-nine in 2018 to forty-three in 2049. It is predicted that from 2018 to 2050, the working population aged fifteen to twenty-four will decrease from 162 million to 131 million and the working population aged twenty-five to fifty-four will decrease from 665 million to 463 million. By contrast, as a result of the third wave of baby boomers (born in 1970–1990) entering their prime

FIGURE 3-4. **Projected Young-Old and Oldest Old Population, 2019–2049**

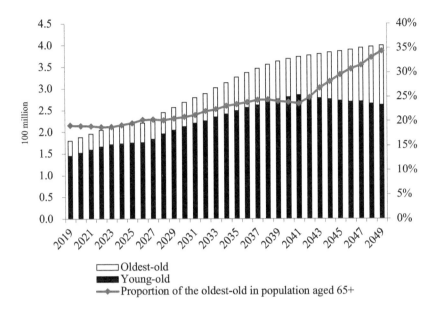

- ☐ Oldest-old
- ■ Young-old
- ◆ Proportion of the oldest-old in population aged 65+

Source: Data from Population and Development Research Center, *China Population Prospects 2018*.

FIGURE 3-5. **Working-Age Population Structure, 1961–2049**

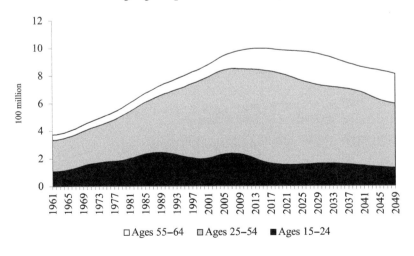

☐ Ages 55–64   ☐ Ages 25–54   ■ Ages 15–24

Source: Data from *Population Estimates and Projections* (database), World Bank Group, 2019.

working age, the proportion of the older workforce (aged fifty-five to sixty-four) to the total working-age population will increase sharply. The older workforce will increase from 164 million to 217 million, and its share in the total working-age population is expected to reach over 26.7 percent in 2049, an increase of 10.2 percent since 2018.

An Increasing Total Dependency Ratio, with the Burden of Care for the Elderly Exceeding That of Child-Raising

In the next thirty years, the total dependency ratio will continue to increase significantly, reaching seventy-two in 2049; that is, every one hundred people in the working-age population will be supporting seventy-two people, including twenty-three children and forty-nine elderly (figure 3-6). At that time, China's dependency ratio (72) will be thirty points higher than it was in 2019 (42), nearly equivalent to the average level of Europe's dependency ratio and much higher than the average developing country's dependency ratio of fifty-seven. The rapid increase in China's total dependency ratio will mainly result from the sharp increase in the elderly dependency ratio. From 2019 to 2049, China's elderly dependency ratio will increase as much as 1.1 percentage points annually and exceed the child dependency ratio by around 2027. Providing eldercare will gradually become the dominant social burden for the working-age population in China. By 2049, the elderly dependency ratio will rise to 49.9, about six percentage points higher than the average level of OECD countries (43.9). In contrast, after a slight increase from around 2019 to 2022, the child dependency ratio will decline steadily, reaching its lowest level by around 2040. After that it will remain relatively stable, in the range of 20–22 percent.

Decreasing Family Size and Greater Proportion of the Elderly Living Alone

The average household size in China started to decrease in 1982, when the strict family planning policy was launched (figure 3-7). Since then the average family size has continued to drop, from 4.4 in 1982 to 2.89 in 2015. According to Y. Zeng's 2019 projections, by 2050 China's average family size will decrease to 2.51, and the downward trend will be most dramatic in rural areas. Although the average size of rural households is usually larger

FIGURE 3-6. Dependency Ratio, 2019–2049

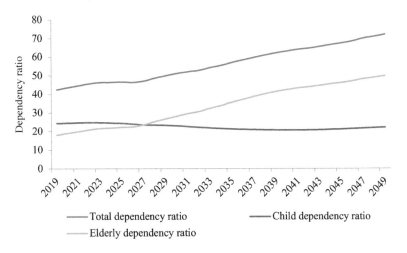

Source: Data from Population and Development Research Center, *China Population Prospects 2018.*

FIGURE 3-7.   Average Number of People per Household, 1982–2050

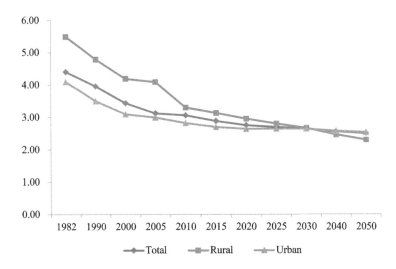

Sources: Data for 1982, 1990, and 2000 from the relevant year Chinese census; data for 2005 from the 1% Population Survey. China's National Bureau of Statistics, http://www.stats.gov.cn/tjsj/ndsj/renkou/2005/renkou.htm.

than that of urban households, this gap will narrow with declining family size in rural areas.

Accompanying the trend toward family miniaturization, the number of empty-nest elderly will be unprecedentedly high in the next thirty years. The number of elderly living alone is projected to increase from 17.5 million in 2010 to 53.1 million in 2050 (figure 3-8), and nearly 10 percent of total households will have at least one elderly person over age sixty-five.

Household miniaturization is taking place much faster in urban areas than in rural areas. As shown in figure 3-9, the number of urban elderly living alone is projected to mushroom sharply, from 7.34 million in 2010 to 39.7 million in 2050, nearly triple that in rural areas.

China is facing a new demographic transition, one that has been triggered mainly by the increasingly aging population. In the next three decades, total population growth will decrease rapidly and turn negative. The low TFR and the large proportion of elderly people as baby boomers age will inevitably combine to aggravate the speed and depth of the population aging process. The change in the population pyramid from 2018 to 2049, which is characterized by "contracting at the bottom and widening at the top," further reflects not only the compression and aging of the working-age population but also the increasingly heavy burden of eldercare. All these factors will undoubtedly pose a series of challenges to the sustainability of China's economic growth.

CHALLENGES

The current rapid and deepening population aging progress will exert a significant influence on all aspects of life in China, among which particular concerns include economic growth, pension sustainability, and the provision of eldercare. The economic challenges will come mainly from the labor supply shortage and slowdown in capital formation due to the structural change of the population. The pressures on pensions and eldercare arrangements will result mainly from China "getting old before getting rich," while its socioeconomic development and social security system are still far behind.

FIGURE 3-8. **Number of Elderly People Living Alone, 2010–2050**

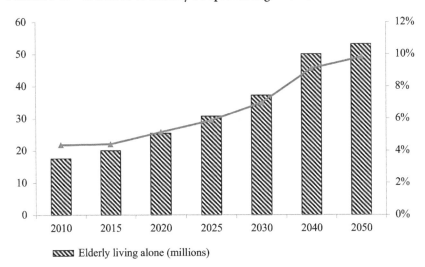

▨▨▨ Elderly living alone (millions)

—▲— Proportion of total households with at least one elderly person aged 65+

Source: Zeng et al. (2019).

FIGURE 3-9. **Number of Elderly People Living Alone, Rural and Urban Areas (Millions), 2010–2050**

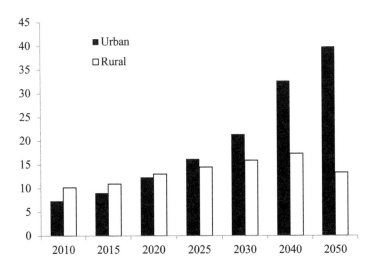

Source: Zeng et al. (2019).

Challenges for Economic Growth

With respect to labor supply, the working-age population in China will undergo a rapid decline in the next thirty years. The total reduction in the working-age population will be more than 200 million by 2049, implying that China will lose nearly a quarter of its current labor force by then. Moreover, under the current compulsory retirement age arrangement (sixty years for men, fifty-five and fifty years for female white-collar and blue-collar workers, respectively), the labor force participation rate will drop significantly from its peak at ages forty-five to sixty years, especially for women, whose participation declines substantially at age forty-five. Thus the aging working-age population (the increase in the proportion of the labor force aged forty-five to sixty years against the total working-age population) may give rise to a continuous decline in the labor force participation rate. That is, over time, more and more of the advancing-age working population will withdraw early from the labor market because of physical, family, or compulsory retirement age reasons.

Population aging will in turn make it more difficult to maintain a high saving rate, thereby inhibiting capital formation in the future. Based on the life-cycle theory, saving takes place mainly among the working-age population and decreases after retirement. With the deepening of the aging process, consumption will dominate saving, terminating the period of high saving that has fueled a long period of high economic growth. As the proportion of the working-age population has decreased, China's gross saving rate has also begun to decline, after reaching a peak of 51 percent (figure 3-10). As these trends continue, the expansion of the elderly population, especially the oldest old, will give rise to a substantial increase in public expenditure on nonproductive sectors, such as pension and medical care provision, thereby narrowing the growth space for public spending on more productive investment. Furthermore, the reduction in the working-age population may lead to a rapid increase in labor costs and contraction of profit margins, lowering the rates of saving and investment, which were among the main factors driving China's capital formation.

For human capital formation, the aging population structure may affect the quality and accumulation of human capital. Human knowledge and skills tend to deteriorate with population aging. In the long run, the fast increase in the elderly population and the aging of the working-age popula-

FIGURE 3-10. **Labor Supply and Capital Formation, 1980–2049**

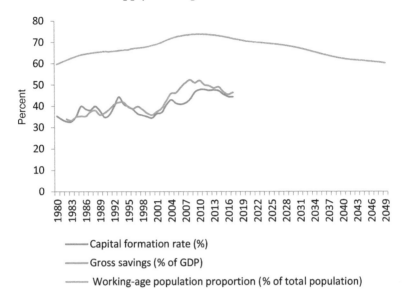

——— Capital formation rate (%)

——— Gross savings (% of GDP)

——— Working-age population proportion (% of total population)

Sources: Data for working-age population proportion from Population and Development Research Center, *China Population Prospects 2018*; gross savings from the World Bank Datasets (data.worldbank.org/); capital formation rate from the World Bank Datasets (data. worldbank.org/).

tion will not be conducive to the accumulation of and quality improvement in human capital. Moreover, as the elderly dependency ratio in China will greatly exceed the child dependency ratio in the next three decades, the increased burden on family and social endowments may crowd out investment in education for the next generation, thus affecting the continuous accumulation of human capital.

Consequently, population aging may accelerate the fading of the demographic dividend for economic growth. According to Cai and Lu's (2016) estimate of the contribution of the demographic dividend to shaping long-run growth performance up to 2050, at a moderate pace of potential growth, the demographic dividend accounted for nearly 20 percent of China's potential economic growth from 1981 to 2010, but the contribution of the demographic dividend will be close to zero during 2016–2021. Even worse, it will turn into a "demographic debt" after 2020 and will continue to deteriorate during the simulation period until 2050.

Financial Pressure on the Pension System

The pension system is the cornerstone of old-age support. As early as the 1980s the Chinese government attempted to improve the pension system by moving from a "pay-as-you-go" approach to the partially funded approach by combining "social pooling accounts" and "individual accounts." However, the reform has not been fully implemented. The risk of a funding gap becomes more obvious as population aging accelerates.

On the one hand, although China's current pension system nominally consists of social pooling accounts and individual accounts, the individual accounts are notional and contain no funds, as the funds accumulated in the individual accounts have been diverted to finance the deficits in the social pooling accounts to pay for current retirees (Li and Lin 2016). Li and Lin (2013) estimate that in 2011, the vacancy ratio of individual accounts was 34 percent, and the shortage of funds in individual accounts was 2.1 percent of GDP. In provinces with large numbers of state-owned enterprises, such as Heilongjiang and Liaoning, the vacancy ratio of individual accounts is even higher. According to the report *China Pension Development Report 2014—Transition to a Nominal Account System*, released by the Chinese Academy of Social Sciences, the debts in social pooling accounts were 83.6 trillion yuan in 2012, and those in individual accounts were 2.6 trillion yuan (Zheng 2014).

On the other hand, in the next thirty years, with the large number of people born in the two baby booms approaching or reaching old age, the number of pension recipients will rise sharply. At the same time, the number of contributors will begin to decrease, which in turn will expand the potential funding gap over the long term and may result in a huge implicit pension debt. Many recent studies have analyzed China's large pension fund gap. For example, according to the World Bank, the size of China's pension fund gap over 2001–2075 will be 9.15 trillion yuan (Sin and Yu 2005). The Chinese Academy of Social Sciences (Zheng 2014) reported that the funding of basic pension will fail to cover its expenditure in 2023, and its accumulated balance will be exhausted in 2029; the cumulative gap will amount to 91 percent of GDP in 2050, and the total pension expenditure will account for 11.85 percent of GDP in that year.

Rising Burden of Eldercare

The growing number of elderly people, the oldest old in particular, with declining physical and cognitive functions will lead to a huge demand for care. This demand is generally measured by difficulty in carrying out activities of daily living (ADLs) and instrumental activities of daily living (IADLs). As people age, they tend to have increased difficulties with ADLs and IADLs. For example, based on the China Health and Retirement Longitudinal Study, Giles and coworkers (2018) report that 9 percent of women aged sixty-five to sixty-nine had an ADL-limited functional ability, compared with 30 percent among cohorts over age eighty. The pattern for men was quite similar. By age seventy-five, all population subgroups average a 10 percent increase in each of five physical functioning disabilities over two years (or 5 percent annually). Under the assumption that five-year cohorts will have similar rates of limited functional ability, and based on current ADL and IADL limited functional ability rates, Giles and coworkers project that the share of the elderly having ADL and IADL deficits will continue to increase. That is, 15 percent of women over age forty-five will have at least slight ADL deficits, as will 8 percent of men.

Currently, informal care provided by a spouse or adult children is the main source of care for the elderly with functional disabilities in China. However, a rapidly aging population in the context of the demographic shift will seriously weaken the household foundation for informal eldercare provided by family members in the next thirty years. According to the national census and Y. Zeng's research group (2019; these results reported in 2018), the number of households with at least one member aged sixty-five or older in China increased by nearly 20 million between 2000 and 2010. The number of households in which a person/couple aged sixty-five or older is living alone is projected to increase from 17.5 million in 2010 to 53.1 million in 2050, when such households will account for nearly 10 percent of total households.

Furthermore, the average Chinese elderly person currently has five or six children, but those born during the second baby boom of the 1950s and 1960s, who will form the main part of the large emerging elderly population over the next thirty years, have on average fewer than two children. It is predictable that as these people become the main corpus of China's accelerated aging population in the next thirty years, the resulting burden of care and the larger scale of "empty-nest" families will severely challenge the traditional family care model. The increasing burden of family care will not only aggravate the burden of social pensions in the future, it will also have a profound impact on China's ability to sustain economic growth because it will suppress the labor supply. Estimates of the relationship between the labor supply of adults ages forty-five to sixty-five and the supply of family care show substantial negative effects of caregiving on the labor supply of rural men and women and declines in women's hours worked in urban and rural areas (Giles et al. 2018).

The effect of relaxing the family planning policy is weakening, and China is falling into the predicament of "population aging with a baby bust." In recent years, relaxation of the family planning policy has served as an important population adjustment policy to address the fast aging trend and increase the supply of labor by releasing potential fertility. As early as 2007, some Chinese provinces started allowing couples in which both adults had been an only child to have a second child. Since 2013, China has continued to relax its family planning policy, and in 2016 it launched a universal two-child policy. By now, the universal two-child policy has been in place for more than three years. However, the impact of relaxing the birth policy on fertility turns out to have been much weaker than expected. The number of newborns has decreased every year since 2016, with only 15.23 million babies born in 2018, which made a new lowest record for any year after the 1960s. Obviously, China has already sunk into the demographic dilemma of population aging with a baby bust, which means a declining fertility rate combined with a rapidly aging population. As figure 3-11 shows, the number of newborns is projected to decrease from 16.87 million in 2019 to 11.99 million in 2049. This decline is attributable not only to a rapid narrowing of the population of childbearing age (ages fifteen to forty-nine years) but also to decreased willingness to have children. Recent surveys of fertility preference show that China has indeed become a low-fertility culture (Zhang and Wang 2015). Nearly 90 percent of women report that they want one or two children, whereas in large cities nearly two-thirds of women state a preference for only one child. This preference reflects the high cost of rearing children, especially the costs for education, and the effect on parental lifestyle and the mother's career.

FIGURE 3-11.   **Projected Births and Women of Childbearing Age, 2019–2049**

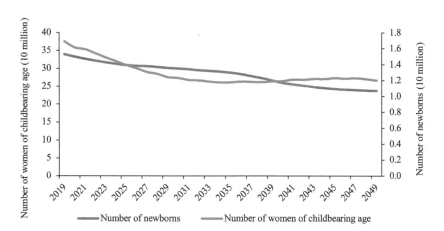

Source: Data from Population and Development Research Center, *China Population Prospects 2018.*

POLICY IMPLICATIONS AND SUGGESTIONS

Acknowledging the challenges addressed in the previous section, China must continue to strengthen reforms along the lines of relieving the pressure of the demographic transition on economic growth, the pension system, and eldercare. Although there are many other potential policy recommendations, a few that are most relevant to this chapter are highlighted below.

Fully Relax the Family Planning Policy and Encourage Childbearing and Child-Rearing

As the effect of implementing the universal two-child policy (i.e., removing the restriction of either parent having only one child and allowing all couples to have two children) since 2015 has been less than expected, other policies are needed to remove the obstacles to having more children. Increasing fertility would serve to promote a more balanced structure of the population and increase the supply of labor in the long run. More important, it is time to relax the family planning policy. The latest results of the 2017 National Fertility Status Survey of the China Health and Family Planning Commission (currently known as the Synergy and Health Committee) show that relaxation of the family planning policy has played a role in increasing the proportion of two-child families from 36.1 percent to 53.9 percent during 2006–2016 and decreasing the high male-female sex ratio at birth from 114.9:100 in 2013 to 112.4:100 in 2016. According to Zeng's 2019 projections, the scheme of "fully relaxing the family planning and encouraging the two-child policy" would contribute to mitigating the population downtrend by improving the negative population growth ratio from –3.35 percent to –2.07 percent over the period 2030–2050. It would also add more than 30 million people to the labor force, compared with the current universal two-child policy. In addition, the rapid acceleration of the aging of the population, especially for empty-nesters who live alone, would be substantially less serious with "fully relaxing the family planning policy and encouraging the two-child policy" than if the two-child policy remained unchanged. Furthermore, according to international experience, a positive direction for population policy would not only relax the family planning policy but also establish a series of service and security systems to support fertility. Specifically, to reduce fertility cost, which proved to be one of the key factors that have an impact on family birth decisions, policies are needed to encourage a supply of more affordable and accessible childcare services. Besides, family-centered fertility policies should also be strengthened to provide more medical and anti-employment discrimination security for pregnant women. Only in this way can we effectively alleviate the external factors that contribute to suppressing female fertility intentions.

Deeply Explore the "Demographic Bonus" and Upgrade the Level of Human Capital

Despite deepening aging and the consequent fading of China's demographic bonus, the comparative advantage of the country's population structure still exists, and there remains much room for improvement in human capital. In 2018, China's working-age population was close to one billion, or about 20 percent of the world's working-age population. Even if this proportion falls to 13 percent in 2049, the working-age population will still be around 800 million, second only to India's 1.1 billion. Yet there is ample room for improvement in the levels of human capital. According to data from the Sixth National Population Census, the average level of education attained by the working-age population in China in 2010 was 9.3 years (including 7.8 years of education for people ages forty-five to sixty-four), and it was estimated to be 10.23 years in 2015—a large gap with the educational achievements of developed countries. Therefore, it is important for China to respond actively to the challenge of population aging by exploring the demographic bonus and promoting the transformation of population development from a "quantity advantage" to a "quality advantage."

First, China should pursue a lifelong learning strategy by expanding education and training resources across a lifetime. In the next thirty years, the decrease in the number of children and adolescents will enable the working-age population to support the population in school. The rise in the proportion of the working-age population aged forty-five to sixty-four means that people in the prime of life, with more mature experience and technology skills, will become the backbone of the labor force. These conditions are ideal for significantly increasing the level of human capital. A lifelong learning strategy should particularly target the relatively older labor force, providing more efficient skill-upgrading and career guidance services to help them better adapt to or participate in the changing working world instead of withdrawing from the labor market prematurely.

Second, the development of the digital economy and technological innovation should be promoted. A fast development of the digital economy should make government become more engaged in improving population quality by expanding the pool of high-tech talent. It also helps create new employment patterns. For example, more than 75 million Chinese workers are employed by various internet platforms, such as Didi and Meituan. Employment in such new technological arenas, many of which offer flexibility, will not only enhance the utilization efficiency of human resources but will also provide more opportunities for the older labor force and elderly to participate. Separately, China has become the largest and fastest-growing market for industrial robots. In 2017, China purchased 138,000 robots, accounting for 36 percent of the global sales volume and exceeding the purchases of Europe and America combined (112,000). Zhuo and Huang (2019) estimate that at least 2.93 million workers were replaced by new industrial robots during 2013 to 2017 in China. The transformation of modern industry from large-scale manual production to automation and artificial intelligence, triggered by technological innovation, may help make up for a shrinking workforce in the next thirty years.

Third, China should improve healthcare provision and promote healthy aging. The extension of life expectancy does not necessarily mean an increase in the stock of human capital. On the contrary, a deteriorating health status will cause more working-age people to leave the labor market early. Therefore, improving healthcare and promoting healthy aging are important prerequisites for human capital upgrading. For the older labor force, much more attention should be paid to the promotion of safe and secure working environments, occupational health services, and occupational disease prevention. The elderly need access to affordable healthcare services. Scaling up the screening, early diagnosis, and control of chronic conditions, cognitive impairment, and depression at the primary care and community health levels may also matter. In addition, the system of eldercare services should be strengthened. With the empty-nest trend and the baby bust, increasing funding for institutional and community services would help reduce the burden of family care. These efforts would also improve the labor force participation rate, especially among women.

Improve the Pension System and Establish a More Flexible Retirement Mechanism

The increasing proportion of the elderly, the growing number of pensioners, and the rapid decline in pension contributors will generate tremendous funding pressure on the current pension system. It will not be sufficient to rely on family support or to reform the pay-as-you-go insurance system. Instead, a multipillar pension system should be established through coordinating government services, market forces, and society for the purpose of efficiently dissolving the implicit pension debt risk caused by population aging. Specifically, besides making further improvements to the basic pension, China needs to enact the Social Insurance Law and complete the regulatory framework for developing its institutional capacity to provide supplementary pensions (employer-sponsored pensions) and individual savings endowment insurance, such as insurance on individual tax-deferred endowments, and so on. A multipillar pension system characterized by greater saving encouragement could not only alleviate the pressure on pension financing but also incentivize saving based on a longer life expectancy. Additionally, a balance should be maintained between rural and urban residents in the matter of pensions. Although the government has declared that a pension arrangement with universal coverage has already been set up in China, it is actually a case of incomplete universalism, particularly in rural areas. The low fertility rate in many rural areas and the continuing rural-to-urban migration of young people mean it will not be practical to leave rural old-age support entirely to families in the coming decades. Currently, the rural pension is very limited, and the incentive to participate is quite low. The old-age security program must be expanded and developed because of the challenges of population aging in rural China.

Postponing the legal retirement age is another measure that has been tried and adopted worldwide as a way to support older worker populations and to stave off the financial crisis looming in various pension schemes. For example, in the United Kingdom, the government raised the retirement age from sixty to sixty-five, and further increases are under way (Holman, Foster, and Hess 2018). The United States has also attempted to raise the age threshold for claiming full government pension benefits from sixty-five to sixty-seven between 2002 and 2027 (Meier and Werding 2010). By contrast, China's legal retirement age is still remarkably low compared with that of most developed countries. Thus, exploring a flexible retirement system by progressively raising the retirement age makes sense. Some quantitative analyses indicate that a flexible retirement system has a stimulating influence on making full use of human resources (Lin and Zhang 2018). Such a system would also help to improve the solvency of the pension system, by reducing pension gaps (Wang, Huang, and Yang 2019).

Develop Long-Term Care Services

As society faces a decline in traditional family support for the elderly, it is of great importance to strengthen China's social services and build a long-term care (LTC) system to cope with the country's aging population and achieve sustainable economic development. China's LTC sector should focus on efficiency and equality, to provide a sustainable solution to the needs of the entire elderly population. Although some pilot projects have emerged, China has no national comprehensive public LTC program for the elderly, and most elderly people have insufficient access to LTC services (Feng et al. 2012). Therefore, in the medium to long run, China may consider establishing a universal public LTC financing system, similar to the universal social insurance models adopted in the Netherlands, Germany, Japan, and Korea.

In addition, it is important to plan and develop an optimal mix of services that meets the needs and preferences of the elderly. According to international experience, a combination of home- and community-based services rather than simply institutional care is preferred by the elderly and recommended, which is consistent with the broad trend across many countries. The government should not only continue to support the public provision of basic care, particularly at the lower end of the market, but should also develop industry regulations and encourage greater participation of the private sector. Moreover, in light of the shortage of high-quality workers in LTC, it will be important to invest in workforce education and training and attract more medical staff and social workers to enter this sector by improving both the economic and social status of eldercare workers.

REFERENCES

Cai, F., and Y. Du. 2009. *The China Population and Labor Yearbook: The Approaching Lewis Turning Point and Its Policy Implications.* Leiden: Brill.

Cai, F., and Y. Lu. 2016. "Take-Off, Persistence and Sustainability: The Demographic Factor in Chinese Growth." *Asia & the Pacific Policy Studies* 3 (2): 203–25.

Cai, F., and D. Wang. 2005. "Demographic Transition: Implications for Growth." In *The China Boom and Discontents*, edited by R. Garnaut and L. Song. Acton: Asia Pacific Press of the Australian National University.

———. 1999. "China's Economic Growth Sustainability and Labor Contribution." *Economic Research Journal* 10:62–68.

Cai, F., and W. Zhao. 2012. "How Is China's Economic Growth after Disappearance of Demographic Dividend?" In *Green Book of Population and Labor,* edited by F. Cai. Beijing: Chinese Academy of Social Sciences Press.

Feng, Z., C. Liu, X. Guan, and V. Mor. 2012. "China's Rapidly Aging Population Creates Policy Challenges in Shaping a Viable Long-Term Care System." *Health Affairs* 31 (12): 2764–73.

Giles, J., E. Glinskaya, Y. Zhao, X. Chen, and Y. Hu. 2018. "Population Aging and Long-Term Care Needs." In *Options for Aged Care in China: Building an Efficient and Sustainable Aged Care System*, edited by E. Glinskaya and Z. Feng. Washington, DC: World Bank Group.

Gribble, J. N., and J. Bremner. 2012. "Achieving a Demographic Dividend." *Population Bulletin* 67 (2): 1–15.

Holman, D., L. Foster, and M. Hess. 2018. "Inequalities in Women's Awareness of Changes to the State Pension Age in England and the Role of Cognitive Ability." *Ageing and Society,* August, 1–18.

Kraay, A. 2000. "Household Saving in China." *World Bank Economic Review* 14 (3): 545–70.

Li, C., and S. Lin. 2013. "China's Social Security Debt: How Large?" Working paper no. 15. Beijing: China Center for Public Finance, Peking University.

Li, S., and S. Lin. 2016. "Population Aging and China's Social Security Reforms." *Journal of Policy Modeling* 38 (1): 65–95.

Lin, Y., and L. Zhang. 2018. "Reward and Punishment Mechanisms of the Flexible Retirement System in China." *Advances in Applied Sociology* 8 (5): 366–77.

Meier, V., and M. Werding. 2010. Ageing and the Welfare State: Securing Sustainability. *Oxford Review of Economic Policy* 26 (4): 655–73.

Population and Development Research Center. 2018. *China Population Prospects 2018*. Beijing.

Sin, Y., and X. Yu. 2005. "China: Pension Liabilities and Reform Options for Old Age Insurance." Working paper, World Bank Group, Washington, DC.

United Nations, Department of Economic and Social Affairs. 2017. *World Population Prospects: The 2017 Revision*. New York.

Wang, H., J. Huang, and Q. Yang. 2019. "Assessing the Financial Sustainability of the Pension Plan in China: The Role of Fertility Policy Adjustment and Retirement Delay." *Sustainability (Switzerland)* 11 (3): 883.

Yang, D., J. Zhang, and S. Zhou. 2011. "Why Are Savings Rates So High in China?" NBER Working Paper no. 16771. Cambridge, MA: National Bureau of Economic Research.

Zeng, Y. 2018. "Fully Relax the Family Planning Policy and Encourage Second Children to Promote National Development and Family Well-Being." Working Paper no. C2018008. Beijing: China Center for Economic Research.

Zeng, Y., et al. 2019. "Research on the Basic Science of an Aging Society." Working project funded by the National Science Foundation of China.

Zhang, L., and G. Wang. 2015. "Research on the Second Childbirth Expectation and the Birth Plan for the Fertility Age Population of Chinese." [In Chinese.] *Population & Economics* 6:43–51.

Zheng, B. 2014. *China Pension Development Report 2014: Transition to Nominal Account System*. [In Chinese.] Beijing: Economic Management Publishing House for the Chinese Academy of Social Sciences.

Zhuo, X., and J. Huang. 2019. "Where Are Manufacturing Jobs Going: Changes and Reflections on China's Employment Structure." [In Chinese.] *Caijing Magazine* 5.

4

China's Green Economic Transition toward 2049

KEJUN JIANG, XIN TIAN, and JINTAO XU

China faces numerous environmental and climate challenges in the coming decades. The country's need for effective pollution control and a reduction in carbon emissions will likely mean a major shift in the economic growth pattern and in how economic policies are utilized. In this chapter, China's growth pattern is characterized according to (1) the environmental Kuznets curve, (2) the "pollution haven" effects that emerged shortly after China's entry into the World Trade Organization (WTO), (3) the carbon footprints of China's main export industries, and (4) the contribution of environmental factors to the growth of China's export sectors. Measures China could adopt to improve environmental performance in the short and intermediate term include improving economic policies and potentially making progress on the technological front. To this end, we offer some policy recommendations to conclude the chapter.

CHINA'S ENVIRONMENTAL PICTURE TODAY: ACHIEVEMENTS AND ONGOING CHALLENGES

Over the past four decades, China has enjoyed phenomenal economic growth. At the same time, welfare loss resulting from a deteriorating environment has been mounting. The ever-growing environmental damage

94 KEJUN JIANG, XIN TIAN, AND JINTAO XU

poses increasing challenges to decision-makers focused on the future direction of China's economy. As noted in *China 2030*, a joint publication by the World Bank Group and the Development Research Center of the State Council, People's Republic of China (PRC) (2013), China's growth model is no longer sustainable, and the country must seek a low-carbon, green growth path. In the same report, using data from 2008, the World Bank estimated that the costs of environmental degradation and resource depletion in China approached 10 percent of GDP, of which air pollution accounted for 6.5 percent, water pollution for 2.1 percent, and soil degradation for 1.1 percent. More than half of China's water is polluted. More than 300 million people are forced to use contaminated water supplies, a third of China's waterways do not meet the government's own safety standards, and about one-fifth of China's farmland has been contaminated with heavy metals (Baidu Baike 2018). An article in the *New York Times* described air pollution as the leading cause of premature death due to illness in China (Wong 2013). In 2010 alone, air pollution caused 1.2 million premature deaths, or one-third of the world total.

The damage doesn't stop there. Heed should also be given to the potential cost of global warming, as China quickly became the world's largest carbon dioxide (CO_2)-emitting country. A 2012 World Bank study noted that China is one of the four countries expected to sustain the greatest damage from sea level rise under a severe climate change regime (Blankespoor, Dasgupta, and Laplante 2012).

China's national goals of development by 2050 include environmental improvement to World Health Organization (WHO) standards. Currently, the national government of China has established development goals for the next thirty years, to occur in three phases. The goal of the first phase is to become an overall well-off society by 2020. The goal of the second phase is to turn China into a modernized country by 2035. The goal of the third phase is to make China a strong international power that still follows socialist principles by the mid-twenty-first century. All these goals have ecological and environmental accompaniments. In the first phase, ecological civilization is one of the five indicators, which requires industrial structure, growth, and consumption patterns to be more in line with the targets of energy and resource saving and ecological and environmental conservation. This transformation will be facilitated by wider adoption of a circular economic model that conserves and makes best use of resources, the derivation of a greater share of energy from renewable sources, effective control of emissions of main pollutants, and substantial improvement in ecological and environmental conditions. The second phase will require fundamental improvement in ecological and environmental conditions (for instance, inhalable fine particulate matter [$PM_{2.5}$] levels < 35 $\mu g/m^3$ in all cities by 2030). The third phase is associated with even more stringent measures, such as air quality in all major cities meeting the tougher WHO standard of 10 $\mu g/m^3$ (annual mean).

China has made tremendous efforts to improve its environmental impact, including committing to global climate actions, such as the Intended Nationally Determined Contributions (INDCs) established by the Paris Agreement. Severe challenges remain, however. In 2013, when air pollution became severe, in particular in Beijing, the State Council issued its Action Plan for the Prevention and Control of Air Pollution, highlighting ten measures to control air pollution. Four measures are considered particularly effective: (1) raising emissions standards and upgrading technologies in key sectors, (2) changing the structure of industry, (3) improving coal-fired boilers, and (4) achieving comprehensive dust control.

It is estimated that the first three measures caused reductions in sulfur dioxide (SO_2) emissions by 39 percent, 29 percent, and 22 percent, respectively, for the period 2013–2015 alone. Estimates of pollutant and greenhouse gas (GHG) reductions were prepared by researchers at the Energy Research Institute of the National Development and Reform Commission, a State Council agency, using their IPAC-AIM low-carbon-technology model.[1] The first two measures contributed 63 percent and 20 percent to the reduction of nitrous oxides (NO_x). An additional 9 percent reduction was achieved by phasing out older-model vehicles that could not meet certain emission standards. The four measures respectively contributed 31.2 percent, 21.2 percent, 21.2 percent, and 15.2 percent to the reduction of $PM_{2.5}$. In Beijing, the phasing out of 1.22 million below-standard vehicles led to the reduction of NO_x by 34,700 tons, or 71 percent of the total reduction, and to the reduction of $PM_{2.5}$ by 2,600 tons, or 16 percent of the total reduction.

A ten-year monitoring data series from the U.S. Department of State reveals evidence of these measures' effectiveness. This data series shows the trends of daily $PM_{2.5}$ concentrations (in units of 10 $\mu g/m^3$) in five Chinese cities from 2008 to mid-2017 (figure 4-1). As shown in the figure, air quality in the major cities covered by the data series has been poor, especially in Beijing, Chengdu, and Shenyang. Beijing had the worst air pollution and saw the greatest improvement in average daily PM$_{2.5}$ indexes. Nonetheless, air quality remains a major challenge. Beijing's yearly average is still far above its goals for 2020, 2035, and 2050.

Challenge One: Air Pollution Control

Air pollution came to the forefront of attention after a bout of smog days in the first half of 2013, though measures to control air pollution had begun much earlier than that. To ensure air quality that would meet the requirements of the International Olympic Committee in 2008, the Chinese government implemented several mitigating measures, including restrictions on driving in Beijing starting just before the Olympic Games; this policy has remained in place up to the present. Later a license plate lottery scheme was adopted to limit the number of licenses permitted. Since 2013, many other powerful air pollution–reducing measures have been launched under

FIGURE 4-1.   Daily PM$_{2.5}$ Concentrations in Five Megacities in China

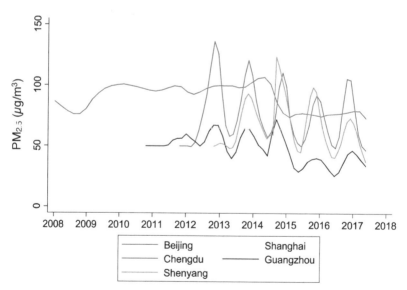

Source: Data from U.S. Embassy & Consulates in China (https://china.usembassy-china.org .cn/embassy-consulates/beijing/air-quality-monitor/).

Note: Bars indicate 95 percent confidence interval.

the rubric "State Council Ten Measures" or "Beijing Ten Measures," a new fuel economy standard has been introduced, and so on. On average, the air quality indexes (AQIs) have been declining since 2013, from more than 80 to below 60 (see figure 4-1). A closer look at the U.S. State Department's data and data from other sources, however, gives less reason to be optimistic.

Figure 4-2A, created from publicly released monitoring data in Beijing, compares air quality in the years 2013 up to mid-2018, using AQIs and without controlling for any conditions. The figures suggest that overall air quality in 2017 and 2018 improved from the years before them. When an important condition is controlled for, however, the results are different. Figure 4-2B charts AQIs for the same period when days with a north wind (beyond 1 degree north, where north is 0) are removed from the data. Basically, we compared AQIs on windless days in the six-year period. The changes in air quality become much less apparent.

Challenge Two: Reducing GHG Emissions

From 1990 to 2001, the annual growth rates of China's annual CO_2 emissions were modest (2–4 percent). After 2001, CO_2 emissions moved onto an accelerated path, for the first few years growing at a rate of more than 9 percent per year. In 2010 this trend produced around four billion tons of additional CO_2 emissions compared to the amount projected based on the 1990–2001 trend. In the meantime, global CO_2 emissions also experienced abnormal growth during the period 2002–2010, amounting to nearly six billion tons of incremental emissions above the trend line projected from the 1990–2001 period. The abnormal increase in CO_2 emissions in China accounted for 70 percent of the world's total abnormal increment (figures 4-3A and 4-3B).

Because of this rapid increase in CO_2 emissions, China surpassed the United States in CO_2 emissions for the first time in 2006, becoming the world's largest CO_2-emitting country. In 2011 China's share amounted to nearly 30 percent of the world's total CO_2 emissions while the U.S. share dropped to nearly 16 percent (figure 4-4). At the twenty-first annual session of the Conference of the Parties to the 1992 United Nations Framework Convention on Climate Change, better known as COP 21 (and also as CMP 11, the eleventh session of the Meeting of the Parties to the 1997 Kyoto Protocol), in 2015 in Paris, China announced its INDCs, which stipulate that

FIGURE 4-2A. **AQIs in Beijing, 2013–2018**

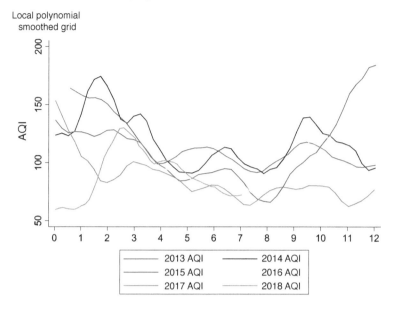

Source: Data from China National Environmental Monitoring Center (http://www.cnemc.cn/sssj/).

Note: All graphs were derived by local polynomial smoothing.

FIGURE 4-2B. **AQIs in Beijing without Windy Conditions, 2013–2018**

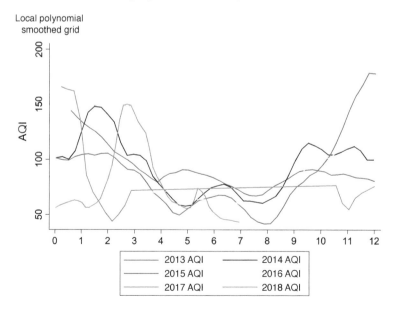

Source: Data from China National Environmental Monitoring Center (http://www.cnemc.cn/sssj/).

Note: All graphs were derived by local polynomial smoothing.

FIGURE 4-3A. **World CO_2 Emissions, 1999 to 2030**

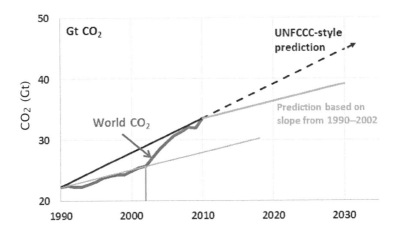

Source: Data from COP 21 Paris Summit website (https://climateparis.org/COP21#china).

Note: Gt, metric gigaton; UNFCCC, United Nations Framework Convention on Climate Change (1992).

FIGURE 4-3B. **China's CO_2 Emissions, 1999 to 2010**

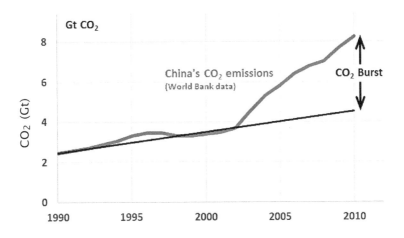

Source: Data from COP 21 Paris Summit website (https://climateparis.org/COP21#china).

FIGURE 4-4.   China's CO_2 Emissions as Proportion of World Emissions, 1960–2011

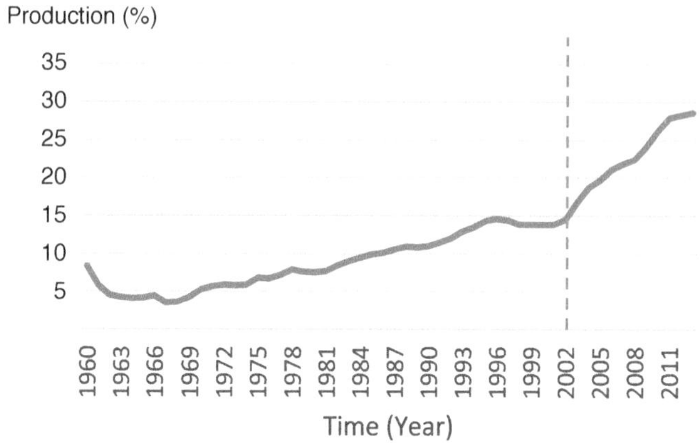

Source: Data from World Bank website (https://data.worldbank.org.cn/indicator/EN.ATM .CO2E.KT?view=chart).

its CO_2 emissions will peak by 2030 and then decline. This emissions goal, by various estimates, does not conform to the goal of containing global temperature rise below 2 degrees Celsius (or, better, 1.5 degrees C). A future worldwide effort to press China to make a stronger commitment to reach its CO_2 emissions peak well before 2030 can be expected.

CHINA'S GROWTH PATTERN SEEN THROUGH AN ENVIRONMENTAL LENS

Paul Krugman (1994, 2011) has argued that the growth of China, along with other emerging Asian economies, was input-driven. Alwyn Young (2000, 2003) has asserted that China's rapid GDP growth could be attributed mainly to intensive capital investment and a massive labor force, with a limited contribution from total factor productivity (TFP) growth. Neither remarked on the environmental damage, which features prominently in the social costs of China's growth. In recent years, the problem of a labor shortage has dominated discussions of China's economic transition. As China approaches a demographic cliff, upgrading industry toward capital-intensive modes has entered mainstream thinking about the country's economic transition. However, the environmental impacts of growth and the importance of incentives for environmental improvement and policy implementation have not received sufficient emphasis. This lack of concern for a quantitative understanding of environmental damage and an appropriate incentive structure will hinder China's achievement of the goals it has set for itself for the next ten to thirty years.

Environmental Kuznets Curve

Many studies have examined the relationship between per capita GDP growth and environmental quality without producing consistent results. In general, most studies have found the expected inverse U-shaped relationship between emissions and per capita GPD for a panel of provinces or cities (Shen and Xu 2000; Zhang et al. 2009, Jiang et al. 2013). Wang and Huang (2015), using measures of air quality across Chinese cities to ascertain environmental change, found different results. Their analysis indicates that AQIs have a U-shaped relationship with the growth of per capita GDP, not the inverse U shape predicted by classical economics (Grossman and Krueger 1995). Conclusions based on emissions data should be taken with a grain of salt, however, as there is some doubt as to the quality of the data. The surprising results of Wang and Huang (2015), based on AQIs, could have two interpretations: (1) Chinese cities are still in an early stage of development and have not grown sufficiently to reach the turning point of a U-shaped curve or (2) these Chinese cities may be representative of a pattern of economic growth specific to China; they may be experiencing greater difficulty in making the economic transition to a low-emissions path than similar cities outside China. The latter possibility raises an alarm over China's growth pattern.

WTO Entry and Pollution Haven Effects in China

Tian and Xu (2019) examined China's growth pattern through the lenses of trade liberalization and environmental changes. They first examined the "pollution haven effects" triggered by China's entry into the WTO in late 2001. Using a CO_2 emissions forecast model and a synthetic control method, they were able to estimate the emissions of a "counterfactual China" (China without entry into the WTO after 2001) and the gap between China's real CO_2 emissions after WTO entry and those of the counterfactual China. The same procedure was used to estimate the gap between the CO_2 emissions of the real United States and those of a counterfactual United States, as well as of China's other main trading partners. The results showed that China's CO_2 emissions increased after its WTO entry, whereas those of its main trading partners, namely, the United States, Germany, and Japan, declined correspondingly. This is clear evidence of the pollution haven effect, according to which strict environmental regulations in developed countries push pollution-intensive production toward developing countries with weaker protections. Tian and Xu proceeded to investigate which sectors were most responsible for China's export boom. Leading the export boom were not the typical labor-intensive industries, such as the textile industry. Rather, the most important sectors were electronic machinery and ordinary machinery. This result was puzzling, as it is generally believed that China's comparative advantage resides in labor-intensive technologies, and labor-intensive industries should be the ones to reap the greatest benefit from free trade. Tian and Xu provided a reasonable explanation by calculating the carbon footprint of all major export industries. They found that China's leading export industries, electronic machinery and ordinary machinery, also led the economy in carbon footprints. If carbon footprints are an indicator of the intensity of use of environmental inputs, then the free use of environmental inputs, such as air and water, could explain the rise of these mid-level capital-intensive sectors in export. Finally, they conducted an export value growth accounting for the top twenty export sectors and further demonstrated that carbon footprints were the main contributor to export value growth, and further, the contribution increased after WTO entry. In the meantime, TFP also grew at a lower rate.

There is thus no convincing evidence that China has reached a Kuznets turning point at this stage. The delayed change can perhaps be attributed to ineffective regulations and a rigid industrial structure. Entry into the WTO gave a major boost to China's economic growth. It also exacerbated China's environmental problems. In the absence of effective environmental regulations, sectors with large carbon footprints grew the most after WTO entry, giving rise to the apparent puzzle that a set of mid-level capital-intensive industries, such as electronic machinery and ordinary machinery, led the export boom after WTO accession. Export growth accounting reinforces the belief that China's growth pattern, exacerbated by entry into the WTO, has been heavily driven by high uses of environmental factors instead of high labor uses. Changing this growth pattern requires correcting price distortions around environmental factors and boosting the contribution of TFP.

TRANSITION TO A GREENER ECONOMY

China's National Goals in Climate Change

China made an important contribution to the Paris Agreement at COP 21 in Paris in 2015 by making it clear that China's CO_2 emissions were expected to peak in 2030 and decline thereafter. This level of commitment, however, is considered by many to be inadequate because China has been responsible for close to a 30 percent share of the world's annual emissions for nearly a decade. Without a significantly better effort, the 2-degree C or 1.5-degree C goals set forth in the Paris Agreement will not be achieved. It is conceivable that upcoming negotiations will seek to have China upgrade its commitment goal from its NDCs.

China also faces another important change. The country has been leading the developing countries in establishing and arguing for the principle of common but differentiated responsibilities. However, as per capita GDP keeps growing, China will soon become a high-income country and is destined to bear the greater responsibilities of other high-income and industrialized countries instead of those borne by developing countries. So, from year 2020 on, it is expected that China's mitigation effort will have to increase, and its responsibility for financing and facilitating international initiatives should increase as well.

Over the past decade, significant efforts have been made to mitigate CO_2 emissions. China has already achieved its goal, set in 2009 at the COP 15 meeting in Copenhagen, of reducing the intensity of CO_2 emissions (per unit of GDP) by 40–45 percent during 2005–2020. Many believe that China's absolute volume of CO_2 emissions began to stabilize after 2013, corresponding to a decline in total coal consumption. If this trend continues, China's CO_2 emissions could peak much earlier.

There is a strong belief that, by 2050, clean energies, such as energy from renewable sources and nuclear power, will become the dominant forms of energy for China. In recent years, the consumption of energy from modern renewable sources has taken a great leap forward, surpassing expectations. In 2016 and 2017, newly installed capacity in solar photovoltaics and wind power accounted for more than 50 percent of the world's total. It is also believed that advanced nuclear energy will also be put on a fast track. The costs of energy from renewable sources and some consumer energy technologies, such as electric vehicles, advanced lighting, and super-high-efficiency household appliances, have been declining drastically.

According to the INDCs China announced in Paris in 2015, CO_2 emissions will peak in 2030, with the carbon intensity decreasing by 60–65 percent from the 2005 level. In 2017, carbon intensity declined by 46 percent from the 2005 level, ahead of the schedule set at the COP 15 in Copenhagen, which stipulated a 40–45 percent decrease by 2020. It is likely that by 2020 the reduction in carbon intensity will reach 50 percent.

Another confidence booster is the reduced cost of producing energy from renewable sources. After two decades of fast development, in 2018 the marginal costs of wind power generation were on par with those of coal-based power generation; solar photovoltaics will be in a similar situation in 2020. The cost of nuclear power generation, after the adoption of third-generation technology, has also declined significantly. Technological changes and tremendous cost reductions have made massive reductions in carbon emissions economically viable. It is also possible that with this technological progress, the need for carbon pricing will be less important after 2020.

Focusing on technological advancement is beneficial for China's future economic growth. Based on the *Global Competitiveness Report of Energy Enterprises (2017)*, by the Center for International Energy and Environment Studies of Renmin University and the International Environmental Research Institute (China), fifty-seven Chinese firms are numerically dominant among the most competitive new energy firms and are much more competitive than the five traditional energy firms. There is great market potential for Chinese new energy firms. Growth in the new energy business will help China's 2025 strategy for restructuring and developing the manufacturing sector.

Our model predictions show that, to achieve the 2-degree C goal, China's CO_2 emission should peak by 2025 and decline by 65 percent in 2050 (Jiang et al. 2013). For the 1.5-degree goal, peak emissions could be reached as early as 2020 (Jiang et al. 2018).

The rapid growth of renewable energies and the changing industrial structure lead us to believe that a peak in CO_2 emissions in 2020 and a 65 percent reduction in CO_2 emissions by 2050 are both feasible. Our analysis indicates that China's end energy demand will grow very slowly after 2020, by 0.7–1.4 percent per year, and perhaps can be entirely met by energy from renewable sources.

Economic Policies to Guide a Green Transition

Environmental regulations have been accompanied by a plethora of administrative measures since 1978, when environmental issues were first seriously addressed. Typical administrative measures include requirements to meet technical standards and obtain permits, and the forced closure of polluting firms. In recent years the central government has often launched national-level campaigns to curb mounting pollution problems. On January 1, 1997, the central government launched a midnight action in the Huai river basin to penalize key water-polluting firms. More than four thousand firms were shut down overnight. Later, firm size limits were established for the top fifteen polluting industries to promote technological upgrading and scale economies in pollution control. During the period 2006–2010, quantitative targets were set on major pollutants with huge government financial supports. A large number of small polluting firms were also shut down to facilitate meeting the set goals. Starting in 2017, prompted by severe air pollution, a third national campaign was launched that featured mandatory central government inspection of pollution-heavy regions, with local officials held responsible for any wrongdoings uncovered. These campaigns, while effective in the short term, have not led to systemic changes in the behavior of the polluting industries or a durable reduction in pollutants.

A serious exploration of economic policies began in 2010, during the twelfth five-year plan. First, seven pilot projects enabling carbon trading were launched. In the meantime, an environmental tax law was drafted, which finally saw passage and full implementation in 2018. Since 2006, large subsidies have been provided to support pollution control, the use of renewable energy, and technological innovations aimed at reducing pollution and carbon emissions.

Only careful evaluation can answer how well these initial attempts at economic policies worked or did not work. A 2018 study by Chen and Xu is perhaps the only rigorous assessment of the seven carbon-trading pilot programs. Their findings indicate that, of the seven pilots, two of them (in Hubei and Guangdong, including Shenzhen) achieved reductions in CO_2 emissions and noticeable trading incidence and prices. No clear evidence is available for the other pilots. The paltry evidence reinforces general concerns with the carbon trading scheme in China. When carbon permits are allocated and traded on the market, local governments have the responsibility to monitor changes in the carbon emissions of the participating firms, which entails significant labor and financial costs. Though the carbon emission permits are free, incentives for local governments to follow through are inadequate. As many studies have found, China's local governments are already charged with executing too many policy mandates with insufficient funding to do so. Additional responsibilities can only mean higher costs and fewer benefits; hence the low expected performance. Despite the unconvincing evidence of the benefits of the carbon-trading scheme, the central government was determined to adopt the scheme nationally. When the nationwide scheme was announced in 2017, only the power sector was initially included.

An environmental tax officially went into effect on January 1, 2018. Prior to that China had a similar policy in the form of a pollution levy that was charged to firms based on a set rate for pollutant emissions. The levy system was long criticized for its rate being set too low and the levy not being seriously implemented even at the very low rate (Qu 1991; Xu, Hyde, and Amacher 2003; Xu, Hyde, and Ji 2010). The most critical weakness of the levy system, perhaps, is that the revenues were distributed within the local environmental agencies to supplement salaries, and therefore did not significantly relieve the local financial situation. Most local government leaders in this circumstance opt to take the side of business, avoiding serious action on pollution control.

The formal environmental tax law made two important improvements to the pollution levy system. First, the tax revenue goes to the local treasury as general fiscal revenue. Second, the local government has a high level of discretion in setting the tax rate, with a base rate equivalent to the previous pollution levy and the ceiling ten times higher. It looks like a textbook taxation design as it both seeks to reap the "double dividend" of environmental taxes and takes into account local heterogeneity.

It is still too early to know the practical results of the newly launched environmental taxes. Previous studies tried to link economic incentives (such as the pollution levy) to firms' behavior. Xu, Hyde, and Ambacher (2003) and Chen (2013) studied the effects of a pollution levy on firms' polluting behaviors. They found that the polluting firms did respond to economic incentives at the margin. Higher charges led to a greater reduction in pollutant emissions. Chen (2013) and Chen and Xu (2019) both estimated firm-level marginal abatement cost curves. The findings of Chen and Xu (2019) indicate that current tax rates are still too low to achieve the established goal of reducing main pollutant emissions. To achieve the reduction goals set by the central government for the current five-year plan period, the average tax rate should be triple the current ceiling rates. With that, revenues generated through environmental taxes could reach 5–10 percent of China's total fiscal revenues.

Subsidies for renewable energy production made it possible for China to become the world's largest producer and supplier and to have the world's largest installed capacity. Technologies also progressed tremendously. The marginal cost of electricity has declined by 90 percent over the course of a decade. And China is ahead of schedule in reaching the planned share of renewable energy in total energy. Nevertheless, financial burdens and lack of access to the electricity grid have been holding back the development of renewable energy sources. To address this problem, the Chinese government changed the scheme and stopped the feed-in tariff requirement for renewable power generation. Instead, an auction scheme was adopted to reduce the financial burden on the central government and stimulate further technological advancement. The auction scheme achieved immediate results. In the spring of 2018, the lowest auction price for energy generated from renewable sources was less than that of power generated from thermal power plants in Qinghai. As a result, Qinghai province has had two periods of power supplied entirely through renewable-source technologies. The most recent one lasted fifteen days.

RECOMMENDATIONS

After four decades of tremendous economic growth, China's economic growth model is considered by many to be no longer sustainable. Environmental damage has mounted. China has been leading the world in criteria pollutant emissions and carbon emission. (Criteria pollutants are those air pollutants designated in the 1970 Clean Air Act as being of concern: carbon monoxide, lead, nitrogen dioxide, ground-level ozone, particulate matter, and sulfur dioxide.) Accordingly, China suffers the most from water and air pollution and from damage attributable to climate change. It would be in China's national interest to take decisive measures to reverse these trends and begin to reduce criteria pollutant and GHG emissions.

We have examined the relationship between China's economic growth and environmental aggravation. Existing studies on the environmental Kuznets curve could not give a clear picture of the environmental trajectory in a context of rapid growth. This lack of clarity or consensus underscores concern that China's green transition faces strong institutional and structural barriers, which in turn emphasizes the need for a concerted effort to enact institutional and structural reforms.

We have also examined China's economic growth pattern using WTO accession as a "shock" event. Our analysis indicates that accession to the WTO did cause China to become a major pollution haven for its main trading partners. CO_2 emissions increased after the event. In addition, an apparent trade puzzle, namely, that medium-capital-intensive sectors led the growth in exports after WTO accession, can be explained by the tremendous increase in China's carbon footprint. This conclusion leads us to believe that sacrificing the environment may be the biggest reason for China's miraculous growth after WTO accession.

This raises the issue of China's international responsibilities. In the process of changing from the world's poorest and largest developing economy to the world's biggest economy, top economy, and a high-income economy, China has acquired commensurate responsibilities. Not only must China improve its domestic environment, it must also lead the way in tackling common environmental threats. A relevant example here is GHG mitigation: for the world to achieve its 1.5- or 2-degree goals, established by the Paris Agreement, China will have to modify its INDCs and try to reach peak CO_2 emissions by year 2025 or even 2020.

Much progress has been achieved over the last decade. China has become the world's largest producer and supplier of energy from renewable sources—indeed, its share of energy from renewable sources in total energy produced has been increasing ahead of schedule. With policy changes to energy schemes, the production of energy from renewable sources is expected to grow faster. This development, together with technological breakthroughs in other sectors, underpins the optimistic assessment that China is capable of moving its CO_2 peak emissions forward in time and move onto a fast reduction path afterward.

The next three decades are critical for China's economic and environmental transition. Moving from a high-pollution-intensity, high-carbon economy to a green, low-carbon economy is perhaps the most important component of China's economic transition. But doing so would require that air and water quality meet the WHO's high standard, carbon emissions fall by more than 60 percent from their current level, and fundamental changes in energy structure be made.

To facilitate a transition of this order requires a systematic policy and regulatory reform package. More important is the change from administrative-oriented approaches to market-based approaches in policy design and implementation. And here some lessons can be drawn from past experience to guide future changes. China has undertaken large-scale policy experiments in setting up the seven pilot projects for carbon trading, with mixed results. The country just launched the environmental tax in 2018, with results awaiting further monitoring and examination. China also switched from a feed-in-tariff scheme to an auction scheme in renewable energy, a change that already shows great promise. This last development has great implications as more and more ecological and environmental programs are launched. All these attempts at developing and fine-tuning economic and market-based policy tools will help China make the transition to a green, low-carbon economy with low social cost and high effectiveness.

NOTE

1. IPAC/AIM is the initialism for Integrated Policy Assessment Model for China/Asia Integrated Assessment Model. The IPAC team at the Energy Research Institute (ERI) has been constructing models for policy analysis since 1992. According to Jiang Ke Jun of the ERI, "After more than twenty years of research and development, IPAC has now become a comprehensive policy evaluation model, with a variety of analytical approaches. Models and methods currently used by the IPAC team include a computable general equilibrium model, a dynamic economic model, a partial equilibrium model, a minimum cost optimization model based on detailed linear programming techniques and industry simulation models. . . . The IPAC-AIM/technology model is a major component of the IPAC model, which aims to give a detailed description of energy services and the current and future development of energy equipment/installation, as well as simulating energy con-

sumption processes." For further information on the process, see the description on the independent climate change think tank E3G's website (https://www.e3g.org/docs/Annex_A_China%E2%80%99s_Investment_Pathways_to_2030.pdf).

REFERENCES

Baidu Baike, 2018. "Ten Major Problems of Chinese Environment," https://baike.baidu.com/item/TenMajorProblemofChineseEnvironment/4868380.

Blankespoor, B., S. Dasgupta, and B. Laplante, 2012. *Sea-Level Rise and Coastal Wetlands: Impacts and Costs.* Policy Research Working Paper WPS6277. Washington, DC: World Bank, November.

Chen, Xiaolan. 2013. "Industrial Enterprise Performance and Environmental Policy in China: Empirical Investigations with Chinese Industrial Plant Level Data." Ph.D. diss., Peking University.

Chen, Xing, and Jintao Xu. 2019. "Estimating Marginal Abatement Cost for Chinese Polluting Industries." Manuscript.

———. 2018. "Carbon Trading Scheme in the People's Republic of China: Evaluating the Performance of Seven Pilot Projects," *Asian Development Review* 35 (2): 131–52.

Grossman, G., and A. Krueger. 1995. "Economic Growth and the Environment." *Quarterly Journal of Economics* 110 (2): 353–77.

Jiang, Kejung, Chenmin He, Hanchen Dai, Jia Liu, and Xiangyang Xu. 2018. "Emission Scenario Analysis for China under the Global 1.5° Target." *Carbon Management*, May.

Jiang, Kejung, Zhuang Xing, Miao Ren, and Chenmin He. 2013. "China's Role in Attaining the Global 2 Target." *Climate Policy* 13 (S01): S55–69.

Krugman, Paul. 2011."Will China Break?" *New York Times*, December 18.

———. 1994. "The Myth of Asia's Miracle." *Foreign Affairs*, November–December.

Qu, G. 1991. *Environmental Management in China.* Beijing: UNEP and China Environmental Science Press.

Shen, M., and Y. Xu. 2000. "A New Style of Environmental Kuznets Curve: A Study of the Relationship between Economic Growth and Environmental Change during the Industrialization Process of Zhejiang Province." *Zhejiang Social Science* 4:53–57.

Tian, Xin, and Jintao Xu. 2019. "The Dividend of Pollution Haven," EfD Discussion Paper MS-918.

Wang, M., and Ying Huang. 2015. "China's Environmental Pollution and Economic Growth." [In Chinese.] *Economics Quarterly* 14 (2): 557–78.

Wong, E. 2013. "Air Pollution Linked to 1.2 Million Premature Deaths in China." *New York Times*, April 1.

World Bank and Development Research Center of the State Council, PRC. 2013.

China 2030: Building a Modern, Harmonious, and Creative Society. Washington, DC: World Bank Group.

Xu, Jintao, William F. Hyde, and Gregory S. Amacher. 2003. "China's Paper Industry: Growth and Environmental Policy during Economic Reform." *Journal of Economic Development* 28 (1): 49–78.

Xu, Jintao, W. F. Hyde, and Yongjie Ji. 2010. "Effective Pollution Control Policy for China." *Journal of Productivity Analysis* 33 (1): 47–66.

Young, Alwin. 2003. "Gold into Base Metals: Productivity Growth in the People's Republic of China during the Reform Period." *Journal of Political Economy* 111 (6): 1220–61.

———. 2000. "The Razor's Edge: Distortions and Incremental Reform in the People's Republic of China." *Quarterly Journal of Economics* 115 (4): 1091–135.

Zhang, H., F. Zhou, H. Yang, and Q. Guo. 2009. "Regulation Performance of the Win-Win of Environmental Protection and Economic Development." *Economic Research Journal* 5:38–47.

5

Constructing a Modern Financial System for China's Future

YIPING HUANG

When the Chinese leadership decided to shift its policy emphasis from class struggle to economic development in the cold winter of 1978, China had only one financial institution, the People's Bank of China (PBOC). At that time, the PBOC served as both the central bank and a commercial bank and accounted for 93 percent of the country's total financial assets. This was primarily because, in a centrally planned economy, transfer of funds was arranged by the state, and there was little need for financial intermediation. Once economic reform started, however, the authorities moved very quickly to establish new financial institutions and to create new financial markets.

Today, forty years after China started economic reform, it has a sizable financial system, which exhibits three distinctive features: gigantic financial volumes, comprehensive government controls, and an inadequate regulatory regime. With respect to the first feature, China has achieved prominence as an important player in the global financial system, including the banking sector, the insurance industry, direct investment, foreign exchange transactions, and bond and equity markets. With respect to the second feature, government interventions in the financial system remain widespread and serious. The PBOC still guides commercial banks' setting of deposit and lending rates through "window guidance," although the final restrictions on deposit rates were removed in 2015. Industry and other policies still play important roles influencing the allocation of financial resources by banks and capital markets. The PBOC intervenes in the foreign exchange markets from time to time by directly buying or selling on foreign exchanges, setting the central parity, and determining the daily trading band. The regulators tightly manage cross-border capital flows. And the state still is the majority owner of most of the large financial institutions. Finally, with respect to the third feature, the regulatory framework is segregated in nature; that is, one regulator is responsible for one sector and focuses exclusively on regulating the institutions, not the functions. The authorities still rely mainly on implicit guarantee rather than on prudential regulation to avert financial crises.

Such a financial system is problematic in many ways, according to conventional assessment. The repressive financial policies, in particular, are subject to criticisms in both academic and policy discussions. Academics believe that state interventions reduce financial efficiency and inhibit financial development (Lardy 1998; McKinnon 1973). Private businesses complain about policy discrimination, which has made it very difficult for them to obtain external funding. China's repressive financial policies are occasionally also a source of controversy in discussions of its outward direct investment (ODI). Some foreign experts argue that the Chinese state-owned enterprises (SOEs) compete unfairly with foreign companies since they receive subsidized funding in China. This issue is also at the center of the current trade dispute between China and the United States (USTR 2018).

Despite all these potential problems, for quite a while this financial system did not stop China from achieving rapid economic growth and maintaining basic financial stability. During the first three decades of economic reform, China's GDP growth averaged 9.8 percent per annum, and its financial system did not experience any systemic financial crisis, although the volume of nonperforming bank loans was quite large in the late 1990s. Unfortunately, during the past decade, this rosy picture faded quickly as economic growth decelerated and systemic financial risks escalated sharply. It appears that what worked before could no longer continue.

China's unique experience of financial reform raises some important intellectual and policy questions. Why did the Chinese government maintain extensive interventions in the financial sector during the reform period? Is financial repression as bad as is commonly believed? Do the costs and benefits of repressive financial policies vary under different circumstances? How should the government respond to changing impacts of financial repression on economic growth and financial stability? In the background of these discussions there is also a more fundamental but somewhat hypothetical question: Had China adopted the "shock therapy" approach to financial reform at the beginning, would the Chinese economy have performed better? Most important, as effectiveness of the current financial system declines sharply, how should the financial system evolve, and what further reforms are necessary to sustain China's robust economic growth in the coming decades?

These are some of the key questions that this chapter addresses. The chapter strives to provide an objective assessment of China's financial reform policies. It also offers recommendations for future reform policies. Wherever possible, it tries to draw some general lessons from the Chinese experience that might be relevant for financial liberalization in other developing countries.

The key findings of this chapter may be summarized as follows. First, China's financial reform and development during the past four decades could be characterized as "strong in establishing financial institutions and growing financial assets, but weak in liberalizing financial markets and improving corporate governance" (Huang and Ge 2019; Huang et al. 2013; Wang and Huang forthcoming). On the one hand, starting with one financial institution in 1978, China has built a very large financial sector, including large numbers of various financial institutions and gigantic accumulations of financial assets. On the other hand, the function of free market mechanisms remains seriously constrained in the financial system, including in pricing and in the allocation of financial resources. This unique pattern of financial liberalization is closely linked with China's gradual dual-track reform approach, which entails maintaining SOEs while creating favorable conditions for the private sector to grow rapidly (Fan 1994; Naughton 1995). In retrospect, this gradual dual-track reform approach worked better than the shock therapy approach might have as it helped maintain economic stability in the transition to the market system. Repressive financial policies, by depressing the cost of capital and discriminatory allocation of financing, provide de facto subsidies to the SOEs. In other words, financial repression is a necessary condition for the dual-track reform approach.

Second, several empirical analyses, using either Chinese data (Huang and Wang 2011) or cross-country data (Huang, Gou, and Wang 2016), confirm that repressive financial policies could have positive effects on economic growth and financial stability during early stages of development. But over time, such positive effects could turn to negative impacts. It is possible that the effects of financial repression are of two types, one being the "McKinnon effect" and the other the "Stiglitz effect" (Huang and Wang 2017; McKinnon 1973; Stiglitz 1994). The McKinnon effect is generally negative, as financial repression hinders both financial efficiency and financial development, while the Stiglitz effect is mainly positive, as repressive financial policies could effectively help convert savings into investment and support financial stability. Both effects exist in all economies, but their relative importance varies. The Stiglitz effect is more important when both the financial market and the regulatory system are underdeveloped. This again validates the observation that financial repression did not disrupt rapid economic growth and financial stability during China's early stage of reform.

Recently, however, repressive financial policies have begun to hurt China's economic and financial performance. Economic growth decelerated persistently after 2010. One of the important reasons is that, as China reached the high middle-income level, its economic growth had to rely more on innovation and industrial upgrading instead of on mobilizing more inputs. But repressive financial policies are not the best way to support corporate innovation. They also are not well suited to provide asset-based income for Chinese households. In the meantime, systemic financial risks also rose markedly, as the two most important pillars supporting financial stability, sustained rapid economic growth and government implicit guarantee, weakened visibly. This suggests that the policy regime that worked quite effectively during the first several decades of the reform era could no longer deliver the same results. Further reforms are urgently needed to support growth and stability in the future. These reforms should probably focus on the development of multilayer capital markets, letting market mechanisms play decisive roles in decisions on allocating financial resources, and improving financial regulation.

These findings have important implications for the general thinking about economic reform, and also for the current trade disputes between China and the United States. In economies where financial markets and the regulatory system are underdeveloped, a certain degree of financial repression could actually be helpful. Had China given up all government interventions at the start of the reform period, it would already have experienced several rounds of financial crises. In this sense, the repressive financial policies in China are transitory measures. They are an integral part of the gradualism approach and are also effective in supporting economic growth and financial stability during a certain stage. Now the Chinese government has decided to push ahead with further financial reforms. The policies to which China has committed, especially increasing the roles of the market and opening to the outside world, are very much in line with demands by its trading partners, especially the United States. There is important common ground for China and the United States to resolve many of their disputes. The only trick is that the Chinese reform will likely remain gradual.

The remainder of the chapter is organized as follows. The next section briefly explains China's process of financial reform and development, summarizes its distinctive features, and explains the logic behind it. The ensuing assessment of the reform policies distinguishes the McKinnon effect and the Stiglitz effect of financial repression on economic growth and financial stability. There follows a discussion of the recent deterioration in China's economic and financial performance, with some suggestions for the future direction of financial reform. The chapter concludes by outlining some directions for future reforms in building a modern financial system for China's future development.

CHINA'S UNIQUE PATTERN OF FINANCIAL REFORM AND DEVELOPMENT

At the end of 1978, the Chinese leadership launched a series of initiatives to rebuild and restructure the financial system. The following four decades may be divided into three stages according to key policy initiatives. The first stage started in 1979, when the authorities quickly reestablished three state-owned specialized banks—the Bank of China (BOC), the Agricultural Bank of China (ABC), and the China Construction Bank (CCB).[1] At the beginning of 1984, the then PBOC was split into two parts, the Industrial and Commercial Bank of China (ICBC) and the new PBOC. The main policy efforts during this stage were to create a large number of financial institutions, especially banks and insurance companies. The second stage began in 1990 when both the Shenzhen Stock Exchange and the Shanghai Stock Exchange were set up at the end of the year. This marked the beginning of China's capital markets. In 1996, the PBOC established the interbank market. China's accession to the World Trade Organization (WTO) at the end of 2001 kicked off the third stage, during which the financial policies focused mainly on financial opening, especially opening of the domestic banking and securities industries to foreign institutions. From 2009, the PBOC also accelerated the pace of internationalizing the renminbi.

China's financial reform and development process exhibits a unique pattern. On the one hand, the government made tremendous progress in establishing financial institutions and growing financial assets. On the other, it continued to intervene in the financial system extensively (Huang et al. 2013).

China already has a very large number of financial institutions, ranging across the banking, insurance, and security industries. At the end of 2017, its broad money supply (M2) was already greater than that of the United States and equivalent to 210 percent of its own GDP, the third highest ratio in the world, after Lebanon's and Japan's. In the same year, total bank assets reached 252 trillion yuan, which was 304.7 percent of GDP. This was much higher than in Japan (165.5 percent), Germany (96.6 percent), or the United States (60.2 percent). The "big four" banks, the ICBC, BOC, CCB, and ABC, are regularly ranked among the world's top ten. China's stock and bond markets are often regarded as "underdeveloped," but they were, respectively, ranked second and third in the world, according to market capitalization measures.

Government interventions can be seen in almost all financial activities, from the determination of bank deposit and lending rates to the allocation of credit and initial public offering quotas, and from the management of cross-border capital flows to majority control of large financial institutions. According to one measure of financial repression, constructed using World Bank data, China's Financial Repression Index (FRI) dropped from 1.0 in 1980 to 0.6 in 2015 (Huang et al. 2018). These various metrics confirm that China made important progress in market-oriented financial reform. Nevertheless, the degree of financial repression has remained high. In 2015, China's FRI was not only higher than the average of the middle-income economies but also higher than that of the low-income economies (figure 5-1). In fact, of the 130 economies for which 2015 data are available, China's FRI ranked fourteenth.

Compared to the international experience, the Chinese financial system not only has a higher FRI but is also more dominated by the banking sector

FIGURE 5-1.   **Financial Repression Index for China and Other Countries, 1980, 2000, and 2015**

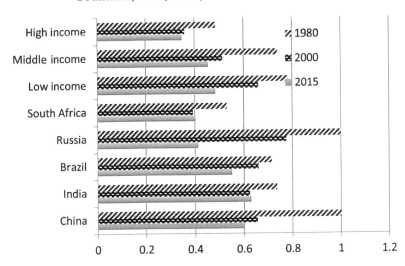

Source: Wang and Huang (forthcoming).

Note: Calculation of the Financial Repression Index used World Bank data on ownership of banks, regulation of interest rates, intervention in credit allocation, and control of cross-border capital flows. The index ranges between 0 and 1, with 0 indicating no repression. The whole sample contains 155 economies, including 41 high-income, 88 middle-income, and 26 low-income economies.

("CHN" in figure 5-2). One common understanding is that financial systems in the United States and the United Kingdom are market-dominated while those in Germany and Japan are more bank-dominated ("DEU" and "JPN," to the right of "USA" in figure 5-2). Cross-country data suggest a possible positive correlation between FRI and the share of the banking sector, probably because banks are more suited to enforce government initiatives.

RATIONALE FOR REPRESSIVE FINANCIAL POLICIES

The high level of financial repression during China's early reform period was likely a result of its unique dual-track reform strategy, divided between the state and the nonstate sectors (Fan 1994). When economic reform started in 1978, the Chinese leadership did not have a blueprint for the reform policy. An urgent task for economic reform at that time was to improve productiv-

FIGURE 5-2.   China's Financial System in International
              Comparison, 2015

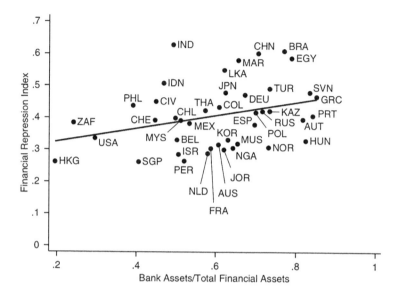

Source: Wang and Huang (forthcoming).

Note: Horizontal axis is the share of the banking sector in total financial assets, and the vertical axis is the FRI.

ity and raise output in both rural agriculture and urban industry. However, the political conditions were not ripe for drastic reform, such as privatization of SOEs. Even the successful household responsibility system reform in agriculture continued with collective ownership of land. This strategy continued to support the SOEs through the old central planning system, which ensured no unemployment and no bankruptcy, at least initially. It also facilitated the growth of private sector and market-oriented activities. This reform approach, once characterized by Naughton (1995) as "growing out of the plan," created a situation of "Pareto improvement"(i.e., nobody is worse off as a result of the reform policy).

As the private sector grows faster than the state sector, this dual-track strategy could, in theory, enable the Chinese economy to transition smoothly from a centrally planned system to a market economy. China's economic performance during the reform period was indeed impressive and was even described as the "China miracle" by Lin, Cai, and Zhou (1995). In addition to rapid economic growth, there was no initial collapse of output and loss of jobs. The SOEs' share in total industrial output declined steadily, from around 80 percent in the late 1970s to around 20 percent in the mid-2010s. However, the state sector's influence on the overall economy did not diminish accordingly. It actually caused some major macroeconomic problems, especially in the 1990s.

The main problem was that the SOEs' financial performance deteriorated continuously. SOEs could not compete with more efficient private enterprises and foreign-invested firms, even though some studies discovered that SOEs' productivity also improved over time (Huang and Duncan 1997). The gradual loss of monopoly power and increased competition quickly eroded the profitability of SOEs. By the mid-1990s, the state sector had become a net loss-maker (Huang 2001). To control bleeding, the government had to adopt a more aggressive reform program, characterized as "grasping the big and letting go the small and medium," in September 1995. The objective of this reform was for the government to focus only on the very large SOEs in strategic industries and to release all small- and medium-sized SOEs in competitive industries. After this round of reform, the SOE sector shrank significantly. Its profitability also improved markedly because most of the remaining SOEs are gigantic and enjoy a certain degree of monopoly. Problems devolving from the so-called soft budget constraint and relative inefficiency, however, continued.

Loss-making by the SOEs around the mid-1990s had at least two types of macroeconomic consequences, one fiscal and the other financial. The government almost suffered a fiscal crisis. Government revenues as a proportion of GDP declined from 36 percent in 1978 to a trough of 11 percent in 1996. This decline was partly a result of the decentralization policy. SOEs, the dominant contributor to government revenues, not only contributed less over time but also demanded more subsidies from the government. Although the private sector grew rapidly, most of the private enterprises were small- and medium-sized enterprises (SMEs), which paid little in tax. Many foreign-invested firms enjoyed preferential policies such as tax exemptions and tax concessions. As a result of the fiscal stress, some local governments were not able to cover their overheads. To alleviate the problem, in 1994 China introduced a new tax-sharing system by dividing taxes into central (such as income tax and customs duty), local (such as resource tax and stamp duty), and sharing taxes (such as value-added tax), both to strengthen tax collection and to raise the revenue share of the central government. Gradually, tax revenues as a proportion of GDP recovered to around 21–22 percent.

The banking sector also suffered severely, as the average bad loan ratio of the Chinese banks reached 30–40 percent around 1997 (Bonin and Huang 2001).[2] This was because SOEs were main borrowers from the banks. As a consequence of the soft budget constraint (i.e., without being subjected to hard market discipline), the government sometimes instructed the banks to make "stability loans" to financially troubled SOEs. Fortunately, there was no bank run, as the banks were also blanket guaranteed by the government. Since then the Chinese government has adopted a series of measures to revamp the banking sector. In 1999 it established four asset management companies to resolve the bad loans. In 2003 the authorities established the Central Huijin Investment Company to inject capital into the banks and other financial institutions. In 2005 the CCB introduced Bank of America as its first foreign strategic investor. Other banks took the same steps in the following years. And in 2006, the BOC and the ICBC became publicly listed companies on the Hong Kong Stock Exchange and the Shanghai Stock Exchange.

All these problems highlight a key difficulty in implementing the dual-track approach to reforms: many of the SOEs are unable to survive without external support. One logical solution is for the government to provide fiscal subsidies to protect the SOEs. However, as the fiscal revenues declined rapidly relative to GDP throughout the 1980s, it became clear that the government would not have enough funding to support the SOEs. An alternative is state intervention in factor markets in favor of the SOEs, in terms of both pricing and the allocation of production factors. For instance, if the government could instruct the banks to continue to allocate large volumes of cheap credit to SOEs, then SOEs could survive even if their performance continued to deteriorate.

This was probably the logic behind the "asymmetric liberalization" of product and factor markets (Huang 2010; World Bank and Development Research Center of the State Council, PRC 2012). On the one hand, the government almost completely liberalized markets for agricultural, industrial, and service products, whereby prices are freely determined by demand and supply. This regime allows producers to identify market demand and profitable opportunities. With an open trade regime, Chinese industries can also easily participate in international competition. On the other hand, markets for production factors, including labor, capital, land, and energy, remained heavily distorted, and the government continued to intervene in their allocation and pricing. These distortions in the factor markets ensure that SOEs receive needed inputs at favorable prices. They are de facto subsidies. For instance, SOEs are often in privileged positions when purchasing energy products from the state power grid or the state-owned oil companies. The private enterprises either would not be able to acquire enough inputs or would have to pay higher prices. The asymmetric liberalization approach between product and factor markets functions as a necessary policy instrument to support the dual-track reform between the state and nonstate sectors.

Repressive financial policies played an essential role in the outcome of factor market distortion and were important instruments to ensure subsidies went to the SOEs. Without these policies, the less efficient SOEs would have been eliminated by competition long ago. Repressive financial policies also led to segmentation of the financial system into a formal sector and an informal sector. In the formal sector, the authorities depressed the cost of capital and allocated funds in favor of the SOEs. This simply pushed a lot of non-SOEs out of the formal sector and caused the funding costs in the informal sector to become exceptionally high. Therefore, though China has developed a very large financial system, undersupply of financial services remains a serious challenge, especially for private enterprises. This is also why, in recent years, shadow banking and the fintech industry have expanded very rapidly. To a large extent, these developments were responses to financial repression in the formal sector. In many cases, they may even be regarded as a form of back-door liberalization of interest rates and other policy distortions because they bypass both regulations and restrictions in the formal sector.

POSITIVE AND NEGATIVE EFFECTS OF FINANCIAL REPRESSION

China's repressive financial policies appeared to represent a policy compromise, at least initially. They were necessary conditions for the SOEs to survive. But how did they affect China's economic performance during the reform period? On the surface, those policies did not prevent the economy from achieving rapid growth and financial stability. But the fundamental question remains: Did the Chinese economy achieve those successes because of or despite the repressive financial policies? Answering this question might help us understand the mechanisms through which repressive financial policies affect economic and financial performance. It could even help us think about policy choices for China today, and for other developing countries.

In an earlier study, Huang and Wang (2011) tried to quantify the impact of financial repression on economic growth in China during 1979–2008 by constructing a financial repression index using provincial data. They first looked at the three-decade period as a whole and found a positive impact; that is, financial repression promoted economic growth. They then looked at three subperiods separately and found that whereas financial repression promoted economic growth in the 1980s and 1990s, it became a negative drag in the 2000s. According to their study, if there had been full financial liberalization, real GDP growth would have been reduced by 0.79 percentage points in the 1979–1988 period and by 0.31 percentage points in the 1989–1999 period. But growth would have increased by 0.13 percentage points in the 1999–2008 period.

The positive effect discovered for the 1980s and 1990s was consistent with George Stiglitz's (1994) reasoning. In the early stages of economic development, financial markets are often underdeveloped, and might not be able to channel savings into investments effectively. Also, financial institutions are often immature and vulnerable to fluctuations in capital flows and financial stability. State intervention in the form of repressive financial policies can actually promote economic growth by building confidence and supporting the effective conversion of saving into investment. Today, China is the only major economy in the world that has never experienced a serious financial crisis. This is mainly because government ownership has anchored investor confidence, despite the various risks that arose in the past decades. For instance, without a relatively closed capital account, the Chinese economy would have been more seriously dampened by both the Asian financial crisis and the global financial crisis of 2008–2009.

The negative impact of financial repression on economic growth discovered for the 2000s is in line with McKinnon's (1973) analysis. State intervention in capital allocation might prevent funds from flowing to the most efficient uses. Protection of financial institutions and financial markets might also encourage excessive risk-taking due to the typical moral hazard problem. Therefore, repressive financial policies would eventually hinder financial development, increase financial risks, reduce investment efficiency, and slow down economic growth. This should be easy to understand. For instance, if less efficient SOEs continued to absorb more and more financial resources, then the efficiency of the overall economy would decline steadily. And if the government continuously provided an implicit guarantee for any financial transactions, the risks could mount quickly and eventually reach a point of blowing up the economy.

In a relatively recent study, Huang, Gou, and Wang (2014) examined the same question by using a cross-country data set for the period 1980–2000. Similarly, they also found different impacts of financial repression on economic growth at different stages of economic development. Statistical analyses revealed that the growth effect of financial repression is insignificant among low-income economies, significantly negative among middle-income economies, and significantly positive among high-income economies. Further, for the middle-income group, repressive policies concerning credit, bank entry, securities market, and the capital account significantly inhibit economic growth.

These empirical results suggest that the mechanisms through which repressive financial policies affect the economy and the financial system are complicated. The negative "McKinnon effect" and the positive "Stiglitz effect" of repressive financial policies on economic growth probably exist simultaneously in any economy (Huang and Wang 2017). The net outcome in an economy depends on the relative importance of these two effects (Huang et al. 2013). And the relative importance of these effects also changes under different economic and financial conditions. For instance, in the early stage of economic development and reform, the contribution of financial repression to economic growth through maintaining financial stability and converting savings into investment is greater than its cost in terms of inefficiency and risks. Therefore, we should observe the Stiglitz effect. As the financial system matures, the negative impact of financial repression in terms of reduced capital efficiency and increased financial risks could outweigh its positive contribution. Then we should observe the McKinnon effect.

The recent transition from the Stiglitz effect–dominated economic situation to the McKinnon effect–dominated economic situation suggests that repressive financial policies have become a main drag on economic growth. After the global financial crisis of 2008–2009, China's GDP growth slowed steadily, from above 10 percent in 2010 to below 7 percent in 2015. There is probably a mixed set of factors responsible for this growth slowdown. Cyclical factors could include sluggish global economic recovery and weak Chinese export growth. Trend factors could refer to slower growth, on average, in more advanced economies. In the meantime, financial repression still favors less efficient SOEs in resource allocation and further impedes economic growth. This points to the urgent need to further liberalize financial policies.

The repressive financial policies actually contributed to the making of the "economic miracle" during the early decades of economic reform in China. Had China completely abandoned government intervention at the beginning of the reform era, the financial system would most likely have experienced dramatic uncertainties and volatilities. Repressive financial policies probably still caused some efficiency losses, but the benefits were far greater. Equally important is that, even during that period, the level of financial repression was static. Financial liberalization continued, which should also generate significant efficiency improvement and strong momentum for growth.

OLD TRICKS NO LONGER WORK

China's economic and financial performance deteriorated markedly, especially after the global financial crisis that began in 2008. After the sharp rebound of GDP growth to 10.3 percent in 2010 following implementation of the massive stimulus package, the economy decelerated persistently to below 7 percent currently. Economists are divided on what caused this persistent slowdown. Some speculate it is part of cyclical fluctuation, while others believe it is a trend change. The most plausible explanation is probably the so-called middle-income challenge. As China's GDP per capita moved from US$2,600 in 2007 to US$8,800 in 2017, it lost the low-cost advantage. Many of the industries that supported Chinese economic development for several decades, especially the labor-intensive manufacturing sectors, are no longer competitive. To continue with robust economic growth, China now needs to develop a large number of new higher-tech and higher-value-added industries that are competitive at high costs. Therefore, what is happening in China is not just a slowdown of growth but a paradigm shift in development.

This is best illustrated by the rapidly rising incremental capital-output ratio (ICOR) in China (figure 5-3). ICOR describes the number of additional units of capital input needed to produce one unit of additional GDP. The ratio was 3.5 in 2007, and it rose to 6.3 in 2015. Rapidly declining capital efficiency is truly worrisome. It might be related to the hangovers of the big stimulus package that the government implemented before. But misallocation of financial resources became an even bigger issue after the global financial crisis. As economic uncertainties remained at escalated levels, private enterprises deleveraged, while the SOEs leveraged up, partly protected by the repressive policies and partly facilitated by the macroeconomic policies. But these led to a sharp deterioration in corporate leverage quality (Wang et al. 2016).

An even more worrisome development is the steady rise of financial risks. Although the Systemic Financial Risk Index (SFRI) fluctuates violently, it has been on the rise since 2008 and remains elevated (figure 5-4). At the macro level, at least three sets of factors contribute to the recent rise in the SFRI. First, persistent growth slowdown led to significant deterioration in the corporate balance sheet, which added to financial risks. The divergence of state and nonstate sectors' corporate leverage ratios further exacerbated the problem. In particular, in the past, the Chinese economy grew at very rapid and stable growth rates. The authorities were able to re-

FIGURE 5-3.   **Incremental Capital-Output Ratio in China, 1985–2017**

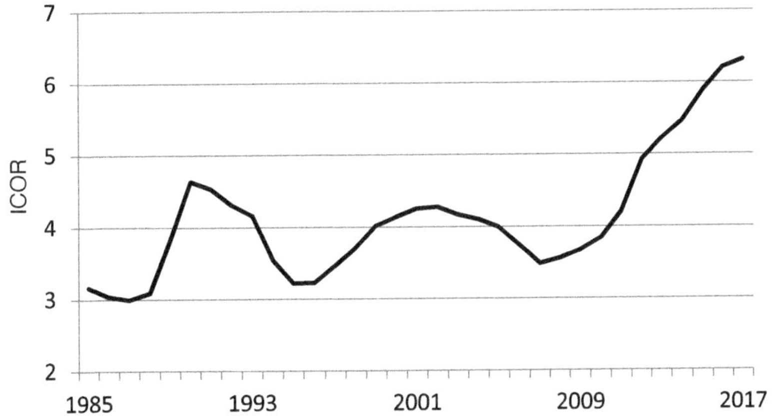

Source: Huang and others (2018).

FIGURE 5-4.   **Systemic Financial Risk Index in China,**
June 2007–June 2017

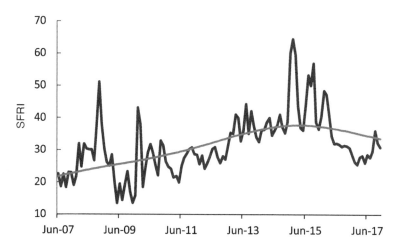

Source: Wang and Huang (forthcoming).

Note: The Systemic Financial Risk Index takes the weighted average of standardized measures of conditional value at risk (CoVaR), marginal expected shortfall (MES), and systemic risk (SRISK), using the stock yield data of 202 listed financial and property developers.

solve, or at least to hide from temporarily, any financial risk factors, even if they did occur. However, that is no longer possible.

Second, the government could no longer guarantee everything. In the past, the government could shield the economy from any major financial shocks. For instance, state ownership ensured that there was no bank run in the late 1990s, even when one-third of banks' loans were nonperforming. This is no longer possible, partly because the potential liabilities are much greater today. Total banking assets are already more than 300 percent of GDP, while corporate debts are about 240 percent of GDP. More important, government liabilities, especially borrowing by the local governments and their affiliated investment platforms, have already become a source of financial risk.

Finally, the segregated financial regulatory regime could no longer keep financial risks under control. The division of labor is for the central bank and the industry regulatory commissions to be responsible for one financial sector and follows the principle that whoever issues the license should be responsible for regulation. This regulatory model worked reasonably well for quite a while. But when shadow banking transactions grew, regulatory gaps quickly emerged. For example, who should be responsible for regulating banks selling insurance products? Even worse, a lot of fintech companies started businesses without applying for a license. In addition, all regulators are responsible for both financial regulation and industry development, which, at times, can create conflict-of-interest situations for the regulatory officials.

The Chinese financial system also became inadequate in serving the real economy. On the one hand, Chinese households receive little return on their financial assets. Total household financial assets rose from 24.6 trillion yuan in 2006 to 118.6 trillion yuan in 2016. Unfortunately, households have very limited options for investment. Currently about 69 percent of household financial assets are in bank deposits, 20 percent are in securities products, and 11 percent are in pension and insurance products. The proportion of total household financial assets held in bank deposits was much lower in other countries: 53 percent in Japan, 36 percent in Western Europe, and 14 percent in the United States. On the other hand, as the growth model shifts from mobilizing inputs to relying on innovation, the traditional bank-dominated and highly repressive financial system is no longer appropriate. Innovation and industrial upgrading are much more uncertain and risky than simple expansion of manufacturing capacity. It requires technical expertise and financial flexibility in providing financial services to support economic development.

BUILDING A MODERN FINANCIAL SYSTEM

These observations explain why, in recent years, complaints about the financial system increased significantly. One complaint frequently heard is that finance no longer strongly supports the real economy; another is that funding for SMEs is too difficult to obtain and too expensive. The real cause behind this shift is that while the economy entered a new phase of development, from input-driven to innovation-driven growth, the financial system has not yet adapted to it. The current financial system, which is characterized by high degrees of both bank dominance and government intervention, is suitable for supporting large enterprises, manufacturing activities, and extensive growth. Its main approaches to risk assessment include historical balance sheet data, collateral assets, and government guarantee. Those approaches were why it worked reasonably well during the early decades of economic reform, despite the potential efficiency losses.

But now the economic growth model is shifting toward being more innovation-driven, and the main contributors of innovation are the private enterprises, which account for about 70 percent of total corporate-level patents. The financial system, however, is not capable of handling the funding needs of such SMEs without historical data, collateral assets, and government guarantee. Some repressive financial policies make the situation even worse. For instance, the banks still face important restrictions in setting lending rates. Even worse, the authorities often require the banks to further lower lending rates to SMEs. Without the ability to conduct market-based risk pricing, it is very difficult for financial institutions to provide financial services to the more risky SMEs.

All these difficulties suggest that whatever financial system worked in supporting economic growth and financial stability in China has reached its limits. Additional reforms are now necessary to support continued robust economic development. China needs to build a modern financial system. The ultimate goal is to establish a system that can both efficiently allocate financial resources and control financial risks. In the near term, the financial system needs to work out ways of supporting innovation, especially innovation by SMEs. But it is also tricky: what does "modern" mean in this case? On the one hand, while China has been pushing ahead with the market-oriented financial reforms for the past four decades, the task is, at most, only half complete. And many nonmarket mechanisms have become obstacles to improving financial efficiency and stability. Therefore, a central mission in building the modern financial system should be to introduce more "market mechanisms." On the other hand, China should probably not implement the forthcoming reforms in a "big bang" fashion. As we demonstrate in this chapter, market-oriented liberalization works well only if market mechanisms and financial regulation can work effectively. But both of these will take some time; therefore, a gradual approach may still be preferred, although in some areas more drastic transitions could be desirable.

Market-oriented financial reforms should focus on three areas, the first being to develop multilayer capital markets. China's financial system is bank-dominated and may remain so for a long time. But it is critical now to increase the role of the capital markets. This is necessary to provide an asset-based income for Chinese households. Direct finance is also critical to support innovation and industrial upgrading. Relatively speaking, venture capital and private equity funds are much more capable of identifying good startup firms and taking informed risks. Larger capital markets might also better serve the long-term capital needs of large enterprises, which would leave more banking resources for the SMEs. Even though China's financial system will likely remain bank-dominated for the perceivable future, non-bank financial institutions should play a greater role in supporting future economic development, especially through funding of innovation-based activities.

The second area is letting market mechanisms play decisive roles in allocating financial resources. The negative consequences of government interventions become clearer now. Artificially extending the life of zombie firms, for instance, not only worsens financial efficiency, it also hinders industrial upgrading (Tan, Huang, and Woo 2016). One critical area of market-oriented reforms is interest rate liberalization. Market-based risk pricing is the basis of commercially sustainable financial services. If the government wants banks to lend more to SMEs, it should not at the same time ask the banks to lower their lending rates. Market-determined interest rates are important not only to improve financial efficiency and reduce financial risks but also to ease the path for financial institutions to serve SMEs. Market-oriented financial reform, however, depends on changes in other areas, particularly SOE reforms.

The third effort is to improve the regulatory system to prevent a systemic financial crisis. A key challenge here is incompatibility between the segregated regulatory system and the growing cross-industry financial transactions. The institution-based regulatory approach leaves many risks exposed, such as cross sales of financial products, shadow banking transactions, and fintech activities. The authorities have started taking actions to reform the regulatory system. The State Council established the Financial Stability Development Committee in mid-2017 and combined the banking and insurance regulatory commission in early 2018 to strengthen policy coordination and improve regulation quality. It is unclear yet which regulatory model China will eventually adopt, but the "twin peak" model, which separates prudential regulation and behavior regulation, looks promising for the moment.

In addition, some financial innovation may also be helpful, especially in the areas of fintech. For instance, the main reason why it is difficult for financial institutions to serve SMEs is because it is difficult both to obtain customers and to assess risks. The Chinese fintech companies, by establishing big-tech platforms and accumulating big data, have found some ways of solving the above problems. MYBank, which was dominated by Ant Financial, was able to serve 15 million SMEs within the first four years after it was established. All the loans were unsecured and uncollateralized. The bank simply relies on big data analysis to make lending decisions, and the nonperforming loan ratio is kept below 1.5 percent. Such new financial models in lending, insurance, and wealth management could be extended to the traditional financial institutions to better serve customers and better manage risks.

NOTES

This chapter was prepared as part of the National School of Development at Peking University and the Brookings Institution Joint Research Project, "China 2049: Dealing with the Challenges of a Rising Global Economic Power," and draws heavily on the author's earlier research, especially Huang and Ge (2019) and Wang and Huang (forthcoming).

1. The CCB was called the People's Construction Bank of China until 1996.

2. At that time, China used a four-category bad loan classification system. After the Asian financial crisis, it adopted the international standard five-category loan classification system.

REFERENCES

Bonin, J. P., and Y. Huang. 2001. "Dealing with the Bad Loans of the Chinese Banks." *Journal of Asian Economics* 12 (2): 197–214.

Fan, G. 1994. "Incremental Changes and Dual-Track Transition: Understanding the Case of China." In "Lessons for Reform," supplement to *Economic Policy* 9 (19): 100–22.

Huang, Y. 2010. "Dissecting the China Puzzle: Asymmetric Liberalization and Cost Distortion." *Asia Economic Policy Review* 5 (2): 281–95.

———. 2001. *China's Last Step across the River: Enterprise and Banking Reforms.* Canberra: Asia Pacific Press.

Huang, Y., and R. Duncan. 1997. "How Successful Were China's State Sector Reforms?" *Journal of Comparative Economics* 24 (1): 65–78.

Huang, Y. and T. Ge. 2019. "Assessing China's Financial Reform: Changing Roles of Repressive Financial Policies." *Cato Journal* 39 (1): 65–85.

Huang, Y., Q. Gou, and X. Wang. 2014. "Financial Liberalization and the Middle-

Income Trap: What Can China Learn from the Multi-Country Experience?" *China Economic Review* 31(C):426–40.

Huang, Y., and X. Wang. 2017. "Building an Efficient Financial System in China: A Need for Stronger Market Discipline." *Asian Economic Policy Review* 12 (2): 188–205.

———. 2011. "Does Financial Repression Inhibit or Facilitate Economic Growth? A Case Study of China's Reform Experience." *Oxford Bulletin of Economics and Statistics* 73 (6): 833–55.

Huang, Y., X. Wang, B. Wang, and N. Lin. 2013. "Financial Reform in China: Progress and Challenges." In *How Finance Is Shaping the Economies of China, Japan, and Korea*, edited by Y. C. Park and H. Patrick, 44–142. New York: Columbia University Press.

Huang, Y., J. Yin, Z. Xu, Z. Ji, L. Hong, G. Sun, and B. Zhang. 2018. *The 2018 Jingshan Report: Strengthening Market Mechanisms to Build a Modern Financial System*. Bejing: China Finance 40 Forum.

Lardy, Nicholas R. 1998. *China's Unfinished Economic Revolution*. Washington, DC: Brookings Institution Press.

Lin, J. Y., F. Cai, and L. Zhou. 1995. *The China Miracle: Development Strategy and Economic Reform*. Hong Kong: Chinese University of Hong Kong Press.

McKinnon, R. I. 1973. *Money and Capital in Economic Development*. Washington, DC: Brookings Institution Press.

Naughton, B. 1995. *Growing Out of the Plan: Chinese Economic Reform 1978–93*. Cambridge: Cambridge University Press.

Stiglitz, J. E. 1994. "The Role of the State in Financial Markets." Washington, DC: World Bank Group.

Tan, Y., Y. Huang, and W. Woo. 2016. "Zombie Firms and Crowding-Out of Private Investment in China." *Asian Economic Papers* 15 (3): 32–55.

USTR. 2018. "Section 301 Report into China's Acts, Policies, and Practices Related to Technology Transfer, Intellectual Property, and Innovation." Office of the United States Trade Representative, Washington, DC, March 27, 2018.

Wang, X., and Y. Huang. Forthcoming. "Large in Size, Strong on Repression and Weak in Regulation: China's Financial Reform during 1978–2018." In *China's Economic Reform and Development: 1978–2018*, edited by F. Cai, Brill Academic Publishers.

Wang, X., Y. Ji, Y. Tan, and Y. Huang. 2016. "Understanding the State Advancing and the Private Sector Retreating in Corporate Leverage in China." Paper presented at the NBER-CCER Conference on China and the World Economy, Peking University, Beijing.

World Bank and Development Research Center of the State Council, PRC. 2012. *China 2030: Building a Modern, Harmonious, and Creative Society*. Washington, DC: World Bank Group.

6

Reforming the Fiscal System

SHUANGLIN LIN

Public finance plays multiple roles in a country. It makes public goods accessible, redistributes income, maintains economic stability, and stimulates economic growth. In addition, public finance in China has a primary role in maintaining political continuity and stability. Thus, public finance serves not only as a means to achieve economic efficiency and distributional equity but also, for China, a political goal. That function, which the government emphasizes, determines the public finance system and its reforms. With population aging, however, China's public finance faces serious challenges in the next three decades. This chapter elucidates these challenges and offers policy suggestions for public finance reform.

The challenges to China's public finance are closely related to the major challenge faced by China in the twenty-first century, population aging. This problem is more severe in China than in other countries, in part because of the strict one-child policy China imposed beginning in the early 1980s to control population growth, and in part because of the declining birth rate of adults born during the two baby booms. As a result, the baby boom generation has produced many fewer children than the baby boom generations of other countries. Meanwhile, life expectancy at birth is increasing rapidly in China, from 65.86 years in 1978 to 76.25 years in 2016.[1] Based on a 2019 projection by the United Nations, the population aged sixty-five or older in China will account for 12 percent of the total population in 2020,

14 percent in 2025, and 20.7 percent in 2035—almost equal to that of the United States (21.2 percent)—and 26.3 percent in 2050, much higher than the 22.1 percent in the United States.[2]

The low growth rate of the population results in low growth of the labor force, which in turn is visible in the slower growth of the economy. Economic growth affects tax revenue growth because many taxes rely on output. In the first decade of the 2000s, the average growth rate of total tax revenues at the constant retail price was 16.9 percent, with real GDP growth at 12.8 percent; from 2010 to 2017, the growth rate of tax revenues at a constant retail price was only 8.9 percent, and average real GDP growth was 8.3 percent (National Bureau of Statistics of China 2019). Clearly, as economic growth slowed, so also did tax revenues. More economic slowing will bring further declines in tax revenue growth. In particular, the growth of social security contributions will decline with the decline in labor force growth.

As more citizens move into senior status, government expenditures on healthcare and social welfare programs will rapidly increase. Because of China's severe pollution problem, government expenditures on environmental issues and technologies will also increase. Meanwhile, infrastructure expenditure will grow as urbanization proceeds. Thus the general fiscal debt, social security debt, and health insurance debt may increase significantly.

China is unprepared for these challenges. Currently the government has accumulated a large amount of social security debt. Li and Lin (2019) show that China's social security debt accounted for 1.6 percent of GDP in 2015. By contrast, in 2016 the accumulated social security fund in the United States accounted for 15.3 percent of GDP (the United States has accumulated a large amount of funds in its social security account) (U.S. Social Security Administration n.d.). China's general fiscal debt has been increasing, accounting for 16 percent of GDP in 2016. Local government debt is very high. Adding up the debt that local government is responsible to pay, local government guaranteed debt, and debt that the local governments are responsible to assist, local government debt reached 35 percent of GDP in 2016. The ability of local governments to repay the debt in some regions is very low since local governments have limited revenues but undertake enormous expenditure responsibilities. Central government branches, government institutes, and the government-run Railway Corporation have also accumulated a large amount of debt, accounting for more than 5 percent of GDP. It is believed that the local governments also have accumulated a large amount of implicit debt in recent years through their private-public partnership investment projects. An article in *The Economist* warned that local government debt is a time bomb that could destroy the Chinese economy if not defused (S.R. 2015). Paul Krugman has argued that the Chinese economy is based on unsustainable levels of investment and has a serious internal debt problem (Haas and Tost 2016). The International Monetary Fund has warned that an economic crisis in China could result in a worldwide recession because of China's close economic links with the rest of the world (Grandhi 2016).

To deal with these challenges, China needs fiscal reforms, including tax reform, social security reform, healthcare reform, local public finance reform, and reform of central and local government's fiscal relationship.

This chapter explores the fiscal challenges China faces now and over the next three decades and discusses various options for coping with these challenges. The chapter first analyzes the problems embedded in the tax system and explains the needed tax reforms. The next two sections take up the problems dogging the urban and rural social security systems and healthcare systems and discuss ways to solve these problems. A discussion of the size and distribution of local government debt among regions follows, with some suggestions for reducing local government debt. The conclusion section summarizes all of the policy recommendations provided in this chapter and looks forward to the prospect of fiscal reforms.

IMPROVING THE TAX SYSTEM

The Slowing Growth of General Fiscal Revenues

The decline in labor force growth will cause a decrease in the GDP growth rate, and thus a decrease in the growth rate of general fiscal revenue. Figure 6-1 shows the level of real general fiscal revenue and the growth rate of real general fiscal revenue at a 1978 constant retail price, as well as the growth rate of GDP. The growth rate of real general fiscal revenue shows a generally declining trajectory: it was 19.16 percent in 2011, 10.67 percent in 2012, 8.67 percent in 2013, 7.56 percent in 2014, 8.38 percent in 2015, 4.02 percent in 2016, and 6.93 percent in 2017. Meanwhile, the growth rate of real GDP was 9.6 percent in 2011, 7.9 percent in 2012, 7.8 percent in 2013, 7.3 percent in 2014, 6.9 percent in 2015, 6.7 percent in 2016, and 6.8 percent in 2017. Clearly, the growth rate of fiscal revenue and the growth rate of GDP are positively correlated. Thus, in the next three decades, fiscal revenue growth is expected to slow further, along with slower growth of the economy.

The Current Tax Structure

China's tax system is based on consumption taxes with the value-added tax (VAT) being the largest tax and the consumption tax, which is similar to the excise tax in the United States, being the third-largest tax. The corporate income tax is large, the personal income tax is small. Figure 6-2 shows the share of major taxes in total tax revenue from 1994 to 2018. In 2018 the share of VAT in total tax revenue was 39.34 percent, the share of the consumption tax was 6.8 percent, the share of the corporate income tax

FIGURE 6-1.   **Real General Fiscal Revenue and Its Growth Rates, 1978–2017 (billions of yuan, at 1978 constant retail price)**

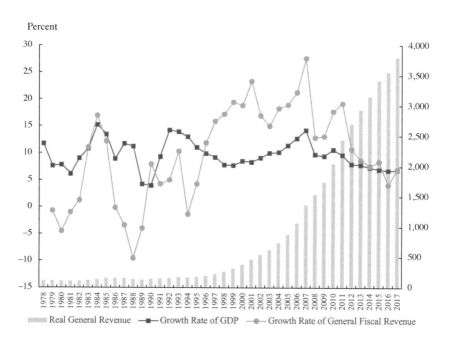

Source: Data from National Bureau of Statistics of China.

was 22.58 percent, the share of the personal income tax was 8.87 percent, and the share of tariffs was only 1.82 percent. The trend of change shows that the share of VAT in total tax revenue began to decline since 1994, then increased after being merged with the business tax in 2016. The consumption tax has remained at a high level. The corporate income tax is growing rapidly, and its share in total tax revenue has increased since the 1994 tax reform. The share of personal income tax in total revenue is increasing but still low compared to that of the corporate income tax.

China's current tax structure favors savings, investment, and growth, but not income redistribution. The reason is clear. Income is equal to consumption plus savings (equal to investment in equilibrium). Taxing income implies that both consumption and savings are taxed, while taxing consumption implies that savings are exempted from taxation. A consumption tax is usually a flat tax, while an income tax is normally a progressive tax. In China, the VAT rate for some products, such as food, is indeed lower than

FIGURE 6-2.   **Share of Major Taxes in Total Tax Revenue, 1994–2018**

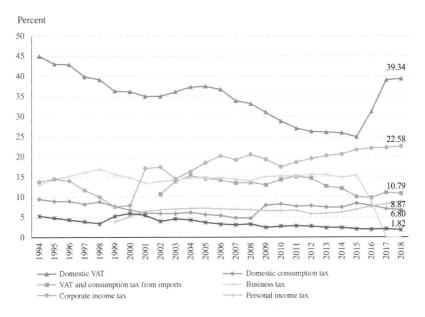

Sources: Data for 1994–2016 are from the China National Bureau of Statistics. Data for 2017 are from the Ministry of Finance of China. Data for total tax revenue and revenue from various taxes in 2018 are from the Ministry of Finance of China.

for other products. Nevertheless, the VAT is much less progressive than the individual income tax and is not effective in redistributing income.

The VAT and other consumption-based taxes are implicit taxes; that is, the tax is included in product prices and consumers just pay the prices listed and do not see the taxes. The individual income tax is an explicit tax, and taxpayers know how much income they earn and how much tax they pay. Like many governments in China's history, the current government prefers implicit taxes.

Currently the government intends to increase the revenue from individual income tax, but also tries to avoid taxpayers' revolt. Thus the exemption level is high and the tax rates for low- and middle-income groups are low. In 2011 only 7.7 percent of income receivers paid income taxes in China (Wang 2011). It might be lower now after the increase in the income exception level in August 2018. If the government keeps doing this, individual income tax revenue may not increase substantially.

Corporate income tax is too high in China. In the last three decades, most countries have lowered their tax rates on corporate income to stimulate economic growth. However, in China, corporate income tax as a share of total tax has increased considerably. The revenue from corporate income tax accounted for 13.86 percent of total tax revenue in 1994, 7.94 percent in 2000, and 22.13 percent in 2016 (NBS 2018). The revenue from corporate income tax accounted for only 5.3 percent of total tax revenue in Germany and 8.3 percent in the United States in 2016 (OECD 2018b). For the purpose of obtaining adequate revenue, the Chinese government is reluctant to reduce corporate income tax.

Prospective Tax Reforms

If the government considers economic efficiency and distributional equity as priorities, then the following tax reforms should occur in China in the future. These reforms may include: making the tax system more transparent, lowering corporate income tax rates, increasing the share of individual income tax in total tax revenue, and establishing a property tax.

Make the Tax System More Transparent. Transparency is one of the principles of taxation proposed by Adam Smith in *The Wealth of the Nations*. As various thoughts of modern public finance are being introduced, China will eventually accept the tax principle of transparency. Instead of treating some information on public finance as secret, the government should let people know clearly what taxes they pay, how much taxes they pay, and how the tax revenues are utilized.

Cut Corporate Income Tax Rates. Studies show that the corporate income tax is most detrimental to economic efficiency (see Chamley 1986; Lucas 1990; OECD 2015). China's corporate income tax rate is 25 percent, which is not especially high compared to other countries' rates. In the United States, the top federal corporate income tax rate was 35 percent in 2017, but it was reduced to 21 percent in 2018; and the state corporate income tax rate was between 0 and 10 percent in 2018. The corporate income tax rate was 29.65 percent in Germany in 2016, 23.4 percent in Japan in 2016, and 20 percent in the United Kingdom in 2016 (OECD 2018b). Although the corporate income tax rate is not high in China, the revenue from corporate income taxes is very high in China because of limited deductions. For example, only 60 percent of entertainment expenditures can be deducted from a company's taxable income, and it cannot exceed 5 percent of revenue. Only donations to nonprofit organizations and government organizations can be deducted from taxable income, and they cannot exceed 12 percent of corporate profit. In the future, China should cut the corporate income tax rate and increase deductions. The revenue from corporate income tax should be reduced by 30–50 percent.

Increase the Share of Individual Income Tax in Total Tax Revenue. Currently the revenue from individual income taxes is low. The starting level of income to be taxed is over 5,000 yuan, which is rather high. With the current deduction of 5,000 yuan, more than 90 percent of income receivers do not pay individual income taxes–and extremely high percentage. In the United States in 2015, about 45 percent of people (including retirees) in the United States did not pay income taxes, and this figure is expected to decline in the future (Williams 2016). The Chinese government should collect individual income tax from more people.

In addition, the top marginal tax rate is too high. The tax rate ranges from 3 percent to 45 percent. The range of the marginal tax rate is 10–37 percent in the United States, 2–22 percent in Singapore, and 2–17 percent in Hong Kong in 2018. Li, Li, and Lin (2016) examined the optimal individual income tax rates and demonstrated that China's individual income tax should be rather flat, with the highest marginal tax rate at about 25 percent. In the next three decades, the highest marginal tax rate should be reduced to below 30 percent, and more people should be required to pay taxes. These steps would significantly increase tax revenues from individual income taxes.

Establish Property Taxes. Personal houses, apartments, and cars, as well as other properties, should be subject to property taxation. Currently, a personal house tax is being levied on an experimental basis in Shanghai and Chongqing. However, with low tax rates and high exemptions, the revenue from property taxes is still small. In the United States in 2018, the effective real estate tax rate varied across states; it was 2.4 percent in New Jersey, 2.32 percent in Illinois, 2.19 percent in New Hampshire, 2.02 percent in Connecticut, 0.43 percent in Alabama, and 0.27 percent in Hawaii (Kiernan 2018). It is expected that property tax will be established in China and property taxes will become a stable source of revenue for local governments.

If the government prefers to prioritize political continuity and stability as the main functions of the taxation system, then it may try to keep the tax system opaque, and tax people implicitly and not explicitly.

REFORMING THE SOCIAL SECURITY SYSTEM

The funding of the social security account is greatly affected by population aging. If current social security systems remain unchanged, in the next thirty years China will start running a large deficit in the social security account every year and accumulate a huge amount of social security debt. For sustainability, the current social security system for urban workers must be reformed and a solid social security system for rural residents must be established.

The Current Systems

China now has two social security systems, one for urban workers and the other for rural residents and urban nonworking residents. China used to have a social security system for government employees; that has been merged with the social security system for urban workers.

Establish a Social Security System for Urban Workers. According to a decision of the State Council in 2005, starting January 1, 2006, the contribution to an individual account became 8 percent of the employee's taxable wage, and the employer contributes 20 percent of the employee's wage to the social pooling account (that is, public finance). Individuals do not contribute anything to the social pooling account. A retiree could withdraw one-120th of the fund from his or her individual account each month. Thus the fund in the personal account could be used up in ten years. The social security system covers workers in all SOEs, collectively owned enterprises, foreign-invested enterprises, and private enterprises. By 2018, 69 percent of urban workers had joined the social security system. However, many rural or migrant workers cannot participate in the urban system. To stimulate economic growth, the State Council decided to reduce the contribution rate of employers from 20 percent to 16 percent beginning May 1, 2019 (State Council of China 2019).

Establish a Social Security System for Farmers. China began to establish the rural social security system in 2009. Everyone aged sixty years or older received social security income of 55 yuan per month. The funds come from the general fiscal revenue of the central and local governments. In exchange, other adult family members must contribute funds to their own individual accounts. The minimum contribution was only 100 yuan per year, with a fixed government subsidy of 30 yuan per year. In 2009 the contribution levels were 100 yuan, 200 yuan, 300 yuan, 400 yuan, or 500 yuan.

In 2014 the State Council announced a new contribution standard, with twelve levels of annual contribution, from 100 yuan to 2,000 yuan (State Council of China 2014). In 2018 the annual contribution to the individual account could be between 1,000 yuan and 9,000 yuan in Beijing; 500 yuan to 5,300 yuan in Shanghai; and 100 yuan to 2,000 yuan in Jilin, Liaoning, Heilongjiang, Zhejiang, and Qinghai. Since the contribution is not mandatory, many people choose to make the minimum contribution.

Over the years, the social security income for the rural old has been increasing. In 2018 the national standard social security income for the rural old was 88 yuan per month. Each province can set its own standard with additional money from its general fiscal revenue. In 2018 the social security income for the rural old was 710 yuan in Beijing, 930 yuan in Shanghai, 295 yuan in Tianjin, 155 yuan in Zhejiang, 148 yuan in Guangdong, 135 yuan in Jiangsu, 175 yuan in Qinghai, 150 yuan in Tibet, 143 yuan in Ningxia, 128 yuan in Inner Mongolia, 118 yuan in Fujian and Shandong, 103 yuan in Jilin, 93 yuan in Sichuan, and only 88 yuan in Shanxi and Yunnan.

In 2014 the social security system for urban nonworking residents and the social security system for farmers were merged. The urban system is for people who are not in the social security system for urban workers.

Problems with the Current Social Security Systems

Serious problems exist in the current social security systems. First, there is a large amount of social security debt in the social pooling account for urban workers. Facing a shortage of funds in the social pooling account, many regions began to appropriate funds from individual accounts, leaving a large vacancy in the personal account. Li and Lin (2019) showed that the debt in the individual accounts reached about 1.59 percent of GDP in 2015, and 23.58 percent of the anticipated funds in individual accounts had been used to pay benefits for retirees in 2015. There is no excuse for China to accumulate such a large social security debt now. China is undergoing industrialization and urbanization. Millions of rural-urban migrant workers have participated in the urban pension system, resulting in more contributors and fewer beneficiaries in the system. China's social security contribution rate for urban workers is high. Employers contribute 20 percent of wages to the social pooling account. In 2014 the pension contribution rate was 10.4 percent of gross earnings in the United States, 9.9 percent in Canada, and 17.5 percent in Japan (OECD 2015). With more young people in the system and with a high contribution rate, China's urban social security system should not have a large debt. Based on Li and Lin (2016), with the benchmark of keeping the system unchanged, the explicit social security debt would reach 68 percent of output in 2050. Recall that the government lowered the contribution rate of employers recently from 20 percent to 16 percent, which means that the social security debt is higher than previously estimated.

Second, rural social security problems are serious. One problem is that the social security income for current rural retirees is too low. According to official statistics, in 2017 the average annual expenditure per urban resident was 24,445 yuan, or 2,037 yuan per month; the average annual expenditure per rural resident was 10,955 yuan, or 913 yuan per month. A social security income of about 100 yuan per month for the rural old is not enough to live a decent life. The government has an obligation to address the current old farmers' social security system, for two reasons arising from China's history. First, China did not have freedom of migration in the 1950s, 1960s, and 1970s, and farmers were forced to stay in rural people's communes, living in poverty. Second, farmers were forced to sell their crops to the government at below-market prices to support SOEs. Thus the government has an obligation to support retired farmers, just as it supports retirees from SOEs.

Another problem with the rural social security system is that contributions by young farmers to the individual accounts are too low. A farmer who contributes 100 yuan a year will, in fifty years (setting aside interest), have accumulated only 5,000 yuan! This is far from adequate to pay basic living expenses in the ten to twenty years after retirement. After economic reforms, farmers have more freedom. They can sell their crops at market prices, and they can migrate to cities to make money. Thus the government has less obligation to younger farmers, who must shoulder more responsibility for their own old-age security. Putting aside a minimal amount of money in an individual account is not a good choice for young farmers.

Traditionally, the Chinese elderly relied on their sons for old-age support, but it is getting harder and harder for children to support their parents. First, as urbanization proceeds, many rural young have migrated to cities, and they cannot remain with their parents and provide needed services. Second, the one-child policy caused a large decline in the number of children, and a single child may not be able to support two parents. (Some provinces strictly followed the one-child policy in rural areas while others allowed a family to have more children until they had a son.) Third, living expenses in urban areas are high, such as the costs of raising children and buying a home, and people in middle age and midcareer may not have extra funds to support their parents. Relying on children for old-age support is no longer sustainable.

Reforming the Current Social Security Systems

Compared to the rates in industrialized countries, China's social security contribution rate is already high, and should not be further increased. Other ways to reduce debt in the social security system for urban workers should be considered. In addition, the rural social security system is undeveloped. The task of reforming the social security systems will be arduous, but some measures seem obvious.

Balance the Social Pooling Account for Urban Workers. This will require raising more revenue and reducing expenditures. Reducing expenditures seems inevitable. The government should reduce inequality in social security payments by reducing the amounts paid to some top social security income receivers. It should also extend the retirement age. This step will increase social security revenue and reduce social security expenditures. The current retirement ages were set several decades ago when China's life expectancy at birth was low. Life expectancy at birth has significantly increased, from 65.86 years in 1978 to 76.25 in 2016 (World Bank 2017). The decision to increase the retirement ages should be announced as early as possible so that individuals can make better retirement plans.

Repay the Debt in the Social Pooling Account and Keep the Funds in Personal Accounts Intact. One way is to rely on the fund accumulation from the social pooling account itself. Another way is to use the assets of SOEs. Theoretically, using government assets in one account to repay the debt in another account will not have any real effect. However, if the return on the SOE assets is lower than the return on social security individual accounts, then such reallocation would improve economic efficiency.

Increase Social Security Payments to the Rural Old. Low social security income for the rural old severely affects rural retirees' well-being. The rural senior cannot live a decent life on 88 yuan (about US$13) per month. In the next thirty years, government expenditure on rural social security is expected to be very large, which will increase the pressure on the general fiscal budget.

Raise the Contribution of the Rural Young to Their Individual Accounts. In 2018, the rural disposable income was 12,363 yuan. If the contribution rate is set at 8 percent, as for urban workers, then the contribution to an individual account would be 989 yuan. Urban workers also need to contribute 20 percent of their wage to social pooling accounts through their employers. Only when the contribution to the individual account is increased can the rural social security system be sustainable.

Accumulate Funds in the Social Security Social Pooling Account. The United States has done this for many years. To do so, the government will need to increase revenues and curtail expenditures. Options include extending the retirement age, reducing the excessively high social security payments to some individuals, particularly government officials, and reducing social security tax evasions.

REFORMING THE HEALTH INSURANCE SYSTEMS

The Current Systems

China has now established four different health insurance programs. In rural areas, a New Rural Cooperative Medical System (NRCMS) exists that is financed by the central and local governments, as well as by farmers, and run by the local government in each region. Three health insurance systems have been established in urban areas: the Health Insurance for Urban Workers (HIUW), which is financed by both employers and employees of enterprises and run by the local government in each region; the Government Health Insurance (GHI), for employees of government agencies and public institutions (for example, public universities and state-owned hospitals), which is financed out of government general budgetary revenue and run by the government in each region; and the Health Insurance for Urban Residents (HIUR). The health insurance program for government employees is the best among all the health insurance programs, while the rural health insurance program is the weakest. All these health insurance programs are run by the central or local governments. Recently the government has merged the NRCMS and the HIUR.

Potential Debt from the Health Insurance System

There are many serious problems with the healthcare systems, such as underdeveloped health insurance programs and high personal expenditure, particularly for rural and urban nonworking residents; underqualified medical providers and poor healthcare services; and excessive and inappropriate government intervention. Here we focus only on the problem of potential healthcare debt for the government.

Currently, all the health insurance programs have surpluses. Low reimbursement rates and low upper limits for reimbursement for catastrophic diseases have resulted in surpluses in the programs for HIUW, HIUR, and NRCMS. Figure 6-3 shows the revenue and expenditure from health insurance programs for HIUW and HIUR. In 2017, there was a surplus from the health insurance programs for HIUW and HIUR, amounting to 1,938.56 billion yuan. The latest statistics on the surplus for the NRCMS program are not available, but the surplus was 6.3 billion yuan in 2013 (Ministry of Health of China 2014).

China's health insurance programs will have deficits and will accumulate a large amount of debt in the future. The current health insurance system is run by government and is pay-as-you-go in nature. Based on current reimbursement rates, contribution rates, the population growth rate, income growth rate, and the elasticity of demand for medical services, a

FIGURE 6-3.   **Surplus in Basic Urban Health Insurance Accounts**

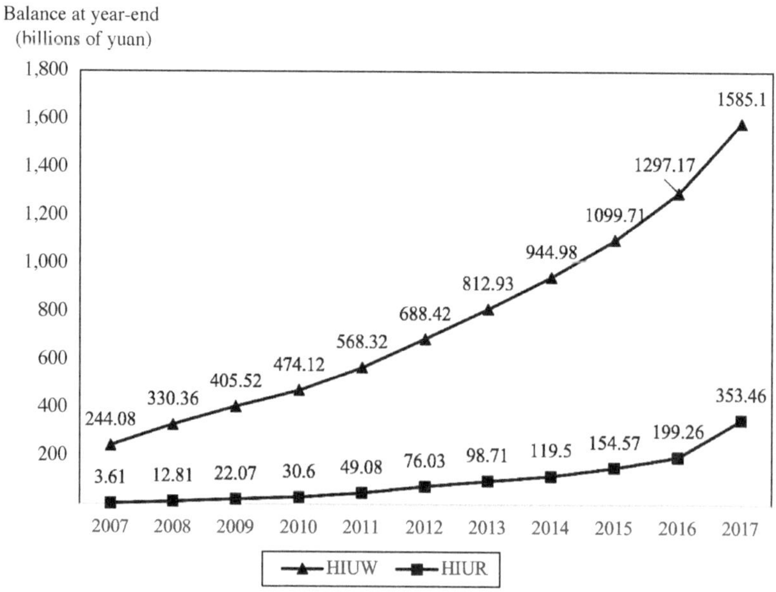

Source: National Bureau of Statistics of China, various years.

Note: HIUW, Health Insurance for Urban Workers program; HIUR, Health Insurance for Urban Residents.

2014 recent study by the Research Group of China, Center for Public Finance at Peking University, has shown that the HIUW program will have a deficit by 2022, the HIUR program will have a deficit by 2034, and the NRCMS program will have a deficit by 2050. When the three programs are combined, a deficit will appear in 2030 and debt will appear in 2041. Both central and local governments have subsidized rural health insurance and health insurance for nonworking urban residents. If the government fills the gap between the receipts and the expenditures of the HIUW program, then total government health insurance subsidies will account for about 2 percent of GDP in 2050.

The reimbursement rates for the NRCMS and the HIUR programs will have to increase in the future. Thus, payment deficits will appear immediately in these accounts. Since these two accounts are heavily subsidized by the government, government subsidies on healthcare will increase dramatically in the future. Subsidies to healthcare programs will no doubt be a heavy burden on China's public finance.

Reforming the Public Financing of Healthcare

In early 2009, the Central Committee of the Chinese Communist Party and the State Council of China announced a comprehensive healthcare reform plan (State Council of China 2009). The goal was to provide the public with safe, effective, convenient, and affordable healthcare and to extend basic healthcare coverage to everyone by 2020. The government is closing in on the goal of universal coverage. However, the following reforms are urgently needed to improve healthcare services, reduce expenditures, and maintain the financial sustainability of the health insurance programs.

Increase the Level of Health Insurance. China's healthcare programs have covered almost all individuals. At the moment, health insurance covers a small portion of expenses for rural and urban residents. In the future, China should increase the level of insurance to cover critical illnesses and severe injuries. Since the insurance premiums are rather low for the rural and urban non-working residents, China should increase the insurance premiums to maintain the sustainability of the healthcare systems. In addition to the government-run health insurance programs, China should allow private insurance companies to participate in health insurance.

Control the Healthcare Expenditures to Make the Healthcare System Sustainable. Recent decades have seen prospective payment systems (PPS), which set a fixed reimbursement level before healthcare is provided. In the United States, Germany, and many other countries, diseases are classified into diagnostic related groups (DRGs). For example, in the United States, there were 999 Medicare severity DRGs in fiscal year 2015 (Center for Medicare and Medicaid Services 2015). Each patient is assigned a DRG on admission to the hospital, and the payment is set according to the DRG classification. This gives hospitals an incentive to conserve costs. Another cost-control method used in developed countries is capitation-based reimbursement, under which hospitals receive annual payments for each patient, regardless of the services used by the patient. This method is used in private insurance programs in the United States, Germany, and other countries. China should use the DRGs and capitation-based reimbursement to control healthcare costs.[5]

Prevent the Accumulation of Debt in the Healthcare Systems. Right now, China's expenditure on healthcare is still low. In 2015, the ratio of the healthcare expenditure to GDP was 16.84 percent in the United States, 9.88 percent in the United Kingdom, 11.15 percent in Germany, 10.9 percent in Japan, 5.56 percent in Russia, and 5.32 percent in China (World Bank 2016). As the healthcare expenditures increase, China may have to increase the health insurance premiums in the future.

CURTAILING LOCAL GOVERNMENT DEBT

China is haunted by high local government debt. As the population ages, tax revenue growth will decline and government expenditures on social welfare programs will increase, resulting in increasing government debt over the next thirty years. In addition, as the population ages, social security debt and healthcare debt will inevitably increase. Thus, dealing with rising government debt is the most troublesome problem associated with structural demographic changes in the coming decades.

The Size of Government Debt

The relative size of China's central government debt is not currently high. The ratio of central government fiscal debt to GDP was 13.12 percent in 2000, 20.62 percent in 2007, and 16.22 percent in 2016 (NBS 2008, 2017). In addition to debt in the general fiscal budget, central government agencies and institutions affiliated with the central government also have debt. By the end of June 2013, the debt that the central government is responsible to pay was 76.854 billion yuan, the central government guaranteed loans were 9.383 billion yuan, and the debt that the central government is obligated to assist in repaying was 16.112 billion yuan (National Audit Office of China 2013). All of this adds up to 102.35 billion yuan, accounting for 0.18 percent of GDP, which was estimated at 56,577.16 billion yuan at the end of June 2013 (NBS 2017). Also, the Railroad Corporation has a debt of 2,294.97 billion yuan (National Audit Office of China 2013), which accounted for 4.07 percent of GDP by June 2013. Given that the debt of affiliative central government agencies and institutions and the debt of the Railroad Corporation remained stable in their ratio to GDP since 2013, it is estimated that the total central government debt-to-GDP ratio was about 20.58 percent in 2016.

Local government debt has been increasing and is high now. Based on the 1994 budget law, local governments did not have the right to issue debt. The central government occasionally issued a small amount of debt for local governments. Thus, local government debt is mainly outside the budget and comes from banks borrowing from local government-owned investment companies and from delayed payments on local government construction projects. Figure 6-4 shows the ratio of local government debt to GDP from 1996 to 2016.

Local government debt is mainly used for infrastructure development. For years, local government officials have had strong incentives to borrow for infrastructure investment. Infrastructure investment can stimulate local economic growth, which increases the chance that officials will be promoted to a higher position. Infrastructure investment also provides opportunities for officials to receive money under the table.

There are three types of local government debt: debt the local government is responsible for repaying, debt guaranteed by the local government, and debt the local government is responsible for assisting in repaying. Total

FIGURE 6-4.   **Ratio of Total Local Government Debt to GDP, 1996–2016**

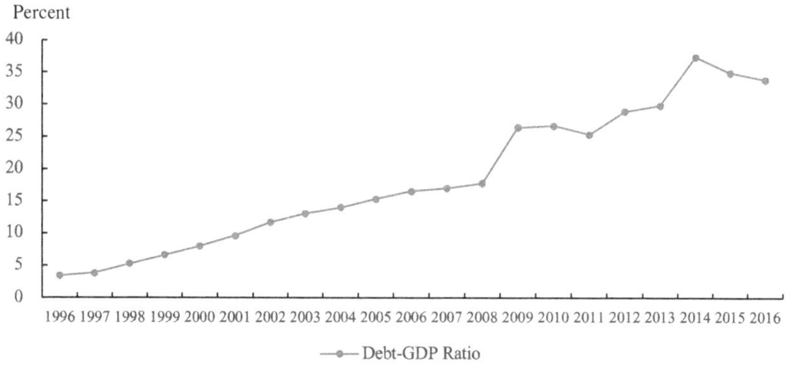

Sources: Figures before 2011 are calculated based on the National Audit Office of China (2011). Figures for 2012 and 2013 are based on the National Audit Office of China (2013). The remaining debt data are from the Wind Information and China Securities Information Network. GDP and fiscal revenue data are from National Bureau of Statistics, *Statistical Yearbook of China 2017.* For 2014, 2015, and 2016, only the data on debt for which the government is responsible to repay are available; the data on debt guaranteed by the government and debt that the government is responsible to assist in repaying are estimated based on the ratio of the debt the government is responsible for repaying in June 2013.

local government debt accounted for 26.45 percent of GDP in 2009, 29.85 percent in 2013, 37.37 percent in 2014, and 33.84 percent in 2016. After 2013, out of concern for high government debt, many local governments only published the debt they were responsible for repaying. The total debt is estimated based on the ratio of debt local governments are directly responsible for repaying and other types of debt.

Local government debt is unevenly distributed among provinces. Figure 6-5 shows the local government debt-to-GDP ratio by province for 2012 and 2016. In 2016, the ratio of debt local governments were responsible for repaying to GDP was 73.96 percent in Guizhou, 52.05 percent in Qinghai, 42.96 percent in Yunnan, 38.49 percent in Hainan, and 38.33 percent in Liaoning, while it was 5.03 percent in Tibet, 10.55 percent in Guangdong, 13.65 percent in Henan, 13.88 percent in Shandong, and 14.1 percent in Jiangsu. Including debt the local government is guaranteed to repay and debt the local government is responsible for assisting in repaying, the debt-to-GDP ratio in some provinces, such as Guizhou, exceeded 100 percent. Many less-developed provinces simply do not have the ability to repay the debt.

FIGURE 6-5.   **Ratio of Government Debt to GDP by Province, 2012 and 2016**

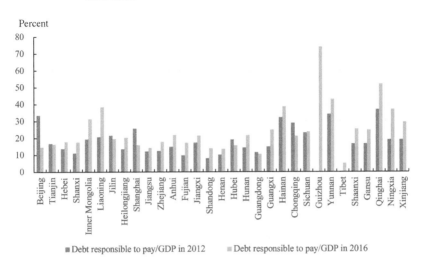

Percent

Debt responsible to pay/GDP in 2012   Debt responsible to pay/GDP in 2016

Sources: The debt data are from the Wind Information and China Securities Information Network. GDP and fiscal revenue data are from National Bureau of Statistics of China, *Statistical Yearbook of China 2017*.

Potential Problems with Government Debt

High local government debt threatens the stability of China's financial system. Currently, banks worry whether local governments will be able to repay the debt, while the local governments worry whether the banks will continue to lend to them. If heavily indebted local governments default, then the banks involved will be in financial trouble and the entire financial system will be affected.

High local government debt may not be sustainable. China's government debt may keep increasing. As the population ages, the social security debt from the social security system for urban workers as well as the system for rural residents will inevitably increase. Meanwhile, government expenditure on healthcare and health insurance will increase, and indebtedness will emerge. To deal with the economic slowdown, the government may continue to use expansionary fiscal policies, which will increase government debt. If the size of debt is large and keeps increasing, the fiscal system is clearly unsustainable.

High government debt implies high annual interest payments by the local governments. Local governments must divert limited fiscal revenues from other productive uses. As debt increases, more and more resources will be diverted to pay the interest. Eventually, the new debt issued will be just to make interest payments, and debt will become a burden on the government.

Government debt affects the economy negatively in the long run. Diamond (1965) has shown that government domestic or foreign debt increases the real interest rate and reduces capital accumulation and per capita output. Reinhart and Rogoff (2010) show that government debt, if greater than 90 percent of GDP, decreases the growth rate of output.

Coping with Rising Local Government Debt

The central government needs to curtail local government debt. First, it is necessary to put an upper bound on debt for local governments. Those with debt-to-GDP ratios higher than the limit should not issue additional debt, while those with debt-to-GDP ratios lower than the limit could still issue debt for needed infrastructure development.

Second, more tax revenue should be allocated to local governments, and local governments should be allowed to establish their own taxes. The central government may allocate more taxes, such as VAT, to local governments. If a property tax is established, the revenue should be given to local governments for infrastructure financing. In addition, the central government may allow local governments to set up taxes or fees on their own, based on local conditions.

Third, the fiscal relationship between the central and local governments should be improved. The high central government budget surplus and high local government deficits should not continue. In the future, the central government should undertake more spending responsibilities, such as taking care of social security programs, health insurance, and social poverty relief, and receive less tax revenue. China may transform from a highly centralized public finance system to a decentralized public finance system, with local governments having a higher degree of fiscal autonomy.

Fourth, the central government should help local governments repay some of the local government debt since the central government's expansionary fiscal policy led to the growth of local government debt.

CONCLUSION

Over the next thirty years, the primary role of public finance in China may change. Instead of prioritizing political continuity and stability as the main functions of public finance, the government may prioritize economic efficiency and distributive equity, just as all the industrialized countries do now. Public finance may go through many reforms.

The current consumption tax–dominated tax system may continue—and should be continued for economic efficiency. The share of individual income taxes in total tax revenue will increase, while the share of corporate income taxes in total tax revenue will decrease. New taxes, such as an individual property tax and an estate tax, will be established mainly for distributive equity, and to help with local infrastructure financing. To cope with the problem of regressiveness resulting from a heavy tax on consumption, the government needs to change the structure of government expenditure from spending an excessive amount on economic construction to spending more on public consumption goods and social welfare.

Social security debt in the social pooling account for urban workers should be eliminated by using the state assets, extending retirement ages, and reducing the excessively high social security payments to some retirees, most of whom are government officials. Social security payments to current retired farmers should be increased since the government owes this group of farmers a great deal because it eliminated the freedom to migrate in search of better-paying work and because it collected excessive amounts of taxes from them when they were young. Younger farmers should contribute more to their individual accounts for their old-age security.

Health insurance programs have a surplus now, but are expected to have deficits and debt in the future. Increases in the health insurance premiums for rural residents and urban nonworking residents are inevitable. Healthcare cost needs to be controlled by using DRGs and capitation-based reimbursement schemes. The government should switch from subsidizing hospitals to subsidizing insurance, or from subsidizing hospitals to subsidizing poor people.

Local government debt is rather high, particularly in some less-developed regions. The central government should set a debt limit for local governments and prevent highly indebted local governments from issuing more debt. The central government may also help local governments repay some local government debt since it is partially responsible for the growth of local government debt. Local governments should also be able to use the assets from local SOEs to repay debt. It is anticipated that the central government debt will be larger than local government debt in the future. Economic growth is crucial, and the debt problem will be eventually solved through economic growth.

If the state adheres to the reform and opening-up policies initiated forty years ago by some prominent reformers, the Chinese economy will continue to grow at a reasonably high rate over the next thirty years, and China will be modernized in all aspects, including public finance.

NOTES

1. World Bank, https://data.worldbank.org/indicator/SP.DYN.LE00.IN?locations=CN, Download 2/21/2019.

2. For a detailed discussion of population aging in China, see Chen, Bai and Xiaoyan Lei (2020), "Aging and Social Policy in an Era of Demographic Transition," chapter 3 in *China 2049: Economic Challenges of a Rising Global Power,* David Dollar, Yiping Huang, and Yang Yao (eds.). Washington, DC: Brookings Institution Press.

3. General Office of the State Council of China (2019).

4. See State Council of China (2009).

5. A diagnosis-related group (DRG) is a patient classification system in which the prospective payment to hospitals for a specific group of patients is standardized to encourage hospitals to contain medical costs. The government-run Medicare and Medicaid programs have been using this approach to classify patients into many different groups. Capitation is a type of healthcare payment system in which a doctor or hospital is paid a fixed amount per patient for a prescribed period by an insurance company. The private health insurance companies in the United States have been using this approach to contain medical cost.

REFERENCES

Center for Medicare and Medicaid Services. 2015. "FY 15 Final Rule Tables/Acute Inpatient PPS." U.S. Government, Center for Medicare and Medicaid Services.

Bai, C., and X. Lei. 2020. "Aging and Social Policy in an Era of Demographic Transition." Chapter 3 in *China 2049: Economic Challenges of a Rising Global Power*, David Dollar, Yiping Huang, and Yang Yao (eds.). Washington, DC: Brookings Institution Press.

Chamley, C. 1986. "Optimal Taxation of Capital Income in General Equilibrium with Infinite Lives." *Econometrica* 54 (3): 607–22.

Diamond, P. A. 1965. "National Debt in a Neoclassical Growth Model." *American Economic Review* 55:1125–50.

Grandhi, Kedar. 2016. "IMF Warns That an Economic Crisis in China Could Cause Global Recession Again." *International Business Times*, April 5.

Haas, Birgit, and Daniel Tost. 2016. "Paul Krugman: "What's Going On in China Right Now Scares Me" (interview). *Business Insider Singapore*, February 25.

Kiernan, John S. 2018. "2018's Property Taxes by State." Wallet Hub, February 26.

Li, C., and S. Lin. 2019. "China's Explicit Social Security Debt: How Large?" *China Economic Review* 53(C):128–39.

Li, C., J. Li, and S. Lin 2016. "Optimal Income Tax for China." *Pacific Economic Review* 20 (2): 243–67.

Li, S., and S. Lin. 2016. "Population Aging and China's Social Security Reforms." *Journal of Policy Modeling* 38 (1): 65–95.

Lucas, R. E. 1990. "Supply-Side Economics: An Analytical Review." *Oxford Economic Papers* 42 (2): 293–316.

Ministry of Finance of China. 2016. *Measures for the Collection and Management of State-Owned Capital Income of the Centrally Owned State Enterprises*. Beijing, July 15.

Ministry of Health of China. 2014. *China Health Statistics Yearbook*. Beijing: China Xiehe Medical University Press.

National Audit Office of China. 2013. *Auditing Report on Local Government Debt*. Beijing, December 30.

———. 2011. *Auditing Report on Local Government Debt*. Beijing, June 27.

NBS (NBS). 2018. *National Data*. Gross National Income and GDP in the Last Decade 2008–2018 (database). Beijing.

———. 2017. *Statistical Yearbook of China* (database). Beijing.

Organization for Economic Cooperation and Development (OECD). 2018. *OECD. Stat* (database). Corporate Income.

———. 2015. "Public Pension Contribution Rates and Revenues." In *Pensions at a Glance 2015: OECD and G20 Indicators*. Paris: OECD Publishing.

Reinhart, Carmen M., and Kenneth S. Rogoff. 2010. "Growth in a Time of Debt." *American Economic Review* 100 (2): 573–78.

Research Group of China, Center for Public Finance at Peking University. 2014. *Deepening the Reforms of China's Health Insurance System* (table 4.8). Beijing.

S.R. 2015. "China's Local Government Debt: Defusing a Bomb." *Free Exchange* (blog), *The Economist*, March 11.

State Council of China. 2019. "Comprehensive Scheme for Reducing Social Insurance Premium Rate." General Office of the State Council Document No. 13. Beijing, April 4.

———. 2015. *Circular on Adjusting the Proportion of the Central and Local Share of Stamp Duty on Securities Transaction*. Beijing, December 31.

———. 2014. *Opinion on Establishing Unified Basic Social Security System for Urban and Rural Residents*. General Office of the State Council Document No. 8. Beijing.

———. 2009. *Opinion on Deepening the Reform of the Medical and Health Care System*, General Office of the State Council Document No. 6. Beijing.

United Nations, Department of Economic and Social Affairs, Population Division. 2019. *World Population Prospects: The 2019 Revision.* New York: United Nations.

U.S. Social Security Administration. n.d. "Financial Data for the Social Security Trust Funds."

Wang, J., 2011. *A Speech at the Press Conference after the 21st Session of the Standing Committee of the 11th National People's Congress of China*, June 30. People.cn (People's Daily Online), http://legal.people.com.cn/GB/15043354.html.

Williams, R. C. 2016. "A Closer Look at Those Who Pay No Income or Payroll Taxes." Washington, DC: Tax Policy Center, July 11.

World Bank. 2017. "Life Expectancy at Birth, Total (Years): China, 1960–2017" (graph). Washington, DC: World Bank Group.

———. 2016. "Current Health Expenditure (% of GDP): World, 2000–2016" (graph). Washington, DC: World Bank Group.

7

Household Consumption in 2049

MIN WANG and XIUMEI YU

Individual consumption is the expenditure on goods and services that are used for the direct satisfaction of individual needs. It is considered one of the most important indicators reflective of people's living standards and welfare, as it reveals how an individual lives, including what she eats, where she lives, how she travels, and so on. Consumption is mainly determined by income, another commonly used welfare measure for individuals, but because of the permanent income hypothesis (Friedman 1957), the literature has suggested that consumption is a better measure of individual welfare because current consumption is a better guide to long-term resources than is current income (Blundell and Preston 1995; Brewer and O'Dea 2012), and income is likely to be underreported by households with low resources (Meyer and Sullivan 2003, 2008). Therefore, studying the consumption of households is crucial to understanding the welfare of the population in China.

Because the final consumption expenditure of households accounts for a large share of the national account of GDP, the study of household consumption can also shed light on China's economic growth in the future. China is now transitioning away from a growth model relying mostly on investment and global trade surplus and toward one that relies more on domestic consumption. According to the Ministry of Commerce, consumption has become the largest driving force for economic growth over the past five years, contributing 76.2 percent to economic growth in 2018, an increase of 18.6 percentage points over the previous year (Zhu and Tong 2019). Meanwhile, China is also going through consumption upgrades, mainly characterized by an increase in the consumption of services and an increase in the quality of goods and services consumed. Thus, studying changes in the structure of consumption can also shed light on the ongoing industry upgrades.

This chapter attempts to forecast household consumption expenditure in the centennial year of 2049, from the perspective of both total consumption and consumption structure. We believe that in the next three decades, economic growth, urbanization, and an aging population will be the three most important forces shaping the economy and society of China, including consumption. This chapter therefore considers the impacts of these three forces on household consumption and consumption structure.

The chapter begins by examining household consumption of the past forty years, followed by a breakdown of the consumption behavior of different population groups by region of residence (urban or rural), income level, and age. Recent household survey data are then used to predict consumption in 2049. The chapter concludes with a discussion of policy implications.

CONSUMPTION DURING THE PAST FORTY YEARS

A quick look at household consumption during the past forty years provides comparative data to use in projecting consumption in China in 2049.

Total Consumption during the Past Forty Years

Since China's reform and opening up in the early 1980s, household income has risen remarkably. One of the results has been a massive improvement in households' living standards as measured by per capita consumption. The national sampling of households conducted by the National Bureau of Statistics of China (NBS) provides comprehensive information on households' income and expenditure. We obtained the per capita income and consumption data for the separate national urban and rural household surveys from the NBS and then calculated national-level household data by using the corresponding population as the weighting factor.

Households' per capita disposable income in China was only 1,548 Chinese yuan (or renminbi) in 1981, but rose steadily to 25,929 yuan in 2017, almost seventeen times the 1981 level. (All income and expenditure data in this chapter are adjusted to 2015 prices.) The average annual growth rate of real per capita disposable income during this period was 8.27 percent. The fast growth in income drove the fast growth in consumption. Residents' per capita consumption expenditure grew from 1,355 yuan in 1981 to 18,188 yuan in 2017, or thirteen times the 1981 level. The average annual growth rate of real per capita consumption expenditure during this period was 7.63 percent.

The difference between growth in household income and growth in consumption reflects the increased household saving rate in China, which grew from 12.5 percent in 1981 to 30 percent in 2017, the world's highest saving rate. By contrast, the personal saving rate in the United States was around 6.7 percent in 2017. An ample economics literature has explored the phenomenon of the high saving rate in China from different angles, such as the dependency ratio (Ang 2009; Horioka and Wan 2007; Kraay 2000; Modigliani and Cao 2004) and future uncertainty–induced precautionary saving (Chamon, Liu, and Prasad 2013; Giles and Yoo 2007; Kraay 2000; Meng 2003).

Consumption Structure during the Past Forty Years

We now turn to examine the trend in consumption structure during the past four decades. The NBS provides data on household expenditures for eight different consumption categories: (1) Food, Tobacco and Liquor; (2) Clothing, including expenditure on clothes, clothing materials, footwear, other clothing and accessories, and processing services related to clothing; (3) Residence, which includes housing rents, water, electricity, fuel, property management, and converted self-owned housing rents; (4) Household Facilities, Articles and Services, a category that includes furniture and interior decoration, home appliances, home textiles, household miscellaneous daily articles, personal articles, and family services; (5) Transportation and Communication, including expenditure on telecommunications and vehicle purchase, maintenance, repairs, and insurance; (6) Education, Culture and Recreation; (7) Healthcare and Medical Services; and (8) Miscellaneous Goods and Services, a category that absorbs all manner of expenditure on other articles and services not included in the previous seven categories. For convenience, we use the categories food, clothing, residence, household facilities, transportation, education, health, and other goods to refer to these eight categories of consumption in this chapter. Of these eight categories, food and clothing are generally considered necessary goods.

Chinese households have undergone a great change in consumption structure over the past four decades. Since 1981, the four fastest-growing categories of consumption have been transportation, health, residence, and education. In 2017 the expenditures on these categories were 247 times, 66 times, 25 times, and 24 times the corresponding levels in 1981. The share of consumption devoted to these categories increased significantly, from 0.7 percent, 1.6 percent, 11.9 percent, and 6.5 percent in 1981 to 13.6 percent, 7.8 percent, 22.5 percent, and 11.4 percent, respectively, in 2017. In contrast, the expenditure on necessary goods, including food and clothing, increased only seven times, and the share of consumption dedicated to food and clothing decreased from 58.6 percent and 13.3 percent, respectively, in 1981 to 29.3 percent and 6.8 percent in 2017. These changes reveal a trend of consumption upgrading.

CONSUMPTION OF DIFFERENT POPULATION GROUPS

Economic growth, urbanization, and the aging of the population are the three most important factors that will determine household consumption in the future. To lay the groundwork for making projections about future consumption, we use data from the NBS and the Chinese Household Income Project (CHIP) 2013 to examine the impacts of these three factors on household consumption by exploring the consumption behavior of different population cohorts analyzed by region of residence (urban or rural), income, and age.

Household Consumption by Region (Urban or Rural)

Since the early 1980s, China has witnessed a rural-to-urban migration unprecedented in world history, with the urbanization rate increasing from 20.16 percent in 1981 to 58.52 percent in 2017. As the rapid urbanization trend is expected to continue for at least the next fifteen to twenty years, urbanization will play an important role in future consumption. In what follows, we use data from the NBS to show the differences in income and consumption between urban and rural populations.

The persistent and widening income inequality between urban and rural China is one of the most notable social phenomena (Démurger, Fournier, and Li 2006; Park 2008; Sicular et al. 2007). As shown in figure 7-1, the urban-rural income ratio was 2.24 in 1981. This ratio fell in the early 1980s as China started the economic reforms in rural areas, abandoning the communal system and adopting a household responsibility system, which gave farmers the freedom to make their own production decisions and greatly improved agricultural productivity. From 1981 to 1984, the per capita disposable income of rural households increased from 1,238 yuan to 1,847 yuan, an increase of 49.1 percent, compared to a 22.1 percent increase for urban households. In 1984 the urban-rural income ratio fell to 1.84, the lowest level of the past forty years. However, the urban-rural income ratio began to increase in 1985 as China expanded its reform into urban areas. With the exception of 1994–1997, the urban-rural income ratio continuously increased until reaching a peak at 3.14 around 2007. Thereafter, owing to the rising labor cost of rural migrant labor and supportive policies in

FIGURE 7-1.   **Income and Consumption Gap between Urban and Rural Areas, 1981–2017**

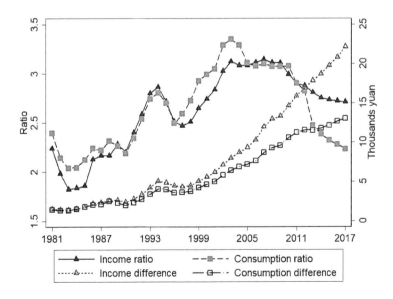

Source: National Bureau of Statistics of China (http://www.stats.gov.cn/english/Statistical-data/AnnualData/).

rural areas, the income inequality ratio continuously decreased to 2.71 in 2017. Although the income ratio between urban and rural households has been falling, the absolute income gap between urban and rural households is still increasing. In 2017, the urban resident on average earned 22,159 yuan more than a rural resident.

Income inequality drives consumption inequality between urban and rural areas. The urban-rural consumption inequality exhibits a similar trend as the income inequality. In recent years, however, the urban-rural consumption inequality has decreased faster. From 2013 to 2017, the urban-rural income ratio fell from 2.81 to 2.71, for a decrease of 0.1, while the urban-rural consumption ratio fell from 2.47 to 2.23, for a decrease of 0.24. The urban-rural consumption inequality is decreasing faster than the income inequality because the average propensity to consume (APC), the fraction of income spent on consumption, in urban areas is decreasing. In 2017, urban households consumed only 67.16 percent of disposable income but rural households consumed 81.55 percent of disposable income.

The consumption structures of urban and rural areas also differ. The share of expenditure on food and on health are both higher in rural areas. In 2017, the expenditure share on food was 31.2 percent in rural areas and 28.6 percent in urban areas, and the expenditure share on health for rural households was 2.4 percentage points greater than for urban households. The large gap in the expenditure share on health implies that, owing to the insufficient coverage of the public healthcare system in rural areas, rural households bear proportionally more out-of-pocket healthcare costs than urban households. By contrast, urban households have larger expenditure shares on clothing, residence, and education.

Household Consumption by Different Income Groups

Income plays a critical role in household consumption behavior as it determines the household's budget constraint. As China's economy continues to grow over the next three decades, income growth will likely be the most important factor determining future consumption. We used the household income and consumption data from the latest survey of the China Household Income Project (CHIP) in 2013 to study the consumption patterns of different income groups. CHIP collects detailed household and individual information in both urban and rural areas in selected provinces in China according to the sampling frame used by the NBS, and thus has national representability. We separated all household samples into five quintiles according to disposable income per capita. We first discuss total consumption by income group and then discuss the consumption structure by income group.

The income and consumption of each quintile are shown in figure 7-2. Just as with total consumption by income group, there are several findings worth noting. First, there is remarkable income inequality within urban and rural areas. In urban areas, the per capita disposable income of the top 20 percent of earners is 63,821 yuan, which is 5.9 times that of the bottom 20 percent of earners, whose per capita disposable income is only 10,842 yuan. In rural areas, the income inequality is even greater: the per capita disposable income of the top quintile is 8.2 times that of the bottom quintile. In rural areas the per capita disposable income of the top quintile is 24,561 yuan, but it is only 3,011 yuan for the bottom quintile.

Second, the consumption inequality among different income groups is smaller than the income inequality because low-income households tend to spend a higher fraction of income on consumption. The consumption ratio of the highest to the lowest quintile is 4.3 in urban areas and 3.3 in rural areas, a difference much smaller than the income ratio of highest to lowest quintiles. In urban areas, the top (bottom) quintile of earners spend 65.3 percent (89.1 percent) of their disposable income on consumption. In rural areas, consumption expenditure accounts for only 63.4 percent of disposable income for the top quintile earners, but this ratio is as high as 156.8 percent for the bottom quintile earners who consume more than what they earn and therefore have negative savings. This implies that wealth inequality is likely to be worse than income inequality because rich people tend to save a larger proportion of their income.

Third, although rural households, having a low income, have a higher APC (or a lower saving rate) than urban households overall, rural households consume less than urban households at the same income level. On average, the APC in rural and urban areas is 78.7 percent and 69.8 percent, respectively.[1] To compare the APC of rural households and urban households at the same income level, we mainly looked at middle quintile households in rural areas and bottom quintile households in urban areas, the disposable incomes of which are comparable and equal to 8,727 yuan and 10,842 yuan, respectively. If rural households share the same consumption pattern as urban households at the same income level, then the APC of rural households in the middle quintile should be larger than that of urban households in the bottom quintile. However, the APC of these two groups is 85.7 percent and 89.1 percent, respectively. This implies that rural households with the same income have a lower APC than urban households. Generally, for the same income group, rural households face greater uncertainty about future income while also lacking in social security coverage and medical care, and therefore have stronger incentive to engage in precautionary saving. This finding is further supported by comparing the APC of households with per capita disposable incomes between 10,000 and 20,000 yuan; the APC is 74.3 percent in rural areas and 79.1 percent in urban areas.

Finally, the saving rate of the lowest income quintile households is negative in rural areas, indicating that their income is not enough to cover current consumption expenditure. Macro data from the NBS also show that the saving rate for rural low-income households was negative during 2002–2012, which underscores that the negative saving rate is unlikely to be caused by year-to-year income fluctuations. The negative saving rate for these low-income households is not sustainable in the long run.

Next of interest is the consumption structure of different income groups. As income increases, the food share of total consumption decreases. This is consistent with Engel's law, which states that the proportion of income spent on food falls as income rises. The share of consumption expenditure devoted to clothing increases with income in rural areas and is an inverted U-shape with income in urban areas. The relationship between expenditure and income of the two consumption categories reveals precisely that both food and clothing are necessary goods, the consumption demand for which increases by less than income increases. In contrast, the expenditure shares on residence and transportation both tend to monotonically increase with income, reflecting that they are luxury goods, the consumption demand for which increases by more than income increases.

The relationship between income and shares of consumption expenditure spent on education and healthcare is not straightforward. An interesting phenomenon is that the consumption share spent on education is lowest for the top quintile households among all income groups in rural areas but is highest for the top quintile households among all income groups in urban areas, which may reflect a lack of relevant infrastructure in rural areas,

FIGURE 7-2.   **Consumption and Saving by Income Group, 2013**

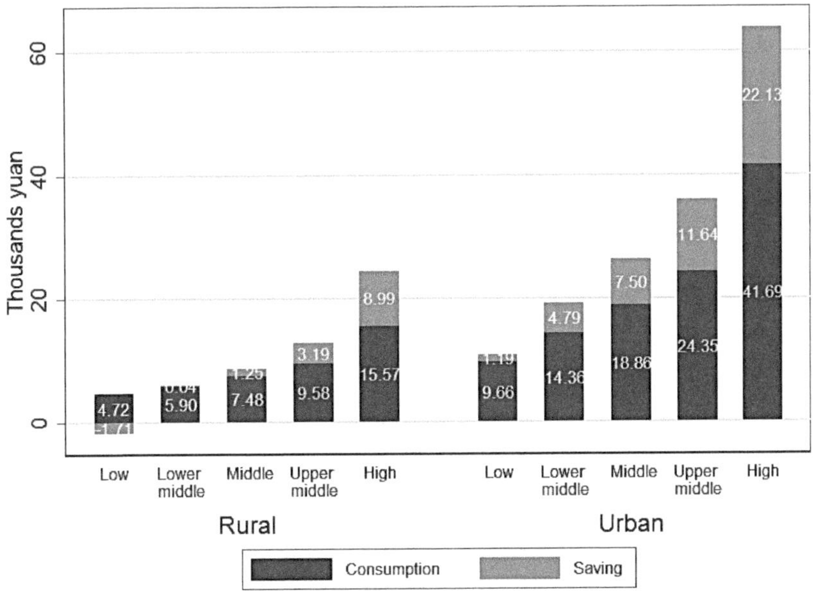

Source: Data from CHIP (2013).

which would constrain consumption. The share of household expenditure spent on healthcare shows a nonlinear relationship with income, and both poor and rich families spend proportionally more on healthcare and medical services than other income groups.

Household Consumption by Different Age Groups

Individuals have different income and consumption patterns across the life cycle. As China's population ages, future consumption will likely be strongly affected. To understand the relationship between age and consumption expenditure, we separated the household sample in CHIP 2013 into five groups based on the age of the head of the household: 20 to 29 years, 30 to 39 years, 40 to 49 years, 50 to 59 years, and those sixty and older.

Figure 7-3 shows the income, consumption, and saving behavior for each age group. For both urban and rural households, per capita income is highest among the youngest cohort (aged twenty to twenty-nine years),

FIGURE 7-3.   **Consumption and Saving by Age, 2013**

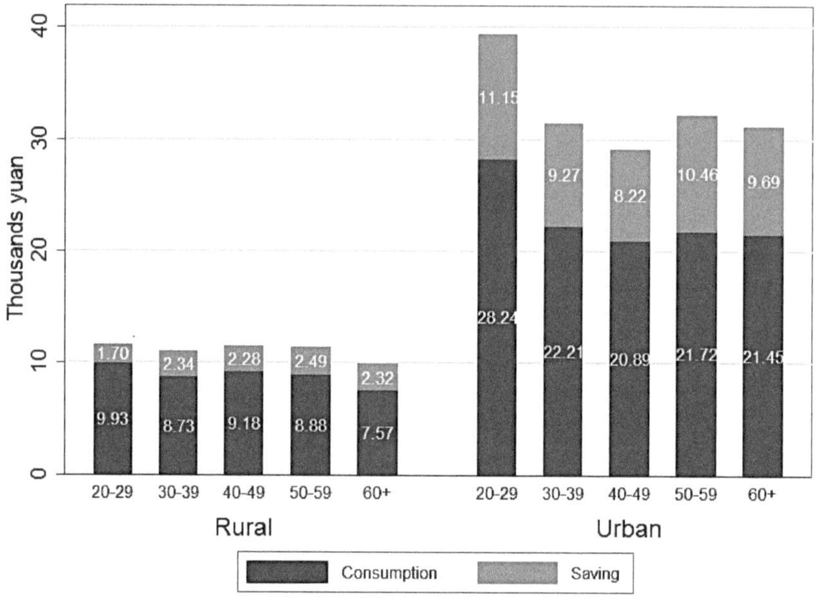

Source: Data from CHIP (2013).

then decreases, then increases a little, and eventually declines among the two oldest age groups. Such an S-shape of per capita income across different age groups may reflect the different dependency ratio during the life cycle. As rural residents generally marry and have children earlier than urban residents, rural households have rather stable per capita income across the life cycle: the per capita disposable income is highest (11,628 yuan) for those aged twenty to twenty-nine years and lowest (9,888 yuan) for those aged sixty and older. In contrast, urban households' per capita disposable income shows more variation across the life cycle. As young adults (those aged twenty to twenty-nine years) have few dependents and a high per capita disposable income, they also have the highest APC. That age cohort in urban areas spends 85.4 percent of its disposable income on consumption, versus the 71.7 percent spent in rural areas, while the average consumption rate across all age groups in urban and rural areas is 78.7 percent and 69.8 percent, respectively. According to the United Nations 2017 *World Population Prospects*, in 2015 the population of twenty- to twenty-nine-year-olds in mainland China was 231 million, second only to the forty- to forty-nine-year-old age cohort, at 243 million. Thus young adults have become an important force in the consumer market.

The consumption structure also varies across age groups. For young adults aged twenty to twenty-nine years, despite having the highest income of all age groups, their expenditure share on necessary items such as food and clothing is not the lowest of all age groups, while the expenditure shares on clothing and transportation are the highest. Unlike clothing and transportation, residence claims a smaller share of young adults' household budget compared with older age groups, though it is still the highest in dollar amount for urban dwellers aged twenty to twenty-nine years. These features may be driven by the fact that as the young just start their career, they spend more income on work-related expenses, such as clothing and a vehicle.

For the population aged sixty and older, the expenditure shares on food, residence, and health are the highest of all age groups, while the expenditure shares on clothing, household facilities, transportation, and education are the lowest. As the body declines over time, the old overall have a lower APC than younger generations and pay more for such basic life needs as food, healthcare, and medical care. The high expenditure share on residence owes to the converted self-owned housing rent, which accounts for a relatively large fraction of the elderly's budget, as houses are indivisible and illiquid assets that the elderly cannot easily exchange for cheaper ones. It's not surprising that healthcare's share in the elderly's budget is the highest of all age groups. As China's elderly population increases, the market demand for healthcare and service will be tremendous in the future.

One feature of the consumption behavior of middle-aged households is that, as they are supporting children in school or at university, education takes a large share of their budget. The education share of those aged forty to forty-nine years is 13.7 percent in rural areas and 14.2 percent in urban areas, making it the third largest consumption expenditure, after food and residence. Education expenditure is likely to be a heavy burden on this age cohort.

PROJECTION OF HOUSEHOLD CONSUMPTION IN 2049

Projection Strategy

One commonly used approach to predict future household behavior is to model households' consumption behavior using current data and then apply the model parameters to predict future values. For example, Zeng and coworkers (2015) used recent survey data to project the future home-based care needs and costs for disabled elders in China. Here we project future household consumption based on household survey data from CHIP 2013.

Our projection assumes that after controlling for income, rural versus urban residence, and age, households' consumption behavior in 2049 will be the same as it is today. In this way, we can first use the CHIP 2013 survey data to study households' consumption behavior. Then, based on the result, we can investigate the consumption changes brought about by future income growth, urbanization, and demographic changes.

We first estimated the following regressions by age and region (urban and rural) for each consumption category using the household-level data of CHIP 2013:

$$C = \alpha + \beta(I)I = \alpha + (\beta_1 + \beta_2 I)I = \alpha + \beta_1 I + \beta_2 I^2, \tag{1}$$

where C and I respectively denote per capita consumption and disposable income, $\beta_1 I + \beta_2 I^2$ is the induced consumption, and   represents autonomous consumption, defined as the minimum level of spending that must take place even if a consumer has zero disposable income. The autonomous consumption of a society is likely to increase with the average income of the whole society because people's minimum living standards rise with the development of the economy. Using China Urban Household Survey data from 2002 to 2009, we found that the average annual growth rate of households' autonomous consumption was only slightly smaller than that of their income. Hence, when making predictions, we adjusted the autonomous consumption by assuming that it has the same growth rate as per capita income.

To use the estimated coefficients in equation (1) to predict the consumption expenditure in 2049, three factors need to be taken into consideration: income growth, urbanization, and population aging.

Income growth. As shown in the previous section, growing income not only expands a household's budget constraint but can also influence consumption behavior, including the propensity to consume and the structure of consumption. Since 1981, China has experienced an astonishing annual growth rate of 8 percent in its households' disposable income per capita and 9.5 percent in real GDP. China's potential GDP is expected to sustain rapid growth in the next thirty years, with an average annual growth rate ranging from 4.8 percent to 5.8 percent (see chapter 2). Because historically, household income grows slower than GDP, we base our predication on three scenarios in which the average annual income growth rate is 3 percent (low growth), 4 percent (moderate growth), and 5 percent (high growth) during 2016–2049.

Urbanization. As discussed earlier, consumption behavior differs between urban and rural households. In concert with China's extraordinary economic boom, the country is also experiencing urbanization at a speed and on a scale that is unprecedented in human history. By the end of 2017, according to NBS data, 58.52 percent of the total population lived in urban areas, a dramatic increase from 20.16 percent in 1981. According to the 2018 *World Urbanization Prospects* (United Nations 2018), by 2050, 80 percent of China's population is projected to be residing in urban areas.

Population aging. Demographic change is another important factor that can shape an economy's consumption behavior. China's population is aging rapidly (see chapter 3). In 1990, the young population aged twenty to twenty-nine years accounted for 33.24 percent of the total population older than twenty.[2] That proportion declined to 21.61 percent in 2015 and is projected to drop to only 12.55 percent by 2050 under the medium-fertility assumption, according to the United Nations (2017). In contrast, the proportion of the population aged sixty or older increased from 14.03 percent in 1990 to 20.08 percent in 2015 and is predicted to reach as high as 43.18 percent in 2050. The proportion of the population aged fifty years or older will be 58.77 percent in 2050, indicating that one in two adults will be more than fifty years old.

Given the above assumptions, we then predicted future household consumption based on the estimated consumption functions. We first obtained the age-by-region coefficients by estimating the consumption function—

that is, equation (1)—by age groups and by region (urban versus rural). In the second step, we used the age-by-region income projections together with the age-by-region coefficients obtained in the first step to calculate the predicted value of age-by-region household consumption, taking into account the growth of both autonomous consumption and induced consumption. This step looked only at the income effect on future consumption. Third, using the predicted age-by-region household consumption calculated in the previous step and the predicted region-specific age structure, we obtained the predicted region-specific household consumption.[3] This step isolated the effects of demographic change on future consumption. Fourth, using the predicted region-specific household consumption and the predicted urbanization rate, we projected per capita household consumption in 2049. This step isolated the effects of urbanization on future consumption. Finally, we multiplied the predicted per capita household consumption by the predicted total population to obtain total household consumption in China in 2049. This step evaluated the effect brought by the change in population size.[4]

Out-Sample Prediction for Household Consumption in 2015

To test how well the forecasting strategy might perform, we first used it to predict household consumption in 2015 and then compared it with the actual, known household consumption.[5]

Estimating equation (1) by the ordinary least squares method by age groups in rural and urban areas separately for each consumption category, we obtained the consumption function for each consumption category and each age group in both rural and urban areas. According to the *China Statistical Yearbook 2016*, the per capita disposable income of rural and urban households in China was 11,422 yuan and 31,195 yuan, respectively, in 2015. Because of the lack of income information on different age groups, we assumed the same disposable income in yuan for each age group. Thus, using the estimated consumption function, we were able to calculate the consumption of each age group by rural versus urban area.

Although we assumed that household income was the same for different age groups, the predicted consumption in 2015 varies with age because of variation in consumption behaviors across age groups. For instance, the elderly, those aged 60 or older, tend to spend more on food and health than other age groups and less on clothing, household facilities, transportation, and education, as noted in the previous section. The residence expenditure of the elderly is also higher than that of other age groups, consistent with the fact that houses are indivisible and illiquid assets that the elderly cannot easily exchange for a cheaper version.

Using the age-by-region consumption and the demographic structure provided by the United Nations (2017), we calculated the per capita household consumption in rural and urban areas separately in 2015. We assumed that the age structure was the same in rural and urban areas since the data provided by the United Nations (2017) are national level. The predicted household consumption turned out to be very close to the actual value. According to our projection, the per capita consumption of rural households in 2015 was 9,244.9 yuan, which is only 0.24 percent higher than the actual value of 9,222.6 yuan. The prediction error can almost be ignored. The predicted per capita consumption level of urban households was 22,022.4 yuan, which is only 2.9 percent higher than its actual value of 21,392.4 yuan. We therefore considered that our forecasting method performed well when estimating household consumption levels. Using the actual urbanization rate of 56 percent given by the 2016 *China Statistical Yearbook*, the projected per capita consumption for the whole country in 2015 was 16,400 yuan, only 2.2 percent higher than the actual value.

We then tested how well our projection strategy performed in estimating the consumption structure. As shown in figure 7-4, the predicted consumption structure differed slightly from its actual value, but the overall trend is consistent. In both actual and predicted consumption, the three categories that account for the largest part of consumption are food, residence, and transportation, while the three categories that account for the smallest shares are other goods, household facilities, and health.

Household Consumption in 2049

We then applied our approach to predicting household consumption in 2049. In terms of household income, we forecasted the income in 2049 based on per capita income in 2015 and annual growth rates of 3 percent, 4 percent, and 5 percent. Specifically, since the per capita disposable income of urban and rural households in 2015 was 31,195 yuan and 11,422 yuan, respectively, then, in the scenario of a 3 percent annual income growth rate,

FIGURE 7-4.   **Predicted Consumption Structure**

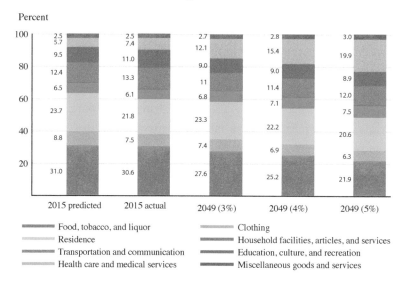

Source: The actual values for 2015 are from *China Statistical Yearbook 2016.* The predicted values represent our projections.

the per capita disposable income of urban and rural households in 2049 would be 85,222 yuan and 31,204 yuan, respectively. A similar approach was used to calculate household income in 2049 under the 4 percent and 5 percent annual income growth scenarios. The urbanization rate and age structure in 2049 were obtained from predictions published by the United Nations (2017, 2018). According to the United Nations (2018), China's urbanization rate will reach 80 percent in 2050.

Per Capita Household Consumption in 2049. We first forecasted per capita household consumption in 2049. To see the impact of different factors on per capita consumption, we changed the income, demographic structure, and urbanization rate from their values in 2015 to their values in 2049, step by step. The results are shown in table 7-1.

In the first step, we allowed disposable income to grow by 3 percent, 4 percent, or 5 percent annually based on actual income in 2015, but kept the demographic structure and urbanization rate unchanged from their actual values in 2015. Under this scenario, the per capita consumption in 2049 is projected to be 44,645 yuan, 61,872 yuan and 85,406 yuan, respectively.

Compared with the predicted consumption level in 2015, the per capita consumption in 2049 is predicted to increase significantly, and the growth of consumption is entirely driven by income growth.[6] Therefore, this part of consumption growth is called the income effect. For example, in the scenario of a 4 percent annual income growth rate, the income effect will increase per capita consumption by 45,472 yuan.

In the second step, we let the age structure of the population change to the level in 2049. Compared with the first calculation, the only additional change in this step is the age structure of the population. Hence the difference between the predicted results of these two steps is the demographic effect. China is aging rapidly, but, as discussed earlier, the consumption attitude of the young population is more liberal and their APC is higher than that of older age cohorts. Therefore, the demographic change is likely to reduce per capita consumption. This is supported by the projected results. In the three income growth scenarios, demographic change will reduce per capita consumption by 1,107, 2,024, and 3,727 yuan, respectively.

Finally, we let the urbanization rate change to the level in 2049. Compared with the second step, the only factor changed in this step was the urbanization rate, so that the difference between the predicted results of the second and third steps is the urbanization effect. There are two channels by which urbanization could affect per capita consumption. First, the consumption behavior of rural and urban households is different. Because urban households consume more than rural households at the same disposable income level, urbanization will increase per capita consumption. Second, rural and urban households have different disposable incomes. The per capita disposable income of urban households is larger than that of rural households. Therefore, the increase in urbanization will increase the proportion of the high-income population, leading to an increase in per capita consumption. From the projected results, the urbanization process will significantly increase per capita consumption. In the three different income growth rate scenarios—3 percent, 4 percent, and 5 percent—the urbanization process will increase the per capita consumption by 8,487, 11,813, and 16,403 yuan, respectively.

With these predictions in hand, we can finally calculate the predicted saving rate in 2049, which is slightly higher than in 2015 and equal to 30.1 percent, 30.7 percent, and 31.4 percent, respectively, in the three income growth rate scenarios. As the future annual household disposable income

TABLE 7-1. **Projected per capita Consumption (yuan)**

	Annual income growth rate		
	3%	4%	5%
Predicted value			
In 2015	16,400	16,400	16,400
In 2049 (age structure and urbanization rate remain the same as in 2015)	44,645	61,872	85,406
In 2049 (urbanization rate remains the same as in 2015)	43,539	59,848	81,679
In 2049	52,026	71,661	98,082
Effect decomposition			
Total effect	35,626	55,261	81,682
Income effect	28,245	45,472	69,006
Demographic effect	−1,107	−2,024	−3,727
Urbanization effect	8,487	11,813	16,403

Source: Based on authors' calculations.

on average grows at 3 percent, 4 percent, and 5 percent per year, the aggregate household saving in 2049 China will be 3.8 to 7.3 times larger than that in 2015, even if the saving rate remains unchanged. Given the fact that the household saving is the main domestic source of funds to finance capital investment, which is the major impetus for long-term economic growth, the high household saving rate in 2049 guarantees the capital supply for the economy and therefore China's long-run sustainable growth.

Aggregate Household Consumption in 2049. We are also interested in China's aggregate household consumption in 2049, as it measures the scale of the consumer markets of China, which will be the largest in the world and thus have nonnegligible impacts on the global economy. As with predicting per capita consumption, we changed factors affecting total consumption from their level in 2015 to their level in 2049 step by step, to see the impact of different factors on total household consumption. In addition to the three factors mentioned earlier—per capita income, demographic structure, and urbanization rate—the total population will also have an influence on total consumption. According to the United Nations (2017), the total population of mainland China in 2015 was 1.397 billion, and it is expected to fall to 1.364 billion by 2050. A decline in total population would be expected to have a negative impact on total consumption.

Table 7-2 presents the forecast results. Total household consumption varies a lot under the different income growth scenarios. When income grows at a rate of 3 percent annually, the total household consumption in 2049 is projected to be 71.0 trillion yuan, which is 3.1 times the predicted value in 2015. If the annual income growth rate is 5 percent, the total household consumption in 2049 will be as high as 133.8 trillion yuan, which is 5.8 times the total consumption in 2015. Both income growth and urbanization will increase total consumption, while population aging and a decline in total population will reduce consumption. Taking the 4 percent annual growth scenario as an example, the income effect and urbanization effect will increase total consumption by 63.5 and 16.5 trillion yuan, respectively. The aging of the population and a decline in total population should reduce total consumption by 2.8 and 2.3 trillion yuan, respectively.

TABLE 7-2. **Projected Total Household Consumption (trillions of yuan)**

| | Annual income growth rate | | |
	3%	4%	5%
Predicted value			
In 2015	22.9	22.9	22.9
In 2049 (age structure, urbanization rate, and total population remain the same as in 2015)	62.4	86.4	119.3
In 2049 (urbanization rate and total population remain the same as in 2015)	60.8	83.6	114.1
In 2049 (total population remains the same as in 2015)	72.7	100.1	137.0
In 2049	71.0	97.8	133.8
Effect decomposition			
Total effect	48.1	74.9	110.9
Income effect	39.5	63.5	96.4
Demographic effect	−1.5	−2.8	−5.2
Urbanization effect	11.9	16.5	22.9
Population effect	−1.7	−2.3	−3.2

Source: Based on authors' calculations.

We can also predict the consumption structure in 2049. Figure 7-4 shows the actual and projected consumption structure for 2015, and the consumption structure for 2049 under different income growth rate scenarios. Compared to the consumption structure in 2015, two significant changes in the consumption structure in 2049 are a decline in the proportion of food expenditure and an increase in the proportion of health expenditure. The share of food consumption declines from around 31 percent to 27.6 percent, 25.2 percent, and 21.9 percent in the three different income scenarios. The decline in the food share is mainly attributable to the increase in disposable income. The health expenditure share will increase to 12.1 percent, 15.4 percent, and 19.9 percent in the three income scenarios. The increase in the health share is driven by both income growth and population aging.

Our estimates of future household consumption are noteworthy in the following respects. First, our projections are based on the assumption that households' consumption behavior in 2049 will be the same as currently exist, after controlling for disposable income, rural versus urban residence, and age. In fact, with the development of society, people's consumption concepts may change. For example, the elderly in the future may have a more liberal attitude toward consumption than the current elderly because of higher educational level and growing up in a more open and wealthier China. What's more, with technological advances, people are likely to have access to more abundant consumption choices, which can also result in changes in consumption behavior. To alleviate concerns that people's minimal standards of living will also increase over time, we have allowed autonomous consumption to grow at the same rate as per capita income.

Second, our projections are based on estimates of future income, age structure, urbanization rate, and total population. Since these four variables can be affected by multiple factors, it is difficult to accurately predict their future values. Therefore, our projected results may differ from the real consumption level in the future because of the prediction error associated with these four variables. For example, the urbanization rate in the future may be higher or lower than expected. If the urbanization rate in 2049 is 75 percent instead of 80 percent, the per capita household consumption will be 3.4 percent lower under the three growth scenarios.

CONCLUSION AND POLICY IMPLICATIONS

This chapter's main goal was to predict household consumption in 2049. We first estimated the consumption functions of households by age groups in urban and rural areas separately, based on household-level data from CHIP 2013. We then projected the household consumption in 2049 based on these consumption functions and on reasonable assumptions about disposable income, demographic structure, urbanization rate, and total population in 2049. The results show that at annual income growth rates of 3 percent, 4 percent, and 5 percent, total household consumption in 2049 will be 71.0, 97.8, and 133.8 trillion yuan, respectively. What's more, the effects of income growth and urbanization on total consumption are positive, while the effects of population aging and a decline in total population are negative. The projected consumption structure shows that the share of food expenditure in total consumption will decrease in 2049 compared to that in 2015, but the share of health expenditure will increase.

Our findings have several policy implications. First, there has been widespread concern that China's rapidly aging population could pose a major threat to the country's economic future, but our work shows that even when the income growth effect is excluded, the increase in future consumption as a result of rapid urbanization is much larger than the consumption lost through population aging. The result highlights that as long as the Chinese government can successfully eliminate institutional constraints on rural-to-urban migration, such as the *hukou* system or the requirement for residency permits in urban areas, aging will not be a major threat to its future development.

Second, the predicted household consumption in 2049 is tremendously large, and Chinese consumers will have large and important impacts on the global consumer markets. This sheds some light on the current trade friction between the United States and China. Since consumption has already replaced investment as the key to China's growth, our prediction shows that China's economic growth can rely more on the domestic market and thus will be sustainable even if the export markets shrink. Moreover, our prediction suggests that the problem of the trade imbalance between the United States and China can eventually be resolved with the rise of China's domestic market. Finally, because of the scale of China's future household consumption, China will be the major export market for most countries and thus will be an important engine of growth for the world.

Third, we project that the medical expenditure share will rise remarkably in the future, but the whole healthcare system in today's China is still overburdened and struggles to cope with rising demand as it is. The large gap between the demand for and the supply of medical and health services implies that the government should deepen and accelerate reforms in the health sector to increase the capacity of the supply, such as by relaxing price regulations on medical services and streamlining the approval procedures for setting up private hospitals.

Fourth, we find that the saving rate of the lowest income group in rural areas is negative, which is not sustainable in the long run. This underscores the need for a poverty alleviation policy in rural areas to increase the income of the rural poor. In particular, the government should expand the social welfare programs, such as social assistance and social security, from the urban areas to the rural areas.

Fifth, because of the poor education infrastructure in rural areas, the households in rural areas in the highest income quintile spend the least on education, which, compared to their urban counterparts, is abnormal. Since human capital drives the growth of an economy as well as the income of households, the government should either increase its investment in education in rural areas or reform the urban-rural dual-track education system and allow rural residents and rural migrants to use and benefit from the high-quality educational services in the cities.

NOTES

1. This is consistent with the findings in the previous subsection using data from the NBS, which show that the consumption ratio in 2013 was 79.4 percent in rural areas and 69.9 percent in urban areas.

2. We consider the age structure of the population aged at twenty and older instead of total population because in the CHIP surveys, the consumption and expenditure data are reported at household level. We divided the CHIP sample into five age groups according to the age of the household head and only seven households had a household head younger than twenty years. These households were excluded from the analysis.

3. United Nations (2017) only predicts the age structure for the whole country without separating the population into the rural and urban. Hence we assume the rural and urban populations have the same age structure as the whole population in 2049, according to the United Nations (2017).

4. When making the prediction, we change per capita income, age structure, urbanization rate, and total population one by one from the 2015 level to the 2049

level. It is worth noting that changing these four variables by different order would modify the values of their effects on consumption change, but the qualitative results always remain unchanged. More specifically, changing the per capita income first would enlarge the effects of the other three variables, but given changing per capita income first, changing the order of the other three variables have rather limited impacts on the effect size. An alternative approach to estimate the effect of one particular variable on future consumption change is to calculate the difference between the consumption at the 2015 level and the consumption in the scenario of changing the value of the interested variable from the 2015 level to the 2049 level but keeping all other three variables at the 2015 level. This approach is kind of like marginal analysis, but its qualitative results again remain unchanged. Because the summation of the individual effects of income, urbanization, and aging cannot be equalized to the total effect in the later approach, we in the main text only report the results obtained from the former approach.

5. Owing to the lack of demographic structure data, we cannot make this out-sample prediction for the year 2017.

6. We compare the predicted value of household consumption in 2049 with the predicted value in 2015 instead of the actual value in 2015 because doing so helps eliminate the impact of forecasting error. Since the projection strategies are the same, the difference between the projected values for 2049 and 2015 are caused only by changes in income, age structure, and urbanization rate. Therefore we can directly decompose the consumption change into different effects. What's more, the difference between the predicted value and actual value of household consumption in 2015 is shown to be quite small in the last subsection of this chapter.

REFERENCES

Ang, James. 2009. "Household Saving Behavior in an Extended Life Cycle Model: A Comparative Study of China and India." *Journal of Development Studies* 45 (8): 1344–59.

Blundell, R., and I. Preston. 1995. "Income, Expenditure and the Living Standards of UK Households." *Fiscal Studies* 16 (3): 40–54.

Brewer, Mike, and Cormac O'Dea. 2012. "Measuring Living Standards with Income and Consumption: Evidence from the UK." IFS Working Paper W12/12. London: Institute for Fiscal Studies.

Chamon, Macros, Kai Liu, and Eswar Prasad. 2013. "Income Uncertainty and Household Saving in China." *Journal of Development Economics* 105:164–77.

Chinese Household Income Survey (CHIP). 2013 Dataset. Published by China Institution for Income Distribution of Beijing Normal University. http://www.ciidbnu.org/chip/index.asp?lang=EN.

China Statistical Yearbook 2016. National Bureau of Statistics of China (Eds.). China Statistics Press.

Démurger, Silvie, Martin Fournier, and Shi Li. 2006. "Urban Income Inequality in China Revisited (1988–2002)." *Economics Letters* 93 (3): 354–59.

Friedman, Milton. 1957. "The Permanent Income Hypothesis." In *A Theory of the Consumption Function*, 20–37. Princeton, NJ: Princeton University Press.

Giles, John, and Kyeongwon Yoo. 2007. "Precautionary Behavior, Migrant Networks, and Household Consumption Decisions: An Empirical Analysis Using Household Panel Data from Rural China." *Review of Economics and Statistics* 89 (3): 534–51.

Horioka, Charles Y., and Junmin Wan. 2007. "The Determinants of Household Saving in China: A Dynamic Panel Analysis of Provincial Data." *Journal of Money, Credit and Banking* 39 (8): 2077–96.

Kraay, Aart. 2000. "Household Saving in China." *World Bank Economic Review* 14 (3): 545–70.

Meng, Xin. 2003. "Unemployment, Consumption Smoothing, and Precautionary Saving in Urban China." *Journal of Comparative Economics* 31:465–85.

Meyer, B. D., and J. X. Sullivan. 2008. "Changes in the Consumption, Income, and Well-Being of Single Mother Headed Families." *American Economic Review* 98 (5): 2221–41.

———. 2003. "Measuring the Well-Being of the Poor Using Income and Consumption." NBER Working Paper No. 9760. Cambridge, MA: National Bureau of Economic Research, June.

Modigliani, Franco, and Shi Larry Cao. 2004. "The Chinese Saving Puzzle and the Life-Cycle Hypothesis." *Journal of Economic Literature* 42 (1): 145–70.

Park, A. 2008. "Rural-urban Inequality in China." In *China Urbanizes: Consequences, Strategies, and Policies*, 41–63, edited by Shahid Yusuf and Anthony Saich. Washington, DC: The World Bank.

Sicular, T., Y. Ximing, B. Gustafsson, and L. Shi. 2007. "The Urban–Rural Income Gap and Inequality in China." *Review of Income and Wealth* 53 (1): 93–126.

United Nations, Department of Economic and Social Affairs, Population Division. 2018. *World Urbanization Prospects: The 2018 Revision*, online edition. New York: United Nations.

———. 2017. *World Population Prospects: The 2017 Revision*. New York: United Nations.

Zeng, Y., H. Chen, Z, Wang, and K. C. Land. 2015. "Implications of Changes in Households and Living Arrangements for Future Home-Based Care Needs and Costs for Disabled Elders in China." *Journal of Aging and Health* 27 (3): 519–50.

Zhu, Jiang, and Zongli Tong, eds. 2019. "Ministry of Commerce: Consumption in 2018 Has Become the First Driving Force for China's Economic Growth for Five Consecutive Years." [In Chinese.] *People's Daily Online*, February 12.

8

Changing Ownership Structure of the Economy

LIXING LI

Ownership transformation has been a cornerstone of China's market reforms over the past forty years. Though ownership reform is key to the successful transition of the rural sector, this chapter focuses on the urban sector and mainly discusses state-owned enterprises (SOEs). The question examined in this chapter is, how should SOEs be reformed?

The share of SOEs in industry, in terms of both output and employment, has continuously declined during the reform era. The private sector now provides a major share of the employment and output in the Chinese economy. Nonetheless, SOEs continue to play a significant role in the economy. In particular, strategic industries are mostly dominated by SOEs. Despite easy access to credit and a more favorable business environment, however, SOEs have a relatively lower efficiency and profitability than non-SOEs. This situation largely results from problems inherent to SOEs, including the principal-agent problem, insider control, state intervention, lack of individual responsibility on the part of leadership, the need to serve multiple objectives, and the soft budget constraint phenomenon (that is, SOEs can count on being bailed out, which affects their behavior and makes them less efficient). Most of these problems are associated with unclear property rights and decision-making authority.

China's past experience with SOE reform can be divided into three stages. Each stage is associated with distinct features or a memorable catch-phrase, such as "internal reform," "Grab the Big, Let Go of the Small," and "Making SOEs bigger and stronger." While some of the problems have been addressed, and SOE profitability and efficiency have greatly improved, many problems remain.

Beginning in 2013, the State-Owned Assets Supervision and Administration Commission (SASAC) has initiated several important reforms. SOEs are divided into two categories and are subject to different modes and degrees of supervision and evaluation. The corporate governance and monitoring of managers have been strengthened with the introduction of boards of directors and a renewed emphasis on the role of the Chinese Communist Party (CCP) in SOEs. A shift from asset management to capital management was adopted by SASAC as a way to give SOEs more autonomy. Meanwhile, a renewed mixed-ownership reform has been proposed, and the social responsibilities previously associated with SOEs are being stricken. The effects of these reforms are as yet unknown.

Over the next thirty years, changing the ownership structure of SOEs will be a key component of the reforms China needs to undertake to successfully transition to a high-income country. In this regard, SOEs will face new challenges from both inside and outside. Rising labor costs and heavy indebtedness are important obstacles to SOEs becoming competitive. The administrative monopoly associated with SOEs and their control of important resources such as capital and land have proved an obstacle to the development of non-SOEs. In addition, critics of "state capitalism" have mounted challenges to SOEs entering the global market. To address old problems and new challenges, this chapter emphasizes competitive neutrality, a principle accepted worldwide, as the guideline for SOE reform.

For China to address the challenges that lie ahead and successfully transition to a high-income country by 2049, we suggest the following policy choices bearing on ownership structure.

First, the role and scope of SOEs should be clearly specified. To improve SOE efficiency and adaptation to global competition, the role and scope of SOEs should be limited. Most social responsibilities associated with SOEs should be removed. The list of strategic industries should be restricted to a minimum through a "negative list." Insofar as most SOEs will still play an important role in executing policy functions in the short run, to improve the efficiency of SOEs and avoid the soft budget constraint problem, it is necessary to draw a bright line between SOEs and the government. Establishing a scheme for the government to buy "services" from the SOEs based on market terms would be a choice.

Second, the playing field should be leveled to enhance competition. Competitive neutrality should be adopted as the basis for government regulations. Non-SOEs should receive equal treatment in terms of business environment and access to production factors such as capital and land. For competitive industries, free entry and market competition should be enforced. Monopoly should be maintained only in a few sectors that have natural monopoly characteristics or are directly related to national security. However, mixed ownership and collaboration between SOEs and non-SOEs should still be encouraged in such sectors.

Third, capital management and the supervision of SOEs should be optimized. The government agencies in charge of state asset management should focus on capital management. Administrative intervention should be minimized and full operational autonomy should be extended to firms. Corporate governance of SOEs should be strengthened according to market rules. The management team of SOEs should be recruited from the market, and it should be clear that they are professional managers instead of government officials. SOE assets and profits should be used more wisely through allocating SOE assets to the social security fund, enforcing profit retention by SOEs, and other ways that have been proven useful by international experience.

SOEs IN THE CHINESE ECONOMY

Some Basic facts of SOEs

At the beginning of the reform era, the Chinese economy was absolutely dominated by state ownership. In the industrial sector, SOEs accounted for nearly 80 percent of output value. By 2013, this figure had declined to around 20 percent (figure 8-1). While the size of employment in SOEs used to be as high as 120 million, this number has declined by half (figure 8-2). In contrast, a rough estimation that is widely cited suggests that private firms now contribute 50 percent of tax revenues, 60 percent of GDP, and 70 percent of innovations; are responsible for 80 percent of employment; and make up 90 percent of the firms in China.

FIGURE 8-1. State Share in Industrial Output

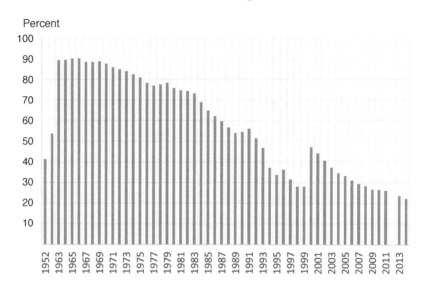

Source: Data from National Bureau of Statistics of China.

Note: The statistical standard was revised in 2000. After that date, statistics are provided for state-holding enterprises, which include state-owned and state-controlled enterprises. For simplicity, we continue to use "SOEs" to represent state-holding enterprises after 2000.

FIGURE 8-2. Urban Employment by Ownership Type, 1988–2014 (millions of workers)

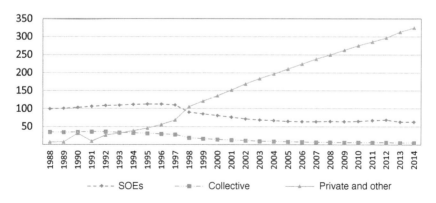

Source: Data from National Bureau of Statistics of China.

Although the importance of SOEs, in terms of both industrial output share and employment share, has continued to decline, the total amount of SOE assets and SOEs' role in the Chinese economy are still substantial. According to SASAC, there were about 120,000 SOEs in China at the end of 2014. They provided a total of 60 million jobs and made 1.2 trillion renminbi (RMB) of profit, of which about 70 percent was contributed by the 112 companies directly controlled by the central SASAC. According to the Ministry of Finance (2019), the total amount of net assets of SOEs in the nonfinancial sector was 52.5 trillion RMB at the end of 2018. According to a report by the minister of finance to the Standing Committee of the People's Congress in October 2018, the total net assets of SOEs in the financial sector amounted to 16.2 trillion RMB. In addition, SOEs control substantial natural resources, including land and mineral resources, which are largely noncapitalized and could potentially have high value (Beijing Unirule Institute of Economics 2015). More important, SOEs maintain a dominant position in industries with strategic importance, such as finance, energy, transportation, and telecommunications. In sum, the huge size of SOEs and their dominant role in important industries imply that SOE reform will be one of the key reforms contributing to China's economic success in the years to 2049.

An important fact is the underperformance of SOEs relative to that of private firms. In particular, despite a more favorite business environment, including easier access to credit, SOEs have a lower rate of return and a higher likelihood of loss-making. According to official statistics published by the National Bureau of Statistics of China (NBS), 24.7 percent of all SOEs made a loss in 2017, whereas only 11.1 percent of non-SOEs made a loss. The average rate of return on assets is 3.9 percent for SOEs but 8.4 percent for non-SOEs.

SOEs have accumulated heavy debt. According to the Ministry of Finance, by the end of 2018, the total amount of debt of SOEs in the nonfinancial sector was 115.6 trillion RMB, with a debt ratio of 64.7 percent.[1] More recently, the "hidden debt" of local government has attracted considerable attention among researchers and policymakers. It mainly refers to the debt borrowed by a special type of SOE, called local government financial vehicles (LGFVs). These SOEs not only conduct business operations but also perform a semigovernmental function in terms of providing urban infrastructure. They borrow from financial institutions, often with an implicit government guarantee. Thus it is somewhat hard to distinguish their debt from local government debt. The financial risk associated with such debt has become increasingly problematic in recent years.

Intrinsic Problems of SOEs

SOEs have a low efficiency and a high likelihood of loss-making. This is true not only in China but also in other economies, including countries with a highly developed market system. In what follows, we briefly review the intrinsic problems of SOEs suggested in the literature.

Principal-Agent Problem and Insider Control. A well-functioning market requires the property rights and decision rights of economic agents to be clearly defined and enforced. With ownership separated from control rights, SOEs are subject to the principal-agent problem. Although this problem is also widespread in non-SOEs, it is especially severe in SOEs because the control rights are not clearly delineated among different government agencies and managers and the monitoring cost is high within a planned system. In short, SOEs suffer from weak supervision and are often troubled by insider control.

State Intervention in Business Operations. Because the government is the de facto owner of both SOEs and public management agencies, both the central and local governments have an incentive to use administrative tools to interfere with the daily operations of SOEs to achieve their specific goals. While state intervention is itself part of the planned system, it is still widespread after many years of transition to a market system. State intervention through administrative orders often makes SOEs operate in a way that is orthogonal to profit maximization.

Lack of Individual Responsibility. Partly because of state intervention, it is hard to hold SOE managers responsible in case of loss-making. Meanwhile, SOEs are traditionally viewed as public organizations that provide permanent jobs. The permanent job guarantee and weak incentives make it equally hard to hold ordinary workers responsible. Shirking is a widespread phenomenon is SOEs.

Multifunctional Social Units. As the owner of SOEs, the government has other objectives in addition to long-term profit maximization. Naturally, SOEs are not profit-maximizing firms but multifunctional social units. An important function of SOEs is to provide social welfare and pursue strategic goals. On the one hand, SOEs suffer from policy burdens, such as providing jobs and social welfare to workers and providing price subsidies to urban residents (Lin, Cai, and Li 1998). Even today, many SOEs are troubled by overstaffing. In regions with an underdeveloped private sector, such as Northeast China, SOEs play an important role in job creation and thus help maintain social stability. On the other hand, SOEs have always had as part of their mission pursuing strategic goals such as national security and building strong Chinese "national champions." Just as with other socialist countries and many nonsocialist countries, state-owned industry in China has always been maintained at the "commanding heights" of the economy in pursuit of the national goal of global competitiveness.[2] With such goals, firm behaviors are often distorted, and profit maximization has to be sacrificed in SOEs.

Soft Budget Constraint. Since the seminal work of Kornai (1980), the soft budget constraint phenomenon has been widely accepted as a major problem afflicting SOEs. Nonperforming SOEs are bailed out by the government, which induces moral hazard and worsens the corporate governance of SOEs. Paternalism and the bearing of policy burdens are often mentioned as reasons for the government to impose a soft budget constraint on SOEs. The accumulation of heavy debt by LGFVs using government as the guarantor is another example of the soft budget constraint in action. Even though most SOEs underwent corporatization after enactment of the Company Law in 1995, the close relationship between SOEs and government has never been severed. Based on the expectation that government will ultimately be responsible for the debt, banks are willing to lend to SOEs and LGFVs, making the soft budget constraint problem prevalent.

A BRIEF HISTORY OF SOE REFORMS

This section reviews the elaboration of China's SOE reforms since 1978. Though some of the problems mentioned in the previous section have been addressed and the profitability and efficiency of SOEs have greatly improved, other problems remain. The existing literature has generally divided the SOE reforms into three stages.

Stage One

The period from the beginning of economic reform in 1978 to the early 1990s has been called the first stage of China's SOE reform. There are two channels through which SOE performance can be improved, the internal channel and the external channel. Reforms in this stage can be summarized along these two dimensions.

Internal Reforms. Reforms inside the state sector mainly focused on providing more discretionary power and stronger incentives to managers and employees of SOEs. Without changing the ownership structure or state control, the decision power over many issues was decentralized from government agencies to SOEs to enable firm managers to better adapt to the market. Meanwhile, various incentive schemes were introduced to SOEs, such as a profit retention system, a manager responsibility system, a contract worker system, and a flexible salary system. These schemes created competition among SOEs and greatly improved efficiency.

Entry and Competition. Reforms outside the state sector can be summarized by "entry and competition." With the gradual removal of barriers to entry, township and village enterprises (TVEs), private firms, and foreign firms (including those invested in by residents of Hong Kong, Macau, and Taiwan) were able to enter the domestic market to compete with SOEs. These non-SOEs, especially TVEs, quickly occupied a significant market share and created a diversified ownership structure for the Chinese economy. By 1993, TVEs have contributed almost one-third of the industrial output and provided a total of 52 million jobs. Entry and competition were conducive to China's industrial growth in the 1980s and early 1990s.

The internal and external reforms improved microlevel incentives and greatly expanded the domestic market. However, the fundamental problems of SOEs listed in the previous section were hardly addressed. In sum, the restructuring was quite limited inside SOEs in this stage.

Stage Two

By the mid-1990s, loss-making had become widespread among SOEs. For example, in 1997, twelve of the thirty provinces in China witnessed a negative total profit for SOEs. Among the 16,000 large and medium-sized industrial SOEs, 39 percent were making losses. It gradually became clear that SOE reform without privatization had reached a dead end. The ideological hostility toward private ownership was alleviated against such a background. The second stage of SOE reforms started with the Third Plenum of the Fourteenth National Congress of the CCP, which took place in 1993. Various dramatic reform measures were adopted, with a focus on ownership restructuring.

Grab the Big, Let Go of the Small. The official policy slogan for reforms during this stage was "Grab the Big, Let Go of the Small." For big SOEs that had a higher importance for the economy and usually had a better performance, the main reform approach was to transform them into profit-oriented modern firms while maintaining state control. Many big SOEs were consolidated to form large conglomerates (Hsieh and Song 2015). In addition, with nonperforming assets being stripped, good assets were restructured and listed on the stock market. During this process, nonstate shares were also introduced to improve corporate governance. In total, about five thousand SOEs were involved in this "grab" approach, with fewer than one thousand SOEs remaining after consolidation and restructuring.

For small and medium-sized SOEs, the restructuring was more dramatic and often involved privatization (also called *gaizhi*). Various restructuring methods were adopted, including public offerings, internal restructuring (incorporation, spinning off, introducing new investors), bankruptcy and reorganization, employee shareholding, management buyout, open sales (to outside private firms or SOEs), leasing, joint ventures, or some combination of the above (Garnaut et al. 2005). In total, about one million small and medium-sized SOEs experienced privatization.

Decentralization of the Oversight Status of SOEs. In addition to privatization, many SOEs were delegated to lower-level governments; that is, they were decentralized. For example, some central SOEs were decentralized to the provincial government, and provincial SOEs were further decentralized

to city or county governments. In light of the importance of local information (Hayek 1945), it is more efficient for upper-level government to decen-
tralize SOEs that are located geographically far away. Among all SOEs in
1998, about 9 percent experienced decentralization of oversight status by
2007 (Huang et al. 2017).

Dealing with Layoffs and Debt. The restructuring induced large-scale
layoffs and exposed huge amounts of nonperforming debt, which posed a
severe challenge to the government. Specifically, there are three categories
of redundant workers in the reform, including unemployment, internal retirement, and *xiagang* (or "losing the position," meaning that a worker stops
working and receives zero or little salary, but nonetheless retains a nominal
tie to the firm). By 2001, the number of lost jobs had reached 15 percent of
urban employment (Garnaut et al. 2005). In total, about 40–50 million SOE
workers lost their jobs during the second stage of the reforms. Large-scale
layoffs quickly posed a threat to social stability. Against this background,
the government provided various reemployment training programs to help
laid-off workers find new jobs. In addition, China's basic pension and medical insurance programs were also established during this period.

Solving the debt problem was equally painful. In fact, the most important impetus for privatization for the local government was the large
amount of debt built up by SOEs. By the end of the 1990s, among all outstanding loans of commercial banks, an estimated 30–40 percent were
nonperforming, with a size equivalent to about 25 percent of GDP. Debt-to-
equity swap was introduced in 1999 by the central government to alleviate
the nonperforming loan problem. Four asset management companies were
established to take over bad loans of SOEs. After the stripping of nonperforming loans and recapitalization by the Ministry of Finance, China's state
banking system soon recovered from the debt crisis.

Improving Performance. After the dramatic restructuring of both large
and small SOEs during this stage, the performance of SOEs continued to
improve. Studies examining the effect of privatization generally find a positive impact on efficiency and financial performance (Hsieh and Song 2015;
Song 2018). In particular, a factor important to successful restructuring has
been found to be the transfer of control rights to managers (Gan, Guo, and
Xu 2018).

Reversal of Privatization. As privatized firms attempted to cut costs and increase labor productivity, privatization often led to large-scale layoffs and induced social unrest. Government officials thus endure tremendous pressure and may have to abandon or even reverse the privatization process in many regions. Among sample firms that were fully owned by local governments in 1998 and then went through privatization by 2006, one-fourth have experienced an increase in government ownership afterward (Huang et al. 2015). While temporarily halting the trend of unemployment, re-nationalization has been found to lead to immediate efficiency loss, labor redundancy, and an increase in firm leverage. The long-term economic impact of re-nationalization appears to be negative and contrary to the aim of SOE reform.

Stage Three

After a ten-year period of dramatic reform, SOE profitability and efficiency have greatly improved. For the central government, profitability is no longer the first priority regarding SOEs. SOE reform has entered a new stage. A key event marking the start of this stage was the establishment of the State-Owned Assets Supervision and Administration Commission in 2003. Several key features of SOE reform emerged after SASAC was established.

Merger of Large SOEs. One mission of SASAC is to make SOEs "bigger and stronger." An important approach to achieving this goal has been forwarding the merger of large SOEs. Initially, SASAC directly oversaw 196 nonfinancial SOEs (the so-called central SOEs). Through mergers of firms in the same industry, this number was reduced to ninety-six by the end of 2018. Large-scale mergers also took place at the local level.

Control of the "Commanding Heights." In 2006, the State Council's document on the reorganization of SOEs stated that "the state should maintain absolute control over important industries that are related to national security and national economic growth" (State Council 2006). The document identified seven such industries: arms and ammunition, electricity and the grid, oil and gas, telecom, coal, aviation, and water transportation. In addition, there are nine "pillar" industries over which the state must maintain "relatively strong control." With the merger of large SOEs and the acquisition of non-SOEs, state-controlled firms have strengthened their dominant position in strategic industries. Through the dominant market power of SOEs in such industries, the government has achieved tight control over the commanding heights of the economy.

Favorable Financing for SOEs. SOEs have had relatively easier access to financing than non-SOEs (see chapter 5). According to the National Economic Research Institute's Business Environment Index 2017 (Wang, Fan, and Ma 2017), SOEs have achieved a significantly higher score than non-SOEs on all eight dimensions of business environment, including financing cost. The presence of a state-dominated banking system and the creation of various government funds designed to promote certain government objectives have contributed to such a financing advantage.

Proliferation of LGFVs. Another important phenomenon during this stage has been the establishment of a large number of LGFVs, which often serve the role of public infrastructure provider and are less focused on business operations and market competition. While LGFVs have played a vital role in China's urban development, they are also an important form of state involvement in the economy. As mentioned earlier, LGFVs have become a key player in generating the huge local government debt. Although LGFVs are not the focus of this chapter, their reform should be regarded as a component of SOE reforms in the future.

RECENT GOVERNMENT POLICIES AIMED AT SOE REFORMS

Central Guidance

The Chinese central government has issued several recent documents aimed at SOE reform. Of these, the resolution of the Third Plenum of the Eighteenth National Congress of the CCP, published in 2013, and the "Guiding Opinions on Deepening the Reform of SOEs," published in 2015, are the most important ones (Chinese Communist Party and State Council 2015). Subsequent documents lay out more specific reform plans.

Differential Supervision of SOEs in Different Categories. The government document requires that SOEs be divided into two categories, public service-oriented and commercial, and receive differential supervision and evaluation by category. The main functions of SOEs in the public service–oriented category include "[to] guarantee people's livelihood, serve society, and provide public goods." It is expected that the government will maintain sole or controlling ownership over SOEs in this category and implement price regulation for their products.

SOEs in the commercial category are to be further divided into two types. SOEs with a main business in the "fully competitive" sectors "should accelerate corporatization, could introduce capital from outside investors and even allow state ownership to become a minority position, and should push forward listing on the stock market." For SOEs in "less than fully competitive" sectors, if the main business is related to "national security or the commanding heights of the national economy," the state's controlling share will be maintained, but a nonstate share is encouraged. If the main business represents a natural monopoly sector, "separation of government and business and separation of government and capital should be the main target of reform." The evaluation of these "less than fully competitive" SOEs should be based not only on profitability but also on how well they "serve national strategies and guarantee national security, and develop forward-looking strategic sectors, as well as any specially assigned responsibilities" (SASAC 2015).

In general, the division of SOEs into two categories seems to move toward the direction of restricting government intervention within a minimum scope, while encouraging the more competitive ones to improve their performance and participate in ownership restructuring (Song 2018).

Stronger Corporate Governance and Monitoring of Managers. Establishment of a board of directors was regarded by SASAC as a key measure to strengthen corporate governance. By the end of 2018, eighty-three of the ninety-six central SOEs had established a board. All the subsidiaries of these central SOEs have established a board. In addition, the CCP will be embedded in the whole process of corporate governance. Meanwhile, managers of SOEs will be subject to stricter monitoring, not only by the SASAC but also by the organization department and the discipline inspection commission of the CCP. The "Method of Evaluation of Central SOE Leaders' Operation Performance," published in 2019, provides specific guidelines on evaluation criteria and incentive schemes for SOEs (SASAC 2019).

Focus on Capital Management. With an unclear delineation of owner-ship and decision-making authority of SOEs, the government has to strike a balance between too much intervention and too little control. An ideal situation for the state asset agency is to give enough autonomy to SOEs so that they have viability to compete on the market, while still retaining the profits of SOEs as their owner. To achieve this goal, the Chinese govern-ment has more or less learned from international experience, particularly the Temasek model, in which a financial holding company manages Sin-gapore's SOEs on behalf of the Ministry of Finance. It has been clear that SASAC will focus on the management of capital instead of the operation of SOEs. By the end of 2018, twenty-one central SOEs had been recognized as pilots of "state capital operation companies and state capital investment companies." At the local level, many more SOEs have joined the reform experiments. The major role of such companies has been designated as financial investors, which leaves space for the relatively independent op-eration of their subordinated firms. With "capital management" becoming the basic function of SASAC, many regulation functions of the SASAC are expected to be eliminated, decentralized to the lower level, or shifted to SOEs.

Mixed Ownership Reform. Mixed ownership reform is one of the most expected reforms related to SOEs. In fact, various types of *gaizhi* in late 1990s could be viewed as mixed ownership reforms. According to SASAC, by the end of 2017, more than two-thirds of the central SOEs had intro-duced mixed ownership. In 2018 alone, nearly three thousand central and local SOEs had started mixed ownership reform. It was required that SOEs in the fully competitive sectors and state capital operation and investment companies should introduce mixed ownership. Despite the large number of SOEs involved, the scale and real impact of mixed ownership were limited at the end of 2018. The mixed ownership reform of China Unicom is the only case that involves high-profile SOEs and private firms. The IPO of SOE subsidiaries and mergers or acquisition of nonperforming private firms have been the major types of mixed ownership reform for central SOEs. In contrast, mixed ownership reform proceeds more quickly at the local level. Among other provinces, Yunnan and Liaoning have conducted more radi-cal reforms in this regard.

Removal of Social Responsibilities. SOEs have long been fulfilling the role of providing jobs, social welfare, and even public goods. Relief of social responsibilities is a necessary step for SOEs to gain viability. In 2017, a document was issued that required all schools and hospitals sponsored by SOEs to be detached by the end of 2018. In 2018 alone, more than 689 fire stations and 1,744 schools were detached from SOEs. However, the detachment of SOE hospitals has slowed. They should either be transferred to the local government and join the public health system or be restructured by commercial hospital groups. However, most of the SOE hospitals have weak technology and human capital stock but heavy burdens such as redundant employees. Both the local government and the hospital investors have been hesitant to take over. This reflects a typical obstacle to the removal of SOE social responsibilities. And though such social responsibilities are being removed, SOEs have taken new responsibilities, such as moving forward the Belt and Road Initiative.

Comment

Since the establishment of SASAC, one of its major goals has been to make SOEs bigger and stronger. It has largely been successful in achieving this goal during the past fifteen years. Allowing the entry of non-SOE competitors, reshaping the incentive structure, and optimizing the information flow within the SOE hierarchies have resulted in efficiency gains for SOEs. Many SOEs, especially those designated central SOEs, have grown to be the largest companies in their respective industries in the world. SOEs have also helped the government achieve certain strategic goals and have provided semipublic goods to society (Jefferson 2017).

However, the intervention of SASAC in the operation of SOEs and the need to meet the nonprofit goals set by the government have greatly affected the performance of SOEs. In fact, an important reason why many SOEs make a profit is the favorable government treatment and the administrative monopoly. SOEs have not only enjoyed a better business environment and cheaper financing than non-SOEs, they have also used many natural resources for free. According to a 2015 report by the Beijing Unirule Institute of Economics, the forgiven rent for land occupied by SOEs was equivalent to US$830 billion each year from 2001 to 2008. If all the opportunity costs are counted, the profitability of SOEs would be even lower.

The recent reform policies made important steps toward solving the fundamental problems of SOEs. However, SOEs are still multifunctional social units that have been assigned multiple objectives by the government. It is important to realize that there is trade-off between achieving different objectives, and some of them seem to be inconsistent. For example, while the establishment of state capital operation and investment companies helps draw a line between government and firm and improve the autonomy of SOEs, it may worsen the principal-agent problem. As pointed out by Naughton (2018), there exists a trade-off between incentive, oversight, and autonomy, and SOEs are tasked with achieving an "impossible trinity" of three goals—make a profit, meet multiple, sometimes conflicting, objectives, and be subject to strong oversight—at the same time.

NEW CHALLENGES AHEAD: 2019–2049

In the next thirty years, as China grows to become the world's largest economy and enters the high-income stage, SOEs will face new challenges. This section summarizes these challenges from both the internal and external perspectives.

Internal Challenges

Becoming a high-income country requires a high level of productivity from the whole economy. The relatively low efficiency of SOEs is an obstacle to meeting this requirement. With weak incentives and complicated goals, managers of SOEs struggle to meet multiple and possibly inconsistent targets, making it hard to prioritize efficiency and profit maximization. Recently, SOEs were vulnerable to economic shocks during the 2008 global financial crisis and the commodity price decline in 2015–2016 (Naughton 2018). It is sometimes argued that China's growth has been below its potential owing to misallocation of capital to SOEs in recent years (Lardy 2018). In the future, population aging will raise China's labor costs and put pressure on the nation's social security system (see chapters 3 and 6). These conditions will make it increasingly challenging for SOEs to improve efficiency.

Another challenge comes from the debt problem. Thanks to the soft budget constraint, China's local government and SOEs have accumulated a huge amount of debt and serious financial risk. For example, the debt-to-equity ratio of SOEs has increased from 132 percent in 2005 to 163 percent in 2015 (Lardy 2018). As was pointed out in chapter 5, there is also a divergence between the leverage ratios of the state and nonstate sectors. The Chinese government has made efforts to tackle the soft budget constraint problem and deal with the debt problem, including implementing a deleveraging policy and forbidding local government to provide guarantees for SOE debt. There is increasing demand for other debt-solving methods, such as introducing mixed ownership, using debt-to-equity swaps, and the capitalization of resources owned by SOEs. In the end, repayment of debt requires SOEs to increase efficiency and make profit.

Private firms have played a major role in generating the high growth rate in the reform era, and will continue to be important to China's industrial upgrading and innovation in the next thirty years. From an opportunity cost point of view, the administrative monopoly associated with SOEs and the control of important resources such as capital and land by SOEs pose a threat to the development of private firms and other non-SOEs. For example, shale gas and oil exploration has been monopolized by the two giant state-owned oil companies. Few oil fields are open to nonstate firms. As a consequence, shale gas and oil exploration has been slow to take off in China as compared with other countries. Meanwhile, the situation makes it hard for private firms to survive in many industries (World Bank and Development Research Center of the State Council, PRC, 2013b). There has been increasing concern over the unfair competition between SOEs and non-SOEs in recent years.

In sum, unleashing the potential of China's economic growth requires substantial reforms to raise the productivity of SOEs, to remove SOEs' monopoly in various industries, and to level the playing field and encourage the development of non-SOEs.

External Challenges

Two major functions of SOEs are to control strategic industries and promote national interests. Thus it is rare for large SOEs in strategic industries to be privatized, even during the dramatic reform period in the late 1990s. Since 2013, it has become clear that SOEs are essential to maintaining the control of the government and achieving strategic objectives (Lardy 2019), some of which are outlined in the China Manufacturing 2025 plan and reflected in other industrial policies. An incomplete list includes pioneering technological development, creating powerful national champions that can promote China's influence, maintaining macroeconomic stability with countercyclical investment, and leading industrial upgrading (Naughton 2018). With the growing influence of the Chinese economy internationally, SOEs are actively entering the global market. The state-dominated expansion has encountered the existing global market order. As it has done so, Chinese SOEs have been criticized for receiving implicit subsidies from the government and thus engaging in unfair competition with international firms (EU Chamber of Commerce in China 2017; Office of the U.S. Trade Representative 2018). Critics even turn to sanctions in high-tech industries. In addition, when conducting foreign acquisitions, SOEs often face difficulties in gaining the approval of regulatory agencies (Li and Xia 2017). These are important external challenges facing SOEs in the future. Recent trade tensions between China and the United States have made such external challenges more explicit.

COMPETITIVE NEUTRALITY: A WELL-ACCEPTED GUIDELINE

All developed countries have SOEs. It is common for SOEs to assume social responsibilities and provide public goods, and to receive government subsidies in exchange. Thus, in the design of ownership reform policies, it is important to examine the experience of other countries. Adopting well-accepted guidelines would help the Chinese government justify policies in response to external critics.

Recently, "competitive neutrality" has been widely cited in policy talks, and even adopted as a principle to guide future policies by the Chinese government. Competitive neutrality initially appeared in Australia in the 1990s. It means that when competing with private firms, SOEs should not rely on government subsidies to achieve advantage. The principle was then adopted by the OECD as an important guideline in the governance of SOEs. Governments were required to follow eight specific components (OECD 2012). In December 2018, China's State Council began requiring that, with regard to government procurement and land allocation, firms with different ownership should be treated equally according to the principle of competitive neutrality. In March 2019, in Premier Li Keqiang's report to the People's Congress, it was formally stated that the government should, "in accordance with the rule of competitive neutrality, treat firms with different ownership equally in terms of factor access, entry permit, operation, and government procurement."

Adhering to competitive neutrality would not only help Chinese government meet its commitment to the world and address external challenges, it would also benefit China's national economy. In fact, competitive neutrality is consistent with China's reform experience since 1978. The opening of the domestic market and competition from nonstate firms have greatly enhanced the efficiency of SOEs. It is also consistent with the document issued by the Third Plenum of the Eighteenth National Congress of the CCP. In this sense, fair competition between SOEs and non-SOEs is the foundation of the "socialist market economy."

Again, it is important to realize there exist trade-offs between different objectives. Meeting the guideline of competitive neutrality would be somewhat counter to the goal maintaining government control over strategic industries and allowing SOEs to pursue national interests. To solve this dilemma, it is necessary to clearly define the scope of "strategic interests" and "strategic industries" and keep them at a limited level. For example, job creation and social welfare provision should be explicitly removed from the goal list of SOEs, especially when China's social security system is adequately developed. The complete removal of such social functions would leave SOEs with no excuse for poor performance and would make the definition of strategic interests clearer. In addition, the government should be cautious when giving SOEs objectives other than those that are directly related to national security. It is reasonable to consider national security when making decisions regarding foreign investment and technology transfer. However, SOEs should not be used as a tool to advance controversial industrial policies, and barriers to entry on the grounds of national security should be restricted to as few industries as possible.

POLICY SUGGESTIONS

For China to address the challenges that lie ahead and successfully transition to a high-income country by 2049, a vibrant domestic economy and a friendly international environment are requisite. While SOEs need to improve efficiency, the private sector needs to continue to grow and innovate. Although an optimal ownership structure is hard to define, the number of

SOEs should be greatly reduced, and the industrial share of SOEs should be further optimized. SOE monopoly should remain in only a few sectors that have natural monopoly characteristics or are directly related to national security. In most sectors, it would be ideal to have a range of firms of diverse size and ownership competing on a level playing field, facing similar market-driven factors and input prices (World Bank and Development Research Center of the State Council, PRC, 2013a).

To achieve these goals, the following policy choices are suggested.

First, clearly specify the role and scope of SOEs. While SOEs have played an important role in achieving multiple objectives, it is important to realize that trade-offs exist in pursuing those objectives. To improve SOE efficiency and adapt to global competition, the role and scope of SOEs should be limited. The list of strategic industries should be restricted to a minimum through a "negative list." Most social responsibilities associated with SOEs should be removed. In the short run, it is likely that most SOEs will still play an important role in terms of executing policy functions. In this circumstance, to improve the efficiency of SOEs and avoid the soft budget constraint problem, a bright line must be drawn between SOEs and the government. For example, establishing a scheme for the government to buy services from the SOEs based on market terms would be a choice.

Second, level the playing field and enhance competition. Competitive neutrality should be adopted as the basis for government regulations. Non-SOEs should receive equal treatment with respect to business environment and access to production factors such as capital and land. For competitive industries, free entry and market competition should be enforced. SOE monopoly should remain in just a few sectors that have natural monopoly characteristics or are directly related to national security. At the same time, mixed ownership and collaboration between SOEs and non-SOEs should be encouraged in such sectors.

Third, optimize capital management and supervision of SOEs. The government agencies in charge of state asset management should focus on capital management, possibly through professional asset management agencies or an investment fund. Administrative intervention should be abandoned and full operational autonomy should be extended to firms. Corporate governance of SOEs should be strengthened according to market rules. The management team for an SOE should be recruited from the market and it should be made clear that professional managers are not government officials. SOE assets and profits should be used more wisely through the allocation of SOE assets to the social security fund, enforcing profit retention of SOEs, and in other ways that have proven useful in international experience.

NOTES

1. For a review of the size of debt, leverage, and debt service burden of various nonfinancial SOE groupings, including by size and extent of state ownership, see Molnar and Lu (2019) and Ferrarini and Hinojales (2018).

2. Many governments across the world have engaged in controlling the "commanding heights" since the end of World War II, including the Attlee Labour government in the United Kingdom, the de Gaulle government in France, India, Germany, Korea, Japan, and many Latin American countries. See Yergin and Stanislaw (1999).

REFERENCES

Beijing Unirule Institute of Economics 2015. *The Nature, Performance, and Reform of State-Owned Enterprises,* 2nd ed. Beijing.

Chinese Communist Party and State Council. 2015. "Guiding Opinions of the Central Committee of the Chinese Communist Party and the State Council on Deepening the Reform of State-Owned Enterprises." [In Chinese.] Xinhua News Agency, August 24.

Ferrarini, Benno, and Marthe Hinojales, 2018. "State-Owned Enterprises Leverage as a Contingency in Public Debt Sustainability Analysis: The Case of the People's Republic of China." Asian Development Bank Economics Working Paper No. 534. Mandaluyong, Philippines: Asian Development Bank.

EU Chamber of Commerce in China. 2017. *China Manufacturing 2025: Putting Industrial Policy ahead of Market Force.* Beijing.

Gan, Jie, Yan Guo, and Chenggang Xu. 2018. "Decentralized Privatization and Change of Control Rights in China." *Review of Financial Studies* 31 (10): 3854–94.

Garnaut, Ross, Ligang Song, Stoyan Tenev, and Yang Yao. 2005. *China's Ownership Transformation: Process, Outcomes, Prospects.* Washington, DC: International Finance Corporation.

Hayek, Friedrich. 1945. "The Use of Knowledge in Society." *American Economic Review* 35 (4): 519–30.

Hsieh, Chang-Tai, and Zheng Song. 2015. "Grasp the Large, Let Go of the Small:

The Transformation of the State Sector in China." *Brookings Papers on Economic Activity* 45:295–346.

Huang, Zhangkai, Lixing Li, Guangrong Ma, and Jun Qian. 2015. "The Reversal of Privatization: Determinants and Consequences." Available at SSRN: https://ssrn.com/abstract=2350053.

Huang, Zhangkai, Lixing Li, Guangrong Ma, and Colin Xu. 2017. "Hayek, Local Information, and Commanding Heights: Decentralizing State-Owned Enterprises in China." *American Economic Review* 107 (8): 2455-2478.

Jefferson, Gary. 2017. "State-Owned Enterprise in China: Reform, Performance, and Prospects." Economics Department Working Paper Series 2017-109R, Brandeis University, Waltham, MA.

Kornai, János, 1980. *Economics of Shortage.* Amsterdam: North-Holland.

Lardy, Nicholas. 2019. *The State Strikes Back: The End of Economic Reform in China?* Washington, DC: Peterson Institute for International Economics.

———. 2018. "Private Sector Development." In *China's 40 Years of Reform and Development, 1978–2018*, edited by Ross Garnaut, Ligang Song, and Cai Fang. Canberra: ANU Press.

Li, Jing, and Jun Xia. 2017. "State-Owned Enterprises Face Challenges in Foreign Acquisitions." Columbia FDI Perspectives No. 205. New York: Columbia Center on Sustainable Development, August 14.

Lin, J. Y., F. Cai, and Z. Li. 1998. "Competition, Policy Burdens, and State-Owned Enterprise Reform." *American Economic Review* 88 (2): 422–27.

Ministry of Finance of China. 2019. "Economic Operation of State-Owned and State-Owned Holding Companies Nationwide from January to December 2018." [In Chinese.] Beijing, January 22.

Molnar, M., and J. Lu. 2019. "State-Owned Firms behind China's Corporate Debt." OECD Economics Department Working Paper No. 1536. Paris: OECD Publishing.

Naughton, Barry. 2018. "State Enterprise Reform Today." In *China's 40 Years of Reform and Development, 1978–2018*, edited by Ross Garnaut, Ligang Song, and Cai Fang. Canberra: ANU Press.

Office of U.S. Trade Representative. 2018. *Section 301 Report into China's Acts, Policies, and Practices Related to Technology Transfer, Intellectual Property, and Innovation.* Washington, DC: Executive Office of the President of the United States, March.

Organization for Economic Cooperation and Development (OECD). 2012. *Competitive Neutrality: Maintaining a Level Playing Field between Public and Private Business.* Brussels: OECD, August 30.

Song, Ligang. 2018. "State-Owned Enterprise Reform in China: Past, Present and Prospects." In *China's 40 Years of Reform and Development, 1978–2018*, edited by Ross Garnaut, Ligang Song, and Cai Fang. Canberra: ANU Press.

State Council. 2006. "Notice on Pushing Forward the Adjustment of State Stocks and Reorganization of SOEs." State Council General Office (国办发) 2006-No. 97. Available at http://www.gov.cn/gongbao/content/2007/content_503385.htm.

State-Owned Assets Supervision and Administration Commission (SASAC), Ministry of Finance and National Development and Reform Commission. 2015. *Views on Demarcating and Classifying SOEs.* [In Chinese.] Beijing, December 29.

State-Owned Assets Supervision and Administration Commission (SASAC). 2019. *Method of Evaluation of Central SOE Leaders' Operation Performance.* [In Chinese.] Beijing, March 1. Available at http://www.sasac.gov.cn/n2588035/c10652592/content.html.

Wang, Xiaolu, Gang Fan, and Guangrong Ma. 2017. *Business Environment Index for China's Provinces.* [In Chinese.] Beijing: Social Sciences Academic Press.

World Bank and Development Research Center of the State Council, PRC. 2013a. "China: Structural Reforms for a Modern, Harmonious, Creative Society." Supporting Report No. 1 for *China 2030: Building a Modern, Harmonious, and Creative Society,* Washington, DC: World Bank Group.

———. 2013b. "Reaching 'Win-Win' Solutions with the Rest of the World." Supporting Report No. 5 for *China 2030: Building a Modern, Harmonious, and Creative Society.* Washington, DC: World Bank Group.

Yergin, Daniel, and Joseph Stanislaw. 1999. *The Commanding Heights.* New York: Simon and Schuster.

PART III

INNOVATION AND INDUSTRY UPGRADING

9

Artificial Intelligence and China's Labor Market

GAOSI CHU and GUANGSU ZHOU

Since the first industrial revolution, technological advances have consistently reshaped labor markets, with outdated occupations disappearing and new employment opportunities emerging, along with higher productivity. Most of what we know about advancing technology's effects on the employment market comes from successful market adaptations. For example, the first and second industrial revolutions resulted in the labor force transitioning from the primary sector to manufacturing and service-oriented industries. Figure 9-1 shows China's employment profile shifting from primary industry to secondary and tertiary industry during the intense industrialization that began in the 1950s. After 2002, though employment almost stopped growing, the trend continued.

Though artificial intelligence (AI) and related automation[1] have been dubbed the fourth revolution, there is growing concern that unlike what followed previous wholesale changes in technology, the widespread application of AI may have substantial negative effects on the employment market. This concern has a sound basis. Even though the adoption rate of AI by industry is low at the moment, in certain industries where AI technology has been widely adopted, strong substitution effects are evident, along with a paucity of new job opportunities, especially those requiring AI skills. In the financial industry, which is a leading adopter of digital and AI technology,

FIGURE 9-1.   China Employment by Sectors, 1954–2017

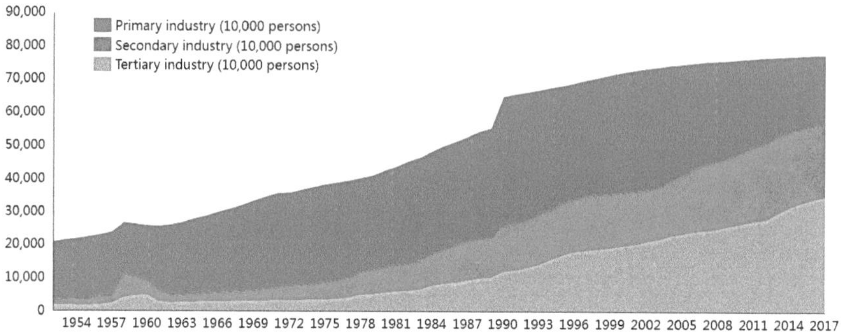

Source: National Bureau of Statistics of China, *China Statistical Yearbook 2018.*

the application of technology has fueled the polarization of employment into low- and high-skill jobs (figures 9-2 and 9-3). From 2016 to 2018 the offline manual handling rate of bank business dropped from 15.69 percent to 11.31 percent. As a result, 26,808 clerks (mainly bank tellers) employed by the Agricultural Bank of China, the second-largest bank in China, lost their jobs, while 638 technical engineers were newly employed by the bank (figure 9-2). What happened with the China Construction Bank is even more telling: after the offline manual jobs rate fell to 3 percent in 2017, both clerk and technical engineer positions decreased in 2018 as "the intelligent level of IT system has been significantly increased after consistent investment in Fintech" (China Construction Bank 2018) (figure 9-3). But there are also many rosy predictions about the future jobs market. The global research and advisory firm Gartner claims that in 2020, AI will become a net positive job creator, creating 2.3 million jobs, while eliminating only 1.8 million jobs (Gartner 2018b).

In light of such conflicting assessments, this chapter aims to provide some preliminary answers to the following questions: What effects will the adoption of AI by industry have on China's employment market? Can AI help solve China's aging problems and the gradual diminishing of the population dividend, or might it instead accelerate job market polarization and amplify income inequality? To answer the first question, we calculated the actual job substitution probability of AI in 2049 using the theoretical substitution probability and offer some predictions about the adoption of AI. Using the substitution probability, we examined the effects of AI on

FIGURE 9-2.   China Agricultural Bank, HR Structural Change 2016–2018

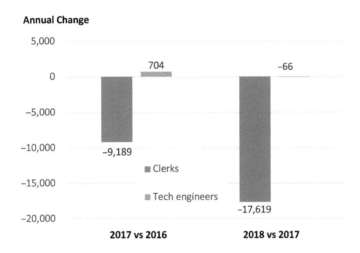

Source: *China Agricultural Bank Annual Report*, 2016, 2017, 2018.

FIGURE 9-3.   China Construction Bank, HR Structural Change 2016–2018

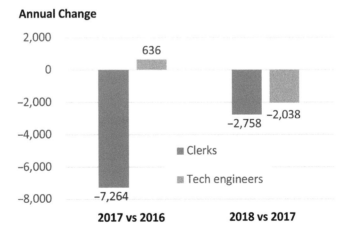

Source: *China Construction Bank Annual Report*, 2016, 2017, 2018.

different sectors of the labor force as a step toward evaluating whether, in the next thirty years, China's employment market can adjust to the structural changes brought about by AI-related technology. The regional migration of jobs and job movement to different sectors, genders, age groups, and industries are highlighted. The chapter concludes with policy suggestions devolving from projections of AI's substitution effects on China's employment market. We emphasize that government and policymakers should seek ways to maximize the positive effects of AI on the employment market, provide relief to those most negatively affected by the industrial embrace of AI, and support the labor force in transition.

CALCULATION OF ACTUAL SUBSTITUTION PROBABILITY OF AI IN 2049

The actual substitution effect of AI on the employment market is decided by two key transformation factors: AI's theoretical substitution rate and the adoption rate in practice. The first factor, AI's theoretical capability, we construed as AI's full potential to replace human intelligence. We developed an AI versus human-level performance matrix (table 9-1) as a scoring system for evaluating that factor. The AI we refer to throughout the chapter aggregates various kinds of technologies corresponding to different human capabilities. For almost each column in the matrix, a gap exists between AI and human intelligence in critical capabilities such as image recognition.

The better the grade that AI technology earned on the human-level performance scorecard, the higher is the theoretical substitution probability of human labor.[2] The replaced workers may need to look for jobs with different

TABLE 9-1. **Main AI Technologies and Corresponding Human Capability**

	Capability		
	Recognition	Analysis	Mass processing
	Vision	Information processing	Handling and control
AI technologies	Audio	Data insights	Navigation and moving
	NLP	Planning/Creating	Image and speech generations

skill capabilities, as the AI substituted for the job by capability rather than by occupation.

One more caveat to observe in the calculation of the theoretical substitution rate is that AI, which has greatly progressed in the past ten years, is still far from fully developed. Many significant AI-related technologies, such as autonomous driving, Edge AI, and Knowledge Graph, are still in the early stage of technology life cycle (TLC) and far from a plateau of market maturity.[3] For the purpose of estimating the theoretical substitution in the future (table 9-2), the calculation was based on the AI in 2049 predicted by experts, which already moves to the plateau of productivity (Frey and Osborne 2017).

The second transformative factor, AI's adoption rate, is a measure of the perceived real-world benefits of the technology, resulting in its acceptance and adoption.[4] As the previous discussion of bank tellers shows, once AI has improved to the point that its performance exceeds human performance, its real-world applications have the potential to explode and replace human labor in related scenarios.

However, practical bottlenecks, such as return on investment, efficiency considerations, modification costs, and even political calculations, limit the pace and extent of adoption of AI in industrial scenarios, and employment substitution is likely to occur far more slowly than the theoretical development of AI, and will also vary by industry and occupation. That is why, when we calculate the actual substitution probability of AI in thirty years, the adoption rate must be considered. A recent Information Technology and Innovation Foundation report on AI's challenges describes AI's status with another interesting analogy, comparing China's stage in the AI innovation cycle with the late 1980s, "when computers, software, and telecommunications were getting better—and people could see where the technology was going—but were not yet good enough or affordable enough to drive what became the Internet revolution after the mid-1990s. As such, societies may not begin to experience and see the full-scale benefits of the next digital wave until the mid-2020s" (Atkinson 2019)—society needs at least thirty years to see the sufficient application of transformative technologies such as digitalization and AI.

TABLE 9-2. Theoretical Substitution Probability for Each Occupation

Code	Occupation	Probability (%)
11	Social science researchers (sociology, literature, economics, etc.)	21.48
12	Scientific researchers (science, engineering, medical science, etc.)	9.55
13	Engineers and technicians (geology, energy science, chemical engineering, space engineering)	15.39
14	Engineers and technicians (TMT, transportation, electrical engineering)	7.14
15	Engineers and technicians (transportation, oceanic science, hydraulic engineering, architecture)	5.38
16	Engineers and technicians (food science, seismology, quality assurance, environmental protection)	14.43
17	Agricultural technicians	1.54
18	Aircraft and ship technicians	20.13
19	Medical technicians	3.08
21	Economic professionals	46.01
22	Financial professionals	47.67
23	Legal professionals	11.86
24	Teachers	7.76
25	Cultural and art professionals	12.76
26	Athletic professionals	24.30
27	Media professionals and publishers	30.46
28	Religious professionals	1.66
32	Security guards and firefighters	41.73
33	Mail and teleservice workers	43.70
39	Other clerical workers	74.88
41	Sales clerks	61.15
42	Stock clerks	46.12
43	Food service workers	74.62
44	Hotels, travel, and fitting service workers	38.74
46	Medical assistant service workers	36.57
47	Social and residential service workers (agencies, photographers, hairdressers, housekeepers)	47.27
48	Social and residential service workers (repairers, dustman, nursery maids)	57.83
51	Agronomic growers	71.08
52	Forestry producers, wild animal and plant protectors	77.92
53	Crop and animal producers	64.55
54	Fishery workers	53.87
55	Water facilities maintainers	88.00
59	Other agricultural, forestry, husbandry, fishery, and water facilities workers	69.33
61	Mining and quarrying workers	53.88

Code	Occupation	Probability (%)
62	Metal producing and processing workers (steel)	87.26
64	Chemical production workers (chemical oil production)	83.58
65	Chemical production workers (fining and compounding)	43.13
66	Machine producing and processing workers	87.67
67	Mechanical and electronic equipment installing workers (common machines)	44.95
68	Mechanical and electronic equipment producing workers (arms)	59.69
69	Mechanical and electronic equipment installing workers (high-precision trajectory)	41.02
71	Machine repairers	45.81
72	Electronical equipment installing, operating, maintaining, and powering workers	57.26
73	Electronic component and equipment producing, installing, testing, and maintaining workers	55.97
74	Rubber and plastic producing workers	44.00
75	Weaving, knitting, and bleaching workers	60.40
76	Tailoring, sewing, and leather and fur producing workers	83.58
77	Oil, food, beverage, and their materials producing and processing workers	84.00
78	Tabacco producing and processing workers	74.67
79	Medicine producing workers	29.16
81	Wood, cabinet, and paper producing and processing workers	63.03
82	Building materials producing and processing workers	75.72
83	Glass, pottery, and enamel producing and processing workers	70.15
84	Media and film producers, cultural relic protectors	58.35
86	Artwork makers	74.72
87	Educational and sport products makers	45.65
88	Construction workers	64.01
89	Construction workers (construction equipment installment)	26.14
91	Transport equipment operators and related workers	60.23
92	Environment monitoring and waste disposal workers	70.48
99	Other production and transport equipment operators and related workers	59.67

Note: This table shows the theoretical substitution probability corresponding to China's two-digit occupation code. The names of some two-digit codes are the same, but that does not mean they are identical occupation categories. (The specific division needs to refer to the three-digit occupation code.)

Calculation of the Theoretical Substitution Probability

The substitution effect of AI on occupations depends on each occupation's attributes, and occupations with lower requirements for perception and manipulation, creative intelligence, or social intelligence are more susceptible to AI substitution. Frey and Osborne (2017) estimated the probability of computerization for 702 detailed occupations according to the U.S. government's Standard Occupational Classification System. They used nine objective variables, corresponding to the defined bottlenecks in computerization, that describe the level of perception and manipulation, creativity, and social intelligence required to perform the job. Together with a group of machine learning researchers, they subjectively hand-labeled seventy occupations, assigning one if automatable and zero if not, and then estimated the function for the determination of computerization. Finally, they predicted the probability of computerization for 702 occupations according to this function.

We estimated the theoretical substitution probability for occupations according to the classification of occupations in China based on the results of Frey and Osborne (2017). We merged the CSCO (Chinese Standard Classification of Occupations) with the SOC (American Standard Occupational Classification) through the code of ISCO88 and ISCO08 (International Standard Classification of Occupations) provided by the U.S. Bureau of Labor Statistics, the International Labour Organization, and the China Family Panel Studies (CFPS) data set (Ren et al. 2012). Finally, we calculated the probability of substitution for sixty-one occupations among the seventy-nine occupations appearing in the Chinese census data. The results are shown in table 9-2.

Calculation of AI Adoption by Industry

To estimate the adoption of AI in practice, we calculated the 2049 AI adoption rate by industry in China by defining and then working out three main evaluation dimensions: the AI adoption rate in 2017, an industry's or occupation's potential for digitization, and a best-fit coefficient.

Adoption Rate in 2017. The AI adoption rate in 2017 was taken as the current AI usage rate in different industries. Based on statistics provided by

China's top AI companies and interviews with key industry personnel, we constructed the index by calculating the relative added value provided by AI.[5] We found that despite the general adoption of multiple AI capabilities in the full value chain in occupations ranging from biological research to wealth management to call center operations, the financial industry was the only one with an adoption rate above 10 percent in 2017. As the starting point for calculating the adoption rate in 2049, the low rate of AI adoption in 2017 proves that AI's solutions contribution in practice is highly limited at the beginning.

Digitization Potential. The accessibility of data, both in cost and amount, is a critical factor in determining the feasibility of AI solutions in a specific industry.[6] In our calculation, *accessibility* is quantified as the *digitization rate*, which is roughly equal to the rate of IT spending as a share of industry revenue. According to AI usage in practice, the greater the IoT (Internet of Things) investment an industry made, the more data availability it owns. Correlation analysis shows a high positive correlation between the AI adoption rate in 2017 and the digitization rate. For many industries, such as agriculture and the medical sector, the low digitization rate turns out to be the main bottleneck in AI adoption.

In the long run of thirty years, however, the current setbacks in digitization pave the way to a higher AI adoption rate in the future. The assumption is that in 2049, the digitization process in China will have concluded and the digitization rate for all industries will have reached the ceiling of full digitization (all main data can be obtained online), which is 8 percent (equal to the current level of Amazon and other top digital companies [CB insights 2018]). A high IoT investment rate will boost the digitization of traditional industries and translate the current drag into a late-mover advantage in the AI adoption process.

Improved Fitting Based on Scenario Limitations. The index shows increased curve fitting with industry characteristics.[7] The analogy with electricity notwithstanding, we found that the adoption of AI solutions by industry relies heavily on deployment customization and varies significantly under different scenario assumptions. With the lessons learned from the practical deployment of AI solutions, the relative pace of different industries' adoption of AI and constraints on adoption are shown in table 9.3.

The projected AI adoption rate in 2049 by industry, based on the three subindexes, is shown in table 9-4. Two assumptions are that the current AI application level we identified may move through the various stages of technology life cycle, and that the coefficient of improved fitting may follow different curves in the next three decades.

Calculation of AI Adoption by Occupations

To analyze the substitution effect of AI on labor forces with different characteristics, we matched the occupations with industries by the corresponding AI adoption rate, grouping them by job categories. As noted at the beginning of the chapter, AI capability is not fully substitutable for human intelligence and occupations. The results show that according to AI adoption degree in industries, the ratio of employment will be affected accordingly.

The occupations list is based on the official two-digit codes, while the correspondence is a rough one based on the occupation definition, as accurate industry employment numbers are not available. Most occupations are connected with only one industry; for example, *Financial professionals* is connected to *Finance Industry.* For one occupation matching with two or more industries, such as *Cultural and art professionals* connecting both to *Education* and to *Culture, sports, and entertainment,* weights measured by

TABLE 9-3. **The Industries' Increase Speed**

Category	Feature
Aggressive later comer advantage	The adoption in scenarios is low as it highly relies on infrastructure, such as sensors' deployment. Once the infrastructure is ready, the adoption rate will increase sharply (e.g., mining and energy plants)
Later comer advantage	Relies on infrastructure and automation progress (e.g., agriculture and transport)
Quick increase	Partially limited by infrastructure and partially limited by commercial motivation (e.g., manufacturing, education, and medical)
Liner increase	Mainly motivated by consumers and users
Slow increase	Limited by alternately high adoption rate and ROI
Sufficient market	Adoption rate is quite high, only motivated by technology upgrade (e.g., finance and security)

TABLE 9-4. AI Adoption Rate in 2017 and 2049 by Industries (China)

Industry code	Industry name	Adoption rate, 2017 (%)	Digitization rate, 2017 (%)	Digitization potential (%)	Increase fitting (to 2049) (%)	Adoption rate, 2049 (%)		
						Low	Medium	High
A	Agriculture, forestry, animal husbandry, and fishery	0.5	0.4	18.14	6.62	42.1	60.0	77.8
B	Mining	0.5	1.0	8.00	11.05	34.3	44.2	60.5
C	Manufacturing	3.7	2.0	4.00	4.34	46.3	64.2	68.7
D	Production and supply of electricity, heat, gas, and water	1.0	2.0	4.09	11.05	35.1	45.1	61.8
E	Construction	1.9	1.0	8.00	4.34	48.4	67.1	71.7
F	Transport, storage, and post	4.5	3.0	2.67	6.62	52.1	55.7	79.4
G	Information transmission, computer services, and software industry	8.0	4.0	2.00	2.57	35.3	41.1	61.4
H	Wholesale and retail trades	5.6	2.0	4.00	3.13	65.3	70.0	85.9
I	Hotel and catering services	5.5	2.0	4.00	2.92	56.6	64.4	84.6
J	Financial intermediation	14.0	5.0	1.60	2.57	49.4	57.3	85.8
K	Real estate	1.9	1.0	8.00	2.57	34.2	39.7	59.4
L	Leasing and business services	2.0	6.0	1.33	4.64	11.6	12.4	17.7
M	Scientific research, technical services, and geological survey industry	3.5	8.0	1.00	2.92	9.0	10.2	13.4
N	Management of water conservancy, environment, and public facilities	2.9	3.5	2.29	6.62	30.8	43.9	56.9
O	Services to households, repair and other services	1.9	1.4	6.93	2.92	34.7	36.4	51.8
P	Education	3.0	3.9	2.05	4.64	26.6	28.5	40.6
Q	Health, social security, and social service	0.5	0.8	9.76	4.64	21.2	22.6	32.3
R	Culture, sports, and entertainment	6.0	5.0	1.60	2.57	21.2	24.6	36.9
S	Public management and social organization	2.0	3.0	2.67	4.34	16.7	23.1	35.3

Source: Baidu & Alibaba AI Reports, IHS, *Harvard Business Review*, Experts Interviews, Gartner Report (Wiles, 2018)

TABLE 9-5. AI Adoption Rate by Occupation in China, 2049 (Projected)

Code	Occupation	Probability (%)
11	Social science researchers (sociology, literature, economics, etc.)	21.48
12	Scientific researchers (science, engineering, medical science, etc.)	9.55
13	Engineers and technicians (geology, energy science, chemical engineering, space engineering)	15.39
14	Engineers and technicians (TMT, transportation, electrical engineering)	7.14
15	Engineers and technicians (transportation, oceanic science, hydraulic engineering, architecture)	5.38
16	Engineers and technicians (food science, seismology, quality assurance, environmental protection)	14.43
17	Agricultural technicians	1.54
18	Aircraft and ship technicians	20.13
19	Medical technicians	3.08
21	Economics professionals	46.01
22	Financial professionals	47.67
23	Legal professionals	11.86
24	Teachers	7.76
25	Cultural and art professionals	12.76
26	Athletic professionals	24.30
27	Media professionals and publishers	30.46
28	Religious professionals	1.66
32	Security guards and firefighters	41.73
33	Mail and teleservice workers	43.70
39	Other clerical workers	74.88
41	Sales clerks	61.15
42	Stock clerks	46.12
43	Food service workers	74.62
44	Hotels, travel, and fitting service workers	38.74
46	Medical assistant service workers	36.57
47	Social and residential service workers (agencies, photographers, hairdressers, housekeepers)	47.27
48	Social and residential service workers (repairers, dustman, nursery maids)	57.83
51	Agronomic growers	71.08
52	Forestry producers, wild animal and plant protectors	77.92
53	Crop and animal producers	64.55
54	Fishery workers	53.87
55	Water facilities maintainers	43.87
59	Other agricultural, forestry, husbandry, fishery, and water facilities workers	60.02
61	Mining and quarrying workers	44.18

Code	Occupation	Probability (%)
62	Metal producing and processing workers (steel)	54.19
64	Chemical production workers (chemical oil production)	54.19
65	Chemical production workers (fining and compounding)	46.35
66	Machine producing and processing workers	64.19
67	Mechanical and electronic equipment installing workers (common machines)	64.19
68	Mechanical and electronic equipment producing workers (arms)	64.19
69	Mechanical and electronic equipment installing workers (high-precision trajectory)	43.66
71	Machine repairers	64.19
72	Electronic equipment installing, operating, maintaining, and powering workers	45.15
73	Electronic component and equipment producing, installing, testing, and maintaining workers	41.06
74	Rubber and plastic producing workers	64.19
75	Weaving, knitting, and bleaching workers	64.19
76	Tailoring, sewing, and leather and fur producing workers	64.19
77	Oil, food, beverage, and their materials producing and processing workers	64.19
78	Tabacco producing and processing workers	64.19
79	Medicine producing workers	22.65
81	Wood, cabinet, and paper producing and processing workers	64.19
82	Building materials producing and processing workers	67.07
83	Glass, pottery, and enamel producing and processing workers	64.19
84	Media and film producers, cultural relic protectors	24.64
86	Artwork makers	64.19
87	Educational and sport products makers	64.19
88	Construction workers	39.68
89	Construction workers (construction equipment installment)	41.93
91	Transport equipment operators and related workers	79.42
92	Environment monitoring and waste disposal workers	43.87
99	Other production and transport equipment operators and related workers	79.42

Note: Table shows the AI adoption rate corresponding to China's two-digit occupation code. The occupation names of some two-digit codes are the same, but that does not mean they are identical occupation categories. (The specific division needs to refer to the three-digit occupation code.)

definition (50:50 percent, for example) would be added to balance the corresponding relation. Based on the calculation, the 2049 AI adoption rate by occupation is shown in table 9-5.

THE IMPACT OF AI ON FUTURE EMPLOYMENT

After estimating the substitution rate for each industry and each occupation, we examined the multilevel effects of AI on employment in the future. We first combined the theoretical substitution probability for each occupation with the adoption rate to estimate the actual substitution probability. We then used China's census data from 2005, 2010, and 2015 to analyze the substitution effect of AI on labor force sectors with different characteristics. Finally, we calculated the employment structure at the industry level to arrive at a prediction of the number of employed people substituted by AI in each industry. The impact of AI on employment in 2049 is shown in table 9-6.

Analysis of the Substitution Effect of AI on Labor Force Subgroups

Although AI has significant impacts on the overall labor market, it has differential effects on different subgroups of the labor force. Therefore we divided our sample into subgroups based on such characteristics as age, gender, level of educational attainment, and income level, and estimated the actual probability of AI substitution for the different worker subgroups. The actual substitution probability equals the theoretical substitution probability multiplied by the adoption rate. For example, to calculate the substitution probability of different age groups, we used each occupation's employment number (calculated from China's 2010 census data) as the weight matrix in each age group, and then calculated the weighted means for the probability of each age group.

Substitution Effect by Age. First we calculated the weighted average of the substitution probabilities by different worker age; the results are shown in figure 9-4. We divided the workers into five age cohorts. Those in the twenty- to twenty-nine-year-old age group are least likely to experience job substitution, while those in the sixty- to sixty-nine-year-old age group are most likely to experience job substitution. The main reason, we believe, is that younger adults are more agile in acquiring new knowledge and new

TABLE 9-6. **Estimated Substituted Employment, 2049 (Projected)**

Industry code	Industry name	Substitution probability (%)	Adoption rate (%)	Urban total employment (10,000)	Urban substituted employment (10,000)	Rural total employment (10,000)	Rural substituted employment (10,000)
A	Agriculture, forestry, animal husbandry, and fishery	70.49	60.02	6,790.73	2,872.91	2,2170.97	9,379.73
B	Mining	52.07	44.18	664.31	152.82	242.59	55.81
C	Manufacturing	63.47	64.19	9,144.04	3,725.66	3,966.79	1,616.23
D	Production and supply of electricity, heat, gas, and water	48.34	45.15	534.05	116.55	85.42	18.64
E	Construction	58.30	67.07	3,273.79	1,280.04	2,364.36	924.46
F	Transport, storage, and post	56.86	79.42	7,676.48	3,466.77	1,950.94	881.06
G	Information transmission, computer services, and software industry	37.07	41.06	2,296.87	349.62	741.42	112.86
H	Wholesale and retail trades	58.14	70.01	2,166.61	881.92	761.92	310.14
I	Hotel and catering services	63.85	64.39	599.18	246.34	54.67	22.48
J	Financial intermediation	46.48	57.33	903.12	240.66	61.50	16.39
K	Real estate	47.61	39.68	707.73	133.71	78.58	14.85
L	Leasing and business services	42.67	12.38	764.17	40.37	136.67	7.22
M	Scientific research, technical services, and geological survey industry	28.60	10.23	364.72	10.67	34.17	1.00
N	Management of water conservancy, environment, and public facilities	52.65	43.87	286.57	66.19	71.75	16.57
O	Services to households, repair, and other services	51.79	36.40	1,497.96	282.39	515.92	97.26
P	Education	12.61	28.50	1,871.36	67.26	300.67	10.81
Q	Health, social security, and social services	12.12	22.65	1,063.77	29.20	167.42	4.60
R	Culture, sports, and entertainment	38.44	24.64	347.35	32.90	44.42	4.21
S	Public management and social organization	42.80	23.13	2,461.86	243.75	413.42	40.93

Source: Based on authors' calculations.

skills, while older workers may be less able to adapt to technological change, or perhaps hold jobs easily substituted by AI technology.

Substitution Effect by Gender. Figure 9-5 shows the weighted average of the substitution probabilities according to worker gender. Female workers are more likely to see their jobs substituted by AI than male workers, but the difference is only about one percentage point. Some studies have shown that women are more likely than men to face discrimination in job searches, promotion opportunities, and compensation (Darity and Mason 1998). If the impact of AI is inevitable, reducing the discrimination against women in the workplace is necessary to prevent widening of the gender gap in the labor market.

Substitution Effect by Level of Educational Achievement. Some studies have shown that AI's substitution effect on employment is not technically neutral, and that it has different impacts on high-skilled versus low-skilled labor (Brynjolfsson and McAfee 2014; Michaels, Natraj, and Van Reenen 2014). Figure 9-6 shows the substitution probability of AI calculated according to level of educational achievement. We divided the sample into five groups based on level of education and report the substitution prob-

FIGURE 9-4.   **Substitution Effect by Age Group**

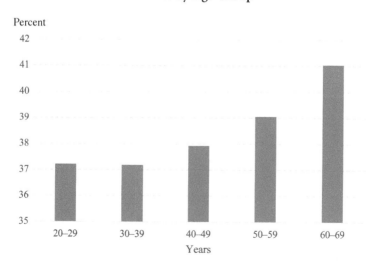

Source: Based on authors' calculations.

FIGURE 9-5.   **Substitution Effect by Gender Group**

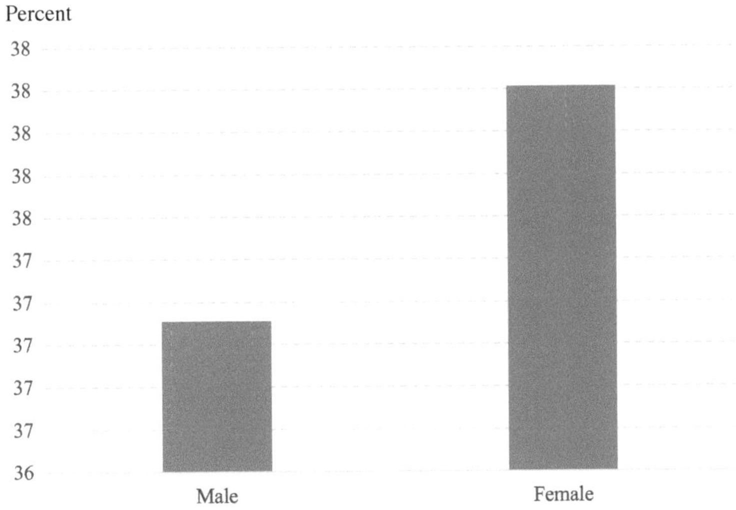

Source: Based on authors' calculations.

ability of each group. It can be seen that the substitution probability by AI decreases with level of education achieved. The illiterate and those with only a primary school or middle school education have a high probability of seeing their jobs replaced, while those with a high school education or better face a much lower substitution probability. Especially for workers with a college degree or higher, the substitution probability is only half that for the lower education groups.

Substitution Effect by Income. Figure 9-7 shows the substitution effect of AI on workers with different income levels. Since the income variable only exists in the 2005 census data, we use the weight matrix calculated by 2005 census data instead of the 2010 data set in this part. We divided workers' income into quintiles, from lowest to highest, and found the substitution probability for each group. The substitution probability of the highest income group is only about 30.5 percent, while that of the lowest income group is as high as 41.1 percent. We also found a significantly negative correlation between income and substitution probability, similar to the conclusions of some other studies (Frey and Osborne 2017). The report by the Executive Office of the President predicts that AI will replace 83 percent of

FIGURE 9-6. **Substitution Effect by Level of Educational Achievement**

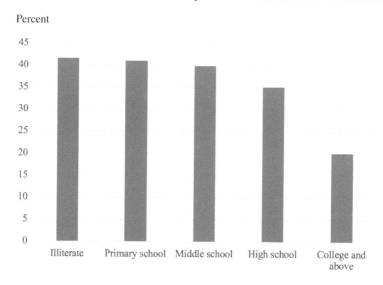

Source: Based on authors' calculations.

jobs paying an hourly rate less than US$20. This proportion is 31 percent for jobs paying between $20 and $40 per hour, but only 4 percent for jobs paying more than $40 per hour (White House 2016).

The Substitution Effect of AI on Employment by Industry

Based on the results of Frey and Osborne (2017), we calculated the average theoretical substitution probability for each industry by using the number of employed people in each occupation in each industry as the weight. Using this calculation, we were able to obtain each industry's AI adoption rate. Multiplying the theoretical substitution probability (by industry) times each industry's expected adoption rate yields the predicted substitution probability of AI for each industry in 2049.

According to China's current industry classification, the employed labor force is mainly distributed among nineteen major industries. We estimated the number of employed people in those industries using the employment structure of 2015 census data and the total employment number of China in 2018. Combined with the actual probability of substitution by AI, it is possible to predict the number of employed people who will be replaced by AI in each industry by 2049.

FIGURE 9-7.   **Substitution Effect by Income Group**

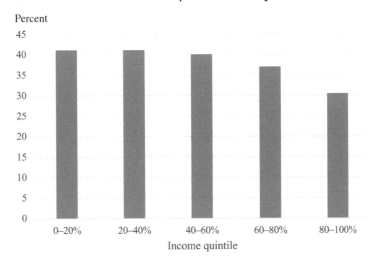

Source: Based on authors' calculations.

Table 9-6 shows the estimated substituted employment in each indus-try. If we add up the results, we find that 142 million people in the urban labor force, or 32.7 percent of the total urban employed (434 million), will have their jobs replaced by AI technology. Meanwhile, 135 million in the rural labor force, or 39.5 percent of the total rural labor force (342 million), will see their jobs replaced by AI technology. In total, 278 million workers, representing 35.8 percent of the currently employed labor force in China, will see their jobs replaced by AI by 2049. The three industries expected to undergo the greatest substituted employment in urban China are manu-facturing; transport, storage, and post; and agriculture, forestry, animal husbandry, and fishery. The three industries with the largest number of substitutions in rural China are agriculture, forestry, animal husbandry, and fishery; manufacturing; and construction.

Based on previous estimates, we also derived the industry adoption rate of AI in a high adoption rate scenario and a low adoption rate scenario. In table 9-7, we present estimates of substituted employment in 2049 accord-ing to the adoption rate in these two scenarios. The results show that the number of jobs that will be substituted in 2049 is 332.6 million under the assumption of a high adoption rate of AI, while this number is 200.7 mil-lion for the low adoption rate.

Thus, China will have 201–333 million laborers replaced by AI technology

TABLE 9-7. Estimated Substituted Employment in Other Scenarios, 2049

Industry code	Industry name	High adoption rate (%)	High substituted employment (10,000)		Low adoption rate (%)	Low substituted employment (10,000)	
			Urban	Rural		Urban	Rural
A	Agriculture, forestry, animal husbandry, and fishery	77.77	3,722.86	12,154.70	42.07	2,014.03	6,575.57
B	Mining	60.46	209.14	76.37	34.31	118.67	43.34
C	Manufacturing	68.67	3,985.53	17,28.97	46.32	2,688.52	11,66.31
D	Production and supply of electricity, heat, gas, and water	61.78	159.50	25.51	35.06	90.51	14.48
E	Construction	71.74	1,369.33	988.94	48.40	923.71	667.11
F	Transport, storage, and post	79.42	3,466.77	881.06	52.08	2,273.21	577.72
G	Information transmission, computer services, and software industry	61.44	523.13	168.87	35.33	300.84	97.11
H	Wholesale and retail trades	85.93	1,082.40	380.64	65.34	823.11	289.46
I	Hotel and catering services	84.58	323.60	29.52	56.61	216.59	19.76
J	Financial intermediation	85.78	360.09	24.52	49.37	207.25	14.11
K	Real estate	59.37	200.06	22.21	34.17	115.14	12.78
L	Leasing and business services	17.65	57.56	10.29	11.57	37.74	6.75
M	Scientific research, technical services, and geological survey industry	13.44	14.02	1.31	9.00	9.38	0.88
N	Management of water conservancy, environment, and public facilities	56.87	85.81	21.48	30.76	46.40	11.62
O	Services to households, repair, and other services	51.82	401.98	138.45	34.68	269.04	92.66
P	Education	40.64	95.91	15.41	26.65	62.88	10.10
Q	Health, social security, and social service	32.29	41.63	6.55	21.17	27.30	4.30
R	Culture, sports, and entertainment	36.86	49.22	6.29	21.22	28.33	3.62
S	Public management and social organization	35.31	372.02	62.47	16.69	175.89	29.54

Source: Based on authors' calculations.

by 2049. However, the impact of AI on China's labor market is also affected by many other factors. First, the effect will depend on the relative costs and benefits of labor performed by AI technology and traditionally, by a human. Although China's current labor costs have increased significantly, they remain relatively low compared with those of developed countries. Once the labor cost is taken into account, industries may be slower in adopting AI technologies. Second, the accelerating population aging process in China will also influence the impact of AI on China's labor market, since it will affect the total amount of the working-age population and labor costs to a considerable degree. On the other hand, adopting AI technology may compensate for the loss of workers as they age out of the workforce. According to He's (2018) predictions, the working-age population is expected to decrease by 167–257 million from 2018 to 2049 (figure 9-8). AI technology might well substitute for the loss of workers from the labor force, and in this way weaken the impact of China's aging population on the labor market. Third, like other technologies, AI technology, while generating a huge substitution effect, at the same time has a large job creation effect. New occupations and new jobs in related occupations can be expected, driven by the development of upstream and

FIGURE 9-8.   **Predictions of Working-Age Population (ages 15–59)**

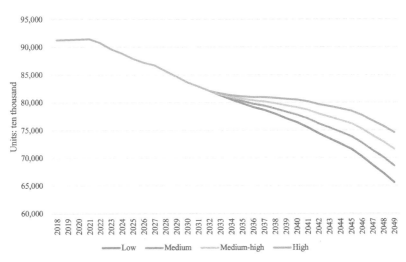

Source: Data from He (2018).

Note: This figure shows the predictions of working-age population under four different total fertility rate scenarios.

downstream industries around AI. Although the available data limit making accurate estimates of new jobs created, AI technology will undoubtedly have both positive and negative impacts on China's labor market, and such a significant change warrants a comprehensive analysis.

CONCLUSION AND POLICY SUGGESTIONS

Automation and AI technology have played pivotal roles in today's economic and social development. They represent a labor-substituted technological progress, with more and more jobs replaced by AI. Using the adoption rate we calculated and the theoretical substitution probability estimated by Frey and Osborne (2017), we estimated the actual substitution probability by AI for various occupations in China. By using this actual substitution probability on an occupation level, we were able to explore the substitution effects of AI on different labor force subgroups. We found that AI has larger substitution impacts on the female workforce, older workers, those with low educational achievement, and those with low incomes. We also predicted the number of employed people who would be replaced by AI in each industry. The results show that China will have 278 million workers (201–333 million under different adoption rate scenarios) replaced by AI by 2049, which is 35.8 percent of the current workforce in China.

Although the research reported in this chapter focused on an analysis of correlation rather than on inferring causality, it provides the first empirical evidence of the impact of automation and AI on China's labor market. Though China considers promoting intelligent industries, represented by AI, one of the important national industrial policies, the potential impacts of AI on the labor market must be handled carefully.

First, it is necessary to comprehensively examine the impact of AI on the labor market, especially on different subgroups of workers. Our study shows that AI has heterogeneous effects on different occupations, different industries, and different subgroups of workers. Only by accurately analyzing the differential effects of AI can we formulate more targeted policies.

Second, more attention should be paid to the importance of human capital investment, and efforts should be made to continuously improve the human capital of Chinese residents. More efforts should be taken to help the relatively vulnerable groups in the labor market (such as women, the low-educated, the old, and the low-income), especially to improve their labor skills and human capital through vocational education or training to avoid the negative impacts of AI. We should also pay attention to AI's impacts on the welfare of workers, to minimize the welfare loss caused by fewer employment opportunities and a slowdown in wage growth.

Finally, the government should pay attention to the social polarization and increased inequality caused by AI. With the development of AI, the labor force will be divided into at least two different groups, a high-skilled group and a low-skilled group, both of which will face different working opportunities and income levels. This division will further increase inequality and intensify social contradictions. To deal with these problems, the government can resort to taxation and transfer payments. For example, taxing AI equipment or robots could be done to subsidize the substituted workers or help improve their working skills. Furthermore, the tax might also be used to deal with the old-age pension shortage caused by aging.

NOTES

1. Regarding the definition of *AI* and *automation* in this chapter, when referring to the influence on the employment market, the two terms are often used interchangeably, which has led to confusion. For example, how should the effects of autonomous driving on the job market be accounted for? After the technology is applied broadly in real practice, professional drivers' job opportunities would decrease sharply, but the result should be attributed to either automation or AI. The fact is that AI is a type of technology while automation is a procedure empowered by various technologies. In different industrial generations, the main driving forces of automation were electrification, digitalization, and even early mechanization, and now the main driving force is AI. So in this chapter, with the purpose of estimating the workforce transition in the next three decades as comprehensively as possible, the substitution probability calculated in the sections that follow is equal to the effects of AI technology and AI-related automation. And by this means the jobs dislocation caused by autonomous driving is due to AI, as autonomous driving is a type of automation mainly empowered by AI technology, such as computer vision and deep learning.

2. Using vision recognition as an example, in 2015 the Microsoft team surpassed human-level performance on ImageNet classification with a convolutional networks algorithm (He et al. 2015). After that achievement, image recognition was widely applied in banking, security, and many other scenarios. According to Gartner, by 2020, 95 percent of video and image content will never be viewed by humans and instead will be vetted by machines that provide some degree of automated analysis (Gartner 2018a). For those occupations that rely on visual recognition, such as a bank teller or security guard, AI's theoretical substitution probability is incredibly high.

3. A technology life cycle, or TLC, is a graphical depiction of various stages for each new technology or other innovation may go through. It describes the costs and profits of a product from technological development phase to market maturity to eventual decline.

4. The influence of the adoption rate on the actual substitution can be explained by the following analogy: As the top agricultural machinery manufacturer, China has an agricultural employment that is more than eight times that of the United States (209.4 million vs. 2.4 million [White House 2019]). The difference is mainly due to the rate of adoption of agricultural mechanized operations and does not reflect an "absolute" technology adoption level.

5. The index mainly relied on Baidu's 2018 study on China's AI market. It calculated the annual revenue of AI solutions businesses and interviewed industry clients to estimate the real value creation to produce the final rate.

6. AI is always defined as the "electricity" of the automation era in empowering industries, and similar to electricity, "coal" is needed to produce the AI power. All AI models require data for automated data analysis capability. Another similarity to electricity is that large amounts of data are required in the adoption of AI, such as with Apple's facial recognition model, which was developed by using more than 5 million real facial image samples and was consistently improved with new data.

7. When we talk about the application, AI is very different from other breakdown technologies, such as electricity, as it cannot be applied generally. Implementation of algorithms in industry scenarios requires the extra work of engineers to deliver the practical solution. And it's true that both scientists and industry experts are working on AGI (artificial general intelligence) to solve the problem, but unfortunately AGI is still far into the future.

REFERENCES

Agricultural Bank of China. 2016–2018. *Annual Reports* (A Share Market). Beijing: Agricultural Bank of China.

Atkinson, Robert D. 2019. "The Task Ahead of Us: Transforming the Global Economy with Connectivity, Automation, and Intelligence." Information Technology and Innovation Foundation, January 7.

Brynjolfsson, E., and A. McAfee. 2014. *The Second Machine Age: Work, Progress, and Prosperity in a Time of Brilliant Technologies.* New York: W. W. Norton.

CB Insights. 2018. *Amazon Strategy Teardown: Amazon's Barreling into Physical Retail, Financial Services, Healthcare, and AI-Led Computing.* CBInsights .com.

China Construction Bank. 2016–2018. *Annual Reports* (A Share Market). Beijing: China Construction Bank.

China Construction Bank, 2018. *Annual Report* (A Share Market). Beijing: China Construction Bank, 17.

Darity, W. A., and P. L. Mason. 1998. "Evidence on Discrimination in Employment: Codes of Color, Codes of Gender." *Journal of Economic Perspectives* 12 (2): 63–90.

Frey, C. B., and M. A. Osborne. 2017. "The Future of Employment: How Susceptible Are Jobs to Computerisation?" *Technological Forecasting and Social Change* 114:254–80.

Gartner. 2018a. *Forecast: The Business Value of Artificial Intelligence, Worldwide, 2017–2025.* John-David Lovelock, Alan Priestley, Susan Tan, Jim Hare, and Alice Woodward (analysts). Available at https://www.gartner.com/en/docu ments/3868267/forecast-the-business-value-of-artificial-intelligence-w0.

Gartner. 2018b. *Predicts 2018: AI and the Future of Work.* Whit Andrews, Svetlana Sicular, Craig Roth, Mike Rollings, Helen Poitevin, Robert Hetu, and John-David Lovelock (analysts). Available at https://www.gartner.com/en/newsroom /press-releases/2017-12-13-gartner-says-by-2020-artificial-intelligence-will-create-more-jobs-than-it-eliminates.

Harvard Business Review. 2018. *The Rise of Intelligent Automation: Turning Complexity into Profit.* Pulse Survey. Harvard Business Review.

He, D. 2018. *China Population Prospects: From Population Size Pressure to Population Structure Challenges.* Beijing: China Population Publishing House Press. (In Chinese.)

He, K., X. Zhang, S. Ren, and J. Sun. 2015. "Delving Deep into Rectifiers: Surpassing Human-Level Performance on ImageNet Classification, Computer Vision and Pattern Recognition." In *Proceedings of the IEEE International Conference on Computer Vision*, 1026–34.

Michaels, G., A. Natraj, and J. Van Reenen. 2014. "Has ICT Polarized Skill Demand? Evidence from Eleven Countries over Twenty-five Years." *Review of Economics and Statistics* 96 (1): 60–77.

National Bureau of Statistics of China, *China Statistical Yearbook 2018.* Beijing: NBS.

Ren, L., L. Li, and C. Ma. 2012. "The Codebook of Occupations and Industries in China Family Panel Studies (CFPS) 2010." In *CFPS Technical Report Series: CFPS-8.* (In Chinese.)

White House. 2016. *Artificial Intelligence, Automation, and the Economy.* Washington, DC: Executive Office of the President.

White House. 2019. *The Annual Report of the Council of Economic Advisers.* "Appendix B: Statistical Tables Relating to Income, Employment, and Production." Washington, DC: U.S. Government Printing Office.

Wiles, Jackie. 2018. "Action Plan for HR as Artificial Intelligence Spreads." Gartner. Available at https://www.gartner.com/smarterwithgartner/action-plan-for-hr -as-artificial-intelligence-spreads/.

10

China's Innovation Capacity in 2049

SHILIN ZHENG, QINQIN ZHUANG, and YONG WANG

Since Deng Xiaoping's announcement of a new Open Door policy in 1978, which marked the start of the era of reform and opening up, China's economy has maintained a relatively high growth rate such that China has now become the world's second-largest economy. Innovation is an important driver of long-term economic growth. China's innovation capacity has improved by leaps and bounds with the remarkable advances of the economy. In 1990 the share of R&D in China's GDP was only 0.67 percent, whereas by 2017 it had reached 2.13 percent, on par with the level of medium-developed countries. The number of patent applications and grants increased from 9,411 and 111 in 1985 to 3,536,000 and 1,721,000 in 2017, making China the world's largest patent holder. According to the Global Innovation Index 2018 (Dutta et al. 2018), jointly released by the World Intellectual Property Organization (WIPO), Cornell University, and the graduate business school INSEAD in July 2018, China has surpassed Canada, Australia, Norway, and other developed countries, ranking among the top twenty (seventeenth) on the index for the first time. In China, new technologies such as high-speed railways, mobile payment systems, e-commerce, and artificial intelligence are widely used.

Although China's innovation capacity has greatly improved, it still lags far behind that of developed countries, especially with respect to the quality of innovation. China holds the most patents in the world, but the quality of the patents is much lower than in the United States, Japan, and other innovative countries. Similarly, China ranks second in the world in the number of research papers published, but the citation rate is low, indicating the research is not as useful to others. The low investment in basic research also means that China lags far behind in basic theory and major inventions, which greatly limits improvement of China's innovation quality. Finally, the misallocation of R&D resources, insufficient protection of intellectual property (IP) rights, and the rise of international trade friction are other important factors holding back improvements in China's innovation capacity.

In the next thirty years, the gap in innovation capacity between China and the developed economies is expected to narrow with respect to the share of R&D spending in GDP. In basic research and in the quality of patents issued and papers published, China will face challenges in catching up with countries known for innovation. The key to China's ability to improve its record on innovation rests on two future efforts. First, China should expect to make major adjustments to the structure of innovation inputs to focus more on basic research, especially for enterprises. Second, the innovation system itself should be reformed to reduce the misallocation of innovation resources and to better protect IP rights.

This chapter addresses China's innovation capacity and its prospects for 2049, the year by which China's leadership wants to accomplish the country's centennial goals. After reviewing the evolution of China's innovation policy, the chapter offers some comparisons of the innovation capacity of China and certain countries known for innovation and looks at China's innovation blueprint for 2049. The discussion then turns to the domestic and foreign challenges China will face in improving its innovation capability and concludes with some policy suggestions.

THE EVOLUTION OF CHINA'S INNOVATION POLICY

China's reform of its science and technology sphere can be divided into five stages. Together, these five stages can be considered China's "great leap forward" in innovation as the institutional guidance moved from a focus on quantity in innovation to a concern with both quantity and quality.

The Experimental Reform Phase, 1978–1984

In the early years after the founding of the People's Republic of China (PRC) in 1949, China's economic foundation was weak. During the first five-year plan period, China established an initial scientific research system, industrial technology system, and national defense science and technology system, which laid the foundations for the further development of science and technology.

In 1978 the Central Committee of the Chinese Communist Party (CCP) convened the National Conference on Science and Technology Work, at which Deng Xiaoping issued the important statement that science and technology are productive forces. In 1982 the strategic principle that "economic construction must rely on science and technology, and scientific and technological work must be oriented toward economic construction," was further clarified. Under this guiding ideology, in 1982 the sixth five-year plan for national economic and social development for the first time included as a component the first National Program for Science and Technology Projects. Since then, China has successively implemented a number of national plans, such as the National Technological Transformation Plan (1982), the National Key Scientific and Technological Breakthrough Plan (1982), and the National Key Laboratory Construction Plan (1984). Technological innovation is constantly developing in exploration.

The Trial Reform Phase, 1985–1994

As the reform of the urban and rural economic systems was being launched, reform of the scientific and technological systems began. In 1985 the "Decision on the Reform of the Science-Technological System" was issued by the CCP's Central Committee. In 1986 the Natural Science Foundation of China (NSFC), the National High-Technology Development Plan (also known as the "863" program, for it was launched in March 1986), and the Spark Program (which takes its name from a Chinese proverb, "A single spark can start a prairie fire"), were put on the agenda. The establishment of the Shenzhen Stock Exchange in 1990 provided effective financing for Chinese companies. In 1988 the national development zone for new and high-technology industries was launched. In August the State Council approved the establishment of the Beijing pilot zone. In 1993, the Law of the

People's Republic of China (PRC) on Scientific and Technological Progress was passed.

During this period, the reform of the science and technology sphere got under way as a major effort, and remarkable advances in innovation were achieved. The number of patents quadrupled in ten years, from 14,372 in 1985 to 77,735 in 1994. In particular, the number of patents for inventions increased significantly, with an average annual increase of 1,051.

The Deepening Reform Phase, 1995–2005

As the reforms took hold, innovation policy focused on optimizing economic growth, improving labor productivity, and increasing the efficiency of economic growth. At the 1995 National Science and Technology Conference, the State Council issued the "Decision to Accelerate the Development of Science and Technology," and the CCP's Central Committee for the first time proposed implementing a strategy to rejuvenate the country through science and education. Since then, China has successively introduced a series of laws, regulations, and policies, further deepened the reforms in the science and technology sphere, and creatively forwarded major policy changes that have had the effect of making research responsive to market needs and of allowing not just Soviet-style institutions but also universities and private industry to do scientific-technological research. From 1996 to 2005, more than a dozen major special plans were issued, such as the National Basic Research Program (the "973" plan), the Knowledge Innovation Program, and the National Science and Technology Innovation Program.

In general, the reforms in the science and technology sphere were solidified during this period. China's overall investment in research and development (R&D) increased rapidly, with an average annual compounded growth of 18.7 percent. In 1995 the R&D input was US$17.2 billion, while in 2005 R&D input had increased to US$95.5 billion, at that point accounting for 1.2 percent of GDP. Meanwhile, the number of patents increased nearly five times from 1995 to 2005, reaching 470,000 in 2005. During this period as well, the central government promoted scientific and technological achievements. The turnover of the technology market, only 26.8 billion yuan in 1995, reached 155.1 billion yuan in 2005, with an annual compounded growth of 19.2 percent.

The Upgrading Reform Phase, 2006–2011

During its attempts to upgrade the reforms, China faced a series of complex and severe challenges at home and abroad, especially the country's lack of capacity for independent innovation. In 2006, the National Medium- to Long-Term Plan for the Development of Science and Technology was unveiled at the National Conference on Science and Technology. This fifteen-year plan was intended to boost the country's capacity for independent innovation. In keeping with the plan, in 2008 a national strategy for IP was formulated to support the development of IP rights, a move expected to incentivize independent innovation. In addition, the State Council issued the "Decision on Accelerating the Cultivation and Development of Strategic Emerging Industries," which focused on seven strategic emerging industries, including the most recent information technology (IT).

On the whole, the reforms were upgraded during this period, and efforts were made to promote independent innovation. According to data from the Organization for Economic Cooperation and Development (OECD), spending on R&D grew at an average annual rate of about 16.7 percent during this period, reaching US$242.8 billion in 2011, or 2.5 times the amount spent in 2006. The share of R&D spending in GDP reached 1.56 percent, almost twice as much as during the period of deepening reforms. Meanwhile, the number of patent applications increased rapidly, from more than 570,000 in 2006 to 1.6 million in 2011. Patents for inventions doubled in six years, to 520,000 in 2006.

The Innovation-Driven Phase, 2012–Present

In 2012 the CCP's Central Committee and the State Council convened the National Conference on Science and Technology Innovation, at which the two bodies emphasized the strategy of innovation-driven development. In 2015 the Central Committee and the State Council issued "Suggestions for Deepening the Reform of Systems and Mechanisms to Accelerate the Implementation of the Innovation-Driven Development Strategy" and various related implementation schemes. To further boost the innovation strategy, the State Council in 2016 formulated the "outline of national innovation-driven development strategy," which clearly put forward the "three-step" development goals of science and technology development from 2020 to

2050. During this stage, the system of scientific and technological innovation has been gradually established, measures for the related reforms have been continuously refined, and institutional innovation obstacles have been gradually removed. The capabilities of China's scientific and technological innovation have reached an unprecedented high level.

During this period, innovation input and output grew rapidly. Since 2012, R&D expenditure has increased by about US$30 billion. By 2017, China's R&D expenditure had reached US$442.72 billion and the ratio of R&D spending in GDP had reached 2.13 percent. The number of patent applications increased by 270,000 per year in 2012–2017, exceeding 3.69 million in 2017. In particular, the number of invention patents doubled and their proportion increased from 31.8 percent to 37.4 percent.

COMPARISONS OF CHINA AND SELECT OTHER COUNTRIES ON INNOVATION CAPABILITY

From the perspective of GDP per capita, under certain conditions, such as opening up to the outside world, the chasing of the leading economies by the following economies is manifested not only in economic convergence (Lucas 2009) but also in the convergence of innovation capabilities (Curran, Bröring, and Leker 2010; Lee 2015; Sharp 2014). Countries such as the United States, Germany, France, and the United Kingdom are representative innovative economies and important references for the economies engaged in catching up. Japan and South Korea are both developed Asian economies that have succeeded in catching up, and they have shown great similarities with China in terms of industrial structure. The following discussion of the differences between China and these successful countries compares and contrasts the inputs to and outputs of innovation, with the goal of providing guidance for China's development of innovation capacity by 2049.

Inputs to Scientific and Technological Innovation

The total amount of R&D investment in China has grown rapidly, but the expenditure is still insufficient. Figure 10-1 shows that from 1991 to 2017, China's total R&D increased rapidly from US$13.44 billion to US$442.72 billion, or an increase in expenditure of 31.9 times over a period of twenty-six years, for an average annual compounded growth of 14.4 percent. During the same period, the total expenditure on R&D in the United States, Japan, and Germany increased by 105.3 percent, 51.5 percent, and 61.5 percent, respectively, while in South Korea it increased by 7.79 times. In 2017 the United States held top place in R&D investment, with US$483.68 billion spent on R&D, followed by China, Japan, Germany, and South Korea, ranking third, fourth, and fifth, at $155.1 billion, $110.08 billion, and $84.25 billion, respectively. Empirically, the higher the GDP per capita of a country, the higher the country's R&D intensity tends to be. R&D investment intensity is measured as the proportion of R&D investment in GDP. During the period 1991–2016, China's R&D intensity showed a clear upward trend. China's R&D intensity was only 0.72 percent in 1991, but broke through 1 percent in 2002 and 2 percent in 2014, respectively. In 2017 the R&D intensity of the United States, Japan, and Germany reached 2.79 percent, 3.20 percent, and 3.02 percent, respectively. South Korea even reached 4.55 percent, far higher than China (2.13 percent). These comparisons show that there is still considerable room for improvement in China's R&D investment.

Besides a large amount of funds, R&D activities also require deep participation of researchers. The total number of Chinese researchers is among the highest in the world, but the density is much lower than in innovative countries such as the United States, Japan, and Germany. In terms of full-time equivalents, the total number of Chinese researchers rose rapidly, from 471,000 in 1991 to 1.692 million in 2016, an increase of 2.59 times, for an average annual compounded growth of 5.15 percent. In 2016 China ranked first in total number of researchers, followed by the United States, Japan, Germany, and South Korea. The density of researchers is measured as the number of researchers per thousand employed. During the period between 1991 and 2016, the density of Chinese researchers increased sharply, from 0.07 to 0.22, with an average annual growth of 4.36 percent. However, the density of Chinese researchers is still significantly lower than in innovative countries. In 2016 the density of researchers in China was only 24.4 percent of that in the United States, 21.9 percent of that in Japan, 23.8 percent of that in Germany, and 15.8 percent of that in South Korea.

Research can be divided into three categories: basic research, applied research, and experimental (or developmental) research. Basic research is the bedrock of innovation. Basic research intensity in China is remarkably low. From 1996 to 2016, China's basic research expenditure as a proportion

FIGURE 10-1. China's Total R&D Expenditure Compared with Other Innovative Economies' Expenditures, 1991–2017 (millions 2010 US$)

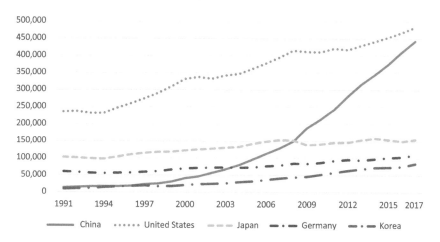

Source: Data from OECD.Stat (database).

of total R&D has been fluctuating around 5 percent, far lower than that of innovative countries (figure 10-2). In 2016 the figure was 5.25 percent, while it was 16.9 percent in the United States, 12.6 percent in Japan, and 16.0 percent in Korea. The intensity of expenditure on basic research is measured as the proportion of basic research input into GDP. The intensity of China's basic research expenditure has increased very little, from 0.047 percent in 2000 to 0.118 percent in 2016, whereas in 2016 the intensity of basic research expenditure in the United States, Japan, and South Korea was 4.01, 3.56, and 5.58 times China's figure.

The government is an important source of R&D funds. The Chinese government's investment in R&D is among the highest in the world. From 1991 to 2017, total R&D investment by the Chinese government increased from US$6.66 billion to US$67.39 billion, or an increase of 8.31 times and an average annual compounded growth of 15.6 percent. Similarly, the government's R&D intensity is expressed as the proportion of government R&D investment in GDP. With rapid economic growth, the Chinese government's R&D intensity has fluctuated but has remained above 0.3 percent of GDP since 2012. In 2017 it reached 0.324 percent, surpassing the figure for the United States (0.271 percent) and Japan (0.25 percent) but still sig-

FIGURE 10-2. **Basic Research Expenditure Ratio, 1996–2016 (%)**

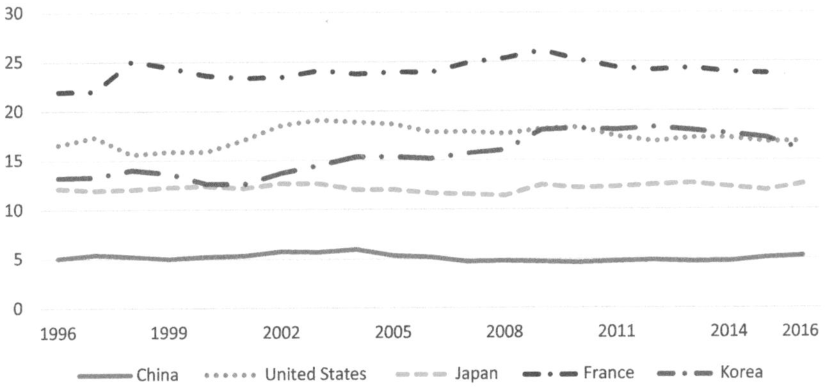

Source: Data from *UIS.Stat* (database, UNESCO Institute for Statistics).

nificantly lower than the R&D intensity of investment in Germany (0.406 percent) or South Korea (0.487 percent).

Colleges and universities play an important role in cultivating talent and carrying out scientific and technological innovation. China's higher education sphere has grown rapidly from a low R&D investment base. During the years 1991–2017, the total R&D investment in higher education increased from US$1.16 billion to US$31.83 billion, for an increase of 26.5 times and an average annual compounded growth of 13.6 percent. Remarkably, the growth rates of 2001, 30.7 percent, and 2009, 20.1 percent, were the stage highs. In 2017 the total R&D investment in China's higher education sphere reached 50.5 percent of that in the United States, making China the second in the world. In sharp contrast, the intensity of China's higher education R&D lags far behind that of the innovative countries used for comparison here. Although the R&D intensity of China's higher education sphere increased from 0.06 percent in 1991 to 0.15 percent in 2017 (1.45 times higher over the period), because of its low initial base, it was only 42.1 percent of that in the United States, 39.8 percent of that in Japan, 29.3 percent of that in Germany, and 39.6 percent of that in South Korea in 2017.

Colleges and universities are key participants in basic research, but they have focused more on the intermediate and back ends of R&D activities in China. In 2016 the basic research funds allotted to China's institutions of higher education amounted to only 40.3 percent of the country's R&D

expenditure, short of the more than 50 percent, on average, in innovative countries (in the United States it was 61.8 percent). Among countries with world-class universities, the United States and the United Kingdom had the largest share of the number of top universities. The gap between China and the two countries remains today. In 2019, of the top two hundred universities listed by the QS World University Ranking, forty-eight were in the United States, twenty-nine in the United Kingdom, twelve in Germany, and nine in Japan. China had only seven on the list, namely, Tsinghua University (seventeenth place) and Peking University (thirtieth), Fudan University (forty-fourth), Shanghai Jiaotong University (fifty-ninth), Zhejiang University (sixty-eighth), the University of Science and Technology of China (ninety-eighth) and Nanjing University (122nd).

Business enterprises are the mainstay of technological innovation, performing the key function of transforming knowledge and patents into goods and services. R&D investment is the source of innovation for technology companies and determines their core competitiveness. The total R&D investment of Chinese enterprises has increased rapidly, from US$5.35 billion in 1991 to US$343.5 billion in 2017, which reflects an increase of 63.2 times and an average annual compounded growth of 17.4 percent. In 2017 the total investment in R&D by Chinese companies reached 97.1 percent of that in the United States, making China second in the world. However, from the perspective of R&D intensity, China is still significantly below the innovative countries. During the period 1991–2017, the R&D intensity of Chinese companies increased from 0.29 percent to 1.65 percent, equivalent to an increase of 4.7 times and an average annual compounded growth of 6.9 percent. As with higher education, because of the low initial R&D intensity of Chinese companies, it was 81 percent of that in the United States, 65.4 percent of that in Japan, 78.9 percent of that in Germany, and 45.7 percent of that in South Korea in 2017.

Chinese companies are actively innovating in areas such as communication technologies, high-speed rail, and internet-plus, and form a new pattern that leads the world in innovation. High-speed rail, mobile payments, e-commerce, and bike-sharing technology have been called China's "Four Great New Inventions" in modern times (An 2017). However, limited by current technology, and driven by short-term interests, most Chinese companies focus on developing new technologies and products with clear commercial prospects rather than products that might be commercially viable in the long term or that seem precarious. In 2016, enterprises' basic research expenditures accounted for only 3.2 percent of total basic research expenditures in China, far lower than in the United States (25.8 percent), Japan (46.7 percent), or South Korea (57.7 percent).

Output of Scientific and Technological Innovation

The number of Chinese patents has grown rapidly, and China has outpaced the innovative countries in this respect. According to WIPO statistics, during the period 1985–2017, the total number of Chinese invention patent applications rose from 8,558 to 1,381,594, an increase of more than 160.4 times and an average annual compounded growth rate of 17.2 percent. In 2017, China's patent applications accounted for 43.6 percent of the total patents in the world, with the United States, Japan, and South Korea coming in second, third, and fourth.

However, the quality of the patents awarded in China is significantly lower than in the innovative countries. China's patents can be broadly divided into three types, invention patents, utility model patents, and industrial design patents, and the proportion of invention patents suggests the average quality of those patents. Figure 10-3 shows that in 2017, the propor-

FIGURE 10-3. **Invention Patent Ratio to Total Patents, China and Other Innovative Economies, 1985–2017 (%)**

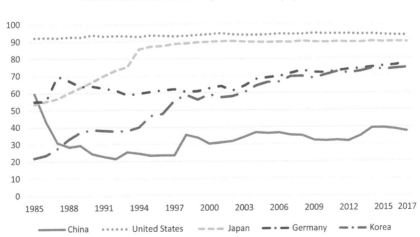

Source: World Intellectual Property Organization Statistics Data Center, Country Profiles.

tion of Chinese invention patents fell to 37.4 percent, which was not only far lower than in the United States (93.3 percent) but also lower than in Japan (89.5 percent), Germany (77.3 percent), and South Korea (74.5 percent). This means that Chinese patents focused on quantity but neglected quality.

The publication of journal articles is another important indicator of a country's innovation output. The number of Chinese scientific papers published annually has grown rapidly, but the gap is still large compared with the number published in the United States. According to the Essential Science Indicators database, between January 2008 and October 2018, the total number of scientific papers published in China was 2,407,339 and Chinese publications were cited 25,047,434 times, both ranking second in the world (table 10-1). The United States was first in total number of papers cited, with the United Kingdom, Germany, and France in third, fourth, and fifth place, respectively. As with patents, the quality of Chinese scientific papers is still below that of research papers emanating from innovative countries. Citation *rate* is another important measure of the quality of a scientific paper. Table 10-1 shows that with respect to number of citations per scientific paper, China has only 10.4, which is far lower than the United Kingdom (18.86), the United States (18.53), and other innovative countries.

TABLE 10-1.   **ESI Index**

Country	Web of Science documents	Cites	Cites per paper	Rank (by cites)
United States	4,067,567	75,366,555	18.53	1
China	2,407,339	25,047,434	10.4	2
England	1,002,004	18,899,104	18.86	3
Germany	1,082,319	18,799,261	17.37	4
France	754,105	12,591,003	16.7	5
Japan	848,977	10,779,183	12.70	7
Korea	542,655	5,948,403	10.96	13

Source: Data from InCites Essential Science Indicators (Clarivate Analytics) (https://esi .clarivate.com).

FORECAST OF CHINA'S MAJOR INNOVATION INDICATORS IN 2049

As discussed in chapter 1, China's GDP per capita in 2040 is expected to reach the level of the United States' GDP per capita in 2017. In accordance with the convergence of innovation capabilities, China's innovation capability in 2040 will likely also reach the corresponding level of the United States in 2017. Owing to factors such as population growth and economic scale, there is no obvious convergence of the innovation quantity index, but the innovation quality index appears to be following the convergence law. Thus the discussion in this section offers predictions of several important indicators related to the quality of China's innovation, with the results shown in table 10-2.

Total R&D Intensity

According to OECD data, the total R&D intensity of China and the United States in 2017 was 2.13 percent and 2.79 percent, respectively. Based on the above analysis, China's total R&D intensity in 2040 should reach the level of the United States in 2017, which means that the average annual growth rate of China's R&D intensity in 2017–2040 will reach 1.18 percent. From 2000 to 2017, the average annual growth rate of China's R&D intensity was as high as 5.24 percent, so it is relatively easy for total R&D intensity in 2040 to be 2.79 percent. The average annual growth rate of total R&D intensity in the United States from 1997 to 2017 was 0.59 percent, and this figure was used to forecast the annual growth rate of China's total R&D intensity in 2040–2049. In that scenario, China's total R&D intensity is expected to reach 2.93 percent in 2049. If China operates in an innovative development pattern, as Japan and South Korea have done, China's total R&D intensity is expected to exceed 3.5 percent in 2049.

Basic Research Expenditure Intensity

In 2017 the expenditure intensity on basic research in China and the United States was 0.118 percent and 0.473 percent, respectively. If China's basic research expenditure intensity in 2040 is to reach that of the United States in 2017, then China needs to grow at an average annual rate of 6.23 percent

TABLE 10-2. **Predicted Values of Main Indicators of Innovation Input and Output**

Indicator	Reference value (%) (Year)	Predicted value (%) (Growth rate, %)			Degree of difficulty
		2035	2040	2049	
Total R&D intensity	2.13 (2017)	2.63 (1.18)	2.79 (1.18)	2.94 (0.59)	Easy
Basic research expenditure intensity	0.12 (2017)	0.35 (6.23)	0.47 (6.23)	0.49 (0.48)	Difficult
Business enterprise basic research ratio	3.16 (2016)	16.65 (9.12)	25.76 (9.12)	27.18 (0.60)	Extremely difficult
Higher education R&D intensity	0.15 (2017)	0.30 (3.83)	0.36 (3.83)	0.40 (1.14)	Easy
Total researcher density	0.22 (2016)	0.67 (6.05)	0.89 (6.05)	1.03 (1.55)	Difficult
Invention patent ratio	37.36 (2017)	76.49 (4.06)	93.33 (4.06)	93.47 (0.02)	Extremely difficult

Source: OECD data.

Note: Growth rate represents the growth rate compared to the previous year's growth.

during 2017–2040, while China's average growth rate between 2000 and 2017 was 5.61 percent. Since 2012, China's economy has entered its "new normal" stage, the role of scientific and technological progress in Chinese economic development has become increasingly prominent, and basic research is the source of scientific and technological progress. Therefore, China's investment in basic research is expected to grow rapidly. If the growth rate of basic research expenditure intensity in China after 2040 is equal to the average growth rate of that in the United States from 1997 to 2017, China's basic research expenditure intensity will reach 0.494 percent in 2049.

Business Enterprise Basic Research Ratio

In 2016, the basic research ratio of China's business enterprises (the proportion of enterprises' basic research investment to basic research in total) was only 3.17 percent, while that in the United States was as high as 25.76 percent. If enterprises' basic research ratio is to reach 25.76 percent in 2040, an average annual growth rate of 9.12 percent during 2016–2040 will be needed. China's corporate basic research investment was affected by the international financial crisis and dropped sharply in 2009, resulting in a decline in the ratio of China's corporate basic research investment from 4.3 percent in 2008 to 1.6 percent in 2009. From 2000 to 2016, the average annual growth rate of the proportion of China's enterprise basic research investment was −0.02 percent. Therefore, in terms of the current growth rate, it is very difficult for China's indicator in 2040 to reach the United States' level in 2016. During the period 1996–2016, the average annual growth rate of the indicator in the United States was 0.60 percent. If that value is used as the growth rate of China after 2040, the proportion of China's enterprise basic research investment will reach 27.18 percent in 2049.

Higher Education R&D Intensity

In 2017, the higher education R&D intensity of China and the United States was 0.153 percent and 0.363 percent, respectively. If the R&D intensity of Chinese higher education in 2040 is to reach the level of the United States in 2017, it needs to grow at an average annual rate of 3.83 percent. From 2000 to 2017, the annual growth rate of R&D intensity of Chinese higher education was as high as 4.16 percent. This shows that it is likely for China to achieve the 2040 target. If the average annual growth rate of R&D intensity of American higher education from 1997 to 2017 is taken as the growth rate of China after 2040, the R&D intensity of Chinese higher education will reach 0.402 percent in 2049.

Total Researcher Density

In 2016, the density of U.S. researchers reached 0.89, while the figure in China was only 0.22. Based on the same analysis, the density of researchers in China in 2040 should reach 0.89, and it will be necessary for China to ensure an average annual growth rate of 6.04 percent during 2016–2040 to reach this figure. However, the average annual growth rate in China between 2000 and 2016 was only 4.92 percent, indicating that it will be a challenge for China to achieve that target. During the period 1996–2016, the density of researchers in the United States increased at an average annual rate of 1.55 percent. If that value is used as the average annual growth rate for China in 2040–2049, the density of Chinese researchers in 2049 will reach 1.03.

Invention Patent Ratio

In 2017, China's invention patent ratio (to total patents issued) was only 37.4 percent, while in the United States it was as high as 93.3 percent. In 2040 the proportion of Chinese invention patents is expected to reach 93.3 percent, but to do so, it will need to grow at an average annual rate of 4.06 percent during the period 2017–2040. However, the average annual growth rate in China from 2000 to 2017 was only 1.22 percent. If the invention patent ratio of China grows at the rate of 0.02 percent, the average annual rate in the United States during 1997–2017, it will reach 93.5 percent in 2049.

In summary, as table 10-2 shows, it is quite possible for China to achieve its convergence goals in terms of total R&D intensity and higher education R&D intensity, namely, 2.94 percent and 0.402 percent, by 2049, but less easy to reach the convergence goals for basic research expenditure intensity (0.49 percent) and researcher density (1.03 percent). Because of the low initial base and low growth rate, it will be a significant challenge for China to achieve the 93.5 percent and 27.2 percent goals of invention patent ratio and business enterprise basic research ratio, respectively.

DOMESTIC AND FOREIGN CHALLENGES FACING CHINA AS IT ENHANCES ITS INNOVATION CAPABILITIES

In quantity of innovation, China is at the world forefront, but it still lags the innovative countries in quality. Therefore, the main point of China's innovation capability improvement lies in the quality of innovation. The weak basic research capabilities, misallocation of R&D resources, insufficient protection of IP rights, and rising international environmental uncertainty have become key factors restricting the improvement of China's innovation quality.

Weak Basic Research Capabilities

Basic research is fundamental to improving the overall quality of a country's innovation. Compared with such innovative countries as the United States, Japan, and Germany, China is deficient in top basic research talent and teams, and major original results are lacking (Wan 2017). This lack is closely related to the configuration of the basic research enterprise in China. China started late on basic research, and the R&D funding is unreasonable. The proportion of basic research funds in R&D funding devoted to basic research has always been low, around 5 percent—far lower than the 15 percent devoted to applied research and the 80 percent going to experimental development. Moreover, funding for basic research comes almost solely from the government. It is allocated to universities and scientific research institutes in the form of state financial appropriations, which account for nearly 90 percent of the basic research funding in higher education, while the proportion of government funds used in basic research in the United States is around 30 percent. Business enterprises' investment in basic research accounts for less than 3 percent of China's total investment in basic research—again, far lower than the roughly 20 percent realized in the United States. Finally, in funding enterprises' research, the Chinese government prefers to support short-term applied research projects rather than long-term basic research.

Misallocation of R&D Resources

The distortion of R&D resource input has also led to the low quality of China's innovation. The misallocation of resources between enterprises with different forms of ownership has led to a diminishment in innovation quality. Generally, state-owned enterprises (SOEs) are less efficient than non-SOEs because of their rigid management system, but SOEs are more heavily subsidized by the central and local governments. It is difficult for non-SOEs with higher innovation quality to obtain government subsidies, making such enterprises' innovation activities vulnerable to market failures. Since R&D resources are not allocated in a market-oriented manner, the innovation capabilities of non-SOEs are not fully utilized, which makes it difficult to quickly improve the quality of national innovation.

We used a database of Chinese industrial enterprises from 2000 to 2007 to examine the effect of government subsidies on innovation. The results show that during this time period, government subsidies (when provided) significantly increased the investment in R&D of non-SOEs but had no significant effect on SOEs. Moreover, the impact on non-SOEs was 3.5 times the impact of SOEs (see appendix table 10A-1). In addition, government subsidies mostly flow to SOEs. From 2000 to 2007, the average subsidy obtained by each SOE was about 4.6 times that obtained by a non-SOE, and the gap widened year by year. Thus government support policy focuses on subsidizing R&D at SOEs with relatively low production efficiency and is inadequate to effectively improve the level of innovation of non-SOE enterprises.

Insufficient Protection of Intellectual Property Rights

Insufficient protection of IP rights is an institutional factor that contributes to the low quality of innovation in China, for several reasons. First, punishment for IP rights infringement is inadequate. Because of the high cost of proving infringement, the long processing period, and difficulty in enforcing judgments, especially in light of the trifling compensation for infringement, enterprises have a high tolerance for infringement and weak enthusiasm for rights protection, which in turn results in substantial losses for innovative enterprises. In particular, it is costly for companies to invest in basic research. Once their rights are infringed, it is difficult for them to reap the rewards for their efforts, which leads Chinese companies to engage in more imitation and application activities than in basic research and product innovation. Second, a patent application review is not enough. On the one hand, patent application has the features of low cost and high returns. Enterprises often split a patent into multiple small patents, resulting in the limited review resources being consumed by a large number of low-quality patents; the high-quality patents easily lose out in such a situation. Utility model patents, on the other hand, do not require substantive examination and the application is easy and cost-effective from a business standpoint. A large number of enterprises apply, resulting in low average patent quality. Finally, there is a notable gap in the degree of IP rights protection across the regions, with local protectionism ensuring no unified IP protection market. China's regions differ greatly in level of economic development level and in market operation efficiency. Enterprises create tax revenues for localities and address local employment. When local enterprises are involved in infringement, local governments often protect them, increasing the difficulty and cost of litigation, and even affecting judgments in IP cases. As a result, IP rights infringements in developing regions are likely to face less legal liability than in more developed regions.

The insufficient protection of IP rights limits the guarantee role of the IP protection system to enterprise innovation. We examined the effect of IP protection on corporate innovation by using the data of the A-share listed companies in 2010–2018 and the provincial intellectual property protection index published by the *Intellectual Property Daily*. The results show that IP rights protection has not brought about a significant increase in corporate R&D investment and patent output, and has had a significant negative effect on design patents (see appendix table 10A-2).

Uncertainty in the International Environment

The low quality of China's innovation puts China in a disadvantaged position with respect to international trade friction. China's innovation faces two main uncertainties internationally. First, the risk of IP-related trade friction has risen. In recent years the number of cases involving China in the 337 investigations launched by the United States has risen sharply, while the number of cases in which China has accused U.S. companies of infringing IP rights is also increasing. Second, the risk of technical barriers has risen as technical trade measures have shifted from traditional industries to high-tech industries. Global trade protectionism has also risen. Because developed countries have technological advantages and have more input into standard setting, technical trade measures have become important trade barriers.

CONCLUSIONS AND POLICY RECOMMENDATIONS

Over the past forty years, China has achieved leap-forward development in innovation and has been at the forefront in terms of quantity of innovation as measured by R&D investment, number of patents issued, and number of publications. However, there remains a huge gap between China and the innovative countries we identified in this chapter in quality of innovation, such as proportion of researchers, intensity of basic research, and proportion of invention patents relative to total patents issued. With the United States as the catch-up target, China's total R&D intensity and the R&D intensity of higher education are more likely to achieve the expected goals. But there exist great challenges in the proportion of basic research investment and the proportion of invention patents. Finally, China's weak basic research capabilities, insufficient protection of IP rights, resource misallocation caused by excessive government intervention, and the increasing uncertainty in the international environment have become key factors constraining the further improvement of innovation quality.

Our recommendations follow.

Increase basic research investment. In the long term, the most effective mechanism to improve the quality of innovation rests on increasing enterprises' and the government's investment in basic research. Enterprises should improve their native innovation ability and master core technologies through massive basic research investment. While playing a guiding role, the government should encourage banks, venture capitalists, institutional investors, and so forth, to stimulate investment in enterprises' basic research and reduce the tax burden of R&D-oriented small and medium-sized businesses. The government should encourage professors and researchers in universities and research institutes to start businesses, and should establish a long-term incentive mechanism for industry-university-research cooperation. In addition, the government should focus on basic research input.

Because of the long duration, high risk, and positive externalities of basic research, the government should expand its investment in basic research.

Optimize the allocation of resources. Improving the quality of China's innovation requires reducing the misallocation of innovation resources; the resources should be fairly distributed among all types of enterprises. Discrimination by type of ownership—that is, SOEs versus non-SOEs—is one of the most important manifestations of China's resource misallocation. China should continue to deepen the reform of SOEs through encouraging mixed formers of ownership and the merger or acquisition of weaker enterprise; break the long-standing discrimination by ownership and make SOEs and non-SOEs participate on an equal footing in the marketplace; and promote the free flow of talents, funds, and physical resources to high-efficiency sectors. The government should reduce the use of selective industrial policies and adopt more inclusive tax incentive policies, giving full play to the decisive role of the market in resource allocation and the screening function of competition.

Strengthen intellectual property rights protections. The institutional guarantee for improving the quality of China's innovation lies in strengthening and optimizing IP rights protection. As a first step, the government should increase the penalties for IP rights infringement. The government should establish a schedule of punitive damages and raise the level of punishment for malicious and repeated infringements, then file the regulations with the National Patent Office and the People's Court. Second, it should strengthen the patent audit. The government assessment should shift from quantity of patents to quality. It should strictly examine the creativity of invention patents to reduce patent splitting and make the patent system focus more on encouraging original inventions. Third, China's central government should impose unified law enforcement standards in the different regions. China should accelerate the construction of specialized IP courts and properly focus on the jurisdiction of patent cases to resolve the problem of nonuniformity of law enforcement standards in the different regions. Finally, China should build an IP rights protection system in line with international standards.

APPENDIX

TABLE 10A-1.   **Impact of Government Subsidies on Firms' Innovation Input and Output**

Variable	R&D intensity			New product output value		
	All	SOE	Non-SOE	All	SOE	Non-SOE
Government subsidies	0.0001‡	0.0001	0.0001‡	0.0350‡	0.0109†	0.0386‡
	(0.0000)	(0.0000)	(0.0000)	(0.0020)	(0.0047)	(0.0022)
Control	Yes	Yes	Yes	Yes	Yes	Yes
Firm FE	Yes	Yes	Yes	Yes	Yes	Yes
Year FE	Yes	Yes	Yes	Yes	Yes	Yes
N	1,301,798	104,754	1,197,044	1,304,151	119,588	1,184,563
R^2	0.0011	0.0007	0.0012	0.0146	0.0069	0.0156

Note: Age, assets, and ownership are controlled for in the whole sample regression. Only age and assets are controlled for in the subsample regression. FE denotes fixed effects. ‡ and † indicates statistical significance at the 1 percent, 5 percent, and 10 percent levels, respectively.

Source: "Above-Scale Industrial Firms Panel (1998–2007)," provided by China's National Bureau of Statistics. Based on author's calculations.

TABLE 10A-2.   **Impact of Intellectual Property Protection on Firms' Innovation Input and Output**

Variable	Innovation input		Innovation output				
	R&D input	R&D density	Patents	Invention patents	Utility model	Design	PCT
IPP Index	-0.061	-0.023	0.019	0.233	-0.052	-0.315†	-0.003
	(0.181)	(0.023)	(0.238)	(0.195)	(0.173)	(0.133)	(0.017)
Control	Yes	Yes	Yes	Yes	Yes	Yes	Yes
Firm FE	Yes	Yes	Yes	Yes	Yes	Yes	Yes
Year FE	Yes	Yes	Yes	Yes	Yes	Yes	Yes
N	16,282	16,290	17,508	17,508	17,508	17,508	17,508
R2	0.420	0.053	0.032	0.029	0.033	0.005	0.002

Notes: Control variables include age, ownership, and lagging value of assets, current ratio, income tax, ROA, and asset-liability ratio. FE denotes fixed effects. PCT denotes Patent Cooperation Treaty. † indicates statistical significance at the 1 percent, 5 percent, and 10 percent levels, respectively.

Source: "A-Share Listed Companies (2010–2018)," provided by Wind Dataset, and *Property Protection Index* published by the Intellectual Property Daily. Based on author's calculations.

REFERENCES

An, ed. 2017. "Spotlight: China's 'Four Great New Inventions' in Modern Times." Xinhuanet, August 8.

Curran, C. S., S. Bröring, and J. Leker. 2010. "Anticipating Converging Industries Using Publicly Available Data." *Technological Forecasting and Social Change* 77 (3): 385–95.

Dutta S., R. E. Reynoso, A. Garanasvili, and others. 2018. "The Global Innovation Index 2018: Energizing the World with Innovation." *Global Innovation Index 2018.*

Lee, K. R. 2015. "Toward a New Paradigm of Technological Innovation: Convergence Innovation." *Asian Journal of Technology Innovation* 23:1–8.

Lucas, R. E. 2009. "Trade and the Diffusion of the Industrial Revolution." *American Economic Journal: Macroeconomics* 1(1): 1–25.

Sharp, P. A. 2014. "Meeting Global Challenges: Discovery and Innovation through Convergence." *Science* 346 (6216): 1468–71.

Wan, G. 2017. "Advance Basic Research for a Country Strong on Science and Technology." [In Chinese.] *China Basic Science* 4:1–8.

Zang, Zezhen. 2018. "2017 Chinese Enterprises Responding to the US 337 Survey Summary (I)." Zhinchanli.com, January 27.

11

Role of Government and Industrial Policies

YONG WANG

Sustainable and healthy economic growth cannot be achieved without continuous industrial upgrading at the disaggregated level, which in turn depends critically on how market and state play their roles (Lin 2011; Lin and Wang 2019b). Over the past forty years, China has worked at developing what is officially referred to as a socialist market economy with Chinese characteristics. Despite a wide array of mistakes and problems, China's central and local governments have played an overall effective and positive role in facilitating structural change and industrial upgrading, promoting market-oriented reforms, embracing trade globalization, and enhancing national power. The average annual GDP growth rate for the past forty years is 9.4 percent, and China is now the second-largest economy in the world, with a per capita GDP equal to US$9,432 in 2018.

Despite the economic achievement, however, the past few years have witnessed a ferocious academic debate over whether China should continue to exercise the industrial policies that undergirded its rise to prominence (Lin et al. 2018). In fact, industrial policies have returned to the spotlight in policy debates and academic research worldwide since the 2008 global financial crisis (see, for example, Aghion and Roulet 2014; Rodrik 2008). Moreover, President Trump's administration keeps criticizing China's government for using inappropriate industrial policies that violate World

Trade Organization (WTO) rules and hurt the U.S. economy; these charges have fueled a trade war between China and the United States. Thus, industrial policies and the role of government in China have become the core controversial policy issues, in theory and in practice.

This chapter addresses the following two questions: What are the major challenges in industrial upgrading that China faces today and will face in the next three decades? And, after forty years of reform and opening up, how should China adjust its industrial policies in the next thirty years?

The chapter is organized as follows. First, I discuss the major challenges China is facing in its industrial upgrading process. Second, I describe theoretically, from the new structural economics point of view, what guiding principles China should follow when formulating appropriate industrial policies. Third, from a practical point of view, I document the basic facts about industrial policies in China's Made in China 2025 initiative, which is a focus of U.S. actions against China under Section 301 of the Trade Act of 1974 in the ongoing trade war between China and the United States. I do so to demonstrate the real-life complexity of formulating and implementing industrial policies in China in the context of today's globalized world. Fourth, I discuss how China should adjust its industrial policies in the next thirty years. A brief conclusion ends the chapter.

MAJOR CHALLENGES IN INDUSTRIAL UPGRADING

The major challenges in industrial upgrading China faces at present and will face in the next thirty years are all structural in nature. The world's largest middle-income country, China is undertaking four structural processes simultaneously—the only country in the history of the world to undertake these processes at the same time (Wang 2017). These changes are being enacted in a country with a vertical structure and facing the sandwich effect—pressure from less-developed and more-developed countries simultaneously—and industrial policies should take all these important elements into account.

Process One: Structural Transformation and Industrial Upgrading.   In almost all countries, as per capita GDP increases, resources are reallocated from agriculture to manufacturing and then to service, as a result of which the employment share of agriculture declines over time, the curve denoting manufacturing's share of employment exhibits a hump shape, and the service share keeps increasing. These changes in sectoral employment and resource use with economic growth are referred to as "Kuznets facts," and together they describe the structural transformation process. In addition, industrial upgrading occurs at the more disaggregated industry level from labor-intensive and low-value-added industries to capital-intensive, high-value-added industries.

Process Two: Economic Transition.   Like other transitional economies, China is still in the process of institutional reform as it moves from a centrally planned economy to a market economy. The more market-oriented reform is being conducted in a gradualist, dual-track approach.[1]

Process Three: Economic Globalization.   Like most other countries, China is deeply engaged in trade globalization, especially after its accession to the WTO in 2001. In fact, China is the largest exporting country in the world. Moreover, the volume of China's cross-border capital flow is also skyrocketing. Liberalization of the capital account and internationalization of the renminbi (RMB) are issues that regularly attract attention from the international community. International technology transfer is the third dimension of the economic globalization in which China is engaged. However, technology transfer faces uphill battles with respect to protection of intellectual property (IP) rights and talent flow.

Process Four: China's Rise as a Global Geopolitical Power.   Together with its economic growth, China's influence can be felt more and more strongly in the international arena in diplomatic, military, and political affairs. In particular, the elaboration of the Belt and Road Initiative (BRI) is perceived by the international community as an important geopolitical strategy of China.

Whereas none of the above four processes is unique to China, what is unique is that China is simultaneously experiencing all four processes as a large country. Consequently, it is much more difficult to understand the appropriate role of the government and the suitable industrial policies that should be implemented.

Challenge One: Developing Production Service

To successfully escape its recent history as a middle-income country, China must accomplish a healthy economic structural transformation from manufacturing to service, and also effect an industrial upgrading from basic manufacturing to high-quality manufacturing, which is related to the first structural process listed above.[2]

In figure 11-1, manufacturing is decomposed to basic manufacturing and high-quality manufacturing, and service is divided into production service and consumption service. There is input-output linkage between these sectors: production service is used as intermediate input for high-quality manufacturing and consumption service.

The production service sector (including financial services, telecommunications, and business services such as R&D) in China exhibits a relatively high administrative barrier to entry, and therefore is inefficient as a result of lack of market competition. The underdevelopment of production service then strangles the structural transformation and industrial upgrading because both consumption service and high-quality manufacturing require production service as a crucial intermediate input. On the other hand, in keeping with Engel's law, both high-quality manufacturing of consumption goods and consumption service have relatively high income demand elasticities, so that consumers' demand for these two increases disproportionately more when income increases. As a result, supply is unable to satisfy demand, which may result in weak domestic demand and even economic stagnation.

FIGURE 11-1.   **Industrial Upgrading and Structural Transformation**

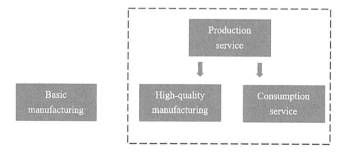

Moreover, there may exist self-fulfilling expectations and multiple equilibria in a laissez-faire market economy. If firms expect optimistically that demand for production service will be high, they might choose to enter the production service sector and produce, as a result of which production service would become cheaper owing to competition, which in turn would also make both consumption service and high-quality manufacturing cheaper relative to basic manufacturing consumption; thus consumers' demand for high-quality manufacturing and consumption service would increase because of both the substitution effect and the income effect, so the induced demand for production service would indeed increase, which would fulfill the initial optimistic belief that the demand for production service will be high. In this case, the economy would reach a high equilibrium featuring more industrial upgrading to high-quality manufacturing and more structural transformation from manufacturing to service. Likewise, a pessimistic belief about future demand is also self-fulfilling and leads to a low equilibrium. Whereas the high-equilibrium position always Pareto dominates the low-equilibrium one, the high-equilibrium position itself is still not the first best choice because of pecuniary externality: each individual firm in the production service sector cares only about achieving its own objective, without taking into account the impact on other firms in the same sector or the impact on the downstream sectors (consumption service and high-quality manufacturing) through the input-output linkage.

As a result, there could be delayed structural change and hindered industrial upgrading or premature deindustrialization and herding industrial upgrading in the laissez-faire market equilibrium. The policy implication, therefore, is that government should overcome the market failure by better coordinating firms' behavior through subsidies or taxation. On the one hand, government should provide the necessary hard infrastructure and policy support to incentivize firms to upgrade to the appropriate new industries to avoid economic stagnation; on the other hand, government should also be alert to speculative investment in "hot" sectors such as real estate markets or premature deindustrialization into low-value-added service sectors. Moreover, China should lower the (administrative) entry barrier to the production service, which is imperative for industrial upgrading and structural transformation at this stage of development.

Challenge Two: Mitigating the Sandwich Effect

As a large middle-income country deeply involved in trade globalization (see the third process in the list above), China faces a sandwich effect in the global market. That is, poorer countries, those with a lower cost of labor than China, chase China by technological imitation and overtaking industries in which China is losing its comparative advantage; meanwhile, richer countries, those with a greater innovation capacity than China, exert pressure on China by extracting monopoly rents on high-technology products that are exported to China or even by reducing the speed of technology diffusion to China by strengthening the enforcement of international IP rights protections or, in extreme cases, by exercising sanctions, especially in cases of high-end key technological products, which may paralyze the whole value chain in China.[3]

To illustrate this idea more formally, imagine there are three countries in the world: North, Middle, and South, denoted by N, M, and S, respectively. There are n different products, all of which are tradable, as shown in figure 11-2.

Different countries have access to different sets of technologies: country S only knows how to produce a subset of products $[0, n_S]$, country M knows how to produce a larger subset $[0, n_M]$, and country N knows how to produce all products. Since labor cost is lowest in South and highest in North, in market equilibrium, all products in the interval $[0, n_S]$ will be produced only in S, all products in the interval $(n_S, n_M]$ will be produced only in country M, and all products in the interval $(n_M, n]$ will be produced only in country N. To be more concrete, S, M, and N could be thought of as Vietnam, China, and the United States.

When Vietnam enhances its technological capabilities by imitation, it can expand the range of products it produces, so n_S becomes larger, which means the total number of products that China will produce be-

FIGURE 11-2. **Sandwich Effect**

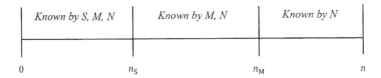

comes smaller. In other words, some industries (products) are reallocated from China to Vietnam because production cost is lower in Vietnam. As a result, China exports less and the world-induced demand for China's labor also becomes smaller, so wages in China would decrease relative to wages in the United States. This in turn would increase the per capita GDP gap between China and the United States. This is the chasing effect. On the other hand, when the United States adopts policies to reduce technological diffusion from the United States to China, n_M becomes smaller, which also increases the per capita GDP gap between China and the United States. This is the pressing effect. Moreover, it can be shown that the larger the country size of a middle-income country, the stronger the sandwich effect it faces.

In addition to technology policies, the sandwich effect may also work through trade policies. For example, when the United States increases the tariff imposed on imports from China, it reduces the demand for China's products and hence increases the GDP gap between the United States and China. Should the United States and Vietnam mutually reduce their bilateral tariff levels while keeping the tariff rates on their imports from China, that would also hamper China's convergence to the U.S. per capita GDP. In reality, trade policies and technology policies are sometimes initiated not merely for economic purposes but also for geopolitical purposes, as described in process four in the list given above.

The policy implications for China are that it should enhance its innovation and imitation capabilities to counteract the pressing effect from the United States. At the same time it should also increase productivity on the goods it knows how to produce in order to counteract the chasing effect from Vietnam. Industrial policies in China must take into account the entirety of the sandwich instead of only focusing only on the interaction with the United States. If China fails to switch quickly enough from an investment-based growth mode to an innovation-based mode, all four structural processes mentioned earlier will inevitably slow down.

Moreover, China should continue to be actively engaged in the world trade system instead of isolating itself. This also suggests that China must be prepared for the possible geopolitical risk of being isolated from the global trade system or the technology diffusion system. In particular, for those high-end products that China imports and that are difficult to substitute, China's government must assess the likelihood of supply termination and the consequent potential damage, as well as determine appropriate actions to take as a backup solution.

Challenge Three: Correcting Government Incentives behind Industrial Policies

China features political centralization and economic decentralization.[4] One important criterion by which to evaluate the performance of local government officials is the regional GDP growth rate. The yardstick competition among local governments fosters market competition in tradable goods among different regions (local governments) and facilitates market-oriented reforms in goods markets, but it is less effective in reforms of factor markets because the latter requires nationwide market integration. Moreover, the practice of local experimentation first and then advocating nationally after success, which works well for reforming the goods markets, may not work for factor market reforms. This is related to the second structural process (economics transition process) mentioned earlier.

China was in a state of shortage when it began its economic reforms after decades of central planning, so the GDP tournament among local governments has proven effective in boosting supply and stimulating growth. After forty years of market-oriented reforms, the bottleneck for most commodities is on the demand side. The key objectives of market-oriented reforms are to reduce resource misallocation (factor market reforms) and to undertake supply-side reforms to meet the changes of effective demand. At this new stage of development, the GDP criterion plus the requirement of maintaining social stability could easily induce local governments to oversubsidize and protect inefficient local industries or firms (especially state-owned enterprises), resulting in industrial overcapacity and resource misallocation, especially when the economy is in recession (Wang 2017).

As a vivid example, during the 2010–2014 period, steel was considered an industry with overcapacity in China, so the central government took stringent measures to reduce the steel output. One policy was to require local governments to shut down steel plants of a size below a certain threshold value. To survive, those small plants tried their best to expand their capacity to meet the minimum size requirement. Local governments knew what was happening, but they had no incentives to stop this expansion behavior because local GDP, employment, and tax revenues all went up with these investments. Consequently, a policy meant to reduce industrial capacity turned out to serve the exactly opposite purpose.[5] As a result of the ferocious domestic competition among steel firms backed by each local government, China's exporting price of steel was so low that it triggered a series of anti-dumping retaliations by the EU and the United States. However, the over-capacity problem of steel came about not because of any purposeful export subsidy policy on the part of the central government but rather because of incentives to local governments to protect local GDP and local employment.

Another political-economic reason behind many failed industrial policies in China is the lack of effective mechanisms to punish government officials for their wrong industrial policies. When the central government issues industrial policies to support a certain industry, it is often safe for local governments to blindly follow these policies even when that industry is not consistent with the comparative advantages of the region. This is because the local government can obtain free financial support from the central government so long as it implements the national policy. There is nothing to lose. All local governments think this way, which naturally leads to investment herding, rent-seeking behaviors, and overcapacity. One such example is the photovoltaics industry in China, which suffered tremendously from this sort of national expansion policy around 2012.

The policy recommendations are to adjust the criteria by which local government officials are evaluated to meet the new challenges in China's new stage of development. In particular, local government should play a greater role in facilitating local industries' growth, and independent third-party post hoc evaluations of industrial policies should be undertaken more seriously and the results made public. Meanwhile, the central government should be more cautious when advocating any industrial policy nationwide; cost-benefit analyses must be more cogent before a policy is announced and implemented. For the central government, the key challenge is how to make the "compelled reform" mechanism continue to work in the future.

HOW TO FORMULATE APPROPRIATE INDUSTRIAL POLICIES

The theoretical rationale for industrial policies is to correct market failures, which are rampant, especially in developing countries. The standard argument against implementing industrial policies is that government failure dominates market failure because government may not have better information than entrepreneurs in the market, or government may be captured by vested interest groups, so industrial policies would be more likely to result in resource misallocation and rent seeking.[6]

In China's case, there still exist tremendous government distortions, the legacy of central planning, that must be eliminated through market-oriented reforms; thus industrial policies become even more controversial. A key challenge is how to distinguish good from bad industrial policies, insofar as China is still going through an economic transition.

From the analytical viewpoint of new structural economics, there are five types of industries: (1) catching-up industries: those whose technologies are still distant from the global technological frontier, such as machinery equipment; (2) leading industries: those that are already on the global technology frontier, such as high-speed rail and home appliances; (3) exiting industries: those gradually losing comparative advantages and moving out of China, such as apparel and footwear; (4) (short-cycle) leapfrogging industries: those overtaking the technological levels of more advanced economies, typically industries that feature rapid innovation and intensive human capital investment, such as online payment systems and 5G technology; and (5) long-cycle strategic industries: those related to national defense and economic security, such as weaponry, warships, and aerospace industries. An industry's type may shift over time, and the relative proportions of these five types change as China develops.

The roles of government and industrial policies are different for different types of industries. For catching-up industries, a category that includes most of China's industries today, government should facilitate technology adoption and diffusion. Setting up industrial parks is an example of a facilitating policy. Foreign firms with better technologies are encouraged to make direct investment by establishing plants in the industrial park, where the infrastructure and business environment are generally better than what is available outside the park.

For China's leading industries, such as household appliances and high-speed railway, we must rely on its own R&D to achieve technological progress, so the government should follow the practices of developed countries, such as improving the patent system, encouraging innovation, and, if necessary, supporting such industries through government purchases. Moreover, the products of these industries are typically aimed at the international market, so the government could help firms find intermediaries overseas and penetrate new markets abroad.

For exiting industries, government should facilitate the geographic redeployment of the firms to places with lower labor costs so that firms can remain viable and continue to be profitable, which increases GNP instead of GDP. Moreover, government could also provide or support training programs for domestic workers in these industries to help them find jobs in other industries or accumulate transferable skills needed to upgrade the industries in a higher-value-added direction.

For leapfrogging industries, human capital is a key factor, and government should facilitate attracting international and domestic talents relevant to those industries, offer tax incentives and R&D subsidies, and provide sufficient hard infrastructure and facilitating policies for those industries.

The firms in long-cycle strategic industries are not necessarily economically viable because the industries may not enjoy a comparative advantage, but the government still needs to support them for national security purposes by providing long-term subsidies for production and R&D, making government purchases, and so on. Likewise, for industries that touch on national economic security, such as certain high-end chip makers, without which the whole supply chain would be paralyzed and the economy would suffer substantial damage, the government should encourage domestic firms to produce these goods to ensure a stable supply, or at least should increase the percentage of domestic content steadily. This industry type differs from the previous four types in that it is typically inconsistent with comparative advantage, but government should still protect it because of geopolitical risks.

China's state capacity may institutionally help the development of strategic industries, but how to incentivize local governments to play appropriate roles in relation to the other four types of industries becomes increasingly difficult owing to regional heterogeneity and the changing international environment.

DISAGREEMENT OVER INDUSTRIAL POLICIES
BETWEEN CHINA AND THE UNITED STATES

Any serious discussion of China's current and future industrial policies must address the current U.S.-China trade war. The Trump administration officially increased its tariff from 10 percent to 25 percent on Chinese imports worth US$200 billion on May 10, 2019. This was followed by a public announcement three days later that the U.S. government planned to impose the 25 percent tariff on a broader array of Chinese imports worth US$300 billion. China's government retaliated by increasing its tariff on U.S. imports worth US$60 billion on June 1, 2019. There is no sign the two sides will be able to reach an effective agreement to permanently end this escalating trade war in the near future. The impact of the trade war between the largest two economies in the world is profound. Negotiations between the two countries go beyond the arena of pure trade. China's industrial policies have become the key target of criticisms the U.S. government has lodged against China and the key subject of negotiations.

The Made in China 2025 strategic plan has been a focus of the Trump administration in its Section 301 actions against China and is frequently cited by the U.S. government as evidence of China's official industrial policies. Made in China 2025 is an initiative formally launched by Prime Minister Li Keqiang in 2015 as a ten-year plan aimed at securing China's position as a global powerhouse in high-tech industries. The initiative establishes nine priority tasks, including (1) improving manufacturing innovation, (2) integrating technology and industry, (3) strengthening the industrial base, (4) fostering Chinese brands, (5) enforcing green manufacturing, (6) promoting breakthroughs in ten key sectors, (7) advancing restructuring of the manufacturing sector, (8) promoting service-oriented manufacturing and manufacturing-related service industries, and (9) internationalizing manufacturing. The ten key sectors that are explicitly listed as strategic ones that China's government should promote are (1) aerospace, (2) robotics, (3) new-energy vehicles, (4) high-technology shipping, (5) artificial intelligence and next-generation information technology, (6) biotechnologies, (7) energy and power generation, (8) advanced railway equipment, (9) new materials, and (10) agricultural machinery. In addition, the initiative also seeks to build forty innovation centers in China by 2025.

The concrete quantitative goal of Made in China 2025 is to reduce China's reliance on foreign technology and increase the domestic market share of key Chinese products. For example, the plan specifies that by 2020, 40 percent of essential spare parts and key materials will have domestic sources, and that figure should increase to 70 percent by 2025. The domestic content goals for different products are shown in more detail in figure 11-3.[7]

FIGURE 11-3. **Domestic Content Goals for Various Products in Made in China 2025**

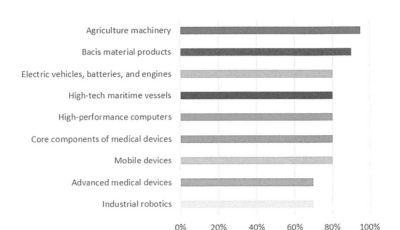

In addition, China's government sets quantitative targets to improve the key performance indexes of the manufacturing sector. For instance, it specifies that R&D as a percentage of sales revenue in the manufacturing sector should increase from 0.95 percent in 2015 to 1.68 percent by 2025, the annual labor productivity growth rate should increase to 6.5 percent by 2025, and so on. Figure 11-4 shows the detailed goals of the key performance indicators of the four categories enumerated by the initiative, Made in China 2025.[8]

From China's point of view, it currently faces the challenge of hitting the middle-income trap, so it must upgrade its industries, enhance its innovative capabilities, and improve the quality of products or risk losing its comparative advantage in labor-intensive industries and low-value-added products because of rapidly rising labor costs. The Made in China 2025 plan explicitly notes that "China's manufacturing sector is large but not strong, with obvious gaps in innovation capacity, efficiency of resource utilization, quality of industrial infrastructure and degree of digitalization. The task of upgrading and accelerating technological development is urgent" (Morrison 2019). This self-assessment is accurate, to the point, and highly consistent with the analyses offered in this chapter. To ensure sustainable growth, China must make its manufacturing stronger along the directions outlined in this initiative. In some sense, this initiative was inspired by Germany's Industry 4.0, a national strat-

FIGURE 11-4.   Key Performance Indicators in Made in China 2025

Category	Manufacturing transformation KPI	2015	2025
Innovation capability	1. R&D cost / revenue (%)	0.95	1.68
	2. Patents / billion RMB of revenue	0.44	1
Quality and value	3. Manufacturing quality competitiveness (index)	83.5	85.5
	4. Manufacturing value-added increase over 2015 (%)	—	4
	5. Average annual labor productivity growth (%)	—	6.5
IT and industry integration	6. Broadband penetration (%)	50	82
	7. Digital R&D and design tool penetration (%)	58	84
	8. Key process control rate (%)	33	64
Green industry	9. Energy decrease over 2015 / industrial value-added (%)	—	34
	10. CO_2 decrease over 2015 / industrial value-added (%)	—	40
	11. Water use decrease over 2015 / industrial value-added (%)	—	41
	12. Industrial solid wastes utilization ratio (%)	65	79

egy launched in 2013 to consolidate German technological leadership in mechanical engineering.

Whereas the legitimacy of China's goals to upgrade its manufacturing and develop its own economy can be hardly challenged by other countries, the U.S. government is very unsatisfied with how China tries to achieve these goals. Moreover, the United States has expressed concern over China's long-term objective, which is that by 2049, the centenary of the founding of the People's Republic of China, China will have become the leader among the world's manufacturing powers. U.S. trade representative Robert Lighthizer issued the following statement on June 15, 2018: "China's government is aggressively working to undermine America's high-tech industries and our economic leadership through unfair trade practices and industrial policies like Made in China 2025."

Critics of Made in China 2025 contend that the domestic content target policy advocates import substitution and violates the WTO rules. They also fear that China's government provides extensive financial subsidies to domestic firms involved in those target sectors, or supports acquisitions of foreign technology companies and IP, because these would give Chinese firms unfair advantages in the global competition and technology upgrading. Overall, this plan is viewed as major evidence that China is still not a free market economy and that state intervention is too comprehensive. The U.S. government, in particular, also fears that Made in China 2025 could empower China to eventually replace the United States as the global leader in the advanced manufacturing areas. These concerns are also shared by other Western developed countries.

In response to these criticisms, the Chinese government defends by arguing that the Made in China 2025 initiative still emphasizes the basic principle that China shall continue to deepen its market-oriented reforms and let markets play the decisive role in resource allocation. Moreover, the government policies mentioned in that initiative are transparent, open, and nondiscriminatory, and they are merely guiding principles instead of concrete execution plans. Those numbers are suggested goals, not mandates. Many even hold the view that the U.S. government criticizes this initiative not because it is wrong but because it can enhance the competitiveness of Chinese firms and therefore jeopardize the leading position of the United States in the global advanced manufacturing arena. Why should China have to stop making progress just because the United States does not like it?

The disparate views of the two sides have already resulted in severe consequences that go much beyond the current trade war between the two largest countries in the world. It fuels national distrust against each other and injects a large degree of uncertainty into the global economy. All countries start to worry about what would happen if the world trading system were to be divided into different blocs or collapsed completely, and what would happen if another cold war commenced. The trend of threats followed by the tit-for-tat imposition of punitive tariffs could easily lead to disaster, and therefore the United States, China, and many other countries must make efforts to put a halt to it.

It is beyond the scope of this chapter to undertake a complete analysis of the U.S.-China disputes over industrial policies and trade policies, but a good understanding of the basic facts involved in this conflict should help us consider what China should do in the future.

HOW SHOULD CHINA ADJUST ITS INDUSTRIAL POLICIES IN THE NEXT THIRTY YEARS?

The largest challenge to China as the country formulates and implements industrial policies is the need to take into account the four co-occurring structural processes, along with China's situation as a large, middle-income country subject to the sandwich effect. Any industrial policy package has to strike an appropriate balance because of potential trade-offs hardwired into those different structural processes at this level of development.

More concretely, China should consider the following points when adjusting its industrial policies.

- Accelerating the market-oriented reforms in factor markets would enable China to reduce its reliance on controversial industrial policies to achieve efficient resource allocation. In contradistinction to the mature market economies of developed countries, China still suffers distortions in factor markets, partly inherited from the central planning regimes and partly resulting from the gap between efficient supplies of pertinent production factors and the changing demand for those factors as the industrial structures endogenously evolve. For example, once the market of venture capital is sufficiently well developed in China, a large fraction of R&D expenditure could be efficiently financed by the market itself, instead of relying on government subsidies. Based on the analysis presented earlier, the fraction of leading industries and leapfrogging industries in the whole economy is expected to increase as China grows, so the financial market should be efficient enough to quickly respond to support this change.

- Except for long-cycle strategic industries, all the other four types of industries should be developed only when they are consistent with comparative advantage (Ju, Lin, and Wang 2011, 2015). Correspondingly, local government should be given more freedom to formulate industrial policies for those four types of industries based on local conditions. This would help to reduce the risks devolving from central planning and overcapacity.

- IP rights protection in domestic markets should be more strictly enforced to encourage indigenous innovation, and the quality of tertiary education must be urgently improved to provide high-skilled talent, which is vital especially for leading industries and leapfrogging industries in China (Tang, Wang, and Zhou forthcoming). How should China go about creating an innovation-friendly business environment, one that could attract global talents and facilitate innovation? Shenzhen sets a good example for other cities in China. How should China encourage firms to make global profits based on hard-core innovation capability instead of merely exploiting arbitrage opportunities in policies? Huawei is a model in this regard.

- The instruments for executing national industrial policies should be improved. Generally speaking, tax rebates should be preferred to additional subsidies, other things being equal, because the former are not only simpler to implement but also are less distorting and less controversial. Moreover, as China approaches high-income status, it should learn from how developed countries formulate and implement their industrial policies to foster innovation, and adapt these approaches to the Chinese environment (Wang and Hua forthcoming).

- Optimal industrial policies are different for the five different types of industries, according to the new structural economics. A given industry may shift from one type to another as it develops and its type may be different in different regions, so some means should be in place to adjust dynamically industrial policies for the same industry and the same location. For example, academic research shows that export-processing zones are overall quite successful as an industrial policy for the labor-intensive stage of production (such as assembly), but as labor costs rise, that policy may become less and less effective, especially in developed regions, so original export-processing zones should be transformed into other types of industrial parks as the comparative advantage changes.

- Based on the vertical structure analyses, production service deserves special attention in China's industrial policies because it is increasingly important for industrial upgrading in manufacturing and for the structural transformation from manufacturing to service. Key obstacles to production service are the relatively high entry barrier and the dominance of state-owned firms (see Du and Wang 2013; Li, Liu, and Wang 2016), so China should give priority to forwarding the market-oriented reforms in this sector to enhance market competition. Otherwise production service is likely to become a universal bottleneck that strangles the downstream private sector and results in stagnation in the aggregate economy (Lin and Wang 2019a).

- Based on the sandwich effect analysis in this chapter, China as a middle-income country should adjust its industrial policies to respond not only to the behaviors of developed economies but also to the behaviors of countries that are closely chasing China. The main thrust of industrial policies is to enhance innovation capacity when China is competing with more advanced economies and to improve efficiency and raise labor productivity when China is competing with countries with lower labor costs. Moreover, the optimal speed at which industrial policies are adjusted should take into account the changes in the chasing effect from the south and the pressing effect from the north (Wang and Wei 2019).

- Instead of emphasizing the domestic content goals of the core industries and products, which may scare other countries if they see them as import substitution policies, China's industrial policies should highlight helping markets identify the key components, products, or industries that not only have higher value added but also are consistent with China's latent comparative advantage, and then provide a facilitating role for industrial upgrading, including the provision of industry-specific infrastructure and the elimination of existing policy impediments, which are academically sound and practically more aligned with market-oriented reforms.

- China should be fully aware of its large size and the resulting global impact of its industrial policies. In the future, it should carefully assess the potential global impact of any of its newly proposed major industrial policies and, when necessary, make serious efforts to maximize the level of acceptance from the international community. For example, the joint concerns over and public criticisms of Made in China 2025 by Western developed countries are partly the result of inadequate advance communication from China to the community of developed countries. China should do more than justify industrial policies based on what China needs; it should also evaluate the likelihood that such policies will generate positive spillover for the rest of the global economy. China would not have to worry about this if it were a small or low-income country.

- With the presence of potential geopolitical risks associated with China's rise as a global geopolitical power, the fourth structural process, China must have a plan B for strategic industries in case of hostile supply cutoff of key components by foreign countries. China should identify such politically vulnerable bottlenecks in its industrial development and support the establishment of backup facilities for national defense and economic security purposes.

CONCLUSION

This chapter revisited an old yet unsettled fundamental question in economics, namely, the role of government and industrial policies, and our analysis is made in the concrete context of China's economic development for the next thirty years. The central point is that challenges to China's industrial upgrading are structural and dynamic in nature, featuring four simultaneous structural processes, a vertical structure, the sandwich effect, and the political-economic interaction between central and local governments. Using the analytical framework of new structural economics, I showed theoretically how different industrial policies should be adopted for five different types of industries, based on each stage of economic development. Then I explored as a real-life case study the international disagreement over the practice and legitimacy of China's industrial policies pertinent to the current trade war between China and the United States and showed how industrial policies in China can be extremely controversial. Based on these analyses, ten guiding principles were proposed for how China should adjust its industrial policies over the next three decades.

NOTES

This chapter is the result of a collaboration between the National School of Development at Peking University and the Brookings Institution. The author gratefully acknowledges the comments and suggestions by Professor Yiping Huang, Professor Yang Yao, and other participants in the workshop for authors. The author is responsible for any remaining deficiencies.

1. Wang (2015) develops a formal model to characterize how endogenous sequential institutional reforms interact with economic growth in China.

2. The discussion in this section is mainly based on Lin and Wang (2019a).

3. The discussion in this section is based on Wang and Wei (2019).

4. Bardhan (2016) is an excellent literature review on the role of state in economic development.

5. Wang (2013) builds a political economy model to show how fiscal decentralization may have a nonmonotonic impact on hierarchic governmental policies toward foreign direct investment based on the experiences of China and India.

6. The discussion in this section draws heavily on Lin and coworkers (2018), especially chapters 1 and 3.

7. This figure is taken from Morrison (2019), who provides a good summary of the Made in China 2025 initiative.

8. This figure is taken from the Institute for Security and Development Policy (2018), which documents important facts about the Made in China 2025 initiative.

REFERENCES

Aghion, Philippe, and Alexandra Roulet. 2014. "Growth and the Smart State." *Annual Review of Economics* 6 (August): 913–26.

Bardhan, Pranab. 2016. "State and Development: The Need for a Reappraisal of the Current Literature." *Journal of Economic Literature* 54 (3): 862–92.

Du, Julan, and Yong Wang (with Julan Du). 2013. "How to Reform SOEs under China's State Capitalism." In *Unfinished Reforms in the Chinese Economy*, edited by Jun Zhang, chap. 1. Singapore: World Scientific Publishing.

Institute for Security and Development Policy (ISDP). 2018. "Made in China 2025." Washington, DC, and Chengdu: ISDP, June.

Ju, Jiandong, Justin Yifu Lin, and Yong Wang. 2015. "Endowment Structure, Industrial Dynamics and Economic Growth." *Journal of Monetary Economics* 76:244–63

———. 2011. "Marshallian Externality, Industrial Upgrading and Industrial Policy." World Bank Policy Research Working Paper No. 5796. Washington, DC: World Bank Group.

Li, Xi, Xuewen Liu, and Yong Wang. 2016. "A Model of China's State Capitalism." Working paper.

Lighthizer, Robert. 2018. "USTR Issues Tariffs on Chinese Products in Response to Unfair Trade Practices," June 15. Available at https://ustr.gov/about-us/policy-offices/press-office/press-releases/2018/june/ustr-issues-tariffs-chinese-products.

Lin, Justin Yifu. 2011. "New Structural Economics: A Framework for Rethinking Development." *World Bank Research Observer* 26 (2): 193–221.

Lin, Justin Yifu, and Yong Wang. 2019a. "Structural Change, Industrial Upgrading and Middle-Income Trap." In "Development Policies," edited by Dani Rodrik. Special issue, *Journal of Industry, Competition and Trade.*

———. 2019b. "Remodelling Structural Change." In *The Oxford Handbook of Structural Transformation*, edited by Célestin Monga and Justin Lifu Lin, chap. 3. Oxford: Oxford University Press.

Lin, Justin Yifu, Jun Zhang, Yong Wang, and Zonglai Kou. 2018. *Industrial Policies: Summary, Reflection and Prospect.* Beijing: Peking University Press.

Morrison, Wayne M. 2019. "The Made in China 2025 Initiative: Economic Implications for the United States." *In Focus* 10964. Washington, DC: Congressional Research Service, April 12.

Rodrik, Dani. 2008. *Normalizing Industrial Policies.* Washington, DC: World Bank Press.

Tang, Heng, Yong Wang, and Qiuyun Zhao. Forthcoming. *Intellectual Property Rights Protection from the Perspectives of New Structural Economics.* Beijing: Peking University Press.

Wang, Yong. 2017. *Thinking and Debates on New Structural Economics.* Beijing: Peking University Press.

———. 2015. "A Model of Sequential Reforms and Economic Convergence." *China Economic Review* 32:1–26.

———. 2013. "Fiscal Decentralization, Endogenous Policies, and Foreign Direct Investment: Theory and Evidence from China." *Journal of Development Economics* 103:107–23.

Wang, Yong, and Xiuping Hua. Forthcoming. "The State as a Facilitator of Innovation and Technology Upgrading." In *The Oxford Handbook of State Capitalism*, edited by Dennis C. Mueller. Oxford: Oxford University Press.

Wang, Yong, and Shang-Jin Wei. 2019. "The Sandwich Effect: Challenges for Middle-Income Countries." INSE working paper. Beijing: Institute of New Structural Economics, Peking University.

PART IV

INTERNATIONAL CHALLENGES

12

China's Opening-Up Policies: Achievements and Prospects

MIAOJIE YU and TENGLONG ZHONG

China began its era of reform and opening up in 1978, which profoundly changed China and has deeply influenced the world. As a result of its opening-up policies, China has become the largest country in the world in goods trade and the second-largest country in services trade. Both inward and outward foreign direct investment (FDI) flow grew fast, reaching US$134.97 billion and US$143.04 billion, respectively, in 2018. Those figures represent 13.3 percent and 14.1 percent of the world FDI flow. Over the past four decades, China's volume of trade in foreign goods has increased 204-fold, whereas its GDP has increased only 34-fold. In this respect, China has successfully pulled off a miracle in foreign trade. This chapter reviews the major practices and achievements of and lessons learned from China's opening-up policy and forwards policy suggestions for China's continued opening in the future.

China's opening-up process can be regarded as having occurred in three stages: a stage characterized by expanding the extensive margin of opening, that is, a stage focused on increasing the quantity of resources, labor, or production, where "margin" denotes the range (before 2001); a stage of expanding the intensive margin of opening, which focused on improving the quality or output per unit of resource or labor (2001–2017); and a general opening (since 2017) after the Chinese Communist Party (CCP) announced a new era of all-around opening up in China at its Nineteenth National Congress.

Before opening, China had followed an import substitution strategy, which was characterized by a lesser reliance on imports and exports. China had also implemented a heavy industry–oriented development strategy, which entailed lowering interest rates, depreciating the renminbi, and distorting the prices of labor, raw materials, and even agricultural products—all to support the development of heavy industry. This strategy led to surplus labor, low incomes, and hence slow economic growth.

After 1978, the Chinese government abandoned the heavy industry–oriented development strategy and began to employ an export-oriented strategy, which lasted until the global financial crisis of 2008–2009. Before China's entry into the World Trade Organization (WTO) in 2001, the major force driving export growth was a comparative advantage based on the country's factor endowment. China is a labor-abundant country and its labor costs are relatively cheap. Accordingly, China exported labor-intensive products and served as the largest "world factory."

Since China's accession to the WTO, however, the cost of labor has increased significantly, and China no longer realizes a cost-saving advantage compared with such countries as Vietnam and other East Asian countries. Indeed, the fundamental force driving China's export boom today is the country's increased market size.

The global financial crisis that began in 2008 had significant negative impacts on the global economy, especially in developed economies. In the context of weakening demand from the developed countries, China's reliance on exports to drive economic growth was no longer tenable. China has begun switching from labor cost advantages to quality, brand, and service to drive exports.

At the Nineteenth National Congress of the CCP, held in October 2017, the State Council made it clear that China's economy was in the process of shifting from a focus on accelerating growth to a focus on high-quality development. As a result, improving the quality of export goods and services has become a top priority. At the same time, trade protectionism and antiglobalization sentiments are on the rise around the world. Against this background, the Chinese government has proposed implementing a new strategy that features opening up across the board, with the twin goals of promoting the development of both the Chinese economy and the global economy.

What's more, the China-U.S. trade conflict provoked by the United States has been escalating since the beginning of 2018. This conflict has had negative effects on both the Chinese and the U.S. economy and contributes to uncertainty about global economic development. Therefore, the external environment China faces has become increasingly complex. China intends to deal with the challenges calmly and confidently. Even as China must fight back against the attacks launched by the United States, the country plans to further open up to the world by broadening market access, improving the investment environment for foreign investors, strengthening the protection of intellectual property (IP) rights, and expanding imports, among other steps.

This chapter explores the historical development of the extensive margin of the opening-up process, reviews the dynamic evolution of the intensive margin of opening up, considers the recent development of the generalized opening up announced by the State Council, and offers a set of policy recommendations.

EXPANDING THE EXTENSIVE MARGIN OF OPENING, 1978–2000

China's opening-up strategy before its accession to the WTO included the following important actions: setting up special economic zones and industrial parks, relaxing market access for foreign investors, reducing tariffs on imports, and encouraging processing trade. The following discussion elaborates on each of these four aspects, with comments particularly on China's expanding the extensive margin during the opening-up process.

Setting Up Open Economic Zones and Industrial Parks

China's establishment of open economic zones was one of the most important changes resulting from the opening-up policy. Before 2000, the establishment of open economic zones can be thought of as occurring in three waves. The first wave, also known as the "point" phase, entailed the adoption of four cities in 1981 as the special economic zones (SEZs): Shenzhen, Zhuhai, and Shantou in Guangdong province and Xiamen in Fujian province. Shenzhen was chosen because of its excellent geographic location; it is a small village near Hong Kong. A similar rationale applied to the selection of Zhuhai, a small town on the western Pearl River near Macau. Shantou was chosen because of its strong network of connections with Chinese immigrants in East Asian countries. Similarly, Xiamen was chosen because it is close to Taiwan province.

The second wave of the establishment of open economic zones brought in many coastal cities, from Dalian, a northern coastal city in Liaoning province, to Beihai, a southern coastal city in Guangxi province. The cities are connected along a "line" and are called coastal open cities. The third wave of open economic zones extended to include zones and parks from the cities along the east coast to the central and western provinces. In particular, the government set up twenty-five high-tech industrial development zones in Shenyang, Tianjin, Wuhan, and Nanjing. Thus, by 1992 China had established six SEZs (the original four point zones, plus Hainan, and Pudong in Shanghai), fourteen coastal open cities, fifty-four national-level economic and development zones, fifty-three high-tech industrial parks, and fifteen tariff-free zones (Naughton 2018).

All of these zones—SEZs, coastal open cities, economic and development zones, and even high-tech development zones—had very similar policy designs. In particular, foreign firms located in the zones were exempt from corporate tax in their first three years. In their fourth and fifth years, they had to pay a corporate tax rate of only 17 percent, which was half the tax rate levied on Chinese domestic firms. This policy lasted for around three decades. After 2007, foreign firms had to pay the same 25 percent corporate tax rate as domestic firms. In addition, wholly owned foreign firms and subsidiaries were permitted in all types of zones.

Relaxing Market Access for Foreign Direct Investment

After 1978, the Chinese government began gradually relaxing access to the Chinese market for foreign investment. In 1979 the Sino-Foreign Equity Joint Venture Law was promulgated, making foreign-invested enterprises legal economic organizations. Later on, more laws and regulations were issued, all of which provided a legal basis for the supervision of foreign investment and protected the rights and interests of foreign investors. Foreign investment grew from almost nothing in 1978 to a cumulative amount of US$23.4 billion in 1991.

In 1992, at the Fourteenth Congress of the CCP, China's leadership announced a market economy would be set up, which markedly improved the willingness of foreign companies and individuals to invest in China. The open areas were extended from the cities along the east coast to the central and even western provinces. To facilitate foreign investors and improve the quality of foreign investment, the Chinese government released its *Catalogue for the Guidance of Industries for Foreign Investment* in 1995. The catalogue assigns all industries to one of four categories: encouraging, allowing, limiting, and forbidding foreign investment. China began to open some service sectors to foreign investment, including its retail, financial, freight, and software industries. After 1992, foreign investment flowed quickly into China, reaching a new high of US$38.9 billion in 1993. From 1994 to 1999, foreign investment topped US$40 billion each year.

Reducing Import Tariffs

Before the economic reforms of 1978, China adopted the import substitution strategy by setting high import tariffs and other nontariff barriers against foreign products. In 1992, at the Fourteenth Congress of the CCP, the State Council announced it would set up a market economy. Thereafter China began actively cutting its import tariffs. The simple import tariff, still 42 percent in early 1992, was reduced to 35 percent in 1994 during the Uruguay round of WTO negotiations. During the next three years, China cut its import tariffs another 50 percent or so. At the end of 1997, the simple import tariff was reduced to around 17 percent. The most important reason for taking such a major step in opening up was that China hoped to accede to the WTO as soon as possible; in 1994, China was still only an observer, rather than a formal member, of the WTO. After its accession to the WTO, China's simple import tariff was reduced from around 17 percent to around 10 percent in 2006. Since 2006, China's import tariff rate has remained stable.

Trade liberalization has been significant for the Chinese economy. To understand the country's economic development, it is essential to understand the realization of firm productivity, since "productivity is not everything, but almost everything," as Paul Krugman has said. It is widely accepted that trade liberalization fosters firm productivity. Yu (2015) finds that trade liberalization has contributed to around 14.5 percent of Chinese firm productivity growth in the twenty-first century.

Encouraging the Processing Trade

The processing trade is a key for understanding China's trade development over the past four decades. "Processing trade" denotes the process by which a domestic firm initially obtains raw materials or intermediate inputs from abroad and, after local processing, exports the value-added final goods (Feenstra and Hanson 2005). As Dai, Maitra, and Yu (2016) note, the iPhone is a perfect example of China's processing trade. Foxconn, a famous iPhone assembler in Shenzhen, imports 155 intermediate components of smart phones from Japan, Korea, and the United States. After producing the final products domestically, Foxconn exports back to the United States and other foreign markets. Governments typically encourage processing trade by offering tariff reductions or even exemptions on the processing of intermediate goods.

Processing imports and exports developed quickly after 1978, especially after 1992, when at the Fourteenth Congress of the CCP it was announced that the state would set up a market economy. Just before China's accession to the WTO, the government decided to establish export processing zones (EPZs) to promote processing trade. Since then, China has set up more than sixty EPZs. Different from the earlier open economic zones and industrial parks, such EPZs are spread across the country. They are located not only in eastern coastal cities but also in western inland cities, such as Urumchi in Xinjiang province. Only processing firms are allowed to enter the EPZs. They also enjoy special tariff treatment. In particular, firms in the EPZs are treated as "inside the territory but outside the customs," as they are exempted from import duty.

Figure 12-1 shows China's export revenues by trade regimes (including ordinary export, processing export, and other exports) after 1978. As can be seen, export revenues in processing regimes increased to US$137.65 billion in 2000 from $1.13 billion in 1981. Processing export revenues increased to $675.1 billion in 2008 from $147.4 billion in 2001, with an annual average growth rate of 29 percent, far outpacing the annual average growth

FIGURE 12-1.   **China's Export and Import Revenue by Trade Regimes,
1981–2017**

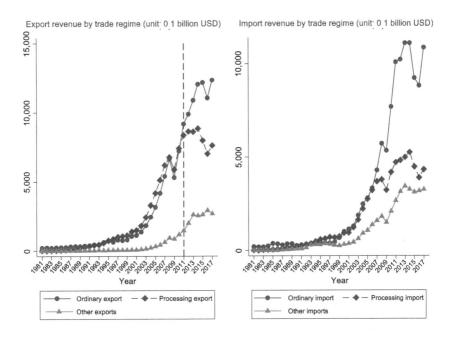

Source: Data from *China's Customs Statistics Yearbook* (various years).

(12.3 percent) during 1992 and 2001. Processing export revenues exceeded ordinary export revenues in 1993, and this situation held until 2010.

Figure 12-1 also shows China's import revenues by trade regimes (including ordinary import, processing import, and other imports) after 1978. Import revenues in processing regimes increased to US$92.56 billion in 2000 from $1.5 billion in 1981. Processing import revenues increased to $378.4 billion in 2008 from $93.9 billion in 2001, with an annual average growth rate of 24.6 percent, also far outpacing the annual average growth (16.1 percent) during 1992 and 2001. Both lines were close before ordinary import revenues began to increase quickly after 2007.

Industries that are intensively engaged in the processing trade are also labor-intensive. The processing trade thus absorbs many workers. In particular, the four major processing industries are household appliances; toys; clothing, footwear, and hats; and leather goods. The four industries employed 13.2 million workers in 2009 and 16.2 million workers in 2014, accounting for more than 10 percent of all employment in manufacturing. The processing trade has also contributed to China's deep integration into global value chains. Accordingly, China has functioned as a nonsubstitutable "world factory." Of course, this also implies that China has naturally maintained a high global trade surplus. Indeed, around two-thirds of China's trade surplus is generated from its processing trade.

Comments on the Stage of Extensive-Margin Opening

Before the era of economic reforms, China had adopted a heavy industry–oriented strategy and import substitution strategy. These strategies led to a surplus agricultural labor force, a low urbanization rate, and low resident income. All these factors laid a strong foundation for the export-oriented strategy implemented after the start of the reforms and opening-up policy.

As one of the most important steps in opening up, China gradually established a series of open economic zones and industrial parks between 1978 and 2000, providing preferential terms for firms locating within the zones or parks and promoting export growth. Meanwhile, the Chinese government also relaxed market access for FDI. With an abundant and cheap labor force but lacking in technological know-how and equipment, China's choice of the processing trade as a way to participate in global trade was almost inevitable. The processing trade increased rapidly, and China became a new "world factory." During this period, China applied to join the General Agreement on Tariffs and Trade (GATT) in 1986, and, beginning in 1992, started actively cutting import tariffs, which decreased by nearly 60 percent between 1992 and 1997. This move shows China's determination to expand its opening up.

However, China was not a member of the WTO during the stage of extensive-margin opening, which posed a serious threat to China's international trade. As an example, the United States granted China only temporary normal trade relations (temporary NTR) status. The U.S. Congress reviews that status annually. Chinese exporters would have faced the punishing non-NTR tariffs had the NTR status not been renewed. Therefore, China's exports still faced great uncertainty. China hoped that accession to the WTO would solve the problem.

FOCUSING ON THE INTENSIVE MARGIN
OF OPENING, 2001–2017

Since the turn of the twenty-first century, China has focused more on open-ing intensively than extensively, as exemplified by the expansion of vari-ous open economic zones or industrial parks. In the twenty-first century, before the Nineteenth Party Congress of the CCP, five important events characterized the features of the intensive margin: accession to the WTO, expanding market access for FDI, the relaxation of outward FDI, establish-ment of free trade pilot zones, and new-economy pilot cities. This section introduces each of the above five actions and comments on the intensive margin of opening up.

Accession to the WTO

Meeting the Tariff Reduction Commitment. As one of the conditions of joining the WTO, China committed to reducing its import tariffs to a cer-tain level before 2006; the highest tariff rate China could set was known as the bound tariff rate. From 2001 to 2006, the applied average tariff rate was always less than the bound average tariff rate set in 2001. In other words, China met its tariff reduction commitment.

Removal of Export Trade Policy Uncertainty. The nominal value of Chi-nese exports increased more than sixteenfold between 1992 and 2008. An obvious acceleration of export growth took place around 2001, when China officially entered the WTO. Before WTO accession, from 1992 to 2001, the annual nominal export growth rate was about 14.1 percent, whereas after accession to the WTO, from 2002 to 2008, the annual nominal export growth rate reached as high as 27.3 percent.

A substantial proportion of the soaring Chinese exports could be attrib-uted to the elimination of the high tariff threat after its WTO accession. Ac-cording to U.S. law, imports from nonmarket economies such as China are subject to relatively high tariff rates originally set under the Smoot-Hawley Tariff Act of 1930. These rates, known as "non-NTR" or "column 2" tar-iffs, are typically substantially larger than the "MFN" (most favored nation) or "column 1" rates the United States offers fellow members of the WTO.

When China joined the WTO on December 11, 2001, the United States effectively assigned China permanent NTR status on January 1, 2002, which completely removed Chinese exporters' concern over possible sudden tariff spikes (Pierce and Schott 2016).

Elimination of Nontariff Measures. China issues nontariff measures (NTMs) mainly focusing on ensuring food safety, human and animal health, product quality and safety, and environmental protection, which together account for about 90 percent of the total NTMs taken.

China is actively following good international practices such as International Organization for Standardization (ISO) and International Electrotechnical Commission (IEC) standards in preparing its own national standards. Of the 1,448 mandatory standards related to NTMs, 555 standards (about 38 percent) are directly adopted from ISO, IEC, and standards promulgated by other international organizations. China is putting increasing effort into streamlining its national standards with international best practices and seeking international cooperation in the standardization process. Especially with China's new Standardization Law, China intends to foster trade, economic, and social development by reducing restrictions.

There are in total 2,071 NTMs identified by the General Administration of Quality Supervision, Inspection and Quarantine (AQSIQ). Of these 2,071 NTMs, only 646 measures apply unilaterally to all countries around the world. The remaining 1,425 measures (about 69 percent) apply bilaterally or plurilaterally to only a certain group of countries. Specifically, 896 (around 63 percent) measures out of the total measures that are bilaterally or plurilaterally applied by AQSIQ were implemented after 2010. This shows that over the years, China is increasingly moving from a unilateral relationship with countries—that is, one in which it applies the same measure to all countries—to a bilateral relationship.

Expanding Market Access for FDI

After the *Catalogue for the Guidance of Industries for Foreign Investment* was first issued in 1995, it has been updated seven times, in 1997, 2002, 2004, 2007, 2011, 2015, and 2017. The number of encouraged categories increased from 115 in 1995 to 153 in 2017; the number of restricted categories decreased from fifty-six in 1995 to seven in 2017; and the number of prohibited categories decreased from ten in 1995 to seven today. This shows that the market access for foreign investment has been constantly expanding. And foreign investment could be guided to the industries China prioritizes for development. For example, foreign investment was expanded from labor-intensive industries to capital- and technology-intensive industries.

Meanwhile, the Chinese government has also introduced preferential policies to encourage more FDI in Central and Western China. In addition, at this point almost all service sectors are accessible by foreign investors. Some of them have a limitation of holding ratio. Thanks to this policy, China's import in services also grew quickly, from US$248 billion in 2011 to US$514 billion in 2018, for an annual growth rate of 11.4 percent.

Figure 12-2 plots China's annual utilized inward FDI from 1982 to 2018. FDI grew to US$134.9 billion in 2018 from US$40.7 billion in 2000, with an average annual growth rate of 7 percent. It is worth noting that the growth rate has slowed in recent years. Specifically, the average annual growth rate was only 3 percent between 2011 and 2018.

FIGURE 12-2.   **China's Annual Utilized Inward FDI, 1982–2018**

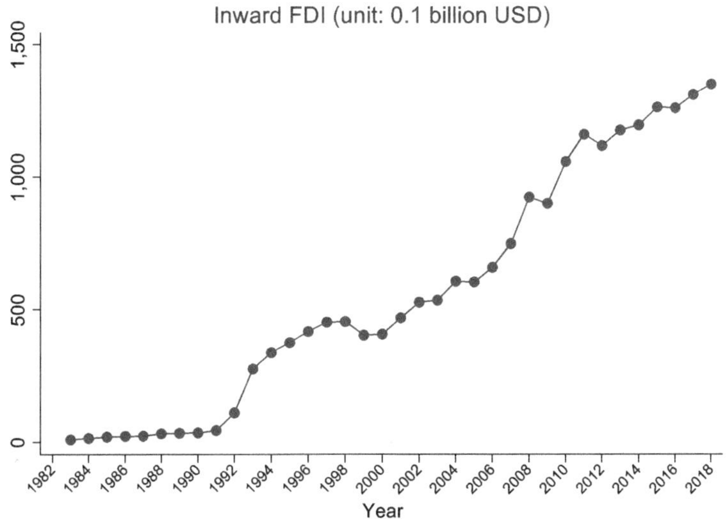

Source: Data from *China's Customs Statistical Yearbook* (various years).

Relaxation of Outward FDI

Before 1991, only state-owned enterprises were allowed to invest abroad, and case-by-case approval was required, regardless of the investment amount (Voss, Buckley, and Cross 2008). In the 1990s, China's foreign reserve holdings increased fast as a result of trade surpluses and high FDI inflow, which promoted outward FDI (OFDI). But OFDI was still stringently restricted in this period by the government issuing the "Opinions on Strengthening the Management of Overseas Investment Projects" in 1991. As can be seen in figure 12-3, China's OFDI had remained at a very low level from 1982 to 1999. The average OFDI from 1982 to 1999 was US$1.5 billion.

In the twenty-first century, the government's policy with respect to OFDI has switched from restriction to relaxation. In 2000 the Chinese government proposed the "Going Out" strategy for the first time. OFDI increased dramatically, to US$6.9 billion in 2001 from US$1 billion in 2000, but fell back in the following three years. In 2004, many implementing rules were introduced by the government, such as the "Decision on Reforming the Investment Systems," issued by the State Council, corresponding to detailed

FIGURE 12-3.   **China's Annual Flow of Outward FDI, 1982–2018**

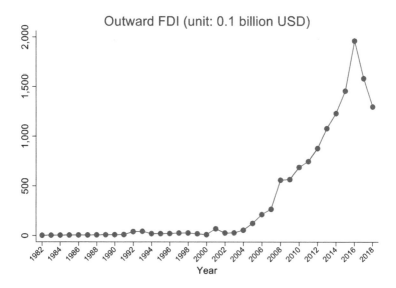

Source: Data from Ministry of Commerce of China; UNCTAD statistics.

policies to simplify the approval procedures, delegate approval authority, and increase approval efficiency promulgated by the National Development and Reform Commission (NDRC) and the Ministry of Commerce (MOFCOM). As a response, China's OFDI more than doubled, to US$12.3 billion in 2005 from US$5 billion in 2004, and grew continuously in the next years.

As a result of the 2008 global financial crisis, global FDI inflows fell by 14 percent in 2008 (UNCTAD 2009), while China's 2008 OFDI flow was double that in 2007. The Chinese government further encouraged OFDI by raising the approval threshold to more than US$300 million for resource development projects and more than US$100 million for other projects.

In 2014, China's OFDI entered a new stage of "registration-based and approval-supplemented" FDI. In this stage, only projects involving sensitive industries or with a value of more than US$1 billion are required to obtain official approval in advance. All other projects need only register with the provincial Development and Reform Commission (DRC). Established Chinese overseas enterprises are exempt from the approval and registration procedures. As a result, China's OFDI increased further, to US$196 billion in 2016 from US$73 billion in 2014. Afterward, China's OFDI fell in the ensuing two years because of escalating trade protectionism and anti-globalization behavior.

Establishment of Pilot Free Trade Zones

In 2013, the government set up a pilot free trade zone (FTZ) in Shanghai. The area of the pilot is not large (its initial area is only around 29 square kilometers), but its economic impact is potentially huge. The whole landscape of the establishment of the pilot FTZ can be summarized as 1 + 3 + 7, achieved in three steps. First, the government set up the first pilot FTZ in Shanghai in September 2013. Second, the pilot was extended to three other FTZs in large coastal provinces in April 2015: Guangdong, Tianjin, and Fujian. Third, in September 2016, the government set up seven more coastal and inland pilot FTZs, in Liaoning, Shaanxi, Henan, Hubei, Chongqing, Sichuan, and Zhejiang provinces. The objective of setting up the pilot FTZs is to replicate them in other non-FTZ places if those places are ready for the reform.

Drawing on the country's earlier experiment with SEZs, the government decided on four roles for the pilot FTZs. First, the pilot FTZs aim to promote further trade and investment facilitation. This goal is consistent with the development of EPZs. For goods within the pilot FTZs, the government requires "release the first line, but hold up the second line." The idea is that the imported intermediate goods used in the FTZs will be exempt from tariffs (that is, released from the first line), but the final products that use such intermediate inputs cannot be sold outside the zones to China's domestic market (hold up the second line).

Second, the pilot FTZs are intended to promote China's "negative list" investment mode. Differing from the previous "positive list," the new negative list investment mode has fewer regulations or restrictions on foreign investment in China. If the products or sectors are listed, foreigners are not allowed to invest in those areas. In other words, foreigners may invest in anything that does not appear on the list. This gives foreign investors huge room to invest in new industries or sectors. It turns out that this policy design has been the most successful policy reform. And because it was so successful in all eleven FTZs, in 2018 the Chinese government decided to expand the policy to the whole country.

Third, the pilot FTZs are intended to give a further push to China's financial reform. In particular, the FTZs aim to promote financial innovation with convertible capital projects and by offering more financial services. This reform so far has had only limited effects. Its limited impact is not difficult to understand, as FTZs make up only a tiny proportion of China's area. Unlike the trade reform, the financial reform cannot be clearly applied separately to entities located inside FTZs but not outside them. It is difficult to undertake a financial experiment in a small area and then apply it to the rest of the country.

Fourth, the pilot FTZs require local governments to reduce bureaucratic procedures and simplify the process of doing business within the zones. Specifically, the FTZs emphasize after-event supervision rather than before-event approval.

New-Economy Pilot Cities Experiment

Different from the establishment of the pilot FTZs, the opening up via the new-economy pilots in twelve cities is less well known. In 2015 the government decided to choose twelve cities located in five city groups, as well as some coastal cities, to experiment with the so-called "new-economy pilot." Jinan, the capital of Shandong province, is the largest of the twelve cities. Zhangzhou, a coastal city in Fujian province, was chosen mainly because of its strong connections with Taiwan province. Fangchenggang, a coastal city in Guangxi province, was chosen because it neighbors one of the SEZs in Vietnam. The government hopes to develop a bilateral border trade by setting up this new-economy zone.

The other eight cities are located around China's five major metropolitan areas. Dalian, in Liaoning, and Tangshan, in Hebei, are the two northern cities closest to the Beijing-Tianjin-Hebei metropolitan area. Xian was chosen because it is the largest city in Northwestern China. Chongqing was chosen because it is one of the core cities among the Chengdu-Chongqing megacities. Wuhan and Nanhang were chosen because they are two large cities in Central China. Finally, Pudong, in Shanghai, and Suzhou, in Jiangsu, are connected to the Yangtze River Delta economic belt.

The experiment of these new-economy zones focuses on six areas. First, it aims at exploring the new management mode of the government. Second, it aims at exploring the coordination of various industrial parks. Third, it hopes to explore new ways to encourage FDI. Fourth, it aims at promoting high-quality exports of domestic products. Fifth, it seeks significant improvement of financial services. Sixth, the zones should focus on promoting all-around opening-up in the regions.

After three years of the experiment, the independent evaluation panel, led by the National School of Development at Peking University, expressed satisfaction with the twelve cities' new-economy reforms. Particularly, the panel recognized that the reforms have successfully improved local economic development and been helpful in the supply-side structural reform.

Comments on the Stage of Intensive Margin of Opening Up

After accession to the WTO, China realized its commitment to reduce import tariffs, and the trade policy uncertainty faced by Chinese exporters was drastically reduced. These moves facilitated the rapid growth of imports and exports. As shown in figure 12-4, China's foreign trade dependence ratio, which is the ratio of total international trade volume to GDP, rose quickly between 2001 (38.1 percent) and 2006 (63.95 percent). This means that the contribution of foreign trade to GDP growth increased significantly. Meanwhile, China further expanded market access for FDI and relaxed restrictions on OFDI, both of which also increased quickly during this period.

After the financial crisis broke out in 2008, foreign markets were badly shocked, facing weak demand and trade protectionism. Since the turn of the twenty-first century, and especially after 2004, the cost of labor in China has increased dramatically and the country's population dividend has shrunk fast. Compared with many East Asian countries, China no longer has a significant comparative advantage on the labor-intensive margin. A not small part of China's foreign markets has been taken over by countries such as Vietnam and Bangladesh. Thus strategies that continue to rely on a simple processing trade to promote China's exports are no longer feasible. Indeed, both processing import and export volumes decreased dramatically after the global financial crisis broke out (see figure 12-1).

At the Eighteenth National Congress of the CCP, China's leadership proposed deepening the reform of China's foreign trade system, promoting openness through institutional reform, and fostering new competitive advantages in foreign trade. To this end, the Chinese government began to establish pilot FTZs in 2013 and to implement the new-economy pilot cities

FIGURE 12-4. **Foreign Trade Dependence Ratio in China, 1978–2018 (%)**

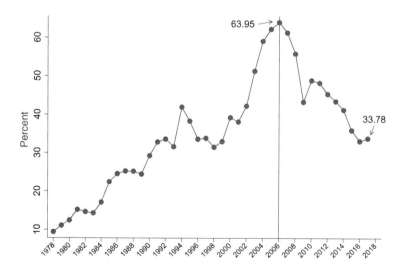

Source: Data from *China's Customs Statistical Yearbook* (various years).

experiment in 2016. These two policy initiatives have succeeded in improving local economic development and have been helpful in the supply-side structural reform.

At the Nineteenth Party Congress, held in 2017, it was emphasized that China's economy has shifted from a high-speed, increasing-volume stage to a high-quality development stage. The Chinese government has proposed the next step, an all-around opening up, that would promote the development of both the Chinese economy and the global economy. The specific measures to implement an all-around opening up are discussed in the next section.

FEATURES OF THE ALL-AROUND OPENING UP

China's strategy of an all-around opening up heavily relies on rolling out the Belt and Road Initiative (BRI), and developing China's free trade ports and the Guangdong–Hong Kong–Macau Greater Bay Area.

Belt and Road Initiative

The BRI, which was initiated by the Chinese government in 2013, is devoted to improving regional connectivity on a transcontinental scale. The initiative aims to strengthen infrastructure, trade, and investment links between China and other countries through which the BRI will pass. Currently, sixty-four countries are actively involved in the BRI. These include ten ASEAN countries, eighteen countries in Western Asia, eight in South Asia, five in Central Asia, seven in the Commonwealth of Independent States, and sixteen in Central and Eastern Europe. The scope of the initiative is still taking shape—recently, the BRI has been interpreted as open to all countries as well as to international and regional organizations.

In addition to trade and FDI, the BRI also concentrates on infrastructure projects. As one of the largest infrastructures and investment projects in history, the BRI addresses the "infrastructure gap" and thus has the potential to accelerate economic growth across the involved countries. The initiative calls for integration of the countries into a cohesive economic area through building infrastructure, increasing cultural exchange, and broadening trade and investment.

Free Trade Ports Experiment

The notion of free trade ports was first brought up in a report to the Nineteenth Party Congress. President Xi Jinping explicitly said that the country will allow more freedom to reform the pilot FTZs and explore the establishment of free trade ports.

The main feature of a free trade port is that, from the perspective of administrative supervision, it is outside the customs jurisdiction of the country. A free trade port combines the features of a port and an FTZ, with many trade-related functions, including product processing, logistics, and warehousing. But it is a more open platform than an FTZ. The construction of free trade ports will help FTZs advance toward the goal of being a more transparent institutional environment, like Singapore and Hong Kong. Meanwhile, breakthroughs in the areas of trade facilitation measures, ship fuel prices, financial support, customs supervision, and inspection and quarantine are necessary for free trade ports. As a result, free trade ports will be able to respond better to the profound changes in the global environment.

Greater Bay Area

The construction of the Guangdong–Hong Kong–Macau Greater Bay Area (GBA) is one of the most urgent tasks facing China in its opening-up process. The GBA includes nine municipal areas and the Special Administrative Regions of Hong Kong and Macau. The nine municipal cities are on the east and west banks of the Pearl River: Shenzhen, Dongguan, Huizhou, Guangzhou, Foshan, Jiangmen, Zhaoqing, Zhongshan, and Zhuhai. In this way the GBA coincides with the Pearl River Delta, which is a top economic development zone (EDZ) in China, along with the Yangtze River Delta.

The development of the GBA should focus on the following perspectives. First, to build the GBA, the real economy and the financial economy should be combined, focusing on the real economy. The services industry can play an auxiliary role to boost the GBA economy. The second goal in constructing the GBA is to facilitate innovation. China is transforming from a manufacturing power to an innovation power. The GBA should play a key role in the formation of an innovative country. The third objective is to achieve institutional innovation. Fourth, the GBA should pay more attention to its ecological environment.

Other all-around opening measures include (1) further widening market access, (2) improving the investment environment for foreign investors, (3) strengthening protection of IP rights, and (4) taking the initiative to expand imports.

POLICY RECOMMENDATIONS

This chapter has reviewed the practices and achievements of China's liberalization of international trade and investment and the country's integration into the international economy since 1978. China has done well so far. However, the internal and external environments in which China must operate have become increasingly complex, with rising labor costs, an aging population, and, in the international arena, accelerating unilateralism and the China-U.S. trade conflict. As emphasized by President Xi, China's opening door will not be closed and will only open even wider. Below are listed several concrete policy recommendations to promote China's continued opening in the future.

Support Multilateralism and Contribute to the Reform of the WTO. Unilateralism and protectionism are on the rise around the world, posing a challenge to the authority and effectiveness of the multilateral trading system. In this context, China should actively participate in WTO reforms. Specifically, China should reinforce the role of the WTO Dispute Settlement Committee and seek to gain a seat on the committee.

Consolidate Existing Regional Free Trade Agreements (FTAs) and Actively Promote New FTAs. To date, China has concluded seventeen FTAs with twenty-five partners in Europe, Asia, Oceania, South America, and Africa. China could deepen its cooperation with these partners in various fields such as trade, investment, and cultural exchange. Thirteen other regional FTAs are in the negotiations stage. The most important of these is the Regional Comprehensive Economics Partnership (RCEP). Since 2012, there have been twenty-two rounds of negotiations on establishing the RCEP. China has been actively communicating with the negotiating parties during the current critical round, hoping to address major disagreements and conclude negotiations sometime in late 2019. In addition, China could also consider participating in the Comprehensive Progressive Trans-Pacific Partnership

(CPTPP), which is now led by Japan, after the United States dropped out. There are two important reasons for China to participate. First, the CPTPP has lower requirements for openness than the Trans-Pacific Partnership (TPP), ones similar to China's existing policies for openness. Second, joining the CPTPP would expand China's circle of friends and offset the negative impacts on China's economy caused by China-U.S. trade frictions.

Deal with the China-U.S. Trade Conflicts by Further Opening Up and Pursuing High-Quality Development. China will be obliged to respond to the attacks launched by the United States by setting high tariff and non-tariff barriers for U.S. exports. The Chinese government should provide necessary subsidies for industries and workers who bear the brunt of the costs of this trade conflict. China's GDP is approaching that of the United States and is expected to surpass it by 2027, when the effects of the China-U.S. trade friction peak. Once China's GDP is 1.5 times that of the United States, the United States may accept China's rise, and China-U.S. relations are expected to shift from competition to cooperation. However, the competition between China and the United States will exist for a long time, potentially for the next thirty years. The Chinese government and Chinese people should be psychologically prepared and concentrate on doing their own jobs well.

Expand Market Access and Improve the Quality of Openness. The Chinese government should try to expand market access for foreign countries by encouraging more foreign investments and imports. Specifically, the negative investment list system should be implemented nationwide, and all companies registered in China should be treated equally. The convenience of doing business in China should also be improved. For example, a secure and effective electronic customs clearance system would speed up the integration of customs and simplify the agency's procedures. Furthermore, developing a better living environment and better services for businesspersons and international talent is a necessary step for China to improve the movement of personnel as well as the ability to attract talent.

China should also strengthen and enforce protections for IP rights. IP rights protection is required by foreign enterprises and should be required by Chinese enterprises. It would provide the biggest boost to the competitiveness of the Chinese economy. To reduce China's technological dependence on foreign countries, the Chinese government should set up special funds to encourage enterprises to develop core technologies.

At present, China has a deficit in its trade in services, which is consistent with China's current stage of economic development. However, in the future, China should vigorously develop the service industry and service trade, making service trade another engine of China's economic growth.

CONCLUSION

This chapter has described China's international trade and investment development and opening-up policies during the four decades since the country began its economic reform. Overall, the opening-up policy has occurred in three waves: expanding the extensive margin, increasing the intensive margin, and an all-around opening up.

International trade is a major focus of China's opening-up policy. China's growing role in international trade before the country's accession to the WTO was driven mainly by the country's cheap labor pool, which gave it a comparative advantage. This was especially useful for labor-intensive industries, where the cost of labor is one of the most important input factors. Moreover, cheap labor to some extent affected the incremental exports of machinery and transport equipment. This is because China's foreign trade in machinery and transport equipment is mainly conducted through its processing trade, which takes advantage of the low cost of labor.

After China's accession to the WTO, the main driving force of China's incremental international trade became the realization of scale economies with the large international market, according to the increasing returns-to-scale theory. One piece of evidence of this is that the share of the processing trade keeps decreasing, whereas total trade volume is increasing (see figure 12-1). This phenomenon is not accounted for in traditional comparative advantage theory.

In recent years, because of increasing labor costs and an expanding domestic market in China, weak foreign demand and trade protectionism in developed countries, and cheap labor costs in other developing countries and their increasing presence in global trade, China's economy has pivoted toward high-quality development and away from high-volume production and the processing trade. In international trade, China is striving to shift from a trader of quantity to a trader of quality. The Chinese government has proposed an all-around opening up as the next major phase. The new driving force of China's international trade will be the dividends of institutional reform achieved by expanding imports, expanding market access for foreign firms, strengthening IP rights protection, and nurturing innovation.

Policy recommendations to ensure China's continuing sustainable and high-quality opening up include (1) supporting multilateralism and contributing to the WTO reform; (2) consolidating existing FTAs and actively promoting new ones; (3) dealing with the China-U.S. trade conflicts reasonably, calmly, and confidentially; and (4) further expanding market access and improving the quality of openness.

REFERENCES

Dai, M., M. Maitra, and M. Yu. 2016. "Unexceptional Exporter Performance in China? The Role of Processing Trade." *Journal of Development Economics* 121:177–89.

Feenstra, R. C., and G. H. Hanson. 2005. "Ownership and Control in Outsourcing to China: Estimating the Property-Rights Theory of the Firm." *Quarterly Journal of Economics* 120 (2): 729–61.

Naughton, B. J. 2018. *The Chinese Economy: Adaptation and Growth*. 2nd ed. Cambridge, MA: MIT Press.

Pierce, J. R., and P. K. Schott. 2016. "The Surprisingly Swift Decline of US Manufacturing Employment." *American Economic Review* 106 (7): 1632–62.

UNCTAD (United Nations Conference on Trade and Development). 2009. *World Investment Report: Transnational Corporations, Agricultural Production and Development*. New York: United Nations.

Voss, H., P. J. Buckley, and A. R. Cross. 2008. "Thirty Years of Chinese Outward Foreign Direct Investment." Paper presented at the Nineteenth Chinese Economic Association Conference, "China's Three Decades of Economic Reform (1978–2008)," Cambridge, April 1–2.

Yu, M. 2015. "Processing Trade, Tariff Reductions and Firm Productivity: Evidence from Chinese Firms." *Economic Journal* 125 (585): 943–88.

13

China's Economic Diplomacy at Seventy: Bifurcation and Future Agendas

DAOJIONG ZHA and TING DONG

China's economic diplomacy has come a long way in the past seventy years. It has served well the purpose of developing the nation and advancing its interests abroad, in addition to making the country a major force of change in the process of globalization. As China moves into the future, several foundational achievements are in place. Internally, opening up the society as a strategy for national development has taken root as an accepted philosophy, tangibly supported by the past forty years of experimentation and practice. Foreign corporate and individual presence and competition in Chinese society receive broad societal endorsement and appreciation. Externally, the country is more integrated into, and more cooperative within, regional and global economic and political systems than in the entire history of the nation. Indeed, on both material and institutional bases, China has achieved a degree of security in the world that is unparalleled in its own history.

Meanwhile, a peculiar predicament is evident as China strives to map out its diplomacy for the future. On the one hand, China sees it as only natural that the country should play a more active role in multilateral economic institutions, through which China can spread its preferences and ideals to other parts of the world, just as other established world economies have done before it. On the other hand, many governments find it difficult to accommodate a larger role for China. Some, including the United States since the start of Donald Trump's presidency in 2017, find it necessary to push back against China's aspirations and methods. No matter what form bilateral ties between China and the United States take in the future, the question of how China and key Western economies can overcome their geopolitical differences will be at the forefront of relations for years if not decades.

Examples of discord between China and key Western economies abound, with as many explanations proffered. A seemingly irreconcilable issue is whether or not conformity in domestic political systems should be treated as a necessary precondition to reducing the geopolitical tension between China and the West. Those who subscribe to the notion of a "Chinese way" of development hold that performance, as evidenced by economic growth and levels of satisfaction with the government, matters (for example, Yao 2010). In contrast, those who subscribe to the notion of a liberal international (that is, Western) order tend to insist that China—by default and by choice—is a source of disruption, and therefore the time has come for a "reckoning" (Campbell and Ratner 2018).

In line with the overall questions the larger project of this book sets out to address, this chapter deals with China's economic diplomacy by asking three questions: What went right with China's economic diplomacy of the past seventy years? What warrants continued serious attention? What future actions can be recommended? In this chapter, we offer a fuller treatment of the bifurcated nature of China's economic diplomacy. This is both useful and necessary, as the English-language literature on global economic diplomacy tends either to dismiss the value of treating China as a separate case[1] or to treat China ahistorically, addressing only China's twenty-first-century initiatives (see, for example, Heath 2016). An ahistorical approach tends to play up the projection of power and influence outside the country (Zhang and Keith 2017) while failing to pay due attention to the counterpart activity, China's adjusting its domestic policies to accommodate foreign demands. We end with a short list of topic areas that we deem merit consideration in thinking about China's future choices in economic diplomacy.

"ECONOMIC DIPLOMACY" AS A FRAMING

Short of an outbreak of catastrophic world-encompassing warfare, the fundamental tenets underpinning China's economic, security, and political situation likely will remain largely unchanged. Rhetoric about the possible Chinese undoing of the global economic system, whether manifesting in expressions of alarm from the outside world or of jubilee from some domestic quarters, is not likely to survive the test of time. A related premise, though beyond the scope of this chapter, is that in the various venues created for international interactions, China will more likely than not stay in its own "club of one"—a euphemism used here to imply pursuit of autonomy but not self-exclusion—in dealing with bilateral, regional, or global affairs.

Projections of and arguments over a purported China-versus-the-West dichotomy enliven the conversation, but whether that framing generates any positive value is questionable. As an alternative approach, we have tried to come up with a narrative designed to stimulate thinking about how, in the future, China and the rest of the world might relate to each other through appreciating the cross-fertilization of ideational input instead of claiming superiority or victory, however that is defined, in one or another dimension.

Our task is made more difficult because, as one observation has it, "Definitions of concepts regarding economic diplomacy have been initially fuzzy and occasionally have made it more difficult to agree on the exact delineation of phenomena to be studied and to decide on what is better left to other scientific disciplines" (van Bergeijk and Moons 2019a, 1). A good part of the complexity derives from the much greater diversity of practitioners and associated viewpoints and recognized responsibilities in economic diplomacy than in the military or political domains of intercountry relations. Based on daily work portfolios of mainstream diplomatic missions posted abroad, truly informed considerations of economic diplomacy should include commerce, trade, finance, migration, and consular work (Lee and Hocking 2010). A fair treatment of any of those topic areas would require broad-based expertise and experience, which we do not claim to have.

"The rise of China" has attracted scholarly and policy attention owing to the increasing share of global trade (international value chains) and investment flows the country captures. One line of argument—which has gained traction in some Chinese-language literature on the topic—holds that "China tends to believe that the major task of its economic statecraft is to translate its national wealth into the exercise of power to institute new international rules that recognize the interests of those, like China, who have arrived late in the process of the definition of the post–Cold War order" (Zhang and Keith 2017, 185). The image is that of a country that seeks—and in some ways can afford—to denounce the very tradition that enabled its growth.

But, as we show in this chapter, there exists a bifurcation in China's economic diplomacy, which exhibits characteristics of both a developing country and a developed one. This bifurcation manifests, on the one hand, in China's agility in adapting to changing economic conditions, and on the other hand in a modus operandi that partners and critics of China will likely continue taking issue with.

BIFURCATION IN CHINA'S ECONOMIC DIPLOMACY

In this section we outline the key features of seventy years of Chinese economic diplomacy. In order to facilitate discussion with those who view China as either an outlier or as uniquely creative in the world, we group Chinese behaviors into two categories—those of a typical developing country and those of a typical developed country. The issues and events we touch upon are not exhaustive and are meant to encourage nuanced appraisal of differences between China and other major economies of the world, regardless of domestic systems.

How China Functions as a Developing Country

A developing country's economic diplomacy can be thought of as occurring in four stages. In the first stage, its government agencies in general and foreign diplomatic missions in particular help sell the country's products and projects abroad, followed by the second stage, that of networking to bring domestic and foreign traders and investors into direct contact. In the third stage they engage in building up the country's image to promote the inflow of investment. In the final stage the country participates in shaping the rules that regulate world economic exchanges. These stages are cumulative: in advancing to a successive stage, the country continues the actions and projects undertaken in earlier stages (Rana 2018).

One facet of the first or sales phase of China's economic diplomacy that deserves special mention is the overseas deployment of Chinese manpower. A vast construction market opened up in the Middle East in the wake of the surge in crude oil prices in 1973. China joined such other developing Asian countries as Bangladesh, India, Pakistan, the Philippines, and Sri Lanka in dispatching contract laborers to the Middle East construction and other labor service markets (Chossudovsky 1982; Ling 1984). The government-organized export of manpower proved key to poverty reduction and continues today, though in far less dramatic fashion. For example, China worked with Japan to create a "trainee visa" category to enable hundreds of thousands of Chinese laborers to take up multiyear manual labor jobs (paying at or below minimum wage levels) in Japan (Zha 2002a). In Israel, the population of Chinese migrant workers, both legal and illegal, is sizable as well (Li 2012).

The 1957 creation of the Canton Fair (renamed the China Import and Export Fair in 2007) is a classic example of government support to get the country's products together with potential consumers abroad. China took advantage of the geographic proximity of Guangzhou to Hong Kong, a British colony until 1997, and managed to gain access to Western products and technologies while the U.S.-led trade blockade was still in effect (Sung 1991). Another example can be found in China's cultivation of "people-to-people trade" with Japan after the war and before the establishment of formal diplomatic ties in 1972 (Soeya 1999). In fact, projects like the first Chinese investment and trade promotion center in Dubai, inaugurated in 2000, could not have materialized without effective salesmanship on the part of China's economic diplomats. The type of retail center that amasses made-in-China products, nicknamed "dragon mart," is considered productive and was thought necessary to replicate outside the Middle Eastern region until an attempt to do so in Cancún, Mexico, ran into serious local opposition (Peters 2016).

In the second, networking phase of economic diplomacy, and especially since the early 1970s, China essentially took an all-of-government approach to maximizing exports, mobilize foreign direct investment, and help Chinese companies access technology. The literature on China's creation and operation of special economic zones and accompanying domestic policy reforms is abundant (Shirk 1994). The published memoirs by such second-tier yet instrumental officials as Gu Mu (2009) and Li Lanqing (2010), both deputy prime ministers in charge of foreign economic management, offer informative clues to answering the question of what went right, as well.

With respect to human networks, Chinese economic policymaking benefited from the advice from Chinese and foreign economists (Bottelier 2018). Chinese embassies and consulates were and continue to be at the forefront of local outreach to foreign corporations, providing them with information and motivating them to embrace the trade-with-China and invest-in-China campaigns. Annual gatherings such as the China Development Forum (since 2000) and the Boao Forum for Asia (since 2001) have become signature events for Chinese and international elites engaged in managing everyday exchanges between China and powerful multinational corporations, international development institutions, think tanks, and universities to take the measure of each other. Numerous other forums, organized by government-affiliated think tanks and universities alike, have helped maintain a steady flow of ideas between China and the rest of the world.

In the third, image-building phase, China has taken actions to improve the country's national brand. Government agencies at the central and local levels make extensive use of the country's cultural heritage to promote inbound tourism, which, particularly against the background of grand narratives about China in the abstract, can be effective in creating the human networks necessary for trade and investment ties. Foreign tourists return home bearing eyewitness accounts of China as an investment destination and trading partner. Another example of Chinese efforts at national branding is activism in hosting international sporting and cultural events (Chen 2012). Such efforts were pioneered by developed countries in their stage of internationalization decades before (Gottwald and Duggan 2008). For China, its campaign to host the Winter Olympics in 2022 is not based on an untapped capacity for winning medals. But that's unlikely to be the last major sporting event China hosts.

Another excellent example of Chinese brand building is evident in how the government chose to relate to the Davos-based World Economic Forum (WEF), a nongovernmental venue that nevertheless has an agenda-setting effect in how the world economy is run. Chinese practices of diplomacy are known to be protocol-conscious. Gradually but surely, Chinese representation at the annual WEF meeting became a matter of high diplomacy for China. Then, in 2007, China agreed to assist the WEF by hosting annual

"Summer Davos" gatherings in Dalian and Tianjian and sending the country's prime minister to speak.

In assessing image branding as a strategy of economic diplomacy, at both the country and firm levels (Ille and Chailan 2011), it is difficult to come up with uniform standards or expectations for either content or effect. For every country or company, image building is a continuous process and requires constant and timely adjustment.

The fourth and final phase of economic diplomacy for a developing country is regulatory management. It is worth noting the process of institutionalized learning that has gone on between China and the rest of the world, especially the developed economies. Agencies such as the China Council for the Promotion of International Trade, created in 1952 (initially mainly to relate to Japan and other "second world" economies), and the China International Center for Economic and Technical Exchanges, created in 1983, were tasked with offering seamless cooperation with the United Nations Development Program's Beijing offices. Less visible but certainly as significant was that a variety of Chinese government agencies, including the legislature, which is nominally the most sovereignty-sensitive, proactively solicited Western input in drafting and revising Chinese laws and regulations (Seidman and Seidman 1996). Exchanges, many of which take the form of technical training by established professionals from the West, helped China formulate new sets of rules for trade and investment dispute resolution, to be conducted in China but with higher levels of convergence with international norms (Song 1992; see also Tao 2012). In short, despite the newsworthiness of Deng Xiaoping's famous tour to the south in 1992, China has more than political determination to offer prospective foreign partners.

Even in East Asia, a region that is a latecomer to institutionalizing regional economic cooperation (compared with Europe and North America), China is one of the latest to take action. It wasn't until May 2001 that China moved to join the Asia Pacific Trade Agreement (also known as the Bangkok Agreement), first established in 1975, with Bangladesh, India, Laos, South Korea, and Sri Lanka as signatories. In January 1991, a group of Southeast Asian countries signed the Association of Southeast Asian Nations (ASEAN) Free Trade Agreement. Were it not for the contagion effect of the Asian financial crisis of 1997–1978, China probably would have taken longer to enter into a free trade agreement with ASEAN (Zha 2002b). In the sixteen-country negotiation toward a Regional Comprehensive Economic Partnership, China has not been as active as some media headlines portray, in part because China would need to move from investment protection to investment liberalization if it were to be accepted as a leader (Wang, 2017).

Undertaking these tasks of economic diplomacy somewhat belatedly does not make developing countries fundamentally different from their developed partners. The point, rather, is that research efforts must not miss the learning process a developing country has gone through and the hurdles it continues to face in navigating myriad challenges around the world. As a developing country, China has added layers of activity to its economic diplomacy as the country has moved forward in its external relations, in addition to making frequent policy adjustments on the domestic front. It should be recalled that in more advanced stages of economic diplomacy, the activities connected with previous phases are not abandoned or minimized. Whether or not some of China's enterprises will continue to need governmental-diplomatic support to enter foreign markets in the future is a major source of contention, in particular between China and the developed countries, and between China and some developing countries as well.

How China Presents as a Developed Country

Features of the economic diplomacy of developed countries can also be observed in Chinese practices. Perhaps the most telling example pertaining to China's posture as a developed country in its foreign economic policy can be found in its development aid policies and practices.

Throughout the 1980s and 1990s, China sought to join multilateral development banks one after another, beginning with the Asian Development Bank. This brought China into the club of creditors. In the early 1990s, China created its own development banks, the China Development Bank and the Export-Import Bank of China in particular. These banks initially focused on the domestic realm but then gradually increased their loan activities abroad. The formal opening of the New Development Bank, in Shanghai, and the Asian Infrastructure Investment Bank, in Beijing, in 2014 sent an unmistakable message of China's intent to start experimenting with a role that had been filled by the developed countries at least since the end of World War II.

In addition to development aid, in 2010, China installed its own generalized system of preferences (GSP) in handling trade with selected developing countries. The GSP regime was in many ways a concrete concession on the part of developed states, especially former colonizers, to address demands for a "new international economic order." It was established to promote the exports of low-income countries to industrialized countries to support the former's economic growth and development. Under the GSP, developed countries offer reduced or zero tariff rates for selected products originating in developing countries. In addition, least-developed countries (LDCs) receive further preferential treatment for a wide range of products. During the 1970s, the first GSP schemes were granted to low-income countries. China was initially a recipient of a GSP granted by several developed economies. Today, around forty industrialized countries grant and more than two hundred states and territories receive GSP import privileges.

In practice, the GSP functions as a handy instrument of economic-political diplomacy by those states that grant it. This is so because the granting party can change the specifics of a GSP arrangement unilaterally, and the temporary withholding of a GSP-related privilege is closely tied to diplomatic maneuvering on bilateral or multilateral fronts. In short, GSP conditionality favors the granting party (Pallavi 2017).

China started to grant duty-free treatment to LDCs that had diplomatic relations with China in 2001. Then, in December 2008, China announced at the United Nations High-Level Event on the Millennium Development Goals that it would gradually increase the coverage of its LDC scheme to reach 95 percent of the country's total tariff lines. This goal was achieved in two steps within three years between 2010 and 2013 (UNCTAD 2016). It can be expected that China will continue using its own version of GSP under the auspices of South-South cooperation and, where applicable, its Belt and Road Initiative.

Much has been written about China's trajectory as a donor and how it differs from developed countries' development finance (Bräutigam 2011). The total amount of aid China provides can only be estimated, principally because of the different accounting standards adopted for reporting purposes (Kitano 2018). A major contributor to the shaping of China's economic aid designs and practices is China's own experience as an aid recipient (Warmerdam and de Haan 2015). As some scholars have noted, there exist discernible levels of commonality in foreign aid among China, Japan, and South Korea, partly resulting from their respective histories of being major benefactors and beneficiaries in economic aid to each other (Stallings and Kim 2017). It helps to remember that the Forum for China Africa Cooperation (FOCAC), initiated by the Chinese government in 2000, drew inspiration from the Tokyo International Conference on African Development (TICAD), a Japanese government initiative launched in 1993. The FOCAC format is heavily modeled after the TICAD, with high-level meetings every third year and aid-based programs of exchange involving all relevant branches of government.

Promotion of national interest by joining multinational economic institutions is another feature of a developed country's approach to economic diplomacy. Beginning in the 2000s, China became progressively more active in joining what official Chinese rhetoric used to dub "rich countries' clubs," that is, informal groupings established by developed countries. Slowly there emerged a broader recognition in China that groupings like the G-7 or G-8 are choices countries make to supplement perceived deficiencies in open-membership international frameworks such as the World Trade Organization (WTO) and various specialized UN agencies for development.

In 2005, China sent its head of state to the first G-8+5 meeting, touted as a "new paradigm for international cooperation," especially with respect to the Doha round of WTO talks and climate change. In the wake of the financial crisis of 2008, the G-8+5 was expanded to become the G-20, again with China as a full member. The new grouping has had its share of the tentative nature of any such project of international governance (Engelbrekt 2015). In 2009 China joined Brazil, India, and Russia to establish the BRICS platform, which meets alongside annual meetings of the G-7 developed countries. Nevertheless, when it came time for China to host the 2016 G-20 summit, the government turned its chairmanship into a yearlong publicity campaign (Kirton 2016).

Although this short list of examples of Chinese economic diplomacy is far from comprehensive, it does offer a discernible picture of China functioning as a developed country. As such, China will likely continue to face demands from other developed countries that it adopt the philosophies and practices they deem fitting, while at the same time being challenged to live up to its official self-designation as a developing country, and therefore to be more sympathetic to the plight of lower-income economies. This is a tall order that demands talent and skill to manage.

AGENDAS FOR THE FUTURE

Our review of several aspects of China's economic diplomacy is meant to highlight two salient points that we feel are essential for conversations about the future direction of China's foreign economic policies: (1) China has been agile in moving up the ladder of economic diplomacy as a developing country and (2) China discernably also tries to function as a developed country.

Understandably, China is likely going to continue to face expectations and even demands from developed countries to adopt a whole range of philosophies and practices (on fronts both domestic and international) deemed commensurate of the weight China carries in the global economy. Concurrently, China likely will continue to be expected to resist pressure from rich and powerful actors domestically but externally demonstrate political solidarity with countries in the lower echelons of world development. Trying to satisfy both streams of expectations is going to be a tall order that demands talent and skill on the part of China.

In many ways, the degree to which China's economic diplomacy resembles that of a typological developing or developed country is not as relevant as the country's capacity to continue adapting to change on both domestic and external fronts with agility. It behooves those considering the future direction of Chinese economic diplomacy to factor in the following four issues, derived from our discussion presented to this point in the chapter. They are listed in no particular order.

Managing the Economic Distance between China and the Rest of the World

China's major position in international product and service trade notwithstanding, the markets under China's jurisdiction remain quite distinct from many markets, for cultural, historical, and institutional reasons. The broadly accepted international characterization of China as an "emerging" player in the world economy is based on the relatively thin history of Chinese participation in global production networks and in multilateral trade and financial systems. China's traditional insistence on developmentalism, that is, on putting economic growth above most if not all other (philosophical) values, has and will continue to meet resistance from developed countries that use market access and regulatory rules as gatekeeping measures for cross-border trade and investment (Laïdi 2008).

Our emphasis on being aware of economic distance is also based on the recognition that globalization has extended the networks of all actors, domestic and external, which accordingly are more vulnerable to changes in the behavior of other jurisdictions. In the digital age, it is tempting to argue that economic distance is set to decay. However, in cross-national trade, physical distance continues to matter, and may actually have started to matter more than in the mid-1990s (Disdier and Head 2008). This is because other forms of distance—cultural, political, and historical—have taken over the trade-reducing role of economic distance. In other words, the cost of transporting goods may be falling, but economic diplomacy related to product quality—standards, trust, and the like—makes China's efforts to improve its image look elementary (van Gorp 2019). This explains why trade in new or nontraditional goods or with "new" trading partners has emerged an important driver of China's international trade (Kehoe and Rule 2013).

The escalation of trade tensions with the United States since 2017 and, as significant, the absence of public expressions of sympathy for China's positions from the developed economies serve as useful reminders that China needs to work toward narrowing those political differences with its major trading partners in the Organization for Economic Cooperation and Development (OECD) club. Better still, China should proactively start exploring expert linkages between the various economic policy research institutions of the OECD and its key member states. It may not be possible (or perhaps even necessary) to win endorsement of Chinese actions and preferences. But it ought to help if those research institutions are better informed about China's plans and the multidimensional domestic challenges China continues to face.

In a similar vein, China should find ways to more effectively relate to the global south (a moniker that has yet to find its way into mainstream Chinese rhetoric on international development) by narrowing economic distances with those markets. Interest in recent Chinese initiatives, such as the Asian Infrastructure Investment Bank and the Belt and Road vision, in some ways validates revival of the notion of South-South cooperation, whose heyday in multilateral economic diplomacy came in the early 1970s (Zha 2018). Yet China would do well to bear in mind that much of the global south has a much wider range of choices to choose from today. China does not claim to be the proverbial locomotive of the developing world, and there is little expectation it would play that role.

Setting Clearer Parameters between Positive and Negative Economic Diplomacy

The bulk of our description and analysis in this chapter focuses on positive interactions between China and other states. This is more in line with standard assumptions in the field of international economics, which tend to see promotion of economic integration as creating a peace dividend. The history of contemporary China's interactions with the rest of the world, especially the four decades since the early 1970s, certainly offers ample evidence to support this line of reasoning. Yet an exclusive focus on trade-enhancing and other positive measures in a country's economic diplomacy is problematic from a policy perspective, especially in view of strategic uncertainties between China and a good number of other countries over a variety of different issues.

Indeed, though not highlighted in this chapter, the historical record of contemporary China's economic diplomacy fits well one dictionary definition: "diplomacy which employs economic resources, either as rewards or sanctions, in pursuit of a particular foreign policy objective" (Berridge and James 2003, 91). In fact, a good deal of the emergent English-language literature on the topic tends to see political, zero-sum competition as the key driver of Chinese economic diplomacy, which is otherwise classified as "economic statecraft" (for example, Li 2017). Examples of negative economic diplomacy in the bilateral context include postponement or cancellation of state visits, curtailing prior agreements on import/export promotion and other forms of economic cooperation, the boycotting or embargoing of products, and the imposition of financial sanctions. In multilateral contexts, a government can choose to exit or not adhere to rules, regulations, or obligations and multilateral sanctions.

Back in April 1970, China's premier Zhou Enlai was reported to have informed a visiting Japanese delegation of four clearly worded political conditions for Sino-Japanese trade. Each of those specific warnings required Japanese traders to choose between mainland China or Taiwan markets (Tao 2008). Today the breadth and depth of China's economic linkages with the rest of the world do not auger any easy repetition of similar demands. But, as indicated in a growing literature on the subject, there is increasing interest in the degree of economic loss China is willing to incur by enacting punitive measures against a trade partner that is deemed to have infringed on China's political interests, in matters ranging from territorial issues to human rights to offending public sentiment in interpreting historical events. For example, one study of trade between Norway and China in the wake of their political dispute over human rights found that China's economic retaliation amounted to "rather less than public discourse suggests" because the Norwegian market holds industrial components that are not easily replaceable in China (Thygeson 2015). Another study similarly found that in the 2000s, when China had difficult political relations with certain governments, "trade deteriorating effects of political tensions [were] only temporary in nature" (Fuchs 2019, 310). In other words, China's intended political message was dismissed as inconsequential on the receiving end. This does not auger well as a message of diplomacy, that is, of trying to get a targeted party to take desired actions.

It is in China's interest to conduct the negative dimension of its economic-political diplomacy in a manner that is transparent, consistent, and predictable. The imposition of economic sanctions is preferable to further accumulation of diplomatic and political acrimony. When it comes to international politics, political line drawing in peacetime can help avoid conflicts down the road.

Making Mobilization of Human Resources a Priority

One of contemporary China's truly remarkable achievements is a shift in its position in the global migration order. From being a nation most notable for its numbers of emigrants, China has increasingly become a destination for immigrants of all nationalities. From Africa to Asia, America to Europe, and Australia, people of all backgrounds are arriving to live and work in the country. As the authors of a book on international immigration note, "China is . . . finally becoming a reciprocal member of the globalized world economy" (Leonard and Lehmann 2019, 1).

In the world of human migration, the transformation of China from a country of origin (net outflow of nationals) to one of destination, in addition to one of transit, puts the country in line with most of its Asian neighbors (Fielding 2016). In 2016, China joined the International Organization for Migration and became its 165th member. A year later, China inaugurated its National Immigration Administration.[2] The creation of a separate bureaucracy to handle immigration is indeed a step forward, as it marks a departure from focusing solely on the illegality of foreign presence in the country.

The regulated and unregulated presence of Chinese labor around the world in the construction sector alone will likely continue to be an issue for China's economic diplomacy. Thus far there continues to exist a general lack of citizenship aims on the part of the foreign population in China, at least for those whose voices manage to find their way to sociological accounts published in English. But, down the road, demands for reciprocity—in terms of employment rights and citizenship-like rights—can be expected to emerge.

In short, it is in China's interest to start preparing for responding to foreign demands for fair treatment at the level of individual laborers, settlers, and even economic refugees. It will not suffice for Chinese government agencies to cherry-pick those whom they classify as talents and who could bring positive added value to specific projects.

Maximizing Cooperation at the Institutional Level

The evolution of China as a club of one over the past seventy years is, in our view, more a result of unique shifts and turns in history than anything that can be theoretically explained as definitive. In the process of catching up economically, China benefited from its agility in handling changing external environments. But China would do well to differentiate between choosing to be its own club and being constrained, so to speak, to be one.

Should China's future economic diplomacy be competitive or cooperative? As the experiences of developed countries indicate, bidding for business will tend to be the former, but working out agreements, whether bilateral, regional, or multilateral, should be approached in a spirit of cooperation (Bayne and Woolcock 2017). Translated into action, the proposition is for China to focus on win-win outcomes during multilateral negotiations at forums such as the WTO. Flexibility, including flexibility on such matters as whether China is designated a developing or developed economy, is ultimately in China's interest. After all, China's practices of economic diplomacy will have to feature a multitude of means characteristic of both developing and developed economies. Insistence on some abstract notions, such as a "common but differentiated treatment" principle, while potentially useful as a bargaining chip in negotiations, may in the end prove costly, as stalling by those group members who in reality disagree is likewise a low-cost choice, politically speaking.

What truly matters, then, is for China—its leadership, bureaucracies, and representatives, in bilateral and multilateral contexts—to be motivated by making avoidance of a middle-income trap the overriding mission of diplomacy. The degree to which the Chinese economy resembles that of a developing or a developed country is less significant and even irrelevant. China should make maximal flexibility in multilateral institutional arrangements a reference point of maturity in its economic actions. Similarly, China's leadership should make preparing a solid domestic societal base a key foundation of economic diplomacy, during both negotiation and implementation phases. By so doing, China would stand a better chance of narrowing conceptual gaps with other developed countries over what constitutes normalcy in diplomacy.

NOTES

1. One indication can be seen in the treatment of China as a separate chapter, for the first time, in *Research Handbook on Economic Diplomacy*, edited by van Bergeijk and Moons (2019)

2. See the official website of the National Immigration Administration at http://www.mps.gov.cn/n2254996/.

REFERENCES

Bayne, Nicholas, and Stephen Woolcock, eds. 2017. *The New Economic Diplomacy: Decision-Making and Negotiation in International Economic Relations*, 4th ed. New York: Routledge.

Berridge, G. R., and Alan James. 2003. *A Dictionary of Diplomacy.* London: Palgrave Macmillan.

Bottelier, Pieter. 2018. *Economic Policy Making in China (1949–2016): The Role of Economists.* New York: Routledge.

Bräutigam, Deborah. 2011. "Aid 'with Chinese Characteristics': Chinese Foreign Aid and Development Finance Meet the OECD-DAC Aid Regime." *Journal of International Development* 23 (5): 752–64.

Campbell, Kurt, and Ely Ratner. 2018. "The China Reckoning: How Beijing Defied American Expectations." *Foreign Affairs* 97 (2): 60–70.

Chen, Ni. 2012. "Branding National Images: The 2008 Beijing Summer Olympics, 2010 Shanghai World Expo, and 2010 Guangzhou Asian Games." *Public Relations Review* 38 (5): 731–45.

Chossudovsky, Michel. 1982. "China's Manpower Exports." *Economic and Political Weekly* 17 (3): 63–64.

Disdier, Ann-Celia, and Keith Head. 2008. 'The Puzzling Persistence of the Distance Effect on Bilateral Trade." *Review of Economics and Statistics* 90 (1): 37–48.

Engelbrekt, Kjell. 2015. "Mission Creep? The Nontraditional Security Agenda of the G7/8 and the Nascent Role of the G-20." *Global Governance* 21:537–56.

Fielding, Tony. 2016. *Asian Migrations: Social and Geographical Mobilities in Southeast, East and Northeast Asia*. New York: Routledge.

Fuchs, Andreas. 2019. "China's Economic Diplomacy and the Politics-Trade Nexus." In van Bergeijk and Moons, *Research Handbook on Economic Diplomacy*, 310.

Gottwald, Jörn-Carsten, and Niall Duggan. 2008. "China's Economic Development and the Beijing Olympics." *International Journal of the History of Sport* 25 (3): 339–54.

Gu, Mu. 2009. *The Memoirs of Gu Mu*. [In Chinese.] Beijing: Party Literature Publishing House.

Heath, Timothy. 2016. "China's Evolving Approach to Economic Diplomacy." *Asia Policy* 22, July 22, 157–91.

Ille, Francis, and Claude Chailan. 2011. "Improving Global Competitiveness with Branding Strategy: Cases of Chinese and Emerging Countries' Firms." *Journal of Technology Management in China* 6 (1): 84–96.

Kehoe, Timothy, and Keith Ruhl. 2013. "How Important Is the New Goods Margin in International Trade?" *Journal of Political Economy* 121 (2): 358–92.

Kirton, John. 2016. *China's G20 Leadership*. New York: Routledge.

Kitano, Naohiro. 2018. "Estimating China's Foreign Aid Using New Data." *Institute of Development Studies Bulletin* 49 (3): 49–71.

Laïdi, Zaki. 2008. "How Trade Became Geopolitics." *World Policy Journal* 25 (2): 55–61.

Lee, Donna, and Brian Hocking. 2010. "Economic Diplomacy." In *The International Studies Encyclopedia*, edited by Robert A. Denemark, vol. 2, 1216–27. New York: Wiley Blackwell.

Leonard, Pauline, and Angela Lehmann. 2019. *Destination China: Immigration to China in the Post-Reform Era*. New York: Palgrave Macmillan.

Li, Lanqing. 2010. *Breaking Through: The Birth of China's Opening-Up Policy*. Oxford: Oxford University Press.

Li, Minghuan. 2012. "Making a Living at the Interface of Legality and Illegality: Chinese Migrant Workers in Israel." *International Migration* 50 (2): 81–98.

Li, Mingjiang, ed. 2017. *China's Economic Statecraft: Cooptation, Cooperation and Coercion*. New York: Elsevier.

Ling, L. Huan-ming. 1984. "East Asian Migration to the Middle East: Causes, Consequences and Considerations." *International Migration Review* 18 (1): 19–36.

Pallavi, Kishore. 2017. "A Critical Analysis of Conditionalities in the Generalized System of Preferences." *Canadian Yearbook of International Law* 54:98–133.

Peters, Enrique Dussel. 2016. "Chinese Investment in Mexico: The Contemporary Context and Challenges." *Asian Perspective* 40 (4): 627–52.

Rana, Kishan, 2018. "Economic Diplomacy: A Developing Country Perspective." In van Bergeijk and Moons, *Research Handbook on Economic Diplomacy,* 317–25.

Seidman, Ann, and Robert B. Seidman. 1996. "Drafting Legislation for Development: Lessons from a Chinese Project." *American Journal of Comparative Law* 44 (1): 1–44

Shirk, Susan. 1994. *How China Opened Its Door: The Political Success of the PRC's Foreign Trade and Investment Reforms.* Washington, DC: Brookings.

Soeya, Yoshihida. 1999. *Japan's Economic Diplomacy with China, 1945–1978.* Oxford: Clarendon Press of Oxford University Press.

Song, Bin Xue. 1992. "China's Civil Procedure Law: A New Guide for Dispute Resolution in China." *International Lawyer* 26 (2): 413–31.

Stallings, Barbara, and Eun Mee Kim. 2017. *Promoting Development: The Political Economy of East Asian Foreign Aid.* Singapore: Palgrave/Development Corporation.

Sung, Yun-Wing. 1991. *The China–Hong Kong Connection: The Key to China's Open Door Policy.* Cambridge: Cambridge University Press.

Tao, Jingzhou. 2012. *Arbitration Law and Practice in China.* Kluwer.

Tao, Peng. 2008. "China's Changing Japan Policy in the Late 1960s and Early 1970s and the Impact on Relations with the United States." *Journal of American-East Asian Relations* 15(1–2):147–71, especially pp. 152–53.

Thygeson, Bjornar Sverdrup. 2015. "The Flexible Cost of Insulting China: Trade Politics and the 'Dalai Lama Effect.'" *Asian Perspective* 39 (1): 104.

UNCTAD (United Nations Conference on Trade and Development). 2016. *Handbook on the Special and Preferential Tariff Scheme of China for Least Developed Countries.* New York and Geneva: UNCTAD. https://unctad.org/en/PublicationsLibrary/itcdtsbmisc76_en.pdf.

van Bergeijk, Peter A. G., and Selwyn J. V. Moons. 2019a. "Introduction." In van Bergeijk and Moons, *Research Handbook on Economic Diplomacy,* 1.

van Bergeijk, Peter A. G., and Selwyn J. V. Moons, eds. 2019b. *Research Handbook on Economic Diplomacy: Bilateral Relations in a Context of Geopolitical Change.* Cheltenham: Edward Elgar.

van Gorp, Desiree, 2019. "Business Diplomacy: Its Role for Sustainable Value Chain." In van Bergeijk and Moons, *Research Handbook on Economic Diplomacy,* chap 3.

Wang, Heng. 2017. "The RCEP and Its Investment Rules: Learning from Past Chinese FTAs," *The Chinese Journal of Global Governance* 3 (2): 160–81.

Warmerdam, Ward, and Arjan de Haan. 2015. "The Dialectics of China's Foreign Aid: Interactions Shaping China's Aid Policy." *Fudan Journal of the Humanities and Social Sciences* 8 (4): 617–48.

Yao, Yang. 2010. "A Chinese Way of Democratization?" *China: An International Journal* 8 (2): 330–45.

Zha, Daojiong. 2018. "Sixty Years of the South-South Cooperation Movement: Lessons for China's Belt and Road Initiative," *Development Finance Review*, 3: 3–11. (In Chinese.)

——. 2002a. "Chinese Migrant Workers in Japan: Policies, Institutions and Civil Society." In *Globalizing Chinese Migration: Trends in Europe and Asia*, edited by Pal Nyiri and Igor Saveliev, 129–57. Farnham, UK: Ashgate.

——. 2002b. "The Politics of China-ASEAN Economic Relations: Assessing the Move toward an FTA." *Asian Perspective* 26 (4): 53–82.

Zhang, Xiaotong, and James Keith. 2017. "From Wealth to Power: China's New Statecraft." *Washington Quarterly* 40 (1): 185–203.

14

Technological Rivalry

PETER A. PETRI

Technology looms large in China's future and its relations with the rest of the world. China has not yet reached broad technological parity with the United States but is the only country likely to do so in the foreseeable future. China's rapid progress, amplified by political differences with the West, has alarmed U.S. politicians and intelligence experts and has led to unprecedented policy reactions. At least for now, a technological cold war is setting in.

Current trends could have far-reaching consequences for global innovation. If many countries see China as an adversary, its contributions to technology at home and abroad will be reduced, slowing progress everywhere. Decoupling Chinese innovation from the West could lead to a bifurcated world with incompatible technologies and limits on the flows of ideas and talent. National security risks would increase, not decrease. Some decoupling is already underway and is shaking global financial markets. Extensive decoupling would be lengthy and costly, with highly uncertain outcomes. There is an urgent need for better pathways to the future.

This chapter builds on the analysis of China's national innovation system presented in chapter 6 by focusing on the role of technology in the international context. China and the United States will be the world's two most innovative countries for some time. The United States will keep its overall lead for some time, but China is catching up and already has frontier technologies in important sectors. U.S.-China relations are crucial to the progress of technology in the decades ahead.

At the optimistic end, an "open innovation" regime—market-based specialization in innovation and trade in technology, subject to rigorous intellectual property rights—would maximize the global pace of innovation and the utilization of knowledge, even as China faces enormous political headwinds. At the more pessimistic end, governments now appear to see competition in zero-sum terms, in part due to security concerns about foreign technology. But intermediate solutions are preferable to either extreme. It should be possible to reduce security risks with sophisticated testing, transparency, and verification and with trust developed over time. A pragmatic strategy is needed to achieve a reasonable level of technological interdependence based on secure foundations.

Attitudes in the rest of the world—countries that produce 60 percent of world GDP—will critically shape the U.S.-China rivalry. The United States and China each account for less than one-quarter of the world output and cannot divide the global economy without extensive support from other countries. Most other countries do not want to be caught in the middle and will be ready to support collaborative solutions. On the one hand, such solutions will require addressing security risks, while on the other hand market-oriented policies are needed to advance global interests.

CHINA IN THE ERA OF INNOVATION

Chinese innovation is moving toward the frontier in a time of exceptional technological change. The McKinsey Global Institute (MGI, 2018) recently estimated that artificial intelligence (AI), just one of the important technologies emerging today, will add US$13 trillion annually to the world economy by 2030. MGI projects that much of the benefits will flow to a handful of countries that are technological leaders.

Innovation is especially important now because productivity growth has slowed worldwide. Chapter 1 has shown that China's average total factor productivity (TFP) growth declined from 6.1 percent between 1996 and 2004 to 2.5 percent from 2005 to 2015. In the United States, TFP growth fell from an annual rate of 1.2 percent in the five years before the onset of the global financial crisis in 2008 to 0.3 percent in the five years ending in 2017 (OECD 2019a). One prominent hypothesis attributes this slowdown to a dearth of large, new innovations (Gordon 2000). Could fields such as AI, genetic engineering, and the "internet of things" become the new electricity?

Meanwhile, countries are increasingly concerned about zero-sum aspects of international technological competition, even if innovations generate positive global returns. It has been long recognized that technologies with scale economies can lead to global monopoly rents that accrue to very few firms and countries. Today network economies create even more dramatic rents for companies that operate online platforms for large groups of users. Concerns about the fairness of such rents have already resulted in international taxes on and outright barriers to online services. Moreover, potential military or intelligence applications of major new innovations add further zero-sum dimensions to international competition.

Technological competition between China and the United States reflects these zero-sum issues and the narrowing technological gap between the two countries, highlights the differences in their economic and political systems, and creates further tension. In both countries, innovations often originate in private firms, but the state plays a much larger role in guiding early-stage technologies in China than in the United States. China's internet sector, for example, now leads the world in many areas, but it was largely shielded from foreign competition in its early stages of development. State-supported research and development (R&D) funding and initiatives to "go out" and attract technology from abroad also play significant roles in promoting innovation.

The engine of American innovation is the private sector, which includes large technology companies with great financial capacity. To be sure, the state plays a significant role through defense expenditures and government research grants to universities, especially in sectors such as aerospace, specialized materials, electronics, and the biological sciences. Still, the bulk of U.S. innovation relies on private capital markets with specialized early-stage investors, advisers, and entrepreneurs concentrated in a handful of innovation hubs, which typically include world-class universities and research institutes to provide basic research and attract talent.

These tensions are intensified because China and the United States are rapidly becoming the "G2" of technology, competing directly for leadership on key technologies such as 5G networks. Their governments want domestic firms to earn rents from new markets, gain experience for future races, and generate state-of-the-art military know-how. In turn, government interventions escalate commercial competition into geopolitical rivalry.

THE STATE OF CATCH-UP

By several indicators—including innovation inputs such as R&D expenditures and outputs such as patents and export competitiveness—China is catching up with the United States, and by some indicators it will pass the United States within a decade or so. But examined more closely, raw data tend to overstate China's capabilities by not fully accounting for differences in the quality and experience of inputs and the value of outputs. Another major difference is that while the United States has access to leading technologies across most major areas of innovation, Chinese technology varies substantially across different sectors. Thus Chinese firms often depend on foreign technologies for some of their activities. The current trade war has "weaponized" these technological gaps.

China's Rapid Progress

The drivers of China's technological progress, already discussed in chapter 6, include large financial investments and an ample, technology-ready workforce. In an international context, the growth of Chinese R&D spending, from US$129 billion to US$443 billion over the decade ending in 2017 (figure 14-1), has made China second only to the United States in global investments in technology (OECD 2019b). Moreover, China's scientific manpower grew to three million workers by 2018, the highest in the world. Even accounting for the relative inexperience of researchers in world competition, China is poised to become a global leader along with the United States.

Further insight into China's role is offered by the Global Innovation Index (GII), a composite indicator of innovation inputs and outputs (Cornell University, INSEAD, World Intellectual Property Organization (WIPO) 2018). Over the five years between 2013 and 2018, China rose from thirty-fifth place to seventeenth as the highest-ranked country in the world, representing the largest advance among the leading countries in the index. Since most GII indicators are expressed in terms of per capita or per dollar of GDP, China's overall importance is even greater once its scale is fully taken into account.

FIGURE 14-1. **China's Expenditures on R&D versus United States's Expenditures, 2000–2017 (2010 US$ millions PPP)**

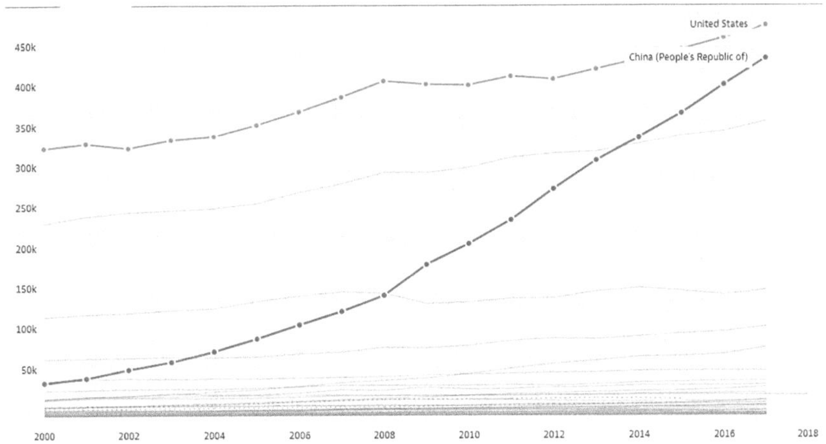

Source: Data from OECD, *Gross Domestic Spending on R&D* (database) (https://data.oecd.org/rd/gross-domestic-spending-on-r-d.htm).

Note: China will soon lead R&D expenditures by OECD members and partners.

Table 14-1 shows the components underlying China's advance. China rose on six of the seven components of the index, including creative outputs (by seventy-five positions), institutions (forty-three positions), business sophistication (twenty-four positions), infrastructure (fifteen positions), and human capital and research (thirteen positions). In this time frame, the rank of the United States declined slightly, from fifth to sixth position. The United States improved in four categories while losing ground in three, including in human capital and research (minus fifteen positions) and infrastructure (minus seven positions). If progress continues at similar rates, China will catch up with the United States within a decade.

China's progress has been particularly rapid in patents, an indicator often cited in discussions of its technological prowess. This indicator needs to be interpreted cautiously. In 2017, China awarded 1.7 million patents to domestic inventors, roughly ten times as many as the United States granted to its domestic inventors. Of these, only 327,000 of Chinese awards were for "invention" patents, as opposed to applications of already existing knowledge in "utilization" and "design" patents (CNIPA 2019), but even this category was twice as large as the number of U.S. patents. Research also

TABLE 14-1. China's Rise in the Global Innovation Indicators Ranking

Indicator	China		United States	
	2018	2013	2018	2013
Overall index	17	35	6	5
Institutions	70	113	13	17
Human capital and research	23	36	21	6
Infrastructure	29	44	24	17
Market sophistication	25	35	1	2
Business sophistication	9	33	8	2
Technology outputs	5	2	6	7
Creative outputs	21	96	14	19

Source: Cornell, INSEAD, WIPO, *Global Innovation Index*, 2013 and 2018 issues.

Note: Rank among 126 (2018) and 142 (2013) countries.

suggests that Chinese inventions are less valuable on average, in part because they often involve modifications of inventions already patented elsewhere (Jefferson 2019).

Chinese innovation does show progress, however, on reasonably selective measures. Registration of patents in foreign patent offices highlights innovations good enough to make it worthwhile to apply for a patent beyond a country's own markets. Table 14-2 shows that from 2010 to 2017 Chinese patents filed abroad grew five times as fast as patents from other countries. These patent registrations abroad are still relatively few they are similar in number to those of the United Kingdom, but well below those of leaders like the United States and Japan. Yet if present growth differentials persist, on this measure too China will catch up with the leaders within a decade.

Catch-Up Is Uneven

Although China's technological capabilities are generally advancing, they vary significantly across fields of knowledge. China's research interests, as measured by scientific publications, have primarily focused on physics, chemistry, and mathematics and are now growing especially fast in engineering and computer science (table 14-3). These interests explain—and are

TABLE 14-2. **Growth in Number of Foreign Patent Registrations, China and Other Leading Innovators, 2010 to 2017**

Country	2010	2017	Growth rate, annualized (%)
United States	80,522	126,321	6.6
China	4,919	25,034	26.2
Japan	99,223	127,005	3.6
South Korea	24,532	40,595	7.5
Germany	46,653	66,271	5.1
UK	11,724	17,272	5.7
France	19,459	27,089	4.8

Sources: Data from Jefferson (2019) and WIPO (2018).

TABLE 14-3. **Share of Applied Physical Sciences Papers in China's Scientific Publications**

Field	China's share of published papers, 2013 (%)	Chinese scientific publications, annual growth rate (2007–2013) (%)
All fields	18.2	18.9
Medical sciences	7.5	15.0
Biological sciences	13.9	14.4
Chemistry	24.5	14.8
Physics	19.6	14.7
Mathematics	18	17.8
Computer sciences	21.1	25.1
Engineering	34.8	22.1

Source: Veugelers (2017), Table 2.

influenced by—production specialization in more applied branches of technology.

Detailed patent data offer insight into variations by field. For this analysis, we use patents registered only in the United States and ask, In what year will the number of patents registered by Chinese inventors reach 25 percent of U.S. patents?[1] To project this catch-up year, we assume that Chinese and U.S. innovations continue to grow at the same pace as patent registrations did in the last five years. (Even if future patent registration trends change, for example due to the U.S.-China trade dispute, the past registration trends still offer a reasonable guess about technological advances in the future.)

Tables 14-4A and 14-4B show these projections and suggest that China will lag behind the United States in new patent production for some decades. China will catch up with U.S. patent awards in about one quarter of sectors by 2030 and in about one-half by 2049. Catch-up will be fastest in industries where China has ample domestic experience, such as tobacco, electric lighting, ceramics, construction, and power generation. China's prospects are best where it has an important role as a supplier or assembler, including in electronics communications and office equipment, but its outlook is weaker in more specialized areas, as listed in table 14-4B.

The January 2019 issue of the *MIT Technology Review* asked "What is China good at?" and identified sectors such as the "shenzhai" manufacturing system (which enabled China to jump ahead in products ranging from drones to electric scooters), the development of large-scale electrical grids, massive construction projects, and niche technology companies (such as electric vehicles and space transport). The article also noted China's progress in payment systems, quantum computing, and microchips specialized in artificial intelligence. In these and other leading fields, foreign components still tend to be important. For example, the McKinsey Global Institute singled out robotics and semiconductors as sectors where China still relies on critical foreign technology (MGI 2019).

China's uneven technological development is not surprising given its relatively recent technological takeoff. Many rapidly advancing countries depend on trade to fill technological gaps. Unfortunately for China, U.S. policies have now turned these gaps into vulnerabilities as China attempts to close remaining gaps with policies such as the Made in China 2025 initiative (State Council 2015) and the New Generation Artificial Intelligence Development Plan (State Council 2017). The sectors targeted by these plans are shown in table 14-5. In many respects, these plans are similar to those proposed in Germany's Plattform Industrie 4.0 (Federal Ministry of Economic Affairs and Energy 2019) and the U.S. *National Artificial Intelligence Research and Development Strategic Plan* (Executive Office of the President of the United States 2016). All define high-level objectives and whole-of-society strategies and even use somewhat similar language.[2] Critics have argued, however, that China relies more directly on self-sufficiency targets and subsidy programs that violate World Trade Organization (WTO) rules.

Risks of Decoupling

Under President Trump, the federal government has begun to limit U.S. connections with the Chinese technology sector in a process often described as "decoupling." The symbol of U.S. criticism is the Made in China 2025 initiative, which U.S. critics interpret as a strategy to achieve technological dominance over the United States through "state capitalism." This interpretation is partly due to the presentational style of Chinese industrial policies, which emphasize national guidance and make relatively little mention of private firms and market competition—factors that in fact will be essential for reaching ambitious targets.

As of July 2019, the United States has applied tariffs to nearly half of Chinese exports, with special focus on areas that require external technology. In May 2019, President Trump also signed an executive order that banned "any acquisition, importation, transfer, installation, dealing in, or use of any information and communications technology or service" (Trump 2019) by companies suspected of acting on behalf of adversaries. Huawei and its subsidiaries were included under this order in the following months and were also added to the U.S. Department of Commerce's "Entity List." Although the implementation of this ban is not clear-cut, it may reduce supplies of Intel processors, Qualcomm chip sets, and Android operating systems to leading Chinese users. The United States is also pressuring allies to adopt similar bans.

The announced purpose of decoupling is to prevent the use of hardware in U.S. communications systems that will make information available to adversaries of the United States. For example, the U.S. government believes that Huawei could be asked to install "back door" equipment in its routers that makes information available to Chinese intelligence agencies. Experts argue, however, that threats from such intrusions are relatively small compared to other risks in U.S. communication systems (Wheeler and Simpson 2019). Illegal access predominantly results from software vulnerabilities due to errors by operators (Cybereason 2019). As argued below, sophisticated ways of testing hardware security are now also becoming available.

TABLE 14-4A.   Sectors Where Chinese Patents Will Catch Up with U.S. Rate by 2049

ISIC 4	Proportion relative to U.S. patents, 2017 (%)	Reach 25% of U.S.[a]	Sector name
1200	77	2017	Tobacco products
2740	31	2017	Electric lighting equipment
2393	20	2019	Other porcelain and ceramic products
2670	18	2021	Optical instruments and photographic equipment
2210	20	2021	Rubber products
2790	17	2022	Other electrical equipment
2610	16	2023	Electronic components and boards
2630	15	2024	Communications equipment
4220	12	2024	Construction of utility projects
2817	14	2026	Office machinery and equipment (except computers and peripheral equipment)
2400	13	2028	Basic metals
2750	12	2029	Domestic appliances
2640	12	2029	Consumer electronics
2680	13	2029	Magnetic and optical media
2310	10	2030	Glass and glass products
2010	10	2030	Basic chemicals, fertilizers and nitrogen compounds, plastics, and synthetic rubber in primary forms
2730	11	2031	Wiring and wiring devices
2710	12	2032	Electric motors, generators, transformers, and electricity distribution and control apparatus
2620	10	2033	Computers and peripheral equipment

1900	7	2035	Coke and refined petroleum products
2420	10	2036	Basic precious and other nonferrous metals
4290	7	2037	Construction of other civil engineering projects
2022	8	2037	Paints, varnishes, and similar coatings, ink and mastics
1600	11	2038	Wood and products of wood and cork, exc. furniture
2813	8	2039	Other pumps, compressors, taps and valves
2652	11	2039	Watches and clocks
2220	5	2040	Plastics products
1300	7	2040	Textiles
2826	7	2040	Machinery for textile, apparel, and leather production
2816	8	2040	Lifting and handling equipment
2100	7	2044	Pharmaceuticals, medicinal chemicals, and botanicals
2300	8	2044	Other nonmetallic mineral products
3290	6	2046	Other manufacturing n.e.c.
2020	7	2046	Other chemical products
2720	11	2047	Batteries and accumulators
2390	8	2047	Non-metallic mineral products n.e.c.

Source: Author's calculations from Patstat data.

Note: [a]Date when China reached or will reach 25 percent of U.S. level of patents registered with foreign offices. ICIS, International Standard Industrial Classification.

TABLE 14-4B. Sectors Where Chinese Patents Will Trail U.S. Rate in 2049

ISIC4	Proportion relative To U.S. patents, 2017 (%)	Sector name
Slow convergence		
1000	6	Food products
1500	5	Leather and related products
1810	3	Printing and service activities related to printing
2021	7	Pesticides and other agrochemical products
2023	6	Soap and detergents, cleaning and polishing, perfumes and toiletry
2029	3	Other chemical products n.e.c.
2200	6	Rubber and plastics products
2510	8	Structural metal products, tanks, reservoirs, and generators
2513	4	Steam generators, except central heating hot water boilers
2520	1	Weapons and ammunition
2591	6	Forging, pressing, stamping, and roll-forming of metal; powder metallurgy
2650	7	Measuring, testing, navigating, and control equipment; watches and clocks
2651	8	Measuring, testing, navigating, and control equipment
2660	2	Irradiation, electromedical, and electrotherapeutic equipment
2810	6	General-purpose machinery
2811	3	Engines and turbines, except aircraft, cycle engines
2815	3	Ovens, furnaces, and furnace burners
2819	7	Other general-purpose machinery

2820	5	Special-purpose machinery
2821	2	Agricultural and forestry machinery
2824	7	Machinery for mining, quarrying, and construction
2829	5	Other special-purpose machinery
2910	3	Motor vehicles
3000	4	Other transport equipment
3100	9	Furniture
3200	4	Other manufacturing
3250	2	Medical and dental instruments and supplies
4300	5	Specialized construction activities
6200	3	Computer programming, consultancy, and related activities

Falling behind

1050	0	Dairy products
1100	1	Beverages
1400	2	Wearing apparel
1700	10	Paper and paper products
2030	13	Man-made fibers
2590	7	Other fabricated metal products; metalworking service
2599	5	Other fabricated metal products n.e.c.
2733	23	Wiring devices
2930	2	Parts and accessories for motor vehicles

Source: Author's calculations from Patstat data.

TABLE 14-5. **Priority Sectors in China's Plans**

Priority sectors
Made in China 2025 (2015)
Integrated circuits and special equipment
Communications equipment
Operating systems and industrial software
High-end digital control machine tools
Robots
Aerospace equipment
Oceanographic engineering equipment and high-technology shipping
Advanced rail transport equipment
Energy efficient and new energy automobiles
Electric power equipment
Agricultural machinery equipment
New materials
Biopharmaceuticals and high-performance medical equipment
High-end equipment innovation projects
New-Generation Artificial Intelligence Plan (2017)
Knowledge computing engine and knowledge service technology
Cross-media analysis and reasoning techniques
The key technology of group intelligence
Hybrid enhancement of new intelligent architecture and new technologies
Intelligent technology for autonomous unmanned systems
Virtual reality intelligent modeling technology
Intelligent computing chips and systems
Natural language processing technology

Source: State Council (2015) and State Council (2017).

Decoupling will also be enormously complicated. U.S. bans will affect not only Chinese producers but also key sectors and firms in the United States and other countries. For example, Huawei holds the largest number of patents among all firms for 5G technologies and, altogether, Chinese companies own 34 percent of standard essential patents (SEP) in 5G networks (China Daily 2019). Engineers envisioned the 5G ecosystem as comprising internationally held patents and Chinese technology leaders actively participated in global standard-setting bodies. Chinese companies may still continue to sell licenses to their patents, although some like Huawei will no longer be able to sell products to U.S. companies that incorporate their own technology. The contributions of Chinese participants will undoubtedly change if technologies continue to decouple. For many countries, the effects may include falling years behind those with access to Chinese 5G technology, as well as substantially higher investment costs.

Meanwhile, U.S. efforts to achieve decoupling have already cast doubt on the reliability of Western partners in product categories that the United States regards as sensitive (table 14-6). Paradoxically, U.S. sanctions increase the urgency of Chinese countermeasures. China will likely accelerate investments in industrial policies, including reforms to facilitate innovation and attract foreign investment and talent. For example, Huawei is committing US$300 million annually, no strings attached, to innovation in universities around the world (Hao 2019).

OPEN INNOVATION: THE IDEAL SOLUTION

Rivalry could either increase or decrease resources directed to innovation in China and the United States, but it will almost certainly result in secretive and less-efficient efforts. For example, recent reports suggest that Chinese companies are already cutting Western-trained staff to prevent information leakages. By contrast, research in management and economics increasingly recommends an open innovation model, that is, the relatively free flow of ideas, capital, and talent. As this section argues, the open model raises the productivity of innovation and almost certainly brings more resources into the technology sector. Unfortunately, in the context of intense rivalry it also poses risks.

Open Innovation in Management and Economics

The open innovation benchmark originated in management research as a tool for making R&D more productive (Chesbrough 2003). The paradigm contrasts with research conducted within specialized R&D units, subject to protection through secrecy and formal intellectual property (IP) rights. The open paradigm has proven to be especially effective in the context of new technologies and now dominates managerial thinking. Some companies and industries even use crowdsourcing to solve problems in technology and product design, widely sharing previous secrets such as source code.

The case for open innovation is equally compelling from an economy-wide perspective. Ideas are non-rivalrous goods; consumption by one "owner" of an idea does not affect consumption by others. In an ideal world, new technologies would be freely available to all users. Modern IP systems offer a second-best compromise to this world by balancing wide dissemination and utilization with incentives for innovation.

There is also evidence that innovations depend increasingly on international collaboration. Branstetter, Glennon, and Jensen (2018) report on an explosion of cross-border research and development efforts, including through nonconventional U.S. research centers located in China, India, and Israel. The scope of these efforts is illustrated in figure 14-2 by the dramatic

FIGURE 14-2. **Share of U.S. Multinationals' USPTO Patents with Cross-border Collaboration**

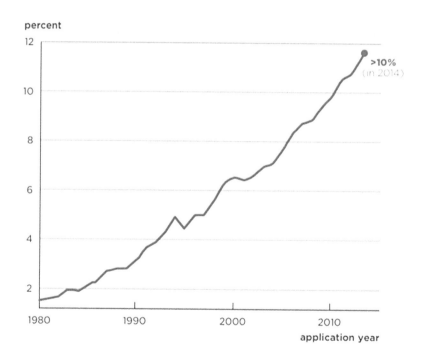

percent

>10%
(in 2014)

application year

Source: Branstatter, Glennon and Jensen (2019).

increase in the share of U.S. multinational patents developed through cross-border collaborations.

Open innovation yields two major kinds of economic benefits. First, it enhances the productivity of innovation investment by enabling researchers to draw on discoveries outside their areas of focus. Research activities often have economies of scale and research clusters have economies of scope by bringing together firms with complementary interests. These clusters attract specialized inputs—talent and innovation services—and facilitate interactions that require geographic proximity. International flows of ideas in turn enable clusters to connect across boundaries, further improving research productivity.

Second, open innovation enhances the utilization of knowledge by enabling firms to draw on ideas originating in a wider economic environment. In an endogenous-growth production function the knowledge stock plays an empirically important role in determining output. If this variable includes not only the sum of commercialized ideas but also ideas from many firms in many economies (even if discounted for distance between them), the effect on productivity will be much larger. Expanded utilization of ideas also encourages standardization and scale economies, further stimulating innovation.

Challenges to Open Innovation

At the same time, open innovation increases risks from zero-sum dimensions of competition among firms and countries, including technology leakages with security applications. It may also increase concerns about the potential uses of technologies for purposes that violate the inventors' values. Consequently, regardless of economic advantages, open innovation systems will be controversial for a variety of reasons.

Economic Risks. An effective IP system allows innovators to transfer inventions to other firms and countries while still retaining value through sales or licensing revenues. Even "forced" technology transfers generate benefits to the transferring firm in the form of access to lucrative markets. But local firms and workers could be negatively affected if local technologies are sold to outside firms or countries. It is important to recognize that this result is not due to open innovation but to innovation externalities for which the inventor is not compensated. Such market failures require a different response (for example, subsidies to inventors that internalize domestic spillover benefits). Erecting barriers against technology outflows is a poor alternative solution because it simply reduces incentives for innovation.

National Security Risks. Knowledge transfers with adverse security implications may be growing with the advent of new general-purpose technologies. For example, image recognition, genetic engineering, and robotics, while general in scope, also have military uses. That is why China identified military-civilian integration as a central goal of its technological efforts. The United States also values these connections. For example, the U.S. Department of Defense has established DIUx (Defense Innovation Unit) in Silicon Valley to contract research from private firms. Similarly, the second largest U.S. defense company—the new combination of Raytheon and United Technologies—will be headquartered in Boston to benefit from cutting-edge research there. Concerns about security spillovers need to be narrowly defined but should affect countries' willingness to transfer technologies abroad.

Risks to Values. Technologies may lead to applications that the inventor's community finds contrary to its values. Since countries cannot ban applications abroad, they may use limits on technology transfers to prevent unwanted applications. Examples of such issues today include some human applications of gene editing, surveillance technology, violations of privacy, and the dissemination of violent and pornographic material. But one cannot underestimate the complexity of such issues—people will differ widely on the acceptability of applications in other countries and even in their own country—and the best solutions may involve limited minimum standards, such as those established in some global environmental agreements.

MANAGING RIVALRY

Given these pitfalls, it will be critical to design mechanisms to keep access to technology as open as possible despite inevitable controversies. There will be no easy way to avoid trade-offs between risks associated with the flow of ideas and the benefits of promoting innovation.

Current Framework for Managing Technology Flows

The current rulebook for managing technological rivalry is badly outdated. The GATT treaty (General Agreement on Tariffs and Trade), drafted decades before current political and technological challenges, is still the main source of relevant rules. It approaches technology transfers from the viewpoint of trade in goods and services and prohibits compulsory licensing and other restrictions that may affect technology products. The plurilateral Information Technology Agreement (ITA), concluded in 1996 and expanded in 2015, further strengthened GATT disciplines for products such as computers, telecommunications equipment, and semiconductors, which now account for 10 percent of world trade. ITA members represent 97 percent of trade in these products and had agreed to bind tariffs at zero (WTO 2019). U.S. bans on trade with Huawei and other Chinese companies would be illegal under WTO rules except as justified by the national security exception discussed below.

International governance is especially unclear on so-called forced technology transfers, that is, requirements for investors to license technology and/or set up joint ventures with the companies of a host economy. China's Accession Protocol to the WTO promised to end licensing requirements (in paragraph 5), but cases seldom involve explicit requirements and there are no established rules for challenging opaque regulatory practices (WTO 2001). The United States and others have brought a case against some Chinese licensing practices under the WTO's Trade-Related Aspects of Intellectual Property Rights (TRIPS) treaty (WTO 2018). China is expanding the list of sectors fully open to foreign investment and plans to restrict administrative interventions in technology licensing.

The case is still murkier on national security. The GATT's all-important national security exception—Article XXI—allows countries to override WTO rules in cases that affect national security. Some even consider the article to be "self-declaratory," allowing a party to invoke it whenever it believes its national security is threatened. If this were correct, Article XXI could arbitrarily nullify any WTO obligation. Because of this dangerous loophole, Article XXI has been used very rarely by GATT members until its recent applications by the United States.

A 2017 case brought by Ukraine against Russia (for refusing to allow the transit of Ukrainian products) was the first to come before a WTO panel.

Significantly, the panel ruled that the WTO, and not individual members, has the right to decide whether Article XXI applies. The test is whether a case represents an "emergency in international relations." However, since appeals to the Appellate Body of the WTO will not be decided in the near future, the issue remains murky.

Trade Controls for National Security

Meanwhile, countries are launching various mechanisms to control exports, imports, and inward investments that are believed to pose national security risks. Ideally these systems will ensure that interventions are limited, transparent, and designed to achieve legitimate objectives. But the United States is rapidly transforming its own system by blurring the distinction between national security risks and economic risks. Peter Navarro, White House trade adviser to President Trump, recently announced that the United States has adopted "a new organizing principle for strategic policy: Economic security is national security" (Navarro 2018). The United States is now using this principle to justify goals as diverse as the sales of weapons to Bahrain, a "whole-of-government assessment" of America's defense industrial base, and tariffs on imports of steel, aluminum, and automobiles.

The United States recently passed the sweeping Export Control Reform Act of 2018 (ECRA) to align its export control authority with its expanded vision of national security. While past controls applied to weapons and "dual use" products, ECRA instructs the president to "identify emerging critical technologies that are not identified in any list of items controlled for export under United States law or regulations, but that nonetheless could be essential for maintaining or increasing" U.S. technological advantage. The controls include an "Entity List" of organizations and individuals that are subject to even stricter reviews. This is the list to which Huawei and other major Chinese companies were recently added.

Between 1980 and 2018, the United States applied import controls for national security only twice. In contrast, it is now making a very broad case. A recent report from the Department of Defense to the White House argues that many conventional manufacturing industries are essential for national security (Department of Defense 2018). Such a definition inevitably requires exceptions and invites "rent seeking" by private firms. For example, as of March 2019, 50,000 applications had been filed by U.S. firms seeking exemptions from steel and aluminum tariffs, and 10,000 had been filed seeking exemptions from tariffs on Chinese products (Mercatus Center 2019).

The new export control list, to be finalized soon, will reverse Obama-era efforts to simplify the system by sharply expanding the range of cases covered. Former Secretary of Defense Robert Gates justified earlier simplification efforts with a quote from Frederick the Great that "He who defends everything defends nothing" (U.S. Department of Defense 2010). The new control system is still under negotiation between the U.S. government and large technology firms.

U.S.-style controls are also spreading to other countries. In 2018, the European Parliament approved a CFIUS-like body (Committee on Foreign Investment in the United States) to review trade and investments on national security grounds. China is also developing such a system. While an early draft of China's control system was similar to the old U.S. system (PwC 2018), recent announcements suggest more aggressive policies that correspond to U.S. changes (Hornby 2019).

Investment Controls for National Security

In parallel with trade controls, the Foreign Investment Risk Review Modernization Act (FIRRMA) of 2018 substantially widened reviews of inward investments. Its goal is to make it difficult for foreigners to acquire technological assets—in the words of a leading U.S. law firm, it is a "euphemism for addressing concerns about Chinese investments" (White & Case 2018). Under the new law, Chinese investments in the United States have declined by 93 percent.

FIRRMA mandates oversight of new categories of investments such as real estate transactions near sensitive installations and sales of less-than-controlling interests to foreigners. The law also mandates oversight of "critical and emerging technologies." An initial list of twenty-seven technologies includes broad sectors such as other basic inorganic chemicals, primary batteries, and semiconductors (table 14-6). As with export controls, this list is still subject to negotiations.

TABLE 14-6. **Priority Sectors in U.S. Export Controls**

No.	Manufacturing industry	NAICS code
1	Aircraft	336411
2	Aircraft Engine and Engine Parts	336412
3	Alumina Refining and Primary Aluminum	331313
4	Ball and Roller Bearing	332991
5	Computer Storage Device	334112
6	Electronic Computer	334111
7	Guided Missile and Space Vehicle	336414
8	Guided Missile and Space Vehicle Propulsion Unit and Parts	336415
9	Military Armored Vehicle, Tank, and Tank Component	336992
10	Nuclear Electric Power Generation	221113
11	Optical Instrument and Lens	333314
12	Other Basic Inorganic Chemical	325180
13	Other Guided Missile and Space Vehicle Parts and Auxiliary	336419
14	Petrochemical	325110
15	Powder Metallurgy Part	332117
16	Power, Distribution, and Specialty Transformer	335311
17	Primary Battery	335912
18	Radio and Television Broadcasting and Wireless Communications	334220
19	Research and Development in Nanotechnology	541713
20	Research and Development in Biotechnology	541714
21	Secondary Smelting and Alloying of Aluminum	331314
22	Search, Detection, Navigation, Guidance, Aeronautical, and Nautical System and Instrument	334511
23	Semiconductor and Related Device	334413
24	Semiconductor Machinery	333242
25	Storage Battery	335911
26	Telephone Apparatus	334210
27	Turbine and Turbine Generator Set Units	333611

Note: NAICS, North American Industry Classification System.

Toward Smarter Controls

The leakage of technologies understandably argues for controls on technology transfers, but excessive controls are inefficient; precision in identifying risky transactions is critical. Such information can be developed through sophisticated cost-benefit analyses and investments in data collection and related technologies. Cybersecurity experts argue that security depends on the likelihood of attacks and the cost of defensive investments, and perfect security simply cannot be achieved. In fact, the control system's focus should be on software, since low-cost efforts to penetrate systems will usually involve standard but difficult-to-stop software vulnerabilities.

Some security can be improved with information from laboratories that test equipment and software. Huawei established such a laboratory in the United Kingdom and has cybersecurity facilities in Germany and Brussels that offer access to equipment and software to local experts. U.K. officials appear to be satisfied with the results (HCSEC 2018). Ex-post verification of transactions can further help to ensure that products reach intended buyers. Huawei is also offering to sign "no spying" agreements and extensive licensing of its technologies to foreign producers, but there is still considerable debate about the commercial value of such promises.

The logic of controlling technology trade is illustrated in figure 14-3. The main insight is that with low levels of information and trust, many potentially safe transactions will have to be prohibited and therefore many beneficial transactions will be denied. With better information and greater trust, the number of prohibited transactions can be reduced and the number of beneficial transactions can be increased while keeping risks at an acceptable level. This is shown in figure 14-3 by shifting from the left side of the diagram (low information and trust) toward the right side (high information and trust). As information and trust increase, more transactions can be moved from the "prohibited" and "controlled" groups into the "controlled" and "free" groups. This increases gains, since benefits depend on the number of approved transactions while risks remain acceptable. The benefits of the system rise as the information-trust variable is increased.

FIGURE 14-3.   **Information and Trust Make Export Controls**
More Efficient

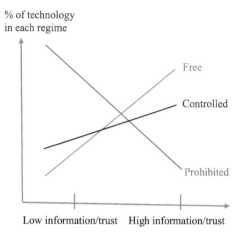

Source: Author's calculations.

POLICIES FOR MOVING BEYOND RIVALRY

The prospects for an open innovation regime have dimmed under U.S.-China clashes on trade and technology. The outlook is especially clouded for Chinese firms that rely on international partners and for Western firms like Qualcomm, Micron, Apple, and Texas Instruments, which heavily depend on China for production or sales. Behind the scenes, firms in both countries are lobbying governments to avoid confrontation. But many are also planning to reduce risks by shifting business away from the U.S.-China nexus.

Thus, decoupling is already underway, with firms and governments replacing vulnerable supply chains and moving toward more secretive innovation regimes. But the extent of decoupling is still unclear. Current production systems rely on interlocking components and technologies from multiple countries and past efforts to "go it alone" have typically failed, often despite heavy investments.[3] Markets do not tolerate inefficiencies; people and ideas learn to jump barriers and find the resources to do so.

In the long run, strategies favorable to technological interdependence will still tend to dominate because they produce better results. Thus, China's rational strategy is to continue its efforts to foster innovation by investing in education and basic research and by adopting flexible ecosystems that support innovative and mostly private firms. To the extent possible, it is also in China's interest to build an open international ecosystem for innovation that leverages its own resources and connects them with those of other leading innovators. This will require solutions to the challenges of zero-sum technological contests and building trust with other countries.

The main elements of such a long-term strategy include the following:

- *Aiming for an open innovation regime.* There is no reasonable long-term alternative to an open, politically coherent global innovation system. International technological interdependence is globally optimal and especially important for emerging technological leaders like China. China should seek to remain a central participant in international innovation and standard-setting systems, a goal that will require transparency and a willingness to share information. International cooperation will require agreements to minimize barriers to technology flows, maintain intellectual property rights, and avoid discrimination among firms of different nationalities. As a leading innovator, China has a large stake in the success of such a regime and needs to help define its directions. To be able to do so, China will also need to win the confidence and support of the global technology community through actions that promote cooperation.

- *Creating national security safeguards.* The international innovation system requires safeguards to prevent technology flows that threaten national security. China has strong incentives to join international efforts to reduce national security risks and to limit how national security exceptions are used to intervene in trade. The transparency of its domestic technology sector, including measures to prevent cybersecurity intrusions into commercial and government systems, is key to this effort.

- *Investing in transparency and information.* China can also contribute to making technology regimes less risky by investing in testing, transparency, verification, and trust. Traded products often face technical or phytosanitary standards, and sophisticated standards and tests for cybersecurity risks are increasingly appropriate in sectors such as finance, communications, and power supply. Recognizing these concerns, China will be in a strong position to lead technical and institutional initiatives to ensure the safety of traded technologies.

- *Engaging the global technology community.* A global regime is especially important for countries that occupy narrow niches in advanced value chains. In a decoupled future, these countries would have to choose between China or the United States and scale back their activities. This large group includes many middle-sized and middle-income countries in Europe and elsewhere in the world that collectively account for 60 percent of world markets. These countries will be harmed by continued U.S.-China confrontations. China needs to contribute actively to international technology policies that serve their interests.

In the long run, China's own interests align with the development of a comprehensive and liberal global technology regime. Many issues in this chapter arise because there is, so far, no such regime. The details of such policies are beyond the scope of this chapter, but the regime will have to include provisions to create an open innovation benchmark; high standards for granting and protecting intellectual property; rules on the digital economy, including taxation, privacy, and data flows; options for security-based controls on technology trade; and high expectations for public and private behavior in cyberspace. Working toward these goals will be important for China as it helps to shape a new global technology regime.

NOTES

1. The 25 percent share of U.S. patents represents a relatively high rate of registrations in the U.S. patent office by the top foreign innovator in an industry. U.S. domestic registrations are obviously more numerous since they include patents of modest quality.

2. Unfortunately, this debate is heavily focused on emotional rhetoric. For example, the Chinese commitment to "mobilize all social forces to work with courage and determination" (State Council 2015) and its "whole-of-nation industrial planning" (Rubio 2019) are widely criticized in the United States, but the U.S. national AI plan similarly refers to a "high-level framework that . . . established priorities for Federally-funded R&D in AI. . . . This coordinated AI R&D effort across the Federal government will help the United States capitalize on the full potential of AI technologies to strengthen our economy and better our society." (Executive Office of the President of the United States 2016).

3. Some examples include video tape recorders, high definition television sets, and mobile telephony devices.

REFERENCES

Branstetter, Lee, Britta Glennon, and J. Bradford Jensen. 2018. "Knowledge Transfer Abroad: The Role of U.S. Inventors within Global R&D Networks." NBER Working Paper No. 24453.

Chan, Kelvin. 2019. "Huawei Opens Brussels Security Lab in Bid to Reassure EU." Associated Press, March 6 (https://apnews.com/870bbded217548c891c4079c4 118a208).

Chesbrough, Henry. 2003. *Open Innovation: The New Imperative for Creating and Profiting from Technology.* Boston, MA: Harvard Business School Press.

China Daily. 2019. "Top 10 5G Standards-Essential Patent Owners Worldwide," June 6 (www.chinadaily.com.cn/a/201906/06/WS5cf844c0a31017657722fbd2 .html).

China National Intellectual Property Administration (CNIPA). 2018. *Comparative Table of Granted Patents* (database) (http://english.cnipa.gov.cn/docs/2018-06/20180629151939027942.pdf).

Cornell University, INSEAD, World Intellectual Property Organization (WIPO). 2018. *Global Innovation Index.* Geneva: WIPO.

Cybereason. 2019. "Operation Soft Cell: A Worldwide Campaign against Telecommunications Providers" (online report) (www.cybereason.com/blog/operation -soft-cell-a-worldwide-campaign-against-telecommunications-providers).

Executive Office of the President of the United States. 2016. *The National Artificial Intelligence Research and Development Strategic Plan.* Washington, DC: National Science and Technology Council.

Federal Ministry of Economic Affairs and Energy. 2019. "What Is the Plattform Industrie 4.0?" (webpage) (www.plattform-i40.de/PI40/Navigation/EN/Home/ home.html).

Gates, Robert. M. 2010. Remarks delivered by the Secretary of Defense at the Ronald Reagan Building and International Trade Center, Washington, D.C., April 20.

Gordon, Robert J. 2000. "Does the 'New Economy' Measure Up to the Great Inventions of the Past?" *Journal of Economic Perspectives* vol. 14, no. 4, 49–74.

Huawei Cyber Security Evaluation Centre (HCSEC). 2018. *Oversight Board: Annual Report 2018* (www.gov.uk/government/publications/huawei-cyber-security-evaluation-centre-oversight-board-annual-report-2018).

Hao, Karen. 2019. "Huawei Is Giving $300 Million a Year to Universities with No Strings Attached." *MIT Technology Review,* July 3 (www.technologyreview.com/s /613917/huawei-is-giving-300-million-a-year-to-universities-with-no-strings -attached/?utm_source=linkedin&utm_medium=tr_social&utm_campaign =site_visitor.unpaid.engagement).

Hornby, Lucy. 2019. "China to Roll Out Export Controls on Sensitive Technology." *Financial Times*, June 8 (https://www.ft.com/content/47562f6-89f6-11e9-a1c1-51bf8f989972).

Jiang, Renai, Haoyue Shi, and Gary Jefferson. 2019. "Measuring China's International Technological Catchup." *Journal of Contemporary China* (doi: 10.1080/10670564.2019.1677362).

McKinsey Global Institute (MGI). 2018. "Notes from the AI Frontier: Modeling the Impact of AI on the World Economy" (discussion paper), September (www.mckinsey.com/featured-insights/artificial-intelligence/notes-from-the-ai-frontier-modeling-the-impact-of-ai-on-the-world-economy).

McKinsey Global Institute (MGI), 2019. *China and the World: Inside the Dynamics of a Changing Relationship* (report) (www.mckinsey.com/featured-insights/china/china-and-the-world-inside-the-dynamics-of-a-changing-relationship).

Navarro, Peter. 2018. "Why Economic Security Is National Security." Real Clear Politics, December 9 (www.realclearpolitics.com/articles/2018/12/09/why_economic_security_is_national_security_138875.html).

Organization for Economic Cooperation and Development (OECD). 2019a. *Multifactor Productivity* (database) (data.oecd.org/lprdty/multifactor-productivity.htm).

Organization for Economic Cooperation and Development (OECD). 2019b, *Gross Domestic Spending on R&D* (database) (data.oecd.org/rd/gross-domestic-spending-on-r-d.htm).

PricewaterhouseCoopers (PwC). 2018. "Who's in Control? China's Proposed Export Control Law," June–July (www.pwc.com/m1/en/services/tax/customs-international-trade/china-proposed-export-control-law-june-july-2018.html).

Mercatus Center. 2019. *Tariff Exclusions: Section 301 Tariffs* (database) (quantgov.org/section-301-tariffs/).

Rubio, Marco. 2019. *Made in China 2025 and the Future of American Industry.* Washington, DC: U.S. Senate Committee on Small Business and Entrepreneurship (Sen. Marco Rubio, chair), February 12.

State Council. 2015. *Made in China 2025*. Beijing, July 7.

State Council. 2017. "New Generation Artificial Intelligence Development Plan." (In Chinese.) (www.gov.cn/zhengce/content/2017-07/20/content_5211996.htm).

Summers, Lawrence. 2016. "The Age of Secular Stagnation: What It Is and What to Do about It." *Foreign Affairs*, February 15.

Trump, Donald J. 2019. "Executive Order on Securing the Information and Communications Technology and Services Supply Chain." Washington D.C.: White House.

U.S. Department of Defense. 2010. Secretary of Defense Speech by Robert M. Gates, April 20. (https://archive.defense.gov/Speeches/Speech.aspx?SpeechID=1453)

U.S. Department of Defense. 2018. *Assessing and Strengthening the Manufacturing and Defense Industrial Base and Supply Chain Resiliency of the United States* (report), September (https://media.defense.gov/2018/Oct/05/2002048904/-1/-1/1/assessing-and-strengthening-the-manufacturing-and%20defense-industrial-base-and-supply-chain-resiliency.pdf).

Veugelers, Reinhilde. 2017. "The Challenge of China's Rise as a Science and Technology Powerhouse." *Policy Contribution* No. 19. Bruegel: Brussels.

Wheeler, Tom, and David Simpson. 2019. *Why 5G Requires New Approaches to Cybersecurity: Racing to Protect the Most Important Network of the 21st Century* (report). Washington, DC: Brookings Institution.

White & Case. 2018. "CFIUS Reform Becomes Law: What FIRRMA Means for Industry." Washington, DC: White & Case, August 13.

World Intellectual Property Organization (WIPO). 2018. *Statistical Country Profiles: United States of America* (database) (www.wipo.int/ipstats/en/statistics/country_profile/profile.jsp?code=US).

World Trade Organization (WTO). 2001. "Protocol on the Accession of the People's Republic of China," November 10 (unpan1.un.org/intradoc/groups/public/documents/APCITY/UNPAN002123.pdf).

World Trade Organization (WTO). 2018. "DS542: China – Certain Measures Concerning the Protection of Intellectual Property Rights," March 23 (www.wto.org/english/tratop_e/dispu_e/cases_e/ds542_e.htm).

World Trade Organization (WTO). 2019. "Information Technology Agreement —An Explanation" (webpage) (www.wto.org/english/tratop_e/inftec_e/itaintro_e.htm).

15

China's Role in the Global Financial System

ESWAR PRASAD

This chapter considers China's evolving role in the global financial system, focusing in particular on the role of its currency. China's economy is now the second largest in the world and a key driver of global growth. But the country's role in global finance, and the prominence of its currency, are not commensurate with its weight in the world economy.

The chapter outlines some of the steps taken in recent years by the Chinese government to promote the international use of the renminbi (RMB), which in turn is linked to moves to open up China's capital account. In light of China's rising share of global GDP and trade, these steps are gaining traction and portend a more prominent role for the RMB in global trade and finance. The chapter then reviews the potential implications of these changes for capital flows into and out of China. This is followed by an evaluation of the progress that China has made in various aspects of financial market development and a discussion of the close relationship between those reforms, capital account openness, and the international role of the currency. Finally, the chapter discusses the prospects for the RMB becoming a major reserve currency.[1]

The RMB has come a long way in a short period. It was only in the early 2000s that the Chinese government began the process of gradually opening up the country's capital account, allowing financial capital to flow more freely across its borders. This process was very gradual at first and picked up pace only a decade later. Over the last few years, the RMB's progress as an international currency has been remarkable in some respects. However, the currency's seemingly inexorable progress stalled in 2014. Starting in mid-2014, the Chinese economy seemed to be losing steam: domestic and foreign investors became less confident about the stability of China's financial markets, and, to compound these problems, China's central bank made some missteps as it attempted to make the currency's value more market-determined.

Nevertheless, in October 2016, the RMB achieved a major milestone in its ascendance as an international currency. That month the International Monetary Fund (IMF) officially anointed the RMB as an elite global reserve currency. The RMB joined the select basket of currencies (previously comprising the dollar, the euro, the Japanese yen, and the British pound sterling) that constitute the IMF's artificial currency unit, the special drawing rights. However, this does not by itself mean that the RMB is already in a position to significantly reshape global finance; it still has a long way to go before it can play a major role in international finance. The Chinese government has taken a number of steps to solidify the RMB's status as an elite global currency by increasing its international use. However, adoption of the RMB in global markets has been limited by the Chinese government's unwillingness to free up its exchange rate and fully open the capital account.

This chapter considers three related but distinct aspects of the role of the RMB in the global monetary system and examines the Chinese government's actions in each of these areas. First, I discuss changes in the openness of China's capital account and the degree of progress toward capital account convertibility. Second, I consider the currency's internationalization, which involves its use in denominating and settling cross-border trades and financial transactions—that is, its use as an international medium of exchange. Third, I trace the RMB's evolution as a reserve currency.

The RMB is likely to become a significant player in international financial markets even if its rise to prominence levels off, yet its full potential may remain unrealized unless the Chinese government undertakes a broad range of economic and financial system reforms. In the long run, what the RMB's ascendance means for the global financial system depends to a large extent on how China's economy itself changes in the process of the country elevating its currency.

CAPITAL ACCOUNT OPENING

In evaluating China's approach to capital account liberalization, one basic question must first be addressed: Why would capital account liberalization be a priority for China given the many domestic challenges the economy faces, including slowing economic growth, a weak financial system, and unbalanced growth that is still heavily dependent on investment? One reason is that such liberalization would generate a number of collateral (indirect) benefits for the domestic economy, particularly in terms of domestic financial market development that, in turn, could facilitate more stable growth (Prasad and Rajan 2008).

Liberalizing outflows provides Chinese households with opportunities to diversify their savings portfolios internationally and stimulates domestic financial reforms by creating competition for domestic banks that currently depend on captive domestic sources of funds (retail deposits of households and corporations). For the RMB to take on a more international role, both portfolio and foreign direct investment (FDI) outflows will need to involve more participation from the private sector.

The liberalization of inflows is also an important part of the overall picture in terms of attaining the collateral benefits of capital account liberalization. This liberalization already has allowed and will continue to allow foreign investors to play a larger role in further developing and deepening China's financial markets. For instance, there is a significant body of evidence that liberalizing portfolio inflows helps improve liquidity in the domestic equity markets of emerging economies. This, along with the entry of foreign banks, would increase competition in the banking sector, which in turn would benefit private savers and borrowers. Other segments of China's financial sector, including the insurance sector, have depended on capital controls and other entry restrictions to stay competitive. These segments will face greater competition with more open inflows. With effective regulation, this could lead to significant efficiency gains.

Capital account liberalization could have broader benefits for China. An open capital account would catalyze progress toward the objective of making Shanghai an international financial center. Capital account opening, especially if accompanied by greater exchange rate flexibility, could also strengthen China's domestic economic structure. It would facilitate financial sector reforms, allowing for a rebalancing of growth away from a reliance on exports and investment-driven growth to a more balanced model of growth with higher private consumption. Financial sector reforms can play a crucial role in this rebalancing effort by promoting a more efficient allocation of resources toward the most productive uses. A more flexible exchange rate would free up monetary policy to facilitate achieving domestic macroeconomic objectives such as maintaining low and stable inflation (Prasad 2016).

Consistent with all these objectives, the government has in recent years removed restrictions on capital inflows and outflows, but in a controlled and gradual manner. These schemes have been designed to generate many of the collateral benefits of financial openness while creating freer movement of capital. For instance, the government has set up a number of schemes to allow foreign investors to invest in China's stock and bond markets. These include the Qualified Foreign Institutional Investor Scheme and the Renminbi Qualified Foreign Institutional Investor Scheme.

At the same time, there are now many channels available for Chinese households, corporations, and institutional investors that wish to invest some portion of their investments in foreign markets. These include the Qualified Domestic Institutional Investor and Qualified Domestic Individual Investor Schemes.

A few channels for two-way flows, such as the Stock Connect and Bond Connect programs, have also been opened up. But the government continues to maintain a tight grip over each of these channels.

How open is China's capital account? De jure measures of capital account openness typically rely on binary indicators from the International Monetary Fund's *Annual Report on Exchange Arrangements and Exchange Restrictions* (AREAER). These binary measures reflect the existence of any restrictions on a large number of categories of inflows and outflows. Conventional measures of de jure financial openness drawing on the AREAER data show little, if any, change for China over the past decade.

An alternative and complementary approach to evaluating an economy's financial openness is to analyze de facto measures of integration into global financial markets. Figure 15-1 shows the levels of China's gross external (foreign) assets and liabilities, along with the net asset position, from 2004 through 2018. At the end of 2018, China had US$7 trillion of external assets and about $5 trillion of external liabilities. Both assets and liabilities have risen sharply over the last decade, and the net asset position stood at $2.1 trillion. Thus the country's capital account is becoming increasingly

FIGURE 15-1. **China's External Assets and Liabilities (in trillions of U.S. dollars)**

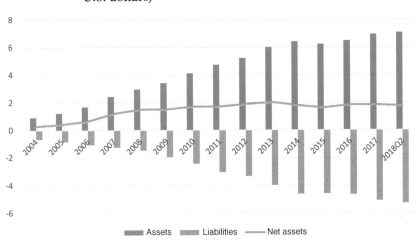

Source: China State Administration of Foreign Exchange (SAFE) and CEIC.

open in de facto terms, although by this measure China is financially less open than many reserve currency economies.

As China opens up its capital account, there have been important shifts in the structure of its capital outflows over the past decade. The change in the composition of gross outflows, from accumulation of foreign exchange reserves by the central bank to nonofficial outflows, reflects China's controlled approach to capital account liberalization but also increasing seepage around remaining controls. Agarwal, Gu, and Prasad (2019) analyzed the allocation patterns of Chinese institutional investors, who constitute the main channel for foreign portfolio investment outflows. They found that, relative to a market-capitalization weighted portfolio, Chinese institutional investors invest smaller fractions of their international portfolios than would be expected in developed countries and high-tech sectors but overinvest in high-tech stocks in developed countries. These results suggest that the acquisition of technology could be an important motivating factor driving Chinese investors' international portfolio allocations. In such ways, unlocking the enormous pool of domestic savings could have a significant impact on global financial markets as China continues to open up its capital account and as domestic investors look abroad for higher returns and diversification.

While the government is taking a number of steps to promote capital account liberalization, its final objective in this regard remains unclear. The end game for the government appears to be a capital account that is largely open but still subject to some degree of administrative control. Joseph Yam, the former head of the Hong Kong Monetary Authority, has argued that the long-term objective for China ought to be full capital account convertibility, which he defines as relaxation of capital controls but maintenance of "soft" controls in the form of registration and reporting requirements for regulatory purposes. He draws a careful distinction between this and an entirely unfettered capital-flow regime, referred to as free capital account convertibility. This is a subtle but important distinction that appears to have resonated well with the Chinese leadership, for full convertibility by this definition provides a path to an open capital account without ceding control entirely to market forces.

INTERNATIONAL USE OF THE RMB

China has promoted the availability of the RMB outside its borders, including sanctioning more than fifteen offshore trading centers where transactions between the RMB and other currencies can be conducted. The government has also set up a payment system to facilitate commercial transactions between domestic and foreign companies using the RMB rather than more widely used currencies such as the dollar and the euro.

These measures have led to the rising internationalization of the RMB. This term signifies its greater use in denominating and settling cross-border trade and financial transactions—that is, its use as an international medium of exchange. By the latter half of 2014, about one-third of China's international trade was being denominated and settled in RMB. Furthermore, according to data from SWIFT (the Society for Worldwide Interbank Financial Telecommunication), by mid-2015 the RMB accounted for nearly 2.8 percent of cross-border payments around the world, a low share but one that already ranked the RMB as among the top five payment currencies in the world (figure 15-2). Other indicators of China's internationalization also showed substantial progress during this period. Such indicators include settlement of trade transactions with RMB, the issuance of RMB-denominated bonds in Hong Kong and other offshore financial centers, and offshore RMB deposits.

But then the currency's progress stalled, as China grappled with a

FIGURE 15-2. **RMB as World Payments Currency by Value (in %)**

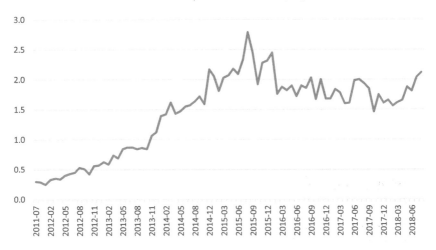

Source: SWIFT RMB Tracker.

growth slowdown, a sharp boom-and-bust cycle in the stock market, and concerns about rising debt levels and financial instability. Since 2015 the RMB's progress as an international medium of exchange has gone into reverse or, at best, flat-lined. At the end of 2018 the RMB accounted for about 2 percent of cross-border payments (see figure 15-2). Other quantitative indicators of the currency's use in international finance, including trade settlement in RMB and the issuance of RMB-denominated bonds offshore, all point to signs of a stalling of the currency's advance as an international currency.

Still, it is important to keep both the upswings and downswings in proper perspective. Despite the constraints on capital flowing into and out of China, the RMB has begun playing a larger, though still modest, role in international finance over a relatively short period. The SWIFT data reveal the rising prominence of the RMB as an international payments currency, although it is still a long way from being a major payments currency that can rival the U.S. dollar. This will be aided by a payments system that China has set up for intermediating transactions. In October 2015, China launched a new cross-border RMB payments system—the China International Payment System (CIPS)—that is organized more in line with internationally accepted standards. This will help facilitate settlement and clearing of cross-border RMB transactions, including trade and investment flows, and bolster the international role of the RMB.

The pace of the internationalization of China's currency depends on its use in international financial transactions as well. The choice of currency for denomination and settlement of trade flows is contingent on the extent to which that currency can also be used in international financial transactions. Bank of International Settlements (BIS) data show that, as of 2016 (when the last BIS triennial survey was conducted), the RMB accounted for only about 4 percent of turnover in foreign exchange markets. This is above the share of any other emerging market currency but well below that of the major reserve currencies.

RESERVE CURRENCY

A different aspect of a currency's role in international finance is its status as a reserve currency, one that is held by foreign central banks as protection against balance of payments crises. This topic might seem premature insofar as China has neither a flexible exchange rate nor an open capital account—two features once considered absolute prerequisites for a reserve currency. Even though the IMF has officially anointed the RMB as a reserve currency, financial market participants' views are more important in determining a currency's status.

The RMB's prospects as a reserve currency will ultimately be influenced by progress on these criteria: (1) capital account openness, (2) exchange rate flexibility, (3) economic size, (4) macroeconomic policies, and (5) financial market development. This section discusses the relative importance of each of these criteria for reserve currency status and summarizes how China measures up on each.

Reserves must be acceptable as payments to a country's trade and financial partners, which requires that the currency be easily tradable in global financial markets. China is gradually and selectively easing restrictions on both inflows and outflows. As noted above, the capital account has become increasingly open in de facto terms, but extensive capital controls remain in place.

Reserve currencies are typically traded freely and their external value is market-determined, although this does not preclude occasional bouts of intervention by the country's central bank in foreign exchange markets. China continues to manage its nominal exchange rate, although it has in principle allowed market forces to play an increasing role in determining the external value of the RMB. The currency is now managed against a trade-weighted basket of other major currencies, although market participants still see China's central bank as playing a major role in influencing the level of the exchange rate in a manner that does not always hew to such a rule. The absence of a fully market-determined exchange rate, especially one that is supported using capital controls, could affect the currency's rise in global finance.

China's economy is now the second largest in the world (based on market exchange rates). In 2018, its annual GDP was about two-thirds that of the United States (at market exchange rates). China is also an important player in international trade, accounting for 13 percent of global trade in goods. China's impact on the world economy is even greater when measured along other dimensions. The country is a net global creditor, to the tune of more than US$2 trillion, as noted earlier, and has accounted for about one-third of global GDP growth since the financial crisis.

Investors in a country's sovereign assets must have faith in its commitment to low inflation and sustainable levels of public debt, so that the value of the currency is not in danger of being eroded. China has a lower ratio of explicit public debt to GDP than most major reserve currency economies and has maintained moderate inflation in recent years.

A country must have broad, deep, and liquid financial markets so that international investors can access a wide array of financial assets denominated in its currency. China's financial markets remain limited and underdeveloped, with a number of constraints such as a rigid interest rate structure. The recent growth and opening up of China's debt markets suggests that the pace of the country's financial market development is consistent with its intention to gradually increase acceptance of its currency as an international currency. Moreover, to satisfy their demand for relatively safe RMB-denominated assets, foreign investors—both official and private—will eventually need to be given greater access to China's debt markets if the RMB is to become a significant reserve currency.

Remarkably, the RMB has already become a de facto reserve currency even though China does not meet some of the traditional prerequisites. China's sheer economic size and the strength of its trade and financial linkages with economies around the world seem to have overridden the other limitations.

Many central banks around the world are gradually acquiring at least a modest amount of RMB assets for their foreign exchange reserve portfolios. The list comprises a geographically and economically diverse group of countries, including Australia, Austria, Chile, Nigeria, South Africa, Korea, Malaysia, and Japan. According to IMF estimates, about 2 percent of global foreign exchange reserves are now held in RMB-denominated financial assets. About thirty-five central banks around the world have signed bilateral local currency swap arrangements with China's central bank. These arrangements give them access to RMB liquidity that they can draw on to defend their currencies or maintain stable imports even if foreign capital inflows into their economies were to dry up.

Although the RMB has managed to attain the status of a reserve currency, its progress is likely to be limited by its lack of well-developed financial markets. Foreign official investors, such as central banks and sovereign wealth funds, typically seek to invest in highly liquid and relatively safe fixed income debt securities, even if such securities have a relatively low rate of return. China's government and corporate debt securities markets are quite large but still seen as having limited trading volume and weak regulatory frameworks.

Thus, strengthening its financial markets is important both for China's own economic development and for promoting the international role of its currency.

FINANCIAL SECTOR DEVELOPMENT AND REFORMS

Financial market development in the home country is one of the key determinants of a currency's international status. Historically, each reserve currency has risen on the international stage under unique circumstances, spurred by a range of motivations, but one constant is that this rise has always required financial markets that can cope with the varied and voluminous demands of private and official foreign investors. There are three relevant aspects of financial market development:

- *Breadth:* The availability of a broad range of financial instruments, including markets for hedging risk.

- *Depth:* A large volume of financial instruments in specific markets.

- *Liquidity:* A high level of turnover (trading volume).

Without a sufficiently large and liquid debt market, the RMB cannot be used widely in international transactions. To make the currency attractive to foreign central banks and large institutional investors, they will need access to RMB-denominated government and corporate debt as "safe" assets for their portfolios. At the same time, both importers and exporters may be concerned about greater exchange rate volatility resulting from an open capital account if they do not have access to derivatives markets to hedge foreign exchange risk. Thus, depth, breadth, and liquidity are all relevant considerations in assessing the readiness of a country's financial sector to cope with an open capital account and elevate its currency to reserve currency status.

China's financial system remains bank-dominated, with the state directly controlling most of the banking system. Domestic credit allocation is controlled largely by state-owned banks and is disproportionately directed toward enterprises, especially state-owned enterprises, rather than households.

Chinese stock markets have been prone to concerns about weak corporate governance, limited transparency, weak auditing standards, and shoddy accounting practices. In the absence of the broad institutional and regulatory reforms that are necessary to support effective price discovery and the overall efficient functioning of stock markets, these markets could remain unstable. The recent bouts of volatility in the stock market and the manner in which the government has addressed volatility has heightened many of these concerns. As a consequence, even with more liberalization of portfolio inflows, international investors may shy away from investing heavily in Chinese equities. Therefore, the country's deep equity markets may be of limited help in promoting the international role of the RMB.

Recognizing the importance of a better financial system to an improved allocation of resources within the economy, the Chinese government has instituted a number of reforms in recent years. For instance, bank deposit and lending rates have now been fully liberalized. Commercial banks can now set these rates freely, although the People's Bank of China still sets reference rates to guide banks. An explicit bank deposit insurance program has been in operation since May 2015. This program is intended to expose banks to some degree of market discipline by replacing the implicit full insurance of all deposits by the government. The system also allows for early intervention by the banking regulator and has an improved resolution mechanism for failing banks. Since the system is relatively new, there have been no test cases as yet.

These reforms are important steps in the right direction. Future reforms and the development of the banking system will have significant implications for the development of China's more nascent financial markets, including the corporate bond market, and also for economic development more broadly. In particular, China's aspirations to make the RMB a global reserve currency rest in large part on the pace of development of its fixed income markets. Reserve currency economies are expected to issue high-quality and creditworthy government debt or government-backed debt instruments that can serve to hedge against foreign investors' domestic currency depreciation during a global downturn.

China's fixed income markets, especially for corporate debt, have developed considerably in the last few years, from both domestic and international perspectives (see table 15-1) The stock of government bonds stood at US$4.9 trillion in September 2018. Nonfinancial corporate debt was practically nonexistent a decade ago, but the outstanding stock has now risen to $2.9 trillion. The size of China's overall fixed income markets, with a capitalization of $12.4 trillion in September 2018, now stands behind only those of the United States, the euro zone, and Japan. However, turnover,

TABLE 15-1. **Stocks of Government and Corporate Bonds: A Cross-Country Perspective (amounts outstanding at end of September 2018, in trillions of US$)**

| | | Corporate bonds | | | |
Country	Government bonds	Financial corporations	Nonfinancial corporations	Total corporate bonds	Total debt
United States	18.35	15.91	6.24	22.15	40.50
Eurozone	9.46	8.57	1.50	10.06	19.53
Japan	9.39	2.50	0.73	3.23	12.62
China	4.89	4.61	2.92	7.53	12.42
United Kingdom	2.63	2.65	0.52	3.17	5.79
Germany	1.85	1.56	0.19	1.75	3.60
India	0.81	0.03	0.03	0.05	0.86

Source: Bank for International Settlements.

a measure of trading volume, remains quite low in China's debt markets. China has recently lifted restrictions on foreign investors' participation in its bond markets, which should improve both the depth and liquidity of these markets over time.

Overall, China's financial markets have improved in some respects during the last decade, but there are still significant gaps, especially in terms of achieving sufficiently large and liquid debt markets. More important, the structure and quality of debt markets will also need to be improved to fully prepare for a currency used widely in international financial transactions and reserve holdings. With relatively low external and government debt positions, China's debt markets can in principle expand rapidly without serious threat to inflation credibility or vulnerability to external risks. Effective regulation of corporate debt markets is an important priority so that these markets can expand without generating financial instability.

The main conclusion of this section is that China has made significant progress in many areas but still falls short on some key dimensions of financial market development. The government's efforts to aggressively promote the RMB's international role are likely to be impeded over the medium term by the weaknesses of China's financial system.

SAFE HAVEN STATUS FOR THE CURRENCY WILL REQUIRE INSTITUTIONAL REFORMS

Since the global financial crisis, a new concept has gained traction in international finance: that of a "safe haven" currency (Prasad 2014). Such a currency is one that investors turn to for safety during times of global turmoil, rather than for diversifying their stores of assets denominated in foreign currencies or seeking higher yields on their investments.

China might have rising economic clout, but whether it will be able to gain the trust of foreign investors is an open question. Such trust is crucial for a currency to be seen as a safe haven. A country seeking this status for its currency must have a sound institutional framework—including an independent judiciary, an open and transparent government with institutionalized checks and balances, and robust public institutions (especially a credible central bank). These elements have traditionally been seen as vital for earning the trust of foreign investors, both private as well as official, including central banks and sovereign wealth funds.

Foreign investors typically want to know that they will be treated fairly according to well-established legal procedures, rather than being subject to the whims of the government. They also tend to value the independence of institutions such as the central bank from government interference, as this is important for maintaining the credibility and value of the currency.

While the Chinese leadership is pursuing financial liberalization and limited market-oriented economic reforms, it appears to have repudiated political, legal, and institutional reforms. In short, while the RMB has the potential to become a significant reserve currency, it will not attain safe haven status in the absence of far-reaching reforms to China's institutional and political structures. Such reforms are apparently not in the cards.

CHINA'S IMPACT ON GLOBAL FINANCIAL MARKETS

This section analyzes the potential impact of the RMB's rise on the competitive balance of global reserve currencies and discusses the effects that the internationalization of the RMB could have on the structure of global capital flows.

Promoting the RMB's international role is tied up with many complex domestic and geopolitical considerations. As with all of its policies, China is working toward multiple objectives. For now, it is likely that China will continue promoting the international use of the RMB using Hong Kong as a platform. When the Chinese government determines that its financial markets are finally strong enough to allow for a more open capital account, it is likely that promotion of Shanghai as an international financial center could take precedence, especially as that would fit better with China's domestic financial market development objective.

While using Hong Kong as the main staging ground for the internationalization of the RMB, the Chinese government is also working to promote competition among financial centers eager to engage in RMB business. Regional and international financial centers such as Bangkok, Frankfurt, London, and Singapore are all being given opportunities to engage in RMB transactions. This competition enables Beijing to continue its program of internationalizing the RMB without having to fully open its capital account.

Why are so many countries eager to sign currency swap lines with China and even hold its currency as part of their reserve portfolios? This may be less a sign of the RMB's inevitable march to global dominance than it is a low-cost bet on a likely outcome of a convertible and more widely accepted global currency. Equally important is the desire on the part of many economies to maintain a good economic relationship with China in anticipation of its rising economic power. Central banks around the world are preparing for a future in which the RMB will start playing an increasingly prominent role in international finance and may ultimately become a reserve currency. A more open capital account will allow the RMB to play an increasingly significant role in Asian as well as global trade and finance, but in a manner that allows the Chinese government to retain some control over capital flows.

There is no clear guidance from economic theory about how many currencies would be best for a world economy that is becoming increasingly closely integrated. Having a system with multiple reserve currencies but with just one principal reserve currency has fueled a number of complications such as persistent global current account imbalances, suggesting that it may not be the optimal situation from the perspective of promoting the stability of the global financial system.

If multiple reserve currencies are indeed desirable, how should one assess the prospects of other currencies that could compete with the dollar? The history of the rise and fall of reserve currencies does offer some useful lessons. The key is for a country to have sound economic policies, well-developed financial markets, and public institutions that are trusted by domestic and foreign investors. These are the relevant criteria that put a country's currency in a position to develop into a reserve currency.

The argument for a world with multiple reserve currencies in a stable competitive equilibrium might be obvious if the world economy was starting with a clean slate. But the argument is far from clear-cut given the present state of financial markets and the level of international financial integration. Events during the financial crisis present a counterargument to the notion that having more reserve currencies is better.

The dollar's dominance has allowed the Fed to act as a credible global lender of last resort, a role that few other central banks are capable of playing. However, there is a risk of confusing cause and effect here. One reason the world was in search of dollar liquidity during the crisis is that many global banks had sought large amounts of cheap dollar funding to finance their worldwide operations. U.S. monetary conditions, which led to an aggressive search for yield through financial innovations, and the fertile ground provided by U.S. financial markets for such sophistry were important elements in making many global banks depend so heavily on dollar liquidity.

While the RMB is likely to become a significant reserve currency over the next decade, it is unlikely to challenge the dollar's dominance. There is still a huge gulf between China and the United States in the availability of safe and liquid assets such as government bonds. The depth, breadth, and liquidity of U.S. financial markets will serve as a potent buffer against threats to the dollar's preeminent status. Rather than catching up to the United States by building up debt, the challenge for China is to develop its other financial markets and increase the availability of high-quality RMB-denominated assets.

CONCLUSION

Despite China's economic might, the international stature of its currency, the RMB, does not yet quite match that of its economy. Among the currencies of the world's six largest economies, the RMB is only now beginning to emerge as a factor in the global economy. The others—the U.S. dollar, the euro (which covers two of the six largest economies, Germany and France), the Japanese yen, and the British pound sterling—all have well-established roles in global finance.

Given its size and economic clout, China is adopting a unique approach to the RMB's role in the global monetary system. As with virtually all other major reforms, China is striking out on its own path to a more open capital account. This move is likely to involve removing explicit controls even while attempting to exercise "soft" control over inflows and outflows through administrative and other measures.

The selective and calibrated approach to capital account liberalization has been effective at promoting the RMB's international presence, but it has generated some risks, since other reforms have not kept pace. Still, the RMB is beginning to play a significant role in international trade transactions. It is making inroads into the global financial system and starting to appear in the reserve portfolios of a number of central banks around the world. It has also become a constituent of the basket of currencies that constitute the IMF's special drawing rights. These shifts, some of which are more symbolic than substantive at present, will develop critical mass over time and have the potential to start transforming the global monetary system. However, the full potential of the RMB's international use cannot be realized without more active onshore development. It will be difficult, for instance, to fully develop China's foreign exchange and derivatives markets in the absence of a more open capital account.

The RMB's prospects as a global currency will ultimately be shaped by broader domestic policies, especially those related to financial market development, exchange rate flexibility, and capital account liberalization. As Chinese financial markets become more fully developed and private investors increase the international diversification of their portfolios, these shifts in China's outward investment patterns are likely to become more pronounced. Thus the various policy reforms that are needed to support the international role of the RMB could also create significant changes in China's economy and the patterns of its capital inflows and outflows.

A number of key reforms could increase the RMB's prominence in global finance and also help in China's own economic development. One is the liberalization of financial markets, including further development of fixed income and secondary (derivatives) markets. Another is the further opening up of the capital account by removing restrictions on both inflows and outflows in a calibrated manner. Fixing the banking system so that it operates on more commercial principles and with better governance structures is also important. A more flexible, market-determined exchange rate should accompany capital account opening. This would provide a foundation for a more autonomous monetary policy regime that emphasizes price rather than quantity instruments. Finally, a more comprehensive and robust regulatory framework that enhances rather than attempts to serve as a substitute for market discipline would help build confidence in China's financial markets.

The RMB is on its way to becoming a widely used currency in international trade and finance. So long as China continues to make progress on financial sector and other market-oriented reforms, it is likely that the RMB will become an important reserve currency within the next decade, perhaps eroding but not displacing the dollar's dominance. For the RMB to become a safe haven currency, however, would require not just economic and financial reforms but also significant institutional reforms.

NOTE

1. A sample of the extensive literature on this topic includes Barry Eichengreen and Masahiro Kawai, *Renminbi Internationalization: Achievements, Prospects, and Challenges* (Washington, DC: Brookings Institution Press, 2015); Jeffrey Frankel, "Historical Precedents for the Internationalization of the RMB," paper presented at a workshop organized by the Council on Foreign Relations and the China Development Research Foundation, Beijing, November 1, 2011; Yiping Huang, Daili Wang, and Gang Fan, "Paths to a Reserve Currency: Internationalization of the Renminbi and Its Implications." ABDI Working Paper No. 482 (Tokyo: Asian Development Bank Institute, 2014); Nicholas Lardy and Patrick Douglas, "Capital Account Liberalization and the Role of the Renminbi," Working Paper 11-6 (Washington, DC: Peterson Institute for International Economics, 2011); and Paola Subacchi, *The People's Money: How China Is Building a Global Currency* (New York: Columbia University Press, 2016).

REFERENCES

Agarwal, Isha, Grace Weishi Gu, and Eswar Prasad. 2019. "China's Impact on Global Financial Markets." Manuscript, Cornell University and University of California, Santa Cruz.

Prasad, Eswar S. 2016. *Gaining Currency: The Rise of the Renminbi*. Oxford: Oxford University Press.

———. 2014. *The Dollar Trap: How the U.S. Dollar Tightened Its Grip on Global Finance*. Princeton, NJ: Princeton University Press.

Prasad, Eswar, and Raghuram Rajan. 2008. "A Pragmatic Approach to Capital Account Liberalization." *Journal of Economic Perspectives* 22 (3): 149–72.

16

China's Evolving Role in the International Economic Institutions

DAVID DOLLAR

Along with China's rise as a trading and investing nation has come greater Chinese participation in the international economic institutions, that is, the World Trade Organization (WTO), the International Monetary Fund (IMF), and the network of multilateral development banks. These institutions have underpinned an extraordinary period of global stability and prosperity. They were established under U.S. leadership with the active participation of advanced capitalist economies in Europe and the Asia-Pacific. One of their achievements is that they have enabled the economic rise of China and other developing economies, which now make up more than half the global economy. If recent trends continue, the developing world will make up an ever-growing share of the global economy. Naturally, these institutions need to evolve to give more voice to this rising population, but that is not happening without controversy.

This chapter focuses on some tensions within the issue areas covered by the WTO, the multilateral development banks, and the IMF. In today's multipolar world, old powers such as Japan and Europe are still relevant, while new powers such as India and countries belonging to the Association of Southeast Asian Nations (ASEAN) come to the fore. But the relationship between China and the United States will be of special importance. These two will be overwhelmingly larger than other national economies in the

period to 2049. Each has some strong preferences about reform of these institutions. The potential exists for compromise between the two that would
modernize the institutions and lay a foundation for a further period of stability and prosperity. It is also easy to imagine a confrontational future in
which compromises are not reached and the world economy devolves into
blocs and competing institutions. The chapter lays out the key challenges
in the trade, development, and finance arenas, and concludes with some
thoughts about what practical compromises might look like.

TRADE, FOREIGN DIRECT INVESTMENT, AND THE WTO

In the case of the WTO, China has become an active member since joining in 2001. Between 2006 and 2015, forty-four cases—representing more
than a quarter of the WTO caseload—involved China as a complainant or
as a respondent. Only the United States and the EU had more active cases
over the period. Furthermore, in general, when China has lost cases it has
changed the necessary laws and regulations and complied with the ruling.
Based on this pattern, one might conclude that China's integration into
trade dispute settlement has been quite successful.

Wu, however, makes a compelling case that the situation is not so rosy.
China presents a number of unique challenges for the trading regime, and
"since the Great Recession WTO litigation has increasingly bifurcated into
an 'Established Powers versus China' dynamic" (Wu 2016, 264). Between
2009 and 2015, China-related cases accounted for 90 percent of the cases
brought by the four large economies against each other. While cases among
the United States, EU, and Japan used to be common, now increasingly
these countries line up together against China.

The problem, according to Wu, is that "China, Inc." is sui generis:

What distinguishes China, Inc.? Contradictions pervade the Chinese economy today. While one might think of the economy as
state-dominated, private enterprises drive much of China's dynamic
growth. In addition, economic intervention does not always flow
through the state. Alongside the state is the Chinese Communist
Party ("Party"), a separate political actor that plays an active role in
the management of state-owned enterprises ("SOEs"). The economy
embraces market-oriented dynamics, yet it is not strictly a free-

market capitalist system. . . . These elements make it difficult to determine certain legal issues under WTO rules—such as whether an entity is associated with the state, or how to characterize the overall form of China's economy. These elements also raise the stakes associated with certain activities that fall outside the scope of the WTO's present jurisdiction (Wu 2016, 265).

It is difficult, for example, for the WTO to deal with investment restrictions, forced technology transfer, and intellectual property (IP) theft. China's policies toward direct foreign investment (FDI) are different from those of other large emerging markets, though the regime for foreign investment has evolved over time, starting with the promulgation of the Equity Joint Venture Law in 1979 (Chen and Song 2003). This law permitted foreign investment through joint ventures, typically with state enterprises. That restriction plus the regulation of foreign exchange resulted in a rather small initial flow of FDI into China, most of it coming from Hong Kong. The second stage, 1986–1991, was characterized by an extension of the FDI openness to more locations in China and enactment of the Law on Wholly Owned Subsidiaries. This set the stage for the third period, 1992–2000. The creation of a legal framework for wholly owned subsidiaries, combined with more market-oriented attitudes following Deng Xiaoping's southern tour of 1992, ushered in a period of rapid inflow of FDI, including from the developed economies. China joining the WTO in 2001 marked the beginning of a fourth phase, in which more sectors were opened, and FDI really took off.

While China's policy has been to gradually open up the economy to foreign investment, it has always retained a policy of requiring joint ventures in some key sectors. In the automotive industry, for example, foreign investors have to operate in 50:50 joint ventures with domestic firms, most of which are state-owned enterprises (SOEs). In financial services such as investment banking, the equity cap has been less than 50 percent. The aim of this restrictive policy is to build up the capacity of domestic firms. The Organization for Economic Cooperation and Development (OECD) calculates an FDI restrictiveness index for its members and key developing countries. Figure 16-1 shows the restrictiveness index for 2018. The overall index for China is 0.3, considerably higher than the level in Brazil or South Africa, each of which has a value around 0.1, similar to that of advanced economies. India is somewhat less open, with an index number around 0.2, but still more open than China. The earliest year for the index is 1997, at which time China's restrictiveness was 0.6. Hence China has become significantly more open in the past twenty years but is still less open to direct investment than other emerging markets.

China's policy is mixed in that many sectors are completely open, and the bulk of the FDI in China in fact comes in the form of 100 percent foreign-owned operations. But the overall index for China is relatively high because the country's economy remains quite closed in a few important sectors. Figure 16-1 shows the restrictiveness toward FDI in media, communications, and financial services, all of which are significantly more restricted than in other emerging markets. These service sectors are of particular interest to many leading U.S. firms, as the U.S. economy is much more a service economy than a manufacturing one. Hence much of the trade tension between the United States and China arises from this mismatch between where China is open and where the United States is strong.

It is also worth noting that China's opening over the past twenty years has come in steps. China undertook considerable liberalization in preparation for joining the WTO and in the immediate aftermath of accession. There followed a ten-year period in which little additional reform took place. Finally, the past few years have seen further significant liberalization, as well as promises for additional moves in the automotive and financial services sectors. Thus the story for China is mixed: it is outside the norm on

FIGURE 16-1. **FDI Restrictiveness, Brazil, India, South Africa, and China, 2018 (Index, 1 = completely closed)**

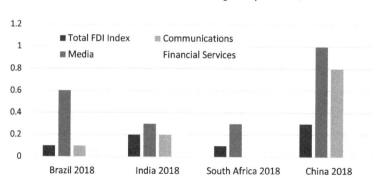

Source: OECD FDI Restrictiveness Index.

FDI openness but has moved significantly in the direction of more openness over time, including in the past few years.

Restrictions on FDI are important because FDI is tied to the issue of "forced technology transfer," which has become a political hot-button issue. International auto firms cannot simply produce and sell in China. They are required to join a 50:50 joint venture and share their technology with their domestic partner in China. In quite a few manufacturing and service industries, foreign firms are basically training their future competitors. The Chinese government does not like the adjective "forced" because the companies are making a choice to enter the China market on these terms. If they want to profit from having their technology in the huge China market, then they must share their technology, which speeds their obsolescence. Many multinational enterprises accept the deal offered and figure they will be able to invent new technologies fast enough to always remain ahead of their Chinese competitors. In general, FDI in China has a high return, so the arrangement is working out well for the average multinational corporation so far. But it remains to be seen what happens in the future.

The issue of forced technology transfer coerced by China's restrictive investment policies is one of the key tensions between China and its main partners—the United States, the EU, and Japan. But there are also more general issues of IP rights protection in China. Aside from sharing technology through joint ventures, many foreign companies have had their patents and brands compromised, and feel they have little redress through the Chinese legal system. As China has developed, foreign investment has gradually moved into higher-tech sectors and services. These are sectors in which there will be more potential disputes than in simple sectors such as clothing and footwear or electronics assembly. A key question for China, then, is whether, as it develops, its legal system is keeping up.

This is not an easy question to answer, but empirically we can look at the Rule of Law index from the World Bank's World Governance database, which "captures perceptions of the extent to which agents have confidence in and abide by the rules of society, and in particular the quality of contract enforcement, property rights, the police, and the courts, as well as the likelihood of crime and violence." The index, which has a mean of zero and a standard deviation of 1.0, is available for a large number of countries starting in 1996.

Figure 16-2 shows the Rule of Law index in 2016 plotted against log per capita GDP in purchasing power parity (PPP) terms, for a large number of countries. China and Korea are identified. The graph also includes the data for those two countries in 1996. China in 1996 had rather poor rule of law (about half a standard deviation below the global mean); however, China was a poor country, and its rule of law was considered to be good for its income level. That is, it was above the regression line by about half a standard deviation. Between 1996 and 2016, China's income grew enormously but its standing in the Rule of Law index barely improved. By 2016 China was well below the regression line, with poor rule of law for its income level. (It bears noting that Korea in 1996 was at about the same income level as China in 2016 but had much better rule of law.)

So, in the matter of investment openness and the related issues of IP rights and rule of law, China is lagging global norms. Its leadership is talking about opening up more sectors of the economy to direct investment. However, if the rule of law is poor, then it is difficult to create a level playing field in complicated sectors that require high technology (in the case of manufacturing) or complex regulation (in the case of modern services).

FIGURE 16-2. **GDP Per Capita and Rule of Law Index, China Compared with Korea (1996 and 2016)**

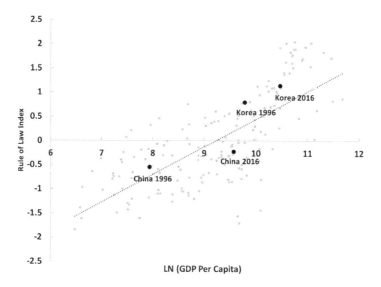

Source: World Development Indicators and World Governance Indicators, World Bank Group.

The Western economies would like to see the WTO evolve to handle these issues, but China would have to agree. Every country in the WTO essentially has a veto, but the large economies are particularly important. If China, the United States, the EU, and Japan can reach an agreement on modernized rules for trade and investment, the rest of the world is likely to go along. Without this kind of evolution there is a risk that the WTO will become increasingly irrelevant and that the established powers plus China will feel free to pursue whatever unilateral measures they deem necessary to address "unfair trade."

It should be noted that the U.S. attitude toward the WTO and trade agreements more generally has been contradictory during the 2010s. The United States negotiated the Trans-Pacific Partnership (TPP) with eleven other Asia-Pacific economies—not including China—and then pulled out just before it was implemented. The TPP included chapters addressing modern issues of investment, services, data, IP rights protection, environment, and labor. Though the United States pulled out of the agreement, it used the negotiated chapters on these issues in the updated NAFTA and U.S.-Korea trade agreements, indicating that it viewed the negotiated agreements as positive steps forward. Concerning the WTO, the United States has refused to agree to the appointment of new appellate judges, threatening to halt WTO dispute settlement by 2020. In the current environment it is hard to imagine China and the United States agreeing on the details of reforms to the WTO. Looking farther out toward 2049, however, this is a key requirement for a stable and prosperous global economy, so there is hope that pragmatism will eventually lead to positive reforms. In 2019 China and the United States were negotiating bilaterally over some of these key issues of openness and IP rights protection. Any bilateral agreement between the two will lack third-party enforcement mechanisms and is highly likely to break down over time. Still, the bilateral discussions may point toward a pragmatic compromise on WTO reform.

MULTILATERAL DEVELOPMENT BANKS AND THE BELT AND ROAD INITIATIVE

With respect to the multilateral development banks, China has had a long and positive relationship with the World Bank, starting with the famous meeting between Deng Xiaoping and Robert McNamara in 1980. Deng told McNamara that China would modernize with or without World Bank assistance, but would do so more rapidly with assistance. For many years China was the largest client of the bank in terms of loan amount and number of projects. The bank started with infrastructure projects in power and transport and moved on to more complicated issues such as watershed management, urban water supply and sanitation, reforestation, and urban transport.

The relationship had some bumps along the way, as Chinese officials came to feel that the bank was moving away from its original mandate to fund infrastructure and growth. It was also getting bogged down in complex rules about environmental and social aspects of infrastructure projects—so much so that many clients stopped approaching the bank for infrastructure funding. In the early years of China's association with the World Bank, infrastructure accounted for 70 percent of lending; that figure has dropped to about 30 percent in recent years. Developing countries have become frustrated with the complex regulations and long delays involved in bank infrastructure projects (Humphrey 2015).

Around the time of the global financial crisis in 2008–2009, an international commission under the chairmanship of Ernesto Zedillo, an economist and former president of Mexico, examined the performance of the World Bank and the other multilateral development banks and made recommendations for modernizing them (Zedillo 2009). This commission had good representation from the developing world (including Zhou Xiaochuan from China) and made a series of practical recommendations: increase the voting shares of developing countries to reflect their growing weight in the world economy; abolish the resident board as an expensive anachronism, in light of modern technology; increase the lending capacity of the multilateral development banks to meet growing developing world needs; reestablish the focus on infrastructure and growth; and streamline the implementation of environmental and social safeguards to speed up project implementation.

China generally shared these criticisms of the World Bank and its sister institutions, such as the Asian Development Bank. In the wake of the Zedillo report, however, there was no meaningful reform. This frustration with lack of reform in the World Bank, combined with a general dissatisfaction with the U.S.-led global financial system, influenced China to launch a new development bank. As He notes,

Indeed, China and other emerging powers have criticized the World Bank and the IMF for their inefficient and over-supervised processes of granting loans. The current gap between the demands for infrastructure investment and available investment from existing international financing organizations in developing countries creates an opportunity for emerging economies to establish a new type of bank with a directed focus in this area." (He 2016, 3–4)

The new bank is also a way for China to put its excess savings to use through a multilateral format in which it has substantial say.

The charter of the Asian Infrastructure Investment Bank (AIIB) is very much in the spirit of the charters of the World Bank and the Asian Development Bank, but it also incorporates virtually all of the Zedillo report recommendations: majority ownership by the developing world, no resident board, authority to lend more from a given capital base, a focus on infrastructure and growth, and environmental and social guidelines that should be implemented "in proportion to the risk" (per the AIIB website).

The issue of environmental and social safeguards was a key factor in the brouhaha surrounding the founding of the new bank. The United States and Japan opposed the effort primarily out of concerns over governance, including the issue of environmental and social safeguards. Other major Western nations such as the United Kingdom, Germany, France, and Australia all chose to fight these battles from the inside. The AIIB has promulgated environmental and social policies that on paper are similar to the principles embodied in World Bank safeguards: environmental and social assessments to analyze risks, public disclosure of key information in a timely manner, consultation with affected parties, and decision-making that incorporates these risks. The AIIB approach, however, differs from that of the World Bank by avoiding detailed prescriptions for how to manage the process. The World Bank's detailed regulations—literally hundreds of pages—inevitably make implementation slow and bureaucratic.

The AIIB's leadership hopes that the bank can meet international standards while being more timely in its responses and more cost-effective. This is largely a matter of implementation, and it will take time and experience on the ground to see whether the effort is a success. In its first two years of operation the AIIB lent US$4.4 billion to twelve different countries, with two-thirds of its projects cofinanced with the World Bank or regional development banks. India has been the largest borrower so far, and the AIIB is now expanding into Africa and Latin America. It will take time for the AIIB to build up a portfolio of projects that it has developed on its own. If the AIIB can meet environmental standards more efficiently, that would be a very positive innovation. If the AIIB's activities can put pressure on the World Bank and the regional development banks to streamline their procedures and speed up their infrastructure projects, that would also be a positive change to the global system that emanated from China. We already have a system in which there are multiple development banks, so China's lead in setting up the AIIB should be seen as an innovation in the global system, not a challenge to it.

The larger context for the establishment of the AIIB is that China in recent years has become a major source of capital for the developing world. China has run a current account surplus that has averaged 2 percent of GDP since the 1980s. As a result, China has emerged as a significant net creditor. Figure 16-3 shows net foreign assets relative to GDP for a large group of countries in 2011 (Lane and Milesi-Ferretti 2007). The China data have also been updated to 2017. China's net foreign asset position in 2017 was not unusual, just modestly above the regression line. But as a high-saving economy, China is likely to continue as a net foreign creditor. As its GDP grows, it is likely to emerge as the world's largest net creditor. This is not assured, because both saving and investment rates are coming down in China as a result of demographic change and the declining return on investment, so it is hard to predict what will happen to the saving-investment gap. We take as our benchmark that China in the medium term continues to have surpluses that average about 2 percent of GDP. With China's GDP continuing to grow, 2 percent now is more than US$200 billion per year. Hence, China is in a position to provide different kinds of financing around the world. Its highest-profile effort is the Belt and Road Initiative (BRI). This is Xi Jinping's vision of providing infrastructure and connectivity along the ancient Silk Road, as well as along a so-called maritime route that goes south from China, past Southeast Asia and South Asia, and on to Europe through the Suez Canal.

China's development finance, that is, loans to developing countries primarily for infrastructure, largely comes from the two policy banks, the China Development Bank (CDB) and the China Export-Import (EXIM) Bank. The CDB and EXIM Bank borrow on domestic and international

FIGURE 16-3. **Net Foreign Assets Relative to GDP (2011)**

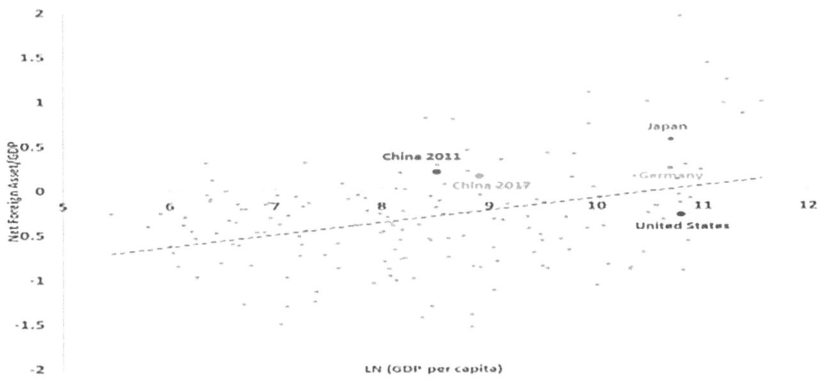

Source: Lane and Milesi-Ferretti (2007).

capital markets and lend with a spread, so they expect to be financially self-sufficient. The EXIM Bank also has access to modest subsidies from the budget in order to make some lending concessional. The motivation for China is partly economic: the economy has excess savings and underemployed construction companies and heavy industry. Also, if infrastructure is improved in partner countries, then China benefits indirectly as trade expands. There is also strategic motivation as China gains friends and influence through these projects.

A valid criticism of China's development finance is that it lacks transparency. There are no official data on loans to different countries, including the projects and the terms. A data set on China's development finance has been compiled by Dreher and coworkers under the title AidData (Dreher et al. 2017). This data set contains project-level information on Chinese official development finance provided to Africa, Asia, Europe, and Latin America from 2000 to 2014. According to AidData, China's development finance was quite modest until the global financial crisis, after which it increased significantly. It reached a peak of $50 billion in 2009 and then moderated to about $40 billion per year. That data set ends in 2014, just as the BRI was gaining traction. Probably the lending amounts have risen in the past few years toward the $100 billion per year range. Certainly the lending from the policy banks far exceeds the amounts coming from the AIIB so far.

About one-half of China's development finance has gone to BRI countries, according to AidData. The data set also has a breakdown of projects by sector. By far the two biggest areas are transport (39 percent of total financing) and power generation (32 percent). Less than 3 percent of the lending is in Chinese renminbi. Most of the lending is in dollars at variable interest rates. Most of these loans would be considered nonconcessional as they reflect the policy banks' borrowing costs plus a spread. However, many developing countries would not be able to borrow from any other source at such attractive rates, so in that sense it is a benefit to those countries. The attraction for borrowing countries is that they get access to a large amount of financing in order to meet their serious infrastructure gaps. The projects are generally carried out by Chinese construction companies, which often bring some of their workers with them.

A look at China's development finance globally shows that 37 percent in the 2012–2014 period went to Africa, 25 percent to maritime Asia, 14 percent to Latin America, and only 14 percent to landlocked Asia (Dollar 2018b). Some additional insight can be gained by focusing on the top twenty recipients of Chinese development finance during the period 2012–2014 (table 16-1). The list does include some Asian economies that are in the BRI project areas, such as Iran, Pakistan, Kazakhstan, and Indonesia. But it also includes eight African countries: Angola, Côte d'Ivoire, Ethiopia, Kenya, Nigeria, South Africa, Sudan, and Tanzania; and three Latin ones: Venezuela, Ecuador, and Argentina. Of the top twenty recipients, several have positions on the Rule of Law index that is above the mean for developing countries, such as Indonesia, Sri Lanka, Kazakhstan, Ethiopia, Kenya, South Africa, and Tanzania, but others are rated very poorly on rule of law: Venezuela, Ecuador, Angola, Nigeria, Sudan, Iran, and Pakistan. This means that significant amounts of Chinese finance are going to risky environments. The lack of any evident geographic pattern of China's development finance suggests that it is more demand-driven, shaped by which countries are willing to borrow, than supply-driven by a Chinese master plan.

China's growing development finance raises several issues of global governance, one of which is debt sustainability. Developing countries have suffered severe external debt crises from time to time, such as the Asian crisis in the 1990s. External debt is different from domestic debt in that it has to be serviced ultimately through exports. Capital flows to developing countries go through cycles: sometimes, in the search for yield, global investors are willing to lend a lot at relatively low interest rates. It is attractive then to

TABLE 16-1. **Chinese Development Finance: Top 20 Borrowers, 2012–2014**

Country	Average annual borrowing, 2012–2014 (billions of US$)	Rule of Law index, 2015
Pakistan	4.16	−0.79
Laos	2.74	−0.75
Ethiopia	1.85	−0.44
Venezuela	1.82	−1.99
Angola	1.65	−1.07
Belarus	1.48	−0.79
Sri Lanka	1.45	0.07
Kenya	1.29	−0.49
Côte d'Ivoire	1.25	−0.62
Ecuador	1.19	−1.03
Ukraine	1.02	−0.8
Cambodia	0.95	−0.92
Nigeria	0.94	−1.04
Argentina	0.92	−0.8
Indonesia	0.91	−0.41
Tanzania	0.86	−0.43
Kazakhstan	0.85	−0.37
Sudan	0.74	−1.18
South Africa	0.73	0.06
Iran	0.71	−0.95

Source: Data from AidData and World Governance Indicators, World Bank Group.

Note: Average Rule of Law index for all developing countries is −0.48.

borrow externally to fund infrastructure. There is always a risk, however, of capital flow reversal and increases in interest rates. Chinese banks are secretive about their lending terms, but most of these loans are in dollars and provided at flexible, commercial rates. Only about one quarter of China's development finance for the period 2012–2014 was concessional enough to meet the standard of "official development assistance." For the nonconcessional lending, as interest rates rise in New York and London, the cost of servicing loans from China will rise.

Some, but not all, of the countries that have borrowed heavily from China in recent years are at risk of debt distress. The World Bank's World Development Indicators include recent data on external debt relative to gross national income (GNI) for most of the countries included in the database for China's development finance, including all of the top twenty borrowers. For these twenty countries, debt to GNI increased from 35 percent in 2008 to 50 percent in 2015. For the other seventy-seven developing countries there was a modest increase in external debt, from an average of 45 percent of GNI in 2008 to an average of 48 percent in 2015. The average level of debt for the major borrowers from China is not alarming. But the rapid increase is something of a concern. More important, the average disguises large variation at the country level. In the last couple of years, large increases in debt, taking countries to risky levels, were experienced by Angola, Belarus, Côte d'Ivoire, Ethiopia, Kenya, South Africa, Ukraine, Venezuela, and Tanzania. A number of these countries have very poor governance, and it is not surprising that debt has not been used productively. The rise in the external debt-to-GDP ratio is an indicator to watch because a strong growth impact would increase GDP and tend to keep the ratio stable, whereas a weak growth effect would show up in the debt-to-GDP ratio rising to unsustainable levels. It should also be noted that China has already rescheduled debts for Ethiopia and Venezuela (and probably others) because the original repayment schedule was too onerous for the country.

Is China violating norms of global development finance? At this point, it would be hard to argue that. Of the countries that have borrowed heavily from China, several currently have IMF programs to help with unsustainable fiscal and balance of payments problems, including Côte d'Ivoire, Kenya, and Ukraine (IMF 2017b). Other countries that have borrowed heavily from China, on the other hand, are in good fiscal and financial shape (Kazakhstan and Indonesia are examples).

On the issue of debt sustainability, a balanced assessment is that most of the developing countries taking advantage of Chinese finance for infrastructure are in sound fiscal condition. A few have taken on excessive amounts of debt, and they have turned to the IMF for the traditional medicine of adjustment policies and emergency finance. Venezuela is the one case in which China's financing may have enabled poor economic policies to persist. But China has reduced its exposure, and it seems likely that Venezuela will go to the IMF in the end.

Key questions for the future are whether China can be more transparent in its bilateral lending for development, whether the AIIB can expand to represent a larger share of China's finance compared to the bilateral efforts, and whether the World Bank and the regional development banks can reform in a way that reflects the preferences of China and other developing countries, rather than the preferences of the rich countries that still dominate shareholding.

INTERNATIONAL FINANCE AND THE IMF

China's relationship with the IMF has undergone an interesting transformation. Beijing took over the China seat at the IMF and the World Bank in 1980 and kept a low profile at these institutions for the next decade. At the time of the Asian financial crisis in 1997, China was one of the many vocal Asian critics that believed that IMF assistance during the crisis was insufficient and IMF conditionality unnecessarily strict and intrusive. China did not need to borrow and suffer this indignity directly, but it voiced concerns similar to those of the affected countries—Thailand, Indonesia, and South Korea. By the mid-2000s, China's relationship with the IMF had become even more antagonistic. As China's currency became undervalued in the mid-2000s and its current account surplus ballooned toward 10 percent of GDP, the U.S. Treasury put pressure on the IMF to highlight the issue of global imbalances and currency misalignment. There were several years in the mid-2000s when the IMF team was not welcome in Beijing to carry out its annual Article IV review of macroeconomic policies.

The background to this difficult relationship between China and the IMF was as follows. In the early years of reform, China had a multiple currency system in which foreign exchange certificates (FEC) were required for certain international transactions. FECs were denominated in yuan but traded at a premium to domestic currency. This was an awkward system and subject to inefficiency and corruption. The currency was unified and the unified rate devalued in 1994. Then began a long period in which the currency was pegged to the U.S. dollar at the rate of 8.3:1. A pegged exchange rate is a reasonable choice for a poor developing country trying to establish macroeconomic stability and credibility with foreign partners and a domestic audience alike. While China had its currency pegged to the dollar, it had substantial trade with other Asian partners such as Japan,

Taiwan, and South Korea, plus Europe. And these areas all had currencies that fluctuated against the dollar.

In examining whether a currency level is appropriate or not, it makes sense to look at the trade-weighted or "effective" exchange rate. Figure 16-4 shows the evolution of China's effective exchange rate from 1994 to today. While pegging to the dollar in 1994 provided stability to the yuan in one sense, ironically, it resulted in fairly rapid appreciation of the effective rate between 1994 and 1998. It turned out to be an appropriate path for China because the country had commenced its rapid productivity growth in tradables. The problem with a fixed exchange rate in an economy with rapid productivity growth is that the country becomes competitive in more and more sectors and starts to run a trade surplus. China avoided this situation initially as the dollar was appreciating from 1994 to 1998. However, after 2001 the dollar began to depreciate, and China chose to follow it down. China's effective exchange rate depreciated 20 percent between 2002 and 2005 (see figure 16-4).

At the end of this period, China started to run large current account surpluses, nearly 6 percent of GDP in 2005, rising to nearly 10 percent in 2007. There was a certain amount of pride in China in this export prowess in the mid-2000s, but large trade surpluses are not necessarily a good thing for a developing country. And, of course, they have to be matched by someone else's deficit, leading to trade friction and questions about sustainability.

China had very large trade surpluses for only four years, 2005–2008, and

FIGURE 16-4. **China's Nominal Effective Exchange Rate, 1994–2019**

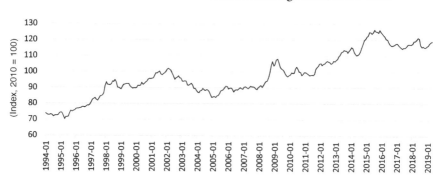

Source: Data from Bank for International Settlements.

it would be a mistake to consider that the trade surpluses resulted only from exchange rate undervaluation. But the exchange rate was crucial because it had so many spillover effects in other areas. To maintain the 8.3:1 peg against the U.S. dollar in the face of rising trade surpluses, the central bank had to buy excess dollars and keep them as reserves. The reserves grew to US$4 trillion. These are low-return assets, and owning more than a country needs for stability has real costs. The central bank was basically borrowing from Chinese people in domestic currency and lending to the U.S. Treasury at low interest rates. The central bank was also reluctant to raise Chinese interest rates to levels that would have been appropriate for a fast-growing developing country because doing so would have complicated its sterilization task. So the effort to maintain the peg led to financial repression in China that encouraged investment and a housing boom, at the expense of consumption.

The undervalued exchange rate was a great stimulus to the export sector. But it created inflationary pressure on the prices of nontradables and on assets, especially housing. In the heyday of the surplus, 2005–2008, China kept its fiscal policy very tight, and put off needed expenditures on health, education, and infrastructure. That was the real cost of the trade surplus. China was making a lot of stuff for Americans and getting paid with IOUs, while underspending on its own domestic needs. This was the period in which China and the IMF were barely talking.

The costs of undervaluation were becoming apparent by 2005, and China moved off the peg that year. It began a period of gradual appreciation against the dollar. Starting in 2005, the effective exchange rate appreciated steadily until 2015 (see figure 16-4). Over that decade it appreciated more than 50 percent. This apparently corrected the earlier undervaluation and accounted for ongoing productivity growth. China's trade surplus dropped during the global financial crisis of 2008–2009, and then continued to drop further, reaching 0.4 percent of GDP in 2018. The IMF and most economists consider the currency fairly valued, as it is keeping any trade imbalance at a very modest level. In the last few years the effective exchange rate has been relatively stable.

Given that background, it is remarkable how the China-IMF relationship has subsequently evolved. As attention shifted away from the exchange rate, starting around 2009, the IMF focused its China program more on financial supervision, with a series of welcome technical interventions and policy advice (Dollar 2018a). Quota reform in the IMF, pushed by the United States, shifted shares toward emerging markets, especially China, primarily at the expense of Europe. While China has gained quota share in the IMF, its share still lags far behind its weight in the world economy. Figure 16-5 shows, for China and the United States, their shares of PPP GDP and IMF quota among G-20 countries, for the period 1984–2016. The basic story is that over this period, China's PPP GDP rose to be similar to the U.S. level; its IMF quota increased but still lagged the U.S. quota—about 10 percent of the quota allocated to G-20 countries versus 25 percent for the United States. Other factors besides economic size are relevant, especially role in global finance, where China is still small; nonetheless, it is clear that China and other emerging markets are severely underrepresented in the IMF.

In recent years the U.S. attitude toward further quota increases for China and other emerging markets has hardened. At the 2019 spring meetings of the IMF, the U.S. treasury secretary publicly opposed quota increases in the foreseeable future. Retired treasury official Mark Sobel has argued that in light of current U.S.-China relations, "Washington is probably supporting the NAB [New Arrangements to Borrow], rather than quotas, partly

FIGURE 16-5. **Chinese and U.S. Shares of PPP GDP and IMF Quota, among G-20 Countries, 1984–2016**

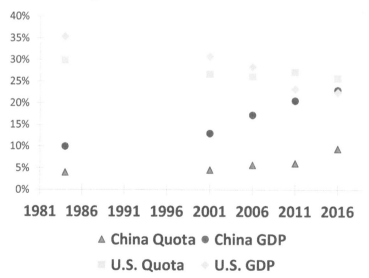

Source: Data from World Development Indicators and International Monetary Fund.

because it does not want to give Beijing more voting power. The administration has legitimate complaints about Chinese industrial policies, massive subsidisation and the like. But China's IMF voting power is around 6 percent, while its global economic weight is around 16 percent. China obviously deserves some increase" (Sobel 2019).

Part of the argument between the United States and China is also about the desirable scale of IMF resources. As noted, China is becoming a major net creditor and has an interest in a well-functioning IMF. U.S. officials have spoken out against using IMF resources to bail out countries that are indebted to China.

Aside from quota issues, China now has a lock on one of the senior positions (deputy managing director) in the IMF. The global financial crisis gave rise to a series of very large IMF bailout packages for European economies. Even with the quota increase, the IMF did not have sufficient resources. So the IMF turned to surplus countries that were willing to contribute to its New Arrangements to Borrow, which was essentially lending in parallel with IMF core resources. This was appealing to China in that it represented a use of reserves that was an alternative to simply buying U.S. treasury bonds.

Because of China's growing role in the IMF, it was natural for the fund to include the yuan in its special drawing rights when the SDR underwent its usual periodic review in 2016. As China becomes an increasingly important creditor in the world, it is natural for the country to deepen its relationship with the IMF, the international institution that oversees international capital flows and comes in with rescue programs when sovereign borrowers are unable to pay their debts.

An interesting recent development is that China is providing US$50 million to fund a China-IMF Capacity Development Center (IMF 2017a). This virtual center will be under IMF administration, will be anchored in Beijing, and will offer courses both inside and outside China on core IMF topics. Roughly half the participants will be Chinese officials and half officials from other developing countries, including countries along the BRI path. One of the important topics that will be emphasized initially is debt sustainability analysis. The People's Bank of China (PBOC) is the driving force behind this initiative, and PBOC represents China in multilateral development banks such as the African Development Bank and the Inter-American Development Bank, which is curious, since normally ministries of finance represent countries in the development banks. In China's case, African and Latin countries are ones to which China lends money and about which it has concerns regarding debt sustainability. The PBOC naturally has more awareness of this issue than other Chinese agencies and wants the knowledge to be spread within China, and also wants to strengthen the capacity of other developing countries. In the end, it is the governments of borrowing countries that need to demonstrate discipline and farsightedness.

CONCLUSION

The international economic institutions are a key foundation of global trade and investment, and hence of growth and prosperity. In the area of trade (WTO) and capital flows (IMF), the key institutions are natural monopolies. That is, it is hard to imagine a world with two or multiple institutions that set the rules for global trade and adjudicate trade disputes among nations. Or it is hard to imagine two lenders of last resort. Such institutional arrangements would likely lead to development of trade and investment blocs, with most exchange occurring within blocs. There would be a large loss in terms of global economic efficiency. Development banks, on the other hand, are not natural monopolies. Even before China's rise the world had a system in which there were multiple development banks that competed to some extent and coordinated well on policy as their major shareholders tended to be the same countries.

In the short run, it is hard to modernize the economic institutions primarily because China and the United States have different interests. These will be the two overwhelmingly largest economies in the period to 2049, and it is hard to see reform without the two cooperating. In the short run, the United States would like to see the WTO police issues such as investment, trade in services, data, and IP rights protection. China is content with the current WTO, which largely focuses on trade in goods and ignores these other issues. In 2018 China put forth a proposal on WTO reform that focused on maintaining special and differential treatment for developing countries and advocated for some specific measures favorable to China, notably fair treatment for SOEs.[1]

In the IMF, there is the opposite dynamic. The United States is content with the status quo. For both ideological and practical reasons, it does not want to see enlarged IMF quotas. On the ideological side, conservatives worry about moral hazard if there are too many resources easily available to bail out countries. On the pragmatic side, quota enlargement would lead to greater influence for China and other emerging markets. China naturally would like IMF reform to enhance its influence. Also, China is likely to become the largest net creditor in the world, so it has a material interest in an IMF that is adequately funded and staffed.

In the case of the multilateral development banks, it is likely that the World Bank and AIIB will emerge as the two dominant players. Unlike other regional banks, the AIIB is already going global. And China, if it wants, can greatly enhance the resources of the AIIB. For the moment, the two institutions are collaborating well, but there is a risk that their practices and orientations will diverge. For now, it is hard to be optimistic about China and the United States cooperating on reform of the international system.

Looking ahead to 2049, on the other hand, one can be a bit more optimistic. The United States and China as the two biggest economies have a large stake in a stable, growing global economy. One can imagine a grand bargain involving all the institutions—this would be easier than one-by-one reform, insofar as U.S. and Chinese interests will continue to be quite different within each institution. The grand bargain would involve Chinese support for the WTO taking on the issues of investment, services, IP rights protection, and data, while the United States accepted the expansion of the IMF and a growing weight for developing countries.

Failure to reform the WTO and the IMF and to coordinate activities of the development banks is likely to lead to a dystopian world in which trade and investment relations devolve into blocs, with the strongest countries extorting favorable terms from the smaller countries in their blocs. This would be a less efficient and prosperous world, and with economic decoupling, it is hard to imagine that military conflicts would not become more common. The United States and China have strong mutual interest in cooperation, but this will require compromise on each side.

NOTE

1. The English version of this document can be retrieved from: http://sms .mofcom.gov.cn/article/cbw/201812/20181202817611.shtml.

REFERENCES

Chen, Jing, and Yuhua Song. 2003. "FDI in China: Institutional Evolution and Its Impact on Different Sources." In *Proceedings of the 15th Annual Conference of the Association for Chinese Economics Studies Australia (ACESA)*. Canberra: Australian National University.

Dreher, A., A. Fuchs, B. Parks, A. M. Strange, and M. J. Tierney. 2017. *Aid, China, and Growth: Evidence from a New Global Development Finance Dataset*, Aid-Data Working Paper No. 46. Williamsburg, VA: AidData.

Dollar, David. 2018a. "China Case Study." In *IMF Financial Surveillance*. Washington, DC: IMF, Independent Evaluation Office.

———. 2018b. "Is China's Development Finance a Challenge to the International Order?" *Asian Economic Policy Review* 13 (2): 283–98.

He, Alex. 2016. "China in the International Financial System: A Study of the NDB and the AIIB." CIGI Papers No. 106, 3–4. Waterloo, ON: Centre for International Governance Innovation, June.

Humphrey, Chris. 2015. "Challenges and Opportunities for Multilateral Development Banks in 21st Century Infrastructure Finance." Washington, DC: Intergovernmental Group of Twenty-Four on Monetary Affairs and Development; Seoul: Global Green Growth Institute, June.

International Monetary Fund (IMF). 2017a. "IMF and the People's Bank of China Establish a New Center for Modernizing Economic Policies and Institutions." Press release, IMF, May 14.

———. 2017b. "IMF Lending Arrangements as of July 31, 2017." Washington, DC: IMF.

Lane, Philip R., and Gian Maria Milesi-Ferretti. 2007. "The External Wealth of Nations Mark II: Revised and Extended Estimates of Foreign Assets and Liabilities, 1970–2004." *Journal of International Economics* 73 (2): 223–50.

Organisation for Economic Co-operation and Development (OECD). 2019. "FDI Regulatory Restrictiveness Index," https://www.oecd.org/investment/fdiindex. htm.

Sobel, Mark. 2019. "U.S. Treasury Misguided on IMF Quotas." Official Monetary and Financial Institutions Forum, April.

World Bank. 2019a. *World Development Indicators*. https://datacatalog.worldbank. org/dataset/world-development-indicators.

World Bank. 2019b. *Worldwide Governance Indicators*. https://datacatalog.world-bank.org/dataset/worldwide-governance-indicators.

Wu, Mark. 2016. "The 'China, Inc.' Challenge to Global Trade Governance." *Harvard International Law Journal* 57 (2): 264.

Zedillo, Ernesto. 2009. "Repowering the World Bank for the 21st Century: Report of the High-Level Commission on Modernization of World Bank Group Governance." Washington, DC: World Bank Group, October.

Contributors

CHEN BAI is an assistant professor in the School of Labor and Human Resources at the Renmin University of China. His research interests lie in the area of healthy aging and social welfare. He has many experiences in consulting programs with the International Monetary Fund, European Union, and Chinese local governments. He is collaborating actively with researchers in the design of the 9th Chinese Longitudinal Healthy Longevity Survey (CLHLS). He received a bachelor's in history and PhD in economics from Peking University.

GAOSI CHU is senior strategy adviser serving in the Corporate Strategy Department of Baidu. Her main responsibilities include AI technology strategy planning, forward research of promising application scenarios, and review of the commercial and societal impact of AI adoption. Before moving to the private sector, she worked in the public and academic sectors in China and the United States. During her time at the Research Center of Chinese Politics & Business, Indiana University, she focused on industrial policy research as well as the initiative on Economic Regulation & Lawmaking in China, such as China's rare earth quota policy and trends in SOE merger and acquisition.

DAVID DOLLAR is a senior fellow in the China Center at the Brookings Institution and host of the Brookings trade podcast, *Dollar & Sense*. From 2009 to 2013, he was the U.S. Treasury's economic and financial emissary to China. Prior to that, Dollar worked at the World Bank, and from 2004 to 2009 was country director for China and Mongolia. From 1995 to 2004, Dollar worked in the World Bank's research department, publishing articles on globalization, growth, and inequality. Prior to his World Bank career, Dollar was an assistant professor of economics at UCLA, spending a semester in Beijing teaching at the Chinese Academy of Social Sciences. He has a PhD in economics from NYU and a bachelor's in Asian studies from Dartmouth College.

TING DONG is a Boya post-doc research fellow in the School of International Studies, Peking University. Her current research interest centers on the roles that technology plays in international affairs, having worked on information and communication technology and infrastructure, including their impact on maritime security in the Asia-Pacific and beyond. She received a PhD from the China Institute of Contemporary International Relations and has more than ten years of experience working in the government.

YIPING HUANG is Jin Guang Chair Professor of Economics and the deputy dean of the National School of Development and director of the Institute of Digital Finance, Peking University. In 2018, he was appointed by the International Monetary Fund's Managing Director Christine Lagarde as a member of the External Advisory Group on Surveillance. He served as a member of the Monetary Policy Committee at the People's Bank of China from 2015 to 2018. Currently he is vice chairman of council at the Public Policy Research Center and research fellow at the Financial Research Center, both at the Counselors' Office of the State Council. He received a bachelor's in agricultural economics from Zhejiang Agricultural University, a master's in economics from Renmin University of China, and a PhD in economics from Australian National University.

KEJUN JIANG is a senior research fellow at the Energy Research Institute of the National Development and Reform Commission and an adjunct professor at the College of Environmental Sciences and Engineering, Peking University. He is an expert in energy and climate modeling, and a leading scholar in forecasting China's carbon emission path. His research interests include the impacts of technological breakthroughs on China's climate strategy and policy choices.

XIAOYAN LEI is professor of economics at the National School of Development, Peking University. She is currently the director of the Center for Healthy Aging and Development Studies at PKU, deputy director of the MOE-PKU Center for Human Capital and National Policy Research, co-editor of *China Economic Quarterly,* and co-editor of the *Journal of Economics of Aging.* Her research spans the areas of labor economics, health economics, and the economics of aging, with publications in the *Review of Economics and Statistics, American Economic Journal: Applied Economics, Journal of Human Resources,* and so on. She is the Co-PI for the Chinese Longitudinal Healthy Longevity Survey (CLHLS) and has been an active member in the China Health and Retirement Longitudinal Study (CHARLS) team. She received a PhD in economics from UCLA.

LIXING LI is a professor of economics at the China Center for Economic Research at the National School of Development, Peking University. He has broad research interests in development economics, public economics, human capital, and political economy. His research projects include SOE reform, taxation and firm behaviors, local government debt, entrepreneurship, and political selection in China. His findings have appeared in journals such as *American Economic Review, Journal of Human Resources, Journal of Comparative Economics,* and *Journal of Population Economics.* He received his bachelor's from Tsinghua University, China, and his PhD in economics from the University of Maryland.

SHUANGLIN LIN is a professor at the National School of Development, Peking University, director of the China Center for Public Finance, Noddle Distinguished Professor at the University of Nebraska–Omaha, and international adviser at the East Asian Institute of the National University of Singapore. His research concentrates on public economics, China's public finance, and economic growth. He has published extensively in academic journals, including the *Journal of Economic Theory* and the *Journal of Public Economics.* He has completed many research projects for China's Ministry of Finance, the World Bank, and the United Nations. He was president of the Chinese Economists Society, chair of the Department of Public Finance of the School of Economics, Peking University, and a member of the Advisory Committee on Healthcare Reforms to the State Council of China.

PETER A. PETRI is Carl J. Shapiro Professor of International Finance at the Brandeis International Business School (IBS), a nonresident senior fellow at the Brookings Institution, and a visiting fellow at the Peterson Institute for International Economics. He served as the founding dean of IBS from 1994 to 2006 and as its interim dean from 2016 to 2018. He has published widely on trade and technology in the Asia-Pacific and has held visiting appointments at Keio University, Fudan University, and Peking University. He is also a Fulbright Research Scholar. He has served as a consultant for the ADB, APEC, OECD, World Bank, WTO, and other international and national governmental organizations. He received his bachelor's and PhD from Harvard University.

ESWAR PRASAD is Tolani Senior Professor of Trade Policy and professor of economics at Cornell University. He is also a senior fellow at the Brookings Institution, where he holds the New Century Chair in International Economics, and a research associate at the National Bureau of Economic Research. He is former head of the IMF's China Division. He is the author of *Gaining Currency: The Rise of the Renminbi* and *The Dollar Trap: How the U.S. Dollar Tightened Its Grip on Global Finance*. His op-ed articles have appeared in the *Financial Times, Harvard Business Review, New York Times, Wall Street Journal*, and *Washington Post*.

XIN TIAN received her bachelor's in statistics from Beijing Normal University, and a PhD in resource economics from Peking University. Her dissertation examined the impacts of China's WTO accession on environmental performance in China and China's main trade partners. She is a researcher at China National Offshore Oil Corporation.

MIN WANG is a tenured associate professor at the National School of Development, Peking University. He is also associate editor of *China Economic Quarterly* and director of the China Center of the Environment for Development Initiative. His research areas are environmental and resource economics, energy economics, climate change, and macroeconomic development. He has published more than twenty academic papers, some of which have been published in top field economics journals, such as *Economic Theory, Journal of Environmental Economics and Management, Journal of Economic Dynamics and Control,* and *Macroeconomic Dynamics.* Besides academic research, he actively participates in policy research and has produced more than ten policy reports that focus on reforming environmental policies, land policies, and energy policies in China. These reports were submitted to the central or local governments, with some of the proposed policies adopted by policymakers.

XUN WANG has been a research fellow at the National School of Development and the Institute of Digital Finance, Peking University, since 2016. He worked as an associate research fellow at the China Center for Contemporary World Studies from 2013 to 2016. He served as a post-doctoral research fellow at the Stockholm China Economic Research Institute of the Stockholm School of Economics from 2011 to 2013. He received a PhD in economics from the National School of Development, Peking University. His research focuses on financial liberalization, financial regulation, and digital finance. He has published academic papers in the *China Economic Review, Journal of the Asia Pacific Economy, Oxford Bulletin of Economics & Statistics, Growth and Change,* and *China Economic Journal.*

YONG WANG is academic deputy dean of the Institute of New Structural Economics, Peking University. His research fields are economic growth, macroeconomics, political economy, and the economies of China and India. He has published academic papers such as the *Journal of Development Economics* and the *Journal of Monetary Economics,* and serves as a co-editor for *China and the World Economy* (SSCI) and associate editor for *Economic Modelling* (SSCI). He is the author of several books, including *Thinking and Debates on New Structural Economics* and *Industrial Policies: Summary, Reflection and Prospect* (Peking University Press). He won the Inaugural Zhang Peigang Young Economist Award in Development Economics in 2018. He received a PhD in economics from the University of Chicago and was a research fellow and consultant at the World Bank.

YONG WANG is a post-doctoral fellow at the National School of Development, Peking University. He received his PhD from the Graduate School of the Chinese Academy of Social Science. His research focuses on macroeconomics, innovative economics, and quantitative economics. His work has published in academic journals, including the *Journal of Financial Research, Studies of International Finance,* and *Journal of Finance and Economics.* He has explored how tight monetary policy impacts the leverage ratios of state-owned and private-owned enterprises in China through the mechanisms of balance sheet recession and financial friction, and whether the central bank should consider the financial factors when implementing monetary policy. A recently published paper examines how the vertical unbundling reform in 2002 affected the productivity of firms in the electricity generation and transmission sectors.

JINTAO XU is Boya Distinguished Professor at the National School of Development, Peking University. He is also the director of the China Center for Energy and Environmental Economics (CCEEE). His research ranges from forest tenure reform, pollution control, and climate change to transportation management. His publications have appeared in the *Journal of Agricultural Economics, Journal of Environmental Economics and Management, Land Economics,* and *World Development.* He has served as associate editor or on the editorial board of the *European Journal of Agricultural Economics, AJAE,* and *JEEM.* He received a bachelor's in engineering from Jilin University of Technology, a master's in forest economics from Beijing Forestry University, and a master's in economics and PhD in natural resource economics from Virginia Tech.

YAO YANG is a Cheung-Kong Scholar and Liberal Arts Chair Professor at the China Center for Economic Research (CCER) and the National School of Development (NSD), Peking University. He currently serves as the director of CCER, the dean of NSD, the executive dean of the ISSCAD, and the editor of CCER's house journal *China Economic Quarterly.* His research interests include economic transition and development in China. He has published widely in international and domestic journals, as well as several books on institutional economics and economic development in China. He received a bachelor's in geography and a master's in economics from Peking University, and a PhD in development economics from the Department of Agricultural and Applied Economics, the University of Wisconsin–Madison.

MIAOJIE YU is the University Liberal Arts Chair Professor, China's Chang-Jiang Scholar, and deputy dean of the National School of Development, Peking University. He received his PhD from the University of California, Davis. He is an expert adviser to China's central and local governments. His research interests include international trade and the Chinese economy. He has published more than one hundred peer-reviewed papers and won the Royal Economic Society prize (2015).

XIUMEI YU is an assistant professor at the School of Public Finance and Taxation, Zhongnan University of Economics and Law. Her research fields are health economics and environmental economics. Prior to joining Zhongnan University of Economics and Law, she obtained a PhD in economics from the National School of Development, Peking University. She also holds a BA in finance and banking and a BS in statistics from Peking University.

DAOJIONG ZHA is a professor in the School of International Studies and Institute of South-South Cooperation and Development, Peking University. His areas of expertise include international political economy and China's international economic relations, particularly the fields of energy and natural resources, development aid, and the economics-political nexus in the Asia-Pacific. His research has extended to political and social risk management for Chinese corporations engaged in infrastructure and manufacturing investments abroad. Prior to joining the faculty of Peking University in 2007, he held academic positions at the Renmin University of China, the International University of Japan, and the University of Macau. He studied at the East-West Center and the University of Hawaii, where he earned a PhD in political science.

SHILIN ZHENG is an associate research professor at the National School of Development, Peking University. He received his PhD in science and engineering management from the University of Science and Technology Beijing. His research interests include industrial organizations, the economics of innovation, and political economics. His research has appeared in several journals, such as *China Economic Review, Telecommunications Policy, Energy Policy,* and *The Economic Journal* (in Chinese).

TENGLONG ZHONG is a post-doctoral fellow at the National School of Development, Peking University. He is also a guest scholar at Aarhus University. His research interests include international trade and industrial organization. He has published more than twenty peer-reviewed papers.

GUANGSU ZHOU is associate professor at the School of Labor and Human Resources, Renmin University of China. He graduated from the National School of Development in Peking University and received a PhD in economics. He has long been dedicated to research on labor economics, focusing on issues such as income inequality, the digital economy, and employment. He has published more than twenty academic papers in Chinese and English journals, such as the *Journal of Population Economics* and the *Review of Economics of the Household*. He has also applied for many research projects through the National Natural Science Foundation of China and the Tianjin Social Science Foundation. His research has won the Liu Shibai Prize in Economics and the Best Thesis Award from *China Economic Quarterly*.

QINQIN ZHUANG is an assistant researcher at the Institute of Quantitative & Technical Economics of the Chinese Academy of Social Sciences. She received her bachelor's in economics from Southwestern University of Finance & Economics and a PhD in economics from Wuhan University. She has engaged in research on innovation economics and has published more than twenty papers in Chinese authoritative journals, such as *Management World* and *China Soft Science*, and has participated in more than ten projects, including through the National Natural Science Foundation and the National Social Science Foundation.

Index